INTRODUCTION TO RURAL MARKETING

R. KRISHNAMOORTHY

Visiting Professor
Management Institutes, Mumbai
and
Formerly National Sales Manager
Sandoz Agro Division
and
General Manager (HR), Syngenta,
Crop Protection Division, Mumbai.

FOURTH REVISED AND ENLARGED EDITION – 2014

Himalaya Publishing House

MUMBAI • NEW DELHI • NAGPUR • BENGALURU • HYDERABAD • CHENNAI • PUNE • LUCKNOW • AHMEDABAD • ERNAKULAM • BHUBANESWAR • INDORE • KOLKATA • GUWAHATI

First Edition	: 2008
Second Edition	: 2009
Third Revised and Enlarged Edition	: 2011
Reprint	: 2012
Fourth Revised and Enlarged Edition	: 2014

Published by : Mrs. Meena Pandey for **Himalaya Publishing House Pvt. Ltd.,** "Ramdoot", Dr. Bhalerao Marg, Girgaon, **Mumbai - 400 004.** Phone: 022-23860170/23863863, Fax: 022-23877178 **E-mail: himpub@vsnl.com; Website: www.himpub.com**

Branch Offices :

New Delhi : "Pooja Apartments", 4-B, Murari Lal Street, Ansari Road, Darya Ganj, New Delhi - 110 002. Phone: 011-23270392, 23278631; Fax: 011-23256286

Nagpur : Kundanlal Chandak Industrial Estate, Ghat Road, Nagpur - 440 018. Phone: 0712-2738731, 3296733; Telefax: 0712-2721216

Bengaluru : No. 16/1 (Old 12/1), 1st Floor, Next to Hotel Highlands, Madhava Nagar, Race Course Road, Bengaluru - 560 001. Phone: 080-22286611, 22385461, 4113 8821, 22281541

Hyderabad : No. 3-4-184, Lingampally, Besides Raghavendra Swamy Matham, Kachiguda, Hyderabad - 500 027. Phone: 040-27560041, 27550139

Chennai : 8/2 Madley 2nd street, T. Nagar, Chennai - 600 017. Mobile: 09320490962

Pune : First Floor, "Laksha" Apartment, No. 527, Mehunpura, Shaniwarpeth (Near Prabhat Theatre), Pune - 411 030. Phone: 020-24496323/24496333; Mobile: 09370579333

Lucknow : House No 731, Shekhupura Colony, Near B.D. Convent School, Aliganj, Lucknow - 226 022. Phone: 0522-4012353; Mobile: 09307501549

Ahmedabad : 114, "SHAIL", 1st Floor, Opp. Madhu Sudan House, C.G. Road, Navrang Pura, Ahmedabad - 380 009. Phone: 079-26560126; Mobile: 09377088847

Ernakulam : 39/176 (New No: 60/251) 1st Floor, Karikkamuri Road, Ernakulam, Kochi – 682011. Phone: 0484-2378012, 2378016; Mobile: 09387122121

Bhubaneswar : 5 Station Square, Bhubaneswar - 751 001 (Odisha). Phone: 0674-2532129, Mobile: 09338746007

Indore : Kesardeep Avenue Extension, 73, Narayan Bagh, Flat No. 302, IIIrd Floor, Near Humpty Dumpty School, Indore - 452 007 (M.P.). Mobile: 09303399304

Kolkata : 108/4, Beliaghata Main Road, Near ID Hospital, Opp. SBI Bank, Kolkata - 700 010, Phone: 033-32449649, Mobile: 7439040301

Guwahati : House No. 15, Behind Pragjyotish College, Near Sharma Printing Press, P.O. Bharalumukh, Guwahati - 781009, (Assam). Mobile: 09883055590, 08486355289, 7439040301

DTP by : Priyanka Mahadik.

Printed at : Geetanjali Press Pvt. Ltd., Nagpur. On behalf of HPH.

Dedicated to the memory of
our beloved Grandfather Late
Shri V.E. Krishna Sastry, a renowned
teacher, who inspired me and the students
of Nallepilly Village, Palghat District,
Kerala State for over three decades and to
our beloved father late Shri S. Rama Iyer, Velonie
Estate, Valparai, Coimbatore District,
Tamil Nadu who demonstrated
that "Work is Worship"
in professional life.

PREFACE TO FOURTH REVISED AND ENLARGED EDITION

It gives me great pleasure to present the **Fourth Revised and Enlarged Edition** of the book on **"Introduction to Rural Marketing"** for the benefit of students and executives engaged in sales and marketing of products and services in rural areas. The book covers the full syllabus on rural marketing of most Indian Universities.

Rural India is emerging as a large market for a number of goods and services such as consumer goods, durables, financial services, health care and telecommunication. We are moving into a new area of development and the base is shifting towards Indian villages. The book contains information on recent developments in Rural Marketing.

The book deals with marketing of Consumer Goods and Services, Agricultural Produce, Agricultural Inputs and provides an integrated approach to Rural Marketing.

It is gratifying to note that the book has been recommended as a reference book on Rural Marketing by Universities of Mumbai, Lovely (Punjab), Acharya Nagarjuna (Andhra Pradesh), Visveswaraya (Karnataka), Anna (Tamil Nadu), Arni (Himachal Pradesh), Gujarat Technological University, M.S. University (Gujarat) and JIS University (Rajasthan).

My deep sense of gratitude to the students, teachers and executives for their warm response to the Third Edition of the book and also for giving me an opportunity to bring out the Fourth Revised and Enlarged Edition within a short period. I request the teachers, students, executives and others to provide constructive suggestions to improve further the contents and quality of the book.

I am thankful to Himalaya Publishing House Pvt. Ltd. for their kind cooperation and excellent service in bringing out the Fourth Revised and Enlarged Edition.

Mumbai

Date: 1st March, 2014

R. Krishnamoorthy

Velonie@yahoo.com

PREFACE TO FIRST EDITION

It gives me great pleasure to present the first edition of the book, **"Introduction to Rural Marketing".**

Rural marketing has been introduced as a subject for Graduate and Postgraduate Studies in Management. I have made a humble effort to meet the needs of students by covering the syllabus instituted by the University of Mumbai and other Universities for Bachelor of Management Studies and Postgraduate Studies in Management. This book will also be useful for executives engaged in sales and marketing of products and services in rural areas.

I am grateful to Mr. S.A. Sherlekar, Retired Professor and Head of the Department of Business Management, R.A. Podar College of Commerce and Economics, Mumbai for his valuable contribution in preparing chapters on Consumer Behaviour and Market Segmentation. I wish to thank Dr. Rakesh Singh, Chairperson – Consultancy, Professor of Economics and Strategy, Narsee Monjee Institute of Management and Higher Studies, Mumbai for his thoughtful suggestions.

I have included a separate chapter on Rural Marketing Initiatives based on information collected from various sources including Praxis published by M/s Kasturi and Sons, Chennai and discussions with some of the sales and marketing personnel across industries. I am grateful to all the companies for the same.

I have travelled extensively in the rural areas of the country during my professional career and have gained practical knowledge in the field of rural marketing. I have been teaching Rural Marketing in Management Institutes for the last eight years. I have tried to combine my teaching and corporate experience in developing various chapters and offer this comprehensive book for the benefit of the students and executives.

I request the professors, students and executives to provide constructive suggestions to further improve the contents and quality of this book.

I am thankful to Himalaya Publishing House Pvt. Ltd. for their kind cooperation and excellent service in bringing out the first edition.

R. Krishnamoorthy

velonie@yahoo.com

Introduction to Rural Marketing

Rural marketing involves flow of goods and services from urban to rural, rural to urban and rural to rural. This comprehensive book deals with marketing of consumer goods, services, agricultural produce and agricultural inputs and provides an integrated approach to rural marketing.

CONTENTS

1 NATURE AND SCOPE OF RURAL MARKETING

INTRODUCTION

It is said that "Bharat mata gram vasini" which means that mother India lives in her villages. According to Census 2011, our country has 6,41,000 villages and total population of 1,210 million. Out of the total population, rural population is 833 million and constitute about 69% of the population. The trust on rural development and the Green Revolution during the late 1960s and early 1970s that focused on the use of high yielding varieties of seeds, increased use of fertilisers and modern pest management practices have resulted in higher yields. From a food deficit nation in the mid-60s, our country became self-sufficient in food production in 1971 and we are now exporting agricultural produce to other countries. The rise in income coupled with increased awareness and the need for possessing modern goods have influenced the rural marketing environment in our country. Expansion of TV network, rising aspirations of rural people and packaging revolution, have contributed to the growth of rural markets.

Further Government has adopted a planned programme for development of village industries and infrastructural facilities. There has been a shift from an agricultural economy to manufacturing and service economy and this development has resulted in increase in job opportunities, income and demand for goods and services in rural markets. However, the general impression among marketers is that the rural markets have potentital only for agricultural inputs like seeds, fertilisers, pesticides, cattle feed and agricultural machinery. Over 50 per cent of the national income is generated in rural India and there are opportunities to market modern goods and services in rural areas and also market agricultural products in urban areas. over 70 per cent of bicycles, mechanical watches and radios and about 60 per cent of batteries, sewing machines and table fans are sold in rural India. At the same time, sales of colour television, washing machines, refrigerators, mobile phones, computers, shampoos, face cream, mosquito repellent and toothpaste are very low and there is tremendous potential for such products in rural markets.

Rural markets have undergone rapid transformation during the last ten years. Today, the rural consumer is exposed to a variety of products and services and specific brands. Rural markets account for about 50 per cent of the consumption of fast moving consumer goods and durables. Even usage of computers is growing in large villages and villages close to towns. While rural markets offer big attractions to the marketers, it is not easy to enter the market and take a sizeable share of the market within a short period. This is due to low literacy, low income, seasonal demand and problems with regard to transportation, communication and distribution. Further, there are different groups based on religion, caste, education, income and age and there is a need to understand the rural markets in terms of buyer behaviour, attitudes, beliefs and aspirations of people. Many of us think that increase in consumption of consumer goods such as mobile phone and television is an indication of the improvement in the quality of life of people in rural areas. But access to sanitation, electricity, education and health care is still lacking in villages and the people should have basic amenities of life such as Roti, Kapda, Makaan, Bijli, Sadak and Pani.

Rural marketing has become a buzz-word among marketing professionals and preachers. Delivering a better standard of living and quality of life will be the new role of rural marketing. The companies entering rural markets have a major role to play by carrying developmental messages to less informed rural population. Late C.K. Prahalad, the Management Guru, in his famous book on "The Fortune at the Bottom of the Pyramid", has rightly said, "the real source of market promise is not the wealthy few in the developing world or even the emerging middle income consumers. It is the billions of aspiring poor who are joining the market economy for the first time." Thus, rural markets offer opportunities and challenges for the marketers.

MARKET

Traditionally, market refers to a physical location where buyers and sellers gather to exchange their goods. In the market, ownership and possession of products is transferred from the seller to the buyer and money acts as a medium of exchange and measure of value. Economists describe a market as a collection of buyers and sellers who transact over a particular product or service. Marketers view sellers as the industry and buyers as the market. Business people use the term market to refer to various grouping of customers, i.e., Product market (***Example:*** Television market), Geographic market (***Example:*** African market) or Non-customer group such as labour market. Market also refers to the aggregate demand of the potential buyers for a product or service. In this sense market means people with needs to satisfy, the money to spend and the will to spend money to satisfy their needs. Therefore the term "Market" has a wider meaning and it is not confined to a particular physical place. It is an area in which forces of demand and supply operate directly or by means of any kind of communication to bring about transfer in the title of the goods.

RURAL MARKET

There are different definitions for the term rural market.

1. Census of India 2011: The rural market has been defined as a place where the population is not more than 5,000, the density of population is not more than 400 per square kilometre and at least 75 per cent of the male working population is engaged in agriculture.

2. Reserve Bank of India: Locations with population up to 10,000 will be considered as rural and 10,000 to 1,00,000 as semi-urban.

3. Planning Commission: Places with population up to 15,000 are considered as rural.

4. NABARD: All locations irrespective of villages or towns, up to a population of 10,000 will be considered as rural.

5. Most Companies in the FMCG would define rural as any place with a population up to 20,000.

6. Consumer Durable Companies would consider any town with a population below 50,000 as rural.

7. A Simple Definition from Marketers' View would be "any market that exists in an area with less than 10,000 population, low density of population and without significant infrastructure facilities is a rural market".

RURAL MARKETING

When we study the evolution of rural marketing in our country, we find the following stages:

1. Agricultural Marketing

In the earlier years, i.e., before the 1960s, the focus was on marketing of agricultural produce such as paddy, wheat, cotton, etc., and the subject was treated as a synonym with agricultural marketing. As per National Commission on Agriculture, "Rural marketing is a process which starts with a decision to produce a salable farm commodity and involves all aspects of market structure or system, functional and institutional, based on technical and economic consideration and includes pre- and post-harvest operations, assembling, grading, storage, transportation and distribution".

2. Agricultural Inputs Marketing

The Green Revolution during 1960s and 1970s led to increase in the use of high yielding seeds, fertilisers, pesticides and agricultural machinery like tractors and a new area of marketing, i.e., agricultural inputs marketing became popular.

3. Consumer Goods Marketing

Focus on rural development and liberalisation in 1980s had a salutory effect on rural economy and the demand for consumables and consumer durables. Companies like Hindustan Unilever, ITC, Colgate, Marico, Parle, Britannia, Godrej, Philips have taken a lead in establishing their products in rural markets. Many marketers and academicians consider rural marketing as the marketing of products and services to rural population. Rural marketing is defined as "the process of developing, pricing, promoting, distributing rural specific goods and services leading to exchange between urban and rural markets which satisfies consumer demand and also achieving organisational objectives".

We can look at rural marketing in two ways:

1. Functional and Product-oriented Concept

Rural marketing is the flow of goods and services from urban to rural and *vice versa*. The flow of goods within the rural areas is also called rural marketing. Therefore, rural marketing is a two-way marketing process and involves three types of transactions.

(a) **Urban to Rural:** Products manufactured in urban areas are marketed in rural areas.

Example: Two-wheelers and television.

(b) **Rural to Urban:** Production takes places in rural areas for consumption in urban markets.

Example: Agricultural produce such as paddy, wheat, cotton, fruits and vegetables.

(c) **Rural to Rural:** Production is carried out in villages and the products are used in villages.

Example: Farm implements (ploughs, pick-axe, sickles, ropes, bamboo mats, baskets, etc.)

"A Craftsman Displaying His Wares"

2. Socio-economic Concept

According to Paul Mazur, marketing is the creation and delivery of standard of living to society. This definition catches the true spirit of the marketing process. It has consumer orientation. It emphasises the major function of marketing, *viz.*, satisfaction of customer and social demand for goods and services. The word 'rural' connotes an environment characterised by low investment, low literacy, low density of population, low infrastructure facilities, low income and low savings and marketing is the process of delivering better standard of living and quality of life to the rural population. A rural salesperson is the carrier of developmental messages to less informed rural population rather than a mere order taker.

Examples:

(a) In the case of oral care products, currently only 47 per cent of the population use toothpaste, 23 per cent use powder and the rest neither. Targeting non-users in rural areas and developing awareness about oral hygiene and converting them into tooth-powder/toothpaste users.

(b) Identifying farmers who are following traditional methods of cultivation and educating them to adopt modern cultivation practices.

(c) The penetration level of soap is about 80 per cent in rural market against over 98 per cent in urban areas and there is a need to educate the non-users on the health benefits of soaps.

In the above cases, the marketers have to invest lot of resources to undertake developmental activities in rural areas. The rural marketing process involves not only business organisations but also public and voluntary organisations associated with rural development process. It deals with all the tangible and intangible things and includes agricultural inputs, products, services and ideas.

RURAL ENVIRONMENT

About two-thirds of the people, especially in the developing countries live in rural areas and depend upon agriculture and related activities for their livelihood. In urban areas, the output from the farm, i.e., food, fibre and other raw materials are processed and made available to the consumers. Rural environment is closely connected to nature as agricultural lands, forests, rivers, mountains, etc., whereas the environment is man-made in urban areas. In rural areas, social contacts are personal and relatively long-lasting. In urban areas, the relations are impersonal, casual and mostly short-lived.

Rural areas refer to countryside, that are sparsely populated places and are distinct from thickly populated urban areas. Rural people live in villages, in farms and in isolated houses. Lifestyle in rural areas are different from urban areas due to limited availability services such as schools, banks, hospitals, libraries, sewerage, street lighting, public transport and telecommunication facilities. The basic facilities such as housing, health, education, water supply, roads, communication and transport are poor in most of the rural areas. Half of the people in rural areas live in unhealthy and unclean environment. Poverty, unemployment and lack of financial resources for modernising agriculture and starting small industries are the other problems faced by rural people. The rural environment is different from urban environment as shown in Fig. 1.1.

Criteria	Rural World	Urban World
Occupation	Majority of the people engaged in agriculture and agricultural related activities.	All the people engaged in manufacturing,mechanical pursuits, trade, commerce, professions, governing and other non-agricultural occupations.
Environment	Direct relationship to nature.	Greater isolation from nature and man-made environment.
Density of population	The density is lower than in urban community.	Greater density than in rural communities.
Heterogeneity and homogeneity of the population	Rural communities are more homogeneous in racial and psychological traits.	More heterogeneous than rural communities.
Mobility	Normally the migration of people takes place from country to the city.	Only in the periods of social catastrophe the people migrate from the city to country.
System of interaction	Fewer contacts with outside world. Simplicity in relations. Speaks through the heart.	Impersonal casual relations, superficial, standardised formality of relations.
Cultural factors	Rigid, conservative, custom based society	Progressive outlook and scientific approach to problems
Status of women	Considered sub-servient	Generally equal status

Fig. 1.1: Criteria for Rural-urban Differentiation

TRANSITION IN RURAL SOCIETY

Due to increase in literacy level, income, reach of mass media, more employment opportunities outside agricultural sector, rural people are leaving caste-based occupations, traditional belief, traditional life, joint family life and servant-master relationship and moving to towns for a better living. Rural people want to replicate the lifestyle of urban people.

One of the problems faced by villagers is unemployment. Agriculture is a seasonal occupation and cannot provide employment throughout the year. The number of people engaged in agriculture is more than what is necessary to carry-out cultivation. There is surplus labour engaged in agriculture, leading to migration of labour to towns and cities in search of employment opportunities. Migrant people are forced to live in slums and there is proliferation of slums in cities. Many of our growing cities are overcrowded and lack basic facilities. Agriculture contributes to about 16 per cent of the GDP and employs 56 per cent of the workforce, i.e., 270 million as shown below:

Table 1.1: Break-up of India's 480 million Jobs

Sector	Contribution to GDP (%)	Workforce (million)	Percentage
Agriculture	15.70	270	56
Manufacturing	28.10	65	24
Services	56.20	145	29

Source: Technopack Analysis – Marketing White Book – 2012-2013.

Agricultural development contributes towards self-sufficiency in food production as well export of agricultural commodities to earn foreign exchange. However, agricultural development may not directly benefit rural population consisting of labourers, petty traders and village artisans. There is mobility of labour from agriculture to industrial sector. This has lead to shortage of labour in villages particularly during peak agricultural season. In the long run, these changes will have an adverse effect on agricultural productivity. Therefore, developments of industries, handicrafts, institutional credit, minimum wages, social security, etc., have to be taken up for overall development of rural sector.

Economic boom in our country has led to lot of developments in urban areas with trickle down gains for the rural areas. Apart from agriculture, we have to focus on development of rural enterprises and rural infrastructure for economic growth of villages.

India 2020: A Vision for the New Millennium, Authored by Dr. A.P.J. Abdul Kalam and Dr. Y.S. Rajan

Vision 2020 has five components, i.e., agriculture and food processing, education and health care, information and communication technology, reliable and quality electric power, surface transport and infrastructure for all parts of country, self-reliance in critical technologies. These five areas are inter-related and will lead to food, economic and national security. Two new situations have emerged: one is PURA (Providing Urban facilities in Rural Areas) and the other is the economic turbulence. To challenge the economic turbulence, our economic development policy has to be wise enough to activate agricultural and rural development. This is possible by establishing PURA complexes covering six lakh villages. PURA calls for establishing physical connectivity (roads), electronic connectivity (information and communication technology) and knowledge connectivity. If these are provided, economic connectivity will be enhanced.

RURAL INFRASTRUCTURE

1. Housing: Rural areas still suffer from poor housing and shelter. According to National Building Organisation, rural housing shortage is about 150 lakh units. In the rural areas, many houses do not have toilets, bathrooms and many are using a part of the living room as a kitchen and the rest are cooking in the open.

Housing is related to other aspects of life like health and hygiene. In many cases cattle sheds are attached to the houses. Inadequate ventilation, poor sanitation and hygiene and inhalation of kitchen smoke affect the health of the people.

"A Kachcha House"

"A Pucca House"

As per Indian Readership Survey (2010), the percentage of Pucca houses is high in Kerala (95 per cent), Punjab (80 per cent) and low in Chhattisgarh (26 per cent) and Madhya Pradesh (31 per cent). The Government has taken initiatives to construct houses on a large-scale. With regard to type of houses, 60 per cent of rural population have Pucca houses, 25 per cent Semi-pucca and 15 per cent Kachcha houses against 22 per cent Pucca, 37 per cent Semi-pucca and 41 per cent Kachcha houses in 1981. But the problem continues due to unchecked growth in population. At present, only 59 per cent of households have access to sanitation in Rural India. The Government plans all rural households would have toilets by 2015 under Total Sanitation Programme. Total sanitation campaign is operational in 590 districts in the country.

Loans for Improvement of Dwellings in Rural Areas

HDFC (Housing Development Finance Corporation Limited), India's largest home loan provider has joined SKS Microfinance in a pilot project to provide loans for improvement of dwellings primarily to low income women clients in Andhra Pradesh. The loans will be in the range of ₹ 50,000-1.5 lakh for a tenure of 3-5 years. The loans would be given to borrowers who have a good credit history of three years. The project will provide loans mainly for extension and improvement of dwelling units which double up for income generating activities like eateries, kirana shops, papad and agarbathi making.

2. Water Supply: Water-borne diseases can be prevented by providing protected water supply. However, only 18 per cent of rural households have tap water facilities compared to 62 per cent in urban areas. Government has initiated rural water supply scheme under Rajiv Gandhi National Drinking Water Mission, an integrated approach to supply clean drinking water to rural population. There are many NGOs who are involved in providing drinking water to the villages. ***Example:*** All women NGO-Swayam Siddha Mahila Utkarsha Sanstha, helps villages with pure drinking water. It has collaborated with National Physical Laboratory, Pune to acquire technology that treat raw water and purify it. The treated water is supplied to villages in Sirur taluka, near Pune for a price as low as one rupee per litre.

"An Open Well"

2. Health: Rural health care system is mostly run by Government and this system is in adequate and has several weaknesses. In our country, availability of health facilities has been poor for various reasons. About 80 per cent of diseases are related to unsafe water supply and inadeqauate sanitation. Health services in rural areas are so poor that many people prefer to go to private practitioners. In primary health centres, there is lack of support staff, doctors, medicines and equipment. Villagers have to travel long distances to avail medical facilities. It is seen that medical personnel are concentrated in urban areas. Around 75 per cent of qualified doctors work in urban areas which account for only 30 per cent of the total population. About 60 per cent of the medical colleges are in South, Maharashtra and Pondicherry and only about 10 per cent are in Bihar, Odisha, West Bengal and North Eastern States. Only about 20 per cent of the hospitals are located in rural areas to cater to the needs of about 70 crore population. Dental hygiene is badly neglected and about 70 per cent of the villagers are affected by dental diseases. There is one dentist for a population of 10,000 in urban areas compared to 2,50,000 persons in rural areas.

National Rural Health Mission aims to provide health care to remotest households in the country through an Integrated Heath Care Service Programme. At present, only 300 out of 604 districts have medical colleges. To overcome acute shortage of doctors in rural areas, the Government has plans to start a unique three-and-a-half-year bachelor course in medicine for students from villages. The Government will select up to 25 students from each of 300 districts which do not have medical colleges. These doctors will be allowed to work only in rural areas.

"Village Pond is Used for Bathing and Washing Clothes by Local People"

"Arogya Parivar"

The Swiss Multinational, Novartis has started "Arogya Parivar" to create awareness about health and hygiene among rural masses. A group of rural health educators move from village-to-village conducting group meeting of villagers. They identify patients and convince them the need for medical treatment. One-to-one meeting is also held to convince the patient and the family. The focus is mainly on women and children. The social business model has treated over 10,000 patients and had built-up rapport with doctors, health workers and medical shops in rural areas.

4. Road Network: There are about six lakh villages and for development of these villages, they have to be connected with towns and cities through road transport system. About 80 per cent of the villages are connected by road and we have to go a long way in developing all-weather roads. During rainy season, about 60 per cent of the villages are not accessible as the roads gets flooded. Road connectivity is rather low to villages having less than 1,000 population. Only states like Punjab, Kerala and Goa have high percentage of rural connectivity. Many farmers use bullock carts for transporting their produce from the village to the market and this method of transport is time-consuming.

"A Kachcha Road from the Village to the Market"

Infrastructure Lapses in Growing Cities

While rural areas suffer due to lack of infrastructure facilities, many of our growing cities are over crowded and lack basic amenities. ***Example:*** The per capital net income of a Mumbaiikar is ₹ 65,000 twice the country's average as per Human Development Report (2009). Mumbai is one of the world's most densely populated cities. Nearly one-third of the population does not get adequate drinking water. The sewerage serves only 50 per cent of the population. Nearly 50 per cent people stay in slums. Study reveals that average vehicular speed on city road has fallen from 30 km/hr in 1962 to 15 km in 2007. Public transport is woefully inadequate. Population density has leapt from 27,000 persons in 2001 to about 48,000 in 2009. More than 4.5 million people per day travel using bus services and another 6.5 million use railway services. During peak hours, people are packed like sardines in railway compartments.

Table 1.2: Mumbai City Homes Lack Toilets, Not Phones

Assets	Island City	Suburbs
No. Households (in lakh)	6.40	20.20
With Tap Water	97.80%	96.50%
With Electricity	98.10	96.90
With Phones	**94.40**	**94.00**
With TV	85.30	85.10
With One Room	62.70	55.50
With Car	12.60	11.80
With Motor Cycle	16.60	15.30
With Bicycle	8.80	11.50
With Toilets	**67.00**	**54.70**

Source: Census 2011(House Listing and Housing Census).

5. Rural Electrification: About five lakh villages have electric supply and this has increased the demand for electric motors, television, pumps, agricultural machinery and consumer durables like transistors, television, electric fans, etc. Kutir Jyoti Programme initiated by Government of India aims to provide single point light connection to rural households. States like Kerala, Tamil Nadu, Delhi, Goa, Haryana, and Punjab have achieved about 100 per cent village electrification. As far as rural household electrification is concerned, about 55 per cent of the households are electrified (2010). However, erratic power supply continues to be a major problem in rural areas. Whenever there is a problem In National Grid, villages are affected since priority is given to urban areas for supply of electricity.

'Bijli Box' Lights Homes in Rural UP with Solar Power

A renewal energy company, OMC Power, lights up rural parts of Uttar Pradesh, delivering solar-charged batteries to homes in an out-of-the-box move that promises cheap and uninterrupted power supply.

A start-up company floated a year ago by three former employees of Ericsson, is supplying electricity to about 3,000 households in remote areas of Hardoi district where conventional power lines are yet to reach. The company's promoters hope to energise another 24,000 homes by the end of the year.

The power distribution of model involves generation of electricity at an 18-kw solar plant at Jangaon, in Hardoi, from where it reaches villagers' homes in rechargeable batteries contained in boxes, popular called 'Bijli Box' (power in a box).

"One charge is enough for 12 hours. Every evening at 6, our employees collect these boxes from the generating unit and deliver them to their subscribers in nearby villages on diesel vehicles," said OMC Power's chief operating officer Rohit Chandra.

The Bijli Box – weighing about 2 kgs. and holding an electronic circuit and accompanying software besides the battery – can power a couple of bulbs, a fan and a specially-made television set. The company has employed youth from the villages to replace the spent boxes with charged ones at daybreak.

In OMC's model there is no security cash deposit or fixed cost and subscribers pay on the basis of usage. The charge for a single electric lantern is ₹ 5 a day or ₹ 120 every month. Charge for the box varies from ₹ 250 to ₹ 500 per month.

The company has already garnered a subscriber base of 3,000 households in and around the village. OMC Power plans to set up 500 units of 18-kw each over the next couple of years, which will produce enough power for about 1.5 million households.

The Bijli Box has started transforming the lives of villagers. Says Radhesham Trivedi, an elderly farmer. "Our community, family and village will be educated. When we are educated, there will be development. If there is development, whatever we are doing – service or agriculture – will give a good income."

Source: *The Economic Times*: November 1, 2012.

6. Communication Facilities: India Post covers rural and semi-urban areas through a network of 1,40,000 post offices. Ending 2011, there were 929 million mobile subscribers. Out of this about 327 million subscribers are from rural (35 per cent) areas. Further there are about 60 lakh public telephones in villages. However, about 20 per cent of the villages are without telephone facility and the Government and Private Sector have taken initiative in developing communication facilities by expanding landline and mobile phone services to interior villages. The Government plans to reach rural teledensity of 40 per cent by 2014.

Example: Nokia Life Tools is a range of services which includes agriculture, education, entertainments designed specially for consumers in small towns and villages. Life Tools will be available even in the entry level model of mobile phone. It gives information on agricultural inputs, market prices of commodities, weather conditions, general knowledge, examination results, etc., at a subscription cost of about ₹ 50 per month.

Warna Wired Village Communication Project (Maharashtra)

Warna is a well-developed rural area situated about 30 kms from Kolhapur in Western Maharashtra. Through the efforts of Late Tataya Saheb Kore, a Cooperative Sugar factory was established in Kadoli (1959), now the main centre for Warna Group of Cooperative institutions. Subsequently new establishments such as Warna Milk Cooperative, Bank Cooperative, Warna Hospital, Warna Bazaar, Warna Fruit Processing, and Warna Shiksha Mandal came up. Warna wired village wired project was started in 1998 for providing internet and intranet within the co-operative institutions and villages. Seventy villages have been connected and each village has information kiosk, computer, printer, modem to aid internet connectivity and operator to provide guidance to users. The total cost of the project was ₹ 2.5 crore and the channels used for the project are V Sat Communication, Dial Up and Radio Frequency. Project partners included National infrastructure centre, Directorate of Information Technology, Government of Maharashtra and Warna Milk Union.

Source: Dhanraj Patil (2010) , Communication for Rural Development in India, Serials Publications, New Delhi.

CHARACTERISTICS OF RURAL MARKET

1. Population: According to Census 2011, our country has 35 States/Union Territories, 640 districts, 5,924 Subdistricts/Talukas, 7,935 towns and 6,41,000 villages and total population of 1,210 million. Out of the total population, rural population is 833 million and constitute about 69 per cent of the population as per Table 1.4. With 168 million households, the rural population is nearly three times of urban. For the first time since independence, the absolute increase in population is more in urban areas than in rural areas. Level of urbanisation has increased from 27.80 per cent in 2001 to 31.16 per cent in 2011. The proportion of rural population has declined from 72.20 per cent (2001) to 68.84 per cent (2011). It is estimated that our country's urban population will reach 600 million by 2030, i.e., 40 per cent of the total Indian population.

India's Rural Population is about 2.5 Times the Population of USA

The estimated global population in 2010 was 6,908 million and our country with 2.4 per cent of the world surface area accounts for 17.5 per cent of the world population. USA accounts for 7.2 per cent of surface area with only 4.5 per cent of the world population. The population of India at 1,210 million is almost equal to the combined population of USA (309 million), Indonesia (238 million), Brazil (191 million), Pakistan (185 million), Bangladesh (164 million) and Japan (128 million) put together. The population of these six countries totals 1,215 million? The combined population of UP and Maharashtra at 312 million is greater than the population of USA, the third most populated country in the world. Our rural population is about 2.5 times the population of USA.

Density of population is defined as the number of persons per square kilometre and it shows the concentration of population in a particular area. The density of population per square km. has gone up from 324 in 2001 to 382 persons 2011. Among the states, population density is high in Bihar and West Bengal and low in Arunachal Pradesh and Mizoram. Among the ten most populous countries of the world, only Bangladesh has higher population density compared to India.

Table No 1.3: State-wise distribution of villages (2011)

State/UT Code	India/State/Union Territory	Percentage of population living in villages of population size						
		Less than 200	200-499	500-999	1000-1999	2000-4999	5000-9999	10,000 and above
	INDIA * +	**0.98**	**4.76**	**12.39**	**23.70**	**34.63**	**14.86**	**8.68**
01	Jammu & Kashmir	0.61	4.89	12.28	25.58	37.85	15.26	3.53
02	Himachal Pradesh	13.16	30.35	27.31	18.31	9.47	1.20	0.20
03	Punjab	0.53	3.92	13.81	28.23	38.13	12.44	2.95
04	Chandigarh #	0.00	0.00	0.00	0.00	28.82	71.18	0.00
05	Uttarakhand	10.18	21.25	17.76	16.04	20.20	9.22	5.36
06	Haryana	0.14	0.97	4.72	17.59	42.76	24.12	9.71
07	N.C.T. Delhi	0.12	0.17	0.97	7.90	43.60	13.46	33.7
08	Rajasthan	0.89	6.13	17.51	28.74	33.05	10.58	3.09
09	Uttar Pradesh	0.45	3.13	11.12	25.82	40.33	14.45	4.70
10	Bihar	0.27	1.76	6.04	15.86	34.00	23.64	18.43
11	Sikkim	0.35	6.02	24.22	38.53	25.19	5.69	0.00
12	Arunachal Pradesh	29.41	29.22	21.16	14.50	5.13	0.58	0.00
13	Nagaland	1.90	10.19	16.87	23.40	33.06	13.78	0.79
14	Manipur+	5.68	13.83	15.24	18.42	31.13	10.85	4.85
15	Mizoram	1.99	15.69	31.70	26.83	21.53	2.27	0.00
16	Tripura	0.05	0.69	2.23	10.93	44.80	32.52	8.78
17	Meghalaya	12.82	33.72	27.65	14.30	9.62	1.89	0.00
18	Assam	1.73	7.18	16.41	30.06	36.07	7.23	1.31
19	West Bengal	0.63	3.84	10.06	20.00	37.24	18.33	9.91
20	Jharkhand	2.28	11.23	22.63	28.90	27.22	5.81	1.94
21	Odisha	3.27	12.85	24.41	31.14	24.52	3.44	0.36
22	Chhattisgarh	1.04	7.70	22.87	38.21	27.34	2.72	0.12
23	Madhya Pradesh	1.05	8.06	22.55	33.18	27.34	7.10	0.73
24	Gujarat	0.18	1.97	8.37	23.26	41.42	18.56	6.24
25	Daman & Diu #	0.00	0.99	4.37	10.77	24.68	59.19	0.00
26	Dadra & Nagar Haveli #	0.06	1.11	2.46	13.96	53.33	20.53	8.55
27	Maharashtra	0.44	3.73	13.36	27.95	33.97	12.77	7.79
28	Andhra Pradesh	0.52	1.95	5.57	16.54	39.43	22.76	13.22
29	Karnataka	0.79	4.95	13.71	24.42	35.31	14.86	5.96
30	Goa	0.53	3.68	7.17	20.62	49.56	15.90	2.54
31	Lakshadweep #	0.40	1.92	0.00	0.00	44.50	53.19	0.00
32	Kerala	0.00	0.00	0.01	0.10	1.17	6.50	92.21
33	Tamil Nadu	0.13	1.13	4.76	16.71	43.02	26.73	7.52
34	Puducherry #	0.00	0.00	0.44	4.76	38.94	47.70	8.16
35	Andaman & Nicobar Islands#	5.03	10.68	18.46	29.97	30.46	5.40	0.00

Source: Census of India Reports – 2011.

Table 1.4: Population in India — Rural vs. Urban

Year	Rural Population in Million	Urban Population in Million	Total Population in Million	Rural Population %	Urban Population %
1951	295	62	357	82.60	17.40
1961	360	79	439	82.00	18.00
1971	439	109	548	80.10	19.90
1981	508	160	668	76.00	24.00
1991	621	215	836	74.30	25.70
2001	742	285	1027	72.20	27.80
2011	8330	3771	12101	68.84	31.16

Source: Census of India Reports — 2011.

Six states, i.e., UP, Bihar, West Bengal, Maharashtra, Andhra Pradesh and MP contribute to 50 per cent of the population. The most populated state is UP with a population of 19.96 core and the least populated state Sikkim has a population of six lakh. States like Maharashtra, Tamil Nadu, Gujarat, Punjab, and Kerala are more urbanised. There are states like Bihar, UP, Rajasthan, Himachal Pradesh, Odisha, Assam, MP where the rural population varies from 70 to 90 per cent as shown in table 1.5. Therefore a large rural population gives us an opportunity for marketing a variety of products and services. However, income and purchasing power play a major role in determining the demand in rural areas.

Table 1.5: Population of India (2011)

India/State/UT	Total Population	Rural Population	Urban Population	Rural Total Population (%) (2011)	Literacy (%) (2011)
India	1,21,01,93,422	83,30,87,662	37,71,05,760	68.84	72.20
Jammu & Kashmir	1,25,48,926	91,34,820	34,14,106	72.79	68.74
Himachal Pradesh	68,56,509	61,67,805	6,88,704	89.96	83.78
Punjab	2,77,04,236	1,73,16,800	1,03,87,436	62.51	76.68
Chandigarh #	10,54,686	29,004	10,25,682	2.75	86.43
Uttarakhand	1,01,16,752	70,25,583	30,91,169	69.45	79.63
Haryana	2,53,53,081	1,65,31,493	88,21,588	65	76.64
Rajasthan	6,86,21,012	5,15,40,236	1,70,80,776	75.11	67.06
Uttar Pradesh	19,95,81,477	15,51,11,022	4,44,70,455	77.72	69.72
Bihar	10,38,04,637	9,20,75,028	1,17,29,609	88.70	63.82
Sikkim	6,07,688	4,55,962	1,51,726	75.03	82.20
Arunachal Pradesh	13,82,611	10,69,165	3,13,446	77.33	66.95
Nagaland	19,80,602	14,06,861	5,73,741	71.03	80.11
Manipur	27,21,756	18,99,624	8,22,132	69.79	79.85
Mizoram	10,91,014	5,29,037	5,61,977	48.49	91.58

Tripura	36,71,032	27,10,051	9,60,981	73.82	87.75
Meghalaya	29,64,007	23,68,971	5,95,036	79.92	75.48
Assam	3,11,69,272	2,67,80,516	43,88,756	85.92	73.18
West Bengal	9,13,47,736	6,22,13,676	2,91,34,060	68.11	77.08
Jharkhand	3,29,66,238	2,50,36,946	79,29,292	75.95	67.63
Odisha	4,19,47,358	3,49,51,234	69,96,124	83.32	73.45
Chhattisgarh	2,55,40,196	1,96,03,658	59,36,538	76.76	71.04
Madhya Pradesh	7,25,97,565	5,25,37,899	2,00,59,666	72.37	70.63
Dadra & Nagar Haveli #	3,42,853	1,83,024	1,59,829	53.38	77.65
Maharashtra	11,23,72,972	6,15,45,441	5,08,27,531	54.77	82.90
Andhra Pradesh	8,46,65,533	5,63,11,788	2,83,53,745	66.51	67.66
Karnataka	6,11,30,704	3,75,52,529	2,35,78,175	61.43	75.60
Goa	14,57,723	5,51,414	9,06,309	37.83	87.40
Lakshadweep #	64,429	14,121	50,308	21.92	92.28
Kerala	3,33,87,677	1,74,55,506	1,59,32,171	52.28	93.91
Tamil Nadu	7,21,38,958	3,71,89,229	3,49,49,729	51.55	80.33
Puducherry #	12,44,464	3,94,341	8,50,123	31.69	86.55

Source: Census of India Reports — 2011.

2. Demography and Economic Growth of States: The last few years have seen tremendous growth in rural areas of the country mainly due to favourable Government policies towards agriculture and rural development. States like Bihar, Madhya Pradesh, and Rajasthan with a large rural population have shown higher growth rates as shown below:

Table 1.6: Demography and Economic Growth of States

State	**2000-2001 to 2005-2006 (%)**	**2006-2007 to 2011-2012 (%)**
Bihar	5.2	13
UP	4.2	7.1
Rajasthan	5.4	8.5
MP	2.7	9
Punjab	4.3	7.4
West Bengal	5.7	7.4
Gujarat	8.4	9.3
Maharashtra	6.7	10.4
Tamil Nadu	6.2	9.5

Source: NSSO.

3. Scattered Markets: The rural population and markets are highly scattered over a wide geographical area as shown in Tables in 1.3 and 1.7.

Table 1.7: Distribution of Villages in India (2011)

Population	No. of Villages	% of Total Villages	% of Population
Less than 200	82149	13.75	.98
200-499	114726	19.20	4.76
500-990	141761	23.73	12.39
1000-1999	139136	23.29	23.70
2000-4999	96388	16.13	34.63
5000 and above	18641	3.12	14.86
Above 10,000	4682	.78	8.68
Total number of initialled villages	597483	100.00	100.00

Source: Census of India Reports — 2011.

Note: Total number of villages 6,40,930 and inhabited villages 5,97,483.

It is seen that nearly half of the rural population lives in 1.2 lakh villages and remining lives in 4.8 lakh villages. For example in Kerla, over 92 per cent of rural population stays in villages of over 10,000 population size.

A small village is known as a hamlet and a group of hamlets form a revenue village with Panchayat. The villages can be categorised based on population, i.e., (a) large villages (> 5,000 population), (b) medium villages (2,000-5,000) and (c) small villages (1,000-2,000) and very small villages (less than 1,000). Practically, there are no shops in villages having less than 500 population and there are about 2 lakh villages in this category. Further, there are about 2.8 lakh villages with a population of 500-2,000 and making products available in these villages involves high distribution costs. Considering the large and scattered population, the marketers have to address two major problems, i.e., (a) How do we reach the scattered market through different media and methods? (b) How do we ensure that goods and services are available at the right time and at the right place as and when required by the rural consumer?

Compared to low density of population in rural areas, there over 50 towns/cities in India having more than 10 lakh population each. The marketers are focusing on these cities even though they contribute to only about 160 million population.

Table 1.8: Population in India: City-wise Population

Sr. No.	City	State	Urban Agglomeration	City Population	Literacy	City Population Ranking
1.	Mumbai	Maharashtra	1,84,14,288	1,24,78,447	90.28	1
2.	Delhi	Delhi	1,63,14,838	1,10,07,835	87.6	2
3.	Kolkata	West Bengal	1,41,12,536	44,86,679	87.14	7
4.	Chennai	Tamil Nadu	86,96,010	46,81,087	90.33	6
5.	Bangalore	Karnataka	84,99,399	84,25,970	89.59	3
6.	Hyderabad	Andhra Pradesh	77,49,334	68,09,970	82.96	4
7.	Ahmedabad	Gujarat	63,52,254	55,70,585	89.62	5

8.	Pune	Maharashtra	50,49,968	31,15,431	91.61	9
9.	Surat	Gujarat	45,85,367	44,62,002	89.03	8
10.	Jaipur	Rajasthan	30,73,350	30,73,350	84.34	10
11.	Kanpur	Uttar Pradesh	29,20,067	27,67,031	84.14	12
12.	Lucknow	Uttar Pradesh	29,01,474	28,15,601	84.72	11
13.	Nagpur	Maharashtra	24,97,777	24,05,421	93.13	13
14.	Ghaziabad	Uttar Pradesh	23,58,525	**16,36,068**	100.54	21
15.	Indore	Madhya Pradesh	21,67,447	**19,60,631**	87.38	14
16.	Coimbatore	Tamil Nadu	21,51,466	**10,61,447**	91.74	39
17.	Kochi	Kerala	21,17,990	**6,01,574**	97.49	51
18.	Patna	Bihar	20,46,652	**16,83,200**	84.71	19
19.	Kozhikode	Kerala	20,30,519	**4,32,097**	96.8	53
20.	Bhopal	Madhya Pradesh	18,83,381	**17,95,648**	85.24	16
21.	Thrissur	Kerala	18,54,783	**3,15,596**	97.24	55
22.	Thane	Maharashtra	18,18,872	**18,18,872**	91.36	15
23.	Vadodara	Gujarat	18,17,191	**16,66,703**	92.37	20
24.	Agra	Uttar Pradesh	17,46,467	**15,74,542**	63.44	23
25.	Visakhapatnam	Andhra Pradesh	17,30,320	**17,30,320**	82.66	17
26.	Pimpri and Chinchwad	Maharashtra	17,29,359	**17,29,359**	90.9	18
27.	Thiruvananthapuram	Kerala	16,87,406	**7,52,490**	93.72	49
28.	Ludhiana	Punjab	16,13,878	**16,13,878**	85.38	22
29.	Nashik	Maharashtra	15,62,769	**14,86,973**	90.96	24
30.	Vijayawada	Andhra Pradesh	14,91,202	**10,48,240**	82.59	42
31.	Madurai	Tamil Nadu	14,62,420	**10,16,885**	91.42	44
32.	Varanasi	Uttar Pradesh	14,35,113	**12,01,815**	80.12	30
33.	Meerut	Uttar Pradesh	14,24,908	**13,09,023**	77.7	26
34.	Faridabad	Haryana	14,04,653	**14,04,653**	84.88	25
35.	Rajkot	Gujarat	13,90,933	**12,86,995**	88.82	27
36.	Jamshedpur	Jharkhand	13,37,131	**6,29,659**	87.5	50
37.	Srinagar	Jammu and Kashmir	12,73,312	**11,92,792**	70.98	31
38.	Jabalpur	Madhya Pradesh	12,67,564	**10,54,336**	88.9	40
39.	Kalyan and Dombivali	Maharashtra	12,46,381	**12,46,381**	93.06	28
40.	Asansol	West Bengal	12,43,008	**5,64,491**	84.82	52
41.	Vasai Virar	Maharashtra	12,21,233	**12,21,233**	91.15	29
42.	Allahabad	Uttar Pradesh	12,16,719	**11,17,094**	86.5	36
43.	Dhanbad	Jharkhand	11,95,298	**11,61,561**	80.78	33
44.	Aurangabad	Maharashtra	11,89,376	**11,71,330**	89.13	32
45.	Amritsar	Punjab	11,83,705	**11,32,761**	85.27	34
46.	Jodhpur	Rajasthan	11,37,815	**10,33,918**	81.56	43
47.	Ranchi	Jharkhand	11,26,741	**10,73,440**	88.49	37
48.	Raipur	Chhattisgarh	11,22,555	**10,10,087**	86.9	45
49.	Navi Mumbai	Maharashtra	11,19,477	**11,19,477**	91.57	35
50.	Kollam	Kerala	11,10,005	**3,49,033**	92.1	54
51.	Gwalior	Madhya Pradesh	11,01,981	**10,53,505**	85.2	41

52.	Haora	West Bengal	10,72,161	**10,72,161**	89.86	38
53.	Chandigarh	Chandigarh	10,25,682	**9,60,787**	86.77	47
54.	Tiruchirappalli	Tamil Nadu	10,21,717	**8,46,915**	91.32	48
55.	Kota	Rajasthan	10,01,365	**10,01,365**	83.65	46
			163306142	**121238744**		

Source: Census of India Reports — 2011.

4. Occupation Pattern: The three sectors that provide employment to rural population are:

(a) **Primary Sector:** Cultivation of crops, dairy farming, cattle rearing, fish culture, poultry, big and small animals' meat production, agricultural labour. They are called primary sector as they produce goods which are necessities for human life.

"A Shepherd"

(b) **Secondary Sector:** Cottage and village industries, quarrying, construction work, rice/flour mill, making toys, baskets, carpets, etc.

(c) **Tertiary Sector:** Wholesale and retail sales, hotels, transport, insurance, banking, community and social services.

Table 1.9: Occupation Pattern

Occupation	Proportion (%)
Self-employed in Agriculture	34
Agricultural labour	30
Non-agricultural labour	11
Self-employed in non-agriculture	11
Others	14

Source: NSSO: 2007-2008.

It is seen from the above table that about 65 per cent of the rural population is engaged in agriculture and agriculture related activities. Out of this 34 per cent consists of cultivators and 30 per cent wage earners. The percentage of rural population self-employed in agriculture is high in Rajasthan (50 per cent), UP (45 per cent) HP (45 per cent) and low in Kerala (17 per cent), Tamil Nadu (17 per cent) and Andhra Pradesh (23 per cent).

5. Rural Economy and Agriculture: The agricultural sector continues to play a major role in rural economy and majority of the rural population is depending upon agriculture and related activities for their livelihood. Further it provides foodgrains to urban population also supplies raw materials like cotton, sugarcane, oilseeds and labour force to industrial sector. Increase in agricultural income leads to considerable demand for consumer goods and services in rural areas of agriculture to GDP has come down during the recent years and there is a need to come out with an integrated approach to accelerate agricultural production in our country and improve the effeciency of agricultural marketing.

Features of Indian Agriculture

- **Dependence on Monsoon:** With the exception of Jammu and Kashmir in the extreme North and Tamil Nadu in South, 80-90 per cent of the rainfall over the country occurs mostly during the south-west monsoon season (Kharif Season). Normally, the south-west monsoon reaches the Kerala coast by the end of May, advances along the Konkan coast in early June and extends over the entire country by the end of July. The rains continue up to the end of September. The north-east monsoon (Rabi Season) is the main contributor to the amount of rainfall over the south eastern portion of the country. In our country, majority of the farmers depend upon monsoon rains for cultivation of crops. Out of total cropped area of 190 million hectares, only about 60 million hectares are irrigated and the balance area is rainfed. In an year when the monsoon rains are good, the farmers get higher yields and higher income and a poor monsoon leads to poor crop yields and low income. Apart from the quantum of rainfall, timely onset of monsoon and distribution of rainfall are important for increasing agricultural production. Further, there are variations in the amount of rainfall received even in the same village. It is rightly said that Indian agriculture is a gamble under monsoon conditions.
- **Irrigation** plays a vital role in agricultural development. Crops growing under irrigated conditions give higher yields, leading to higher farm income. Also efficiency of other farm inputs largely depends on quantity and timing of water supply. There is considerable difference in irrigation facilities from state-to-state. About 95 per cent of the cultivated area is irrigated in Punjab compared to Maharashtra (15 per cent), West Bengal (22 per cent), Andhra Pradesh (40 per cent) and Karnataka (23 per cent).
- **Land Use Pattern:** Nearly 60 per cent of the area under cultivation is occupied by food crops. An average farmer would prefer to cultivate crops like paddy, wheat, jowar, etc., to meet the family consumption requirements. Nearly 50 per cent of the produce is retained for consumption and balance made available for sale. Cash crops like cotton, chillies, vegetables and fruits give higher returns compared to food crops and these farmers have high disposable income.
- **Small Holdings:** About 75 per cent of the land holdings consist of small and marginal farmers. The income from the farm is not sufficient to meet household expenses. When the holdings are small, cultivation becomes uneconomical and therefore it

is not a remunerative occupation. Most of these farmers follow traditional methods of cultivation leading to low yields from the farm. The requirements of small and marginal farmers are very basic, i.e., food, clothing and shelter. They spend less on non-food items.

- **Low Productivity:** The yield per hectare is very low compared to foreign countries. While there are very progressive farmers in states like Punjab, Andhra Pradesh, Tamil Nadu who are able to obtain very high yields comparable to developed countries, most of the small and marginal farmers continue to follow traditional methods of cultivation. These farmers lack support in the form of agricultural credit, crop insurance, inputs and marketing of agricultural produce.
- **Seasonal Employment:** Agriculture is a seasonal activity and depends upon agro-climatic conditions. About 80 per cent of the rainfall over the country is received mostly during Kharif season, i.e., the south-west monsoon season. The farmers do not have sufficient work throughout the year. Agricultural labourers remain unemployed for more than four months in an year. They are unorganised and unskilled and are not governed by any rules and regulations.
- **Semi-commercial Nature of Agriculture:** Under traditional farming practices, the production from the farm mainly caters to the requirements of the members of the family. As we have seen, majority of farmers have small holdings and bulk of the food production goes to meet personal domestic consumption. Under commercial farming, production of cash crops like cotton, sugarcane, fruits and vegetables is undertaken for sale. Changes in the cropping pattern from food crops to cash crops have enabled farmers to increase their income. Therefore we can say that Indian agriculture is neither completely traditional nor fully commercial.
- **Use of Agricultural Inputs:** Modern agricultural inputs such as high yielding varieties of seeds, chemical fertilisers and plant protection chemicals have helped our country to become self-sufficient in food production. The use of inputs depend upon a number of factors such as size of the farm, type of crops grown, irrigation facilities, output prices, etc. Further there are variations within the farming community in terms of education, age, income, values, beliefs, lifestyle and these factors influence the use of agricultural inputs. The use of hybrid wheat and rice is very low in our country. Fertilisers are used by large and medium farmers. About 25 per cent of the farmers do not use fertilisers regularly and such farmers are high in Bihar, Odisha and Rajasthan. There is a need to evolve integrated agricultural input management along with modern farming practices in our move towards sustainable agriculture.
- **Marketing of Agricultural Produce:** The farmers may sell the produce in the village itself or in the nearby market. Small farmers and the farmers living in interior villages not connected by road prefer to sell the produce in the village market. Large farmers and the farmers from the villages that are connected to the market by road normally sell the produce in the nearby market. Normally half of the marketed surplus of grains reaches the market during the first three months after harvest of the crop and the balance

during the remaining nine months. During harvesting reason, the prices of commodities come down in the market. The farmers would be motivated to increase yields only if they receive remunerative prices for their produce. Vagaries of monsoon, unorganised markets and superfluous middlemen are the major reasons for wide fluctuations in the prices of agricultural commodities and we are yet to develop an efficient system that will benefit all sections of the society, i.e., the farmers and consumers.

- **Need for Second Green Revolution:** Green Revolution took place some 40 years back. Economists and agricultural technologists are of the opinion that we need a second Green Revolution to meet the food requirements of the growing population and ensure the livelihood and survival of the rural people. National Commission on Farmers has stated that the agricultural progress has to be measured not in terms of the growth in production and growth rates, but in terms of growth in the real income of farmers. Today, the farmers are not getting remunerative prices for their produce. Many farmers would like to quit farming if there are other alternatives. The policy stresses the importance of income generation at farm level. The commission has further recommend that Minimum Support Price (MSP) for essential commodities like paddy and wheat should be cost of production plus 50 per cent. This will help us to overcome rural poverty and attract younger generation to enter farming.

6. Rural Income: It is seen that major income still comes from agriculture though the share of non-farm sector has gone up during the recent years. Increase in yields of crops and encouraging output prices will lead to increased income of rural people. Demand is seasonal and fluctuates depending upon agricultural situation. Demand is more after harvest of crops, during festivals and marriage seasons.

Table 1.10: Rural Income

Source of Income	Proportion (%)
Agriculture	53%
Business, crafts, Non-agricultural wages, Salaried class and Others	47%

Recent studies show that out of a rural population of about 800 million, there are 50 million people having per capita income of over ₹ 6,750 per month. Although the amount looks low, disposable income is high due to low cost of living in villages. It is this segment of the population that offers opportunities for marketing of consumer goods and services.

Examples:

(a) The demand for LPG in rural areas is highly seasonal and there is high demand during harvesting season and festivals. It is not affordable for daily use and alternatives such as cowdung, firewood, coal, etc., are available.

(b) The demand for durables like TV, transistors and two-wheelers is high after harvest of crops and during festivals.

(c) The gold buying season starts in October and continues till March in rural areas.

7. Literacy: Literacy level and educational attainment are vital indicators of development in a society. There has been marked improvement in the population of literates. At the time of independence, the rate of literacy was only about 14 per cent, which rose to 74 per cent for the whole country in 2011. The rural literacy has grown from 59 per cent in 2001 to 69 per cent in 2011 due to initiatives taken by Government. The pace of increase in female literacy is higher in rural areas. Female literacy has increased from 47 per cent in 2001 to 59 per cent in 2011. Of course there are wide variations within the country. ***Example:*** Literacy in Kerala (90 per cent), Mizoram (81 per cent), Goa (80 per cent), Maharashtra (70 per cent), UP (53 per cent), Arunachal Pradesh (48 per cent) and Jharkhand (46 per cent), Bihar (44 per cent).

Due to low levels of education, the demand for magazines, calculators, computers and English newspapers are generally low in rural areas. However, changes are taking place in villages near towns and semi-urban areas due to increase in educational facilities.

It has been observed that level of education coupled with increase in income has significant influence on usage of colour TV, refrigerator and two-wheelers. For example, penetration of refrigerator is only 4.8 per cent, whereas it is 33 per cent among graduate rural consumer.

"A Village Middle School – In Existence for Over Hundred Years"

Table 1.11: Literacy Levels

Literacy Levels (%)

Gender	1971		1981		1991		2001		2011	
	R	U	R	U	R	U	R	U	R	U
1. Male	34	61	41	66	58	81	71	87	79	90
2. Female	13	42	18	48	31	64	47	73	59	80
Total	24	52	30	57	45	73	59	80	69	85

R. Rural, U. Urban

Source: Census of India — 2011.

Empowerment of Women

Shama Khan (29 years) after completing a degree in law entered Grassroot level politics as a member of Chohtan Panchayat Samiti in 2005. She was elected Pradhan in 2010. In 2012, Chohtan was declared as the best Panchayat Samiti in the State and was awarded ₹ 15 lakh by the Government. She focused on girls' education and enrolment increased from 550 to 6,500 in two years. She persuaded women to attend Panchayat Samiti meetings. Rajasthan Government is impressed with her dedicated work and the way she conducts herself despite the fact she is from a community in which education of women is not a priority.

Source: *India Today*, December 24, 2012.

8. Many Languages and Dialects: As many as 18 major languages and 850 dialects add to the complexities in rural communication. Some of the important languages together with the number of people who speak the language are given in Table 1.12.

Table 1.12: Major Languages

Language	Percentage to Total population	Number of People who Speak the Language (Million)
Hindi	33	352
Bengali	18	133
Telugu	7.20	74
Marathi	6.99	72
Tamil	5.91	60.7
Urdu	5.01	51.5
Gujarati	4.48	46
Kannada	3.69	38
Malayalam	3.21	33
Oriya	3.21	33
Punjabi	2.83	29
Assamese	1.28	13.2
Maithili	1.18	12
Bhili/Bhilodi	0.95	9.6
Santats	0.64	6.4
Sindhi	0.25	2.5
Konkani	0.24	2.4

Source: Census of India – 2011.

9. Education: Most educational institutions in rural areas suffer from inadequate building and staff. It has been observed that in many cases, a single teacher handles more than one class. The teacher spends less time in the school as he has to look after his farm and many schools remain without teachers for a long period. Even adult education programmes have suffered due to frequent transfers and postings of key functionaries. Children from poor families work in the fields to add to family income.

"An Open Air School"

The Noon Meal Scheme, initiated by many State Governments, has motivated the parents to send their children to school and 14 crore children have been covered under this programme.

"Mid-day Meal Scheme"

In a village environment, religion, caste, cost of schooling, poverty, child labour, gender disparities, and family size influence education of children. Indian households are focusing on children's' education and household budget share on education has increased from 2 per cent to 7 per cent from 1993-1994 to 2011-2012. For example, during 2004-2005, 40 per cent of rural and 57 per cent of urban households were spending on education. The numbers moved to 63 per cent rural and 73 per cent urban as per National Sample Survey in 2009-2010. Sarva Shiksha Abhiyan, aims to provide access to education for school children. About 80 per cent of children are able to attend elementary school within 3 kms. radius from their houses.

Building the Poor Man's Doon School

Driving out of the Delhi National Capital Region on a spanking new highway to Agra, glitzy hotels, fancy apartments and fountains quickly give way to a narrow, four-metre wide road, heading into Bulandshahr, a district in Uttar Pradesh. An hour's drive into the countryside and you won't miss the distinct two storey brick building on 30 acre plot. It's the Vidya Gyan School, one of the two free schools that the Shiv Nadar Foundations has set-up. The building has been deliberately kept low rise to merge with the surrounding fields and villages.

Inside, the school could be mistaken one in any big city. Sprawling sports grounds, neat assembly areas, boys and girls hostels and residences for teachers are part of this boarding school. Thirty-one-year-old Roshni Nadar Malhotra set it up three years ago to help build future leaders from among India's bottom of the pyramid population. She believes this could do to poor students in UP what Doon School and the like do to India's elite.

The Foundation offers free education from class six to the 12th standard. The spend covers student stay, uniforms, books, *et. al.* "We take the brightest lot from the bottom of the pyramid and want to give them the best education that any child in India can get," says Roshni.

Fifth grade toppers across UP, among the underprivileged, can get admission to Vidya Gyan. The school has 703 students (will scale up to 1,400) and 39 teachers and gets students mainly from western UP. The other school in Sitapur, near Lucknow, attracts students from central UP. The Foundation is planning a third school, to be located in east UP, and thus cover the whole state.

Biswajit Banerjee, principal, Vidya Gyan, Bulandshahr: "Coaching schools have come up to train kids for admission to Vidya Gyan. Roshni has the perseverance and patience to see results." Banerjee is an academician with 25 years of experience was previously principal of DPS Lucknow and head of Physics department at DPS Noida.

Roshni's plan is not to take philanthropy to the masses, but rather focus on the brighter students among the poor. "At present we are serving 1,400 students through the two Vidya Gyan schools and that's really a drop in the ocean. We can't do and don't want to do everything", says Roshni.

Mahatma Gandhi has righty said: Educate one-man, you educate one person, but educate a woman and you educate a whole civilisation. Many State Governments have initiated special schemes for education of girl children. ***Example:*** Madhya Pradesh Government has attached special importance to women empowerment under Beti Bachao Campaign. Girl's education is promoted in big way – free bicycles to go to school, free uniforms, free textbooks, scholarship for higher studies and reservation of jobs in Government service.

Regarding educational level, about 29 per cent of the rural population has studied up to primary school, 31 per cent up to middle school, 21 per cent up to matriculation, 16 per cent are matriculates and only about 3 per cent of the people have graduate and postgraduate qualifications.

"A Village High School"

10. Standard of Living: The average annual rural household income has gone up from ₹ 52,000 in 2005 to ₹ 76,000 in 2010. Due to increase in income, rural consumers are spending more on education, travel, recreation and personal care. However, expenditure on non-food items continues to be low compared to urban areas. ***Example:*** Share of food in consumer expenditures 57 per cent for rural against 45 per cent in urban areas. Of course, there are wide variations among states. The food share is rural Kerala is 46 per cent compared to 65 per cent in Bihar and Assam.

11. Cultural Factors: Villagers in India show a deep loyalty to their villages and even people who have lived in a city for a very long time refer to their ancestral village as "our village". People in rural areas share use of common facilities such as village pond (tank), temple, school, cremation ground, well, school ground and sitting space under large shade trees. Each village normally has a deity, i.e., the village protector and villagers join together in worshipping the deity. Festivals such as Deepavali, Durga Pooja bring people together in villages. Along with unity comes conflicts, rivalries and violence arising out of caste, religion, politics and other socio-economic factors. There are prosperous and powerful people living side-by-side with weak dependent agricultural labourers and underdeveloped fellow villagers. The dwellings of low caste are generally located away from the houses of upper caste and people who enjoy high income in villages.

Traditional outlook of rural people has been preventing them from taking full advantage of the incentives offered by the Government. There are different groups based on religion, caste, occupation, income, age, education and politics and each group exerts influence on the behaviour of the people in the villages.

12. Mass Media: Television has made great impact and large audience has been exposed to the medium. Regional television channels have become popular among rural population. However, reach of television differs from state-to-state. Many consumer goods' companies are using television as a medium to reach large villages and semi-urban markets. While English newspapers and magazines have very low circulation in rural areas, regional language newspapers and magazines are becoming popular among educated families in rural areas. Radio reaches a large population at a relatively low cost. The villagers have the habit of listening to regional news/agricultural news in the morning and late evening and advertisement could be released during this time to get maximum coverage. Now that private operators have been given licences, radio, as a medium is bound to become more popular with rural audience. Cinema continues to be the main source of entertainment in the villages. Film viewing habits are high in southern states. Village theatres do roaring business during the season by having four shows per day. The companies can organise screening of product films in rural cinema houses through local distributors and dealers.

13. Rural Poverty: Rural poverty is characterised by malnutrition, primitive shelter and poor health. Unemployment and underemployment are the basic problems of rural areas. As per Nutrition Advisory Committee of the Government, the required minimum calorie intake per day for rural and urban person is 2,400 and 2,100 respectively. The monthly income required to meet this minimum calorie requirement is ₹ 1,840 for a family of five in rural areas and ₹ 2,795 in urban areas (year 2005). The majority of the rural poor are landless agricultural workers who earn a daily wage ranging from ₹ 60 to ₹ 150. The agricultural labourers are hired for undertaking activities such as land preparation, transplanting of seedlings, weeding, application of fertilisers, pesticides, water management and harvesting of the crop. The landless agricultural labourers are unorganised and unskilled and are not governed by any rules and regulations. Agricultural labourers remain unemployed for more than four months in a year. Besides, there are small farmers with large families. They do not have access to land, irrigation and credit facilities. A large per cent of the poor households are illiterate. About 75 per cent of landholders are small and marginal farmers and are forced to avail credit facilities from moneylenders at exorbitant rates to meet cultivation and household expenses.

"Agricultural Labourers"

The incidence of poverty is 21 per cent in rural areas compared to 14.60 per cent in urban areas as shown below.

Table 1.13: The Percentage of Populate below Poverty Line

Area	1972-73	1977-78	1887-88	1993-94	1999-2000	2007-08
Rural	54.10	51.20	39.09	37.27	27.09	21.00
Urban	41.20	38.20	36.20	32.36	23.62	14.60
All India	51.50	48.30	38.86	35.97	26.10	19.20

However, there are variations between the states. Rural poverty is low in Punjab (9.10 per cent), Andhra Pradesh (11.20 per cent) and Kerala (13.20 per cent).

The National Rural Employment Guarantee Programme is an initiative to provide minimum number of days of work in an year to unemployed people. During the year 2007-2008, Government has provided guaranteed employment for 100 days a year for 34 million households, in rural areas.

"Rural Employment Guarantee Programme"

As per National Sample Survey Office report (2013), a large percentage of households are not receiving food subsidy while significant number of households with relatively high purchasing power are able to avail food and kerosene subsidy through Public Distribution System. Government of India launched the Direct Benefits Transfer (DBT) scheme in January 2013 in 20 districts covering 25 Government sponsored schemes. The DBT scheme is expected to cover the entire country by end of 2013 and it aims to improve the delivery of welfare benefits targeted recipients and lower the burden on Government finances by reducing leakages. The DBT scheme relies on the Aadhar number as a means to establish personal identity and the Aadhar number will be linked to the bank accountant. Cash benefits under various schemes will be directly transferred into the Aadhar linked bank account of the beneficiary. The beneficiaries can withdraw this cash from ATMs or with the help of business correspondents after biometric authentication, i.e., iris scan plus fingerprint.

Banking Correspondent

Pan Singh Tomar was a national athlete who took to the Chambal ravines in Madhya Pradesh after land disputes. His great grandson Anuj Singh Tomar moves around their ancestral village dispensing money to those at the bottom of the pyramid. While senior Tomar resorted to guns for the latter part of his life, Anuj Singh Tomar has his handheld biometric machine that helps identify beneficiaries of schemes so that he can open bank accounts, verify account holders and distribute cash. Tomar Jr. works as a Banking Correspondent in village Kosarikalam in Morena, near Gwaliar. He makes nearly ₹ 2,500 a month plus commission. He is a part of a new army that forms the last mile in Madhya Pradesh Government's ambitious financial inclusion programme in rural areas.

14. Rural Enterprises: The Ministry of Small-scale Industries and Agro and Rural Industries is involved with policy formulation, promotion, development and protection of small-scale industries. It plays a major role in providing employment, improving productivity and earnings and poverty alleviation programme. Rural industries provide maximum employment per unit of capital employed comparable to large industries. Important cottage industries are Khadi and Village Industries Commission. Khadi is the cloth woven on handlooms from yarn which is spun by hand from cotton or silk or mixture of cotton and silk. Village industries include crushing of oilseeds to produce oil, manufacture of gur, gobar gas, pottery, handmade paper, making soap, etc. Handicrafts are articles produced by hand with great skill and years of experience. The handicrafts are made out of wood, marbles, soap stone, ceramic, clay, cotton, bamboo, silk, etc. We are one of the key suppliers and exporters of handicrafts and earning from exports during 2012-2013 was about ₹ 18,000 crore as shown below:

Table 1.14: Export of Handicrafts (Value in Crore)

Number	Product	2011-12	2012-13
1	Art metal wares	2,603	3,328
2	Wood wares	1,560	2,745
3	Hand printed textiles	1,655	2,234
4	Embroidered and crocheted	3,924	4,665
5	Shawls	254	448
6	Zari and Zari goods	240	286
7	Imitation jewellery	575	1,020
8	Misc. handicrafts	2,164	3,244
	Total	**12,975**	**17,970**

Bihar Innovation Forum

The Bihar Innovation Forum is an initiative of the State Rural Livelihoods Mission, Government ofBihar which offers social innovations and enterprises a unique opportunity to participate in the transformation of the lives and livelihoods of the rural poor in Bihar. The forum encourages high impact innovations that can lead to sustainable and scalable rural livelihood solutions. The livelihood scheme covers agriculture, livestock, rural energy; IT based solutions, Skill development in non-farm sector, financial services, access to entitlements and access to services.

15. Rural Artisans: The rural artisans constitute an important segment of the rural economy. The rural artisans are skilled workers in village crafts and they are engaged in producing a wide variety of products like carpets, brassware, earthenware, textiles and artistic pieces for the local people. They also supply a wide range of implements to agriculturalists. The artisans suffer from lack of financial resources. They face problems in procuring raw materials and the middlemen who supply these materials usually tend to exploit the artisans. They require a package of services which include training, new designs, raw materials, credit, marketing and general guidance.

The Ministry of Textiles, Government of India has come out with "Human Resource Development Scheme" for building a creative workforce in the field of handicrafts. The objective is to provide qualified and trained workforce capable of establishing a strong production base to meet the present-day market requirements. Training will be imparted to handicrafts artisans in the following areas:

(a) Crafts related skill such as wood carving, embroidery, POP moulds, wooden blocks, etc., through short-term and long-term courses varying from one to nine months' period based on the type of craft.

(b) Non-technical skills such as microfinance, preparation of business plan, project report, export procedure, packaging, etc.

(c) Upgrade the skills of semi-skilled artisans; add additional skills through master craft persons.

KVIC
The Government has set up Khadi and Village Industries Commission (KVIC) in 1957 with the main objective of promoting village industries. With a turnover of over ₹ 20,000 crore, KVIC markets a variety of products, i.e., honey, soaps, hand-made paper, agarbathi, khadi, pottery, textiles, etc., through 20,000 stores spread across the country. It offers technical, financial and marketing support to village entrepreneurs to set up small-scale factories in rural areas. KVIC has generated employment for about one crore people and has supported 5,000 cooperative institutions and 3 lakh village entrepreneurs and has taken a lead in rural development.

कामये दुःखतप्तानाम्।
प्राणिनाम् आर्तिनाशनम्॥

KHADI AND VILLAGE INDUSTRIES COMMISSION
MINISTRY OF MICRO, SMALL AND MEDIUM ENTERPRISES,
GOVT. OF INDIA
GRAMODAYA, 3, IRLA ROAD
VILE PARLE (WEST), MUMBAI - 400056
Tel: 022-26714320,26716323
E-mail: kvichq@bom3.vsnl.net.in Website: www.kvic.org.in

"Khadi and Village Industries Commission"

16. Rural Credit: During pre-independence days, there was practically no institutional source for availing loans and the villagers were forced to borrow money from local moneylenders. Realising the need for rural credit, the Government decided to expand institutional credit. Nationalisation of fourteen banks took place in 1969. In 1980, six more banks were nationalised. In 1975, Regional Rural Banks were established. Subsequently, National Bank for Agriculture and Rural Development was set-up in 1982.

SBI-TINY

State Bank of India is looking to expand the reach of its retail products such as personal loans, life and medical insurance to rural areas, through its latest initiatve 'SBI Tiny'. Tiny is the bank's no frills savings account for the rural areas, under which depositors can open accounts with zero balance and deposit amounts as small as ₹ 5. Through this deposit scheme, the bank plans to develop a relationship with the villagers. Once they have a savings account, they can create assets by taking credit and then move on to other relationships such as insurance. The aim is to see that every villager becomes an accountholder with the bank.

For Tiny, SBI has introduced the concept of **SBI Mitras**, people who would assist the villagers in opening accounts and also collect deposit from them through deposit boxes. Branch managers in areas where Tiny is offered would be given decentralised decision making powers.

In our country, the credit cooperatives have been able to develop a unique delivery system at the doorsteps of the farmers by providing credit and supply of agricultural inputs to farmers. The financial institutions have come out with Kisan Credit Card, a unique credit facility to meet cultivation expenses as well as living expenses. The card aims to provide hassle-free credit assistance for a smooth, happy and profitable agriculture. As a result of these measures, the share of institutional credit has increased from 7.3 per cent in 1951 to 61 per cent in 2002.

17. Urban Orientation denotes the degree to which a rural consumer would like to replicate the lifestyle of urban consumer. The higher the urban orientation, the higher will be the requirements of consumer goods and services. The villages close to towns/cities and villages connected by public transport facilities have high level of urban orientation compared to villages not connected by public transport.

"Display of Ready-made Garments in a Village Shop Close to the City"

18. Heterogeneous Rural Markets: Rural markets are highly heterogeneous due to the following reasons:

- Social and Cultural factors
- Variations in village wise population and population density
- Infrastructure differences between large and small villages
- Reach of mass media among villages
- Literacy level
- Degree of urbanisation

A Few Myths about Rural Markets

1. Rural consumers are very price sensitive and are not concerned about branded products.
2. Rural consumers are illiterate and printed materials like leaflets and mailers have no role in rural promotion.
3. In rural areas, head of the family is the decision maker.
4. Rural consumers use cheap products.
5. Rural areas lack electricity and therefore there is limited scope for electrical goods like TV sets.
6. There are several barriers like low income, low quality consciousness, traditional outlook and low infrastructural facilities and therefore I do not want to work in rural areas.

Note: Heterogeneity in lifestyles of rural consumers is mainly due to variations in literacy, income and cultural factors. Therefore classroom teaching, followed by field visits will enable the students to understand rural realities and dispel some of the myths about rural markets.

CONCLUSION

Rural markets are growing at a faster pace and offer tremendous opportunities for marketing a variety of consumer goods and services. However, rural markets and rural marketing have special features as compared to urban markets. The marketers have to understand the characteristics, the buyer behaviour and the business potential of rural markets. Further, companies with long-term plans and high level of commitment to rural markets will only be successful in the marketplace.

QUESTIONS

1. 'Rural markets lack of infrastructural facilities'. Discuss the initiatives taken by Government for development of infrastructural facilities?
2. 'Many marketers feel that rural markets are similar to urban markets and implement similar strategies in rural areas.' Do you justify this? Give reasons.
3. Do you think that rural markets are heterogeneous? Discuss.

✿ ✿ ✿

2 EXPLORING THE GROWING RURAL MARKET

INTRODUCTION

With over 80 crore population, rural market has great potential for expansion and growth. The segment, popularly known as the "Bottom of the Pyramid" presents huge opportunities for the creative marketers. Rural income is going up and infrastructural facilities are being developed. Rural people are being exposed to urban way of living and they value material comforts. Even premium brands of consumer goods have entered the rural market. However marketers have to face challenges such as scattered location of villages, seasonal rural income, relatively low awareness about products and services, low reach of mass media and low transport facilities while exploring the rural market.

FACTORS CONTRIBUTING TO THE GROWTH OF RURAL MARKET

1. Favourable Government Policies

Mahatma Gandhi has rightly said "India lives in villages and to become a developed nation, villages have to be developed". The Government has taken the initiative for economic development of rural areas and through Five Year Plans have invested heavily in development of agriculture, animal husbandry, irrigation, electricity, dairy and khadi and village industries and infrastructure facilities. In the Tenth Five Year Plan, high priority was given to the development of agriculture and rural areas, transportation, communication, electricity and social services like health, education, employment generation.

Dr. Manmohan Singh recently talked about his vision for rural India. "My vision for rural India is of modern agrarian, industrial and services economy co-existing side-by-side, where people can live in well-equipped villages and commute easily to work, be it on the farm or in the non-farm economy. There is much that modern science and technology can do to realise this vision. Rural incomes have to be increased. Rural infrastructure has to be improved. Rural health and education needs have to be met. Employment opportunities have to be created in rural areas."

Rural development is a comprehensive programme and includes growth in agriculture, village industries, service sector, and development of housing, public health, literacy, transport, education and communication. The Government has initiated a holistic and integrated approach to rural development consisting of the following:

- **Rural Infrastructure Development Programme** under the umbrella of **'Bharat Nirman'**.
- **National Food for Work Programme** which focuses on Employment Guarantee Programme. The work relates to water conservation, land development, flood control and rural connectivity.
- **Sampoorna Gramin Rozgar Yojana** (1993) with the aim to provide additional wage employment in rural areas and also food security.
- **Pradhanmantri Gram Sadak Yojana:** Launched in 2000, with the objective of constructing new roads and connecting about one lakh villages and upgrading existing roads.
- **Rashtriya Bal Swasthya Karyakram (2013) provides:** Free Treatment of Childhood Illnesses under National Rural Health Mission.
- **Swarnajayanthi Gram Swarojgar Yojana:** Launched in 1999, the programme aims at developing self-employment among villagers through mix of need-based credit and subsidies. The earlier programmes such as Intensive Rural Development Programme, Million Wells Scheme, Development of women and children in rural areas have been merged under this scheme.
- **National Rural Employment Guarantee Scheme (2006).**
- **Rural housing project** or providing shelter to rural people.
- Stepping up **credit flow** to farmers and others.
- **Insuring** against risks in agriculture.
- **Creating market** for agricultural produce.
- Providing **agricultural market information** through IT and internet connectivity.
- **National Food Security Mission** to increase production of wheat, rice and pulses.
- **Rastriya Krishi Vikas Yojana** to increase public investment in agriculture.
- **National Agricultural Extension System** towards extension training to farmers.
  - ***Example:*** Bihar has become the first state in the country to start e-Krishi Bhavans at block level. These fully computerised e-Krishi Bhavans would provide a package of services such as technical advice, soil testing and training to farmers. These centres have internet facilities to provide updated information on prices of agricultural commodities, arrivals in the market, weather conditions, etc.

- **National Horticulture Mission (NHM)** is being implemented by the Ministry of Agriculture with effect from 2005-2006. The objectives of the mission are to increase production and productivity of horticulture crops (fruits, vegetables and flowers), reduce post-harvest losses, improve nutritional security, increase exports, increase farmers' income and generate employment opportunities for the unemployed. The floriculture exports have touched ₹ 1,000 crore by 2010. The domestic market is estimated at about ₹ 3,000 crore and is growing at 40 per cent per annum. The Government is setting up flower auction centres in Bengaluru, Kolkata, Noida and Mumbai and is improve cargo-handling facilities in Goa, Calicut and Coimbatore.

The latest report from Central Statistical Organisation shows that states like Bihar, Uttaranchal, Uttar Pradesh, Chhattisgarh and Jharkhand have shown higher growth between 2004-05 and 2008-09 compared to All India growth for the same period. ***Example:*** Bihar has recorded a growth of 12.10 per cent in the 11th Plan period ending 2012 compared to country's average growth of 7.90 per cent.

2. Agricultural Development

Agriculture contributes to about 16 per cent of GDP of our country but over 65 per cent of the rural population is depending on agriculture for their livelihood. The agricultural sector plays a major role in the Indian economy as it provides foodgrains to urban population and also supplies raw materials like cotton, sugarcane and labour force to industrial sector. Agricultural prosperity generates considerable demand for consumer goods in rural areas. States like Madhya Pradesh has shown agricultural growth of 9.04 per cent compared to all India growth rate of 3.20 per cent during the 11th Five Year Plan. Madhya Pradesh has 16 lakh hectares under irrigation compared to 7 lakh hectares in 2003. The following initiatives have lead to growth and development of agriculture.

(a) Agricultural Education and Research: Establishment of agricultural colleges and research stations has ensured availability of technical manpower and technological developments in agriculture.

(b) The Green Revolution during late 60s and early 70s focused on increasing yields of crops through modern cultivation practices. From a food deficit nation in mid-60s, our country became self-sufficient in food production in 1971 and we are now exporting agricultural produce to other countries. There has been an increase in disposable income of rural people.

(c) Crop Diversification: Change in cropping pattern from food crops to cash crops like cotton, chillies, fruits, vegetables, flowers and production of seeds have enabled the cultivators to increase their income.

"The Author in a Marigold Farm" – Marigold is a Lucrative Crop

(d) Diversification of Agriculture: Considering the dependence on monsoon, many farmers have taken up production of poultry, fish culture and dairying to supplement income.

"EMU Farming"

(e) White Revolution was initiated by the Government for achieving self-sufficiency in milk production. The policy envisaged producing milk through rural cooperatives and moving the processed milk products to urban areas. Milk production increased from 17 Mio tonnes in 1950 to 123 Mio tonnes in 2012 and increase in rural income.The Indian dairy industry is now the world's largest, accounting for a 20 per cent share in world milk production. At present, only about 20 per cent of the milk produced is processed. The demand for dairy products can be easily met by processing a major portion of milk produced. There are opportunities for export of high quality dairy products and rural India can be converted into a dollar India.

"Milk Producers' Cooperative Society"

Example: Gujarat has taken a lead in dairy development, followed by states like Punjab, Andhra Pradesh, Maharashtra and Tamil Nadu.

"Mother Dairy – Milk Booth"

3. Development of Indian Economy

In an underdeveloped country, a large part of national income is contributed by primary sector (Agriculture) and as the country develops, share of primary sector declines and that of secondary (Manufacturing) and tertiary sector (Services) increase. There has been changes in the contribution of primary, secondary and tertiary sectors to total national income as shown below:

Table 2.1: Sectorwise Share (per cent) of GDP (At 1993-1994 Prices)

Year	Agriculture	Industry	Services
1980-81	39.71	23.70	36.59
1993-94	30.97	26.26	42.77
2001-02	24.23	26.67	49.10
2003-04	21.71	26.86	51.43
2005-06	19.66	26.23	54.11
2009-2010	15.70	28.10	56.20

There has been expansion of industrial and service sectors leading to more employment opportunities. Therefore, Indian economy has undergone a change from underdeveloped economy to a developing economy.

4. Rising Aspirations of Rural People and Attraction for High Standard of Living

The average household income has increased from ₹ 52,000 (2005) to ₹ 76,000 (2010). Further it has been observed that monthly salary earners have high income compared to income from the farm. The rise in income coupled with increased awareness and the need for possess modern goods have influenced the rural marketing environment in the country. The mobility towards higher income group has been higher in rural area compared to urban. The rural consumer is quickly moving from basic necessities to branded products. Rural consumption share is 50 per cent of total consumption as shown below.

Table 2.2 India's Consumption Centres (2011-2012)

Number of towns/cities	Consumption (Per cent)	Population (Per cent)
48 cities/towns	25 per cent	12 per cent
7,834 small towns	25 per cent	18 per cent
6,40,000 villages	50 per cent	70 per cent

Examples:

(a) The rural youth forms a distinct segment of the population. They are modern, knowledgeable and receptive to changes than their elders. They value material comforts and are quick in adopting fashionable lifestyle. Marketers of two-wheelers, TVs, ready-made garments, soft drinks, cosmetic, etc., are targeting the youth market.

(b) Premium brands like Denim Talc and Pantene have entered the market though current volumes are low.

(c) The consumption of instant noodle, an urban product, is growing fast in rural areas.

5. Media Explosion

Expansion of TV network and more channels have contributed to the growth of rural markets. Through several TV channels and internet, rural consumer is also exposed to the global village.

There are about 6 lakh inhabited villages and about 80 per cent of the villages have been connected through Village Public Telephones. Ending 2011, there were 929 million mobile subscribers. Out of this 327 million subscribers are from rural (35 per cent) areas. Further there are about 60 lakh public telephones in villages. The Government plans to reach rural teledensity of 40 per cent by 2014. Regarding internet users, at the end of 2013, the number of total internet subscribers in rural India stood at 68 million (All India 205 million). Total internet subscribers is expected to reach 243 million by 2014. (More than in the US the second largest internet base in the world after China).

(a) Many states have implemented E-governance projects. Karnataka's Bhoomi Project aims at computerisation of land records and the documents are made available through bhoomi kiosks.

Bhoomi Project – Karnataka

The Karnataka Bhoomi Project, has computerised 20 million land records. It is becoming the nucleus that will connect the village with the world.

Talks are on with BSNL to provide the much needed connectivity to set up kiosks in a few villages. The Simputer Trust is in final discussions to supply the 'simple common man's computer' to revenue officials. And, the revenue department will provide content, i.e., details of the land to the village kiosk owner.

This is the way it works: Today, the Bhoomi Project which connects 177 taluks (distribution points) earns a revenue of ₹ 1 crore a month with about 7 lakh people shelling out ₹ 15 each to get a printout of their land record. If you take this amount (₹ 1 crore) and divide it by 1,000 villages, each village gets ₹ 10,000. On a revenue sharing basis of say 60:40, ₹ 6,000 would go to the revenue department for the content it is giving to the village while the rest (₹ 4,000) will go into the villager's kitty. No doubt, how will have to pay the rental and 50 paise for each printer paper but at least some money is ensured every month as well as ease of access to records at the village level itself.

Says Additional Secretary in the Revenue Department Rajiv Chawla, "if a villager is willing to set up a kiosk in his village by paying BSNL the initial deposit of ₹ 1,000 for a telephone connection, we will see that he gets access to the land record details of his own village and, through this, he can earn a minimum of ₹ 4,000 per month by giving a printout of the records to the land owners in the village".

The Senior BSNL officials are excited about the project. "Once we have worked out the virtual private network (VPN) rates, this project should get going", they said.

Meanwhile, Simputer is also gearing for its rural onslaught, "with about 9,000 revenue officials going to around 27 thousand villages and getting crop information thrice a year by using the Simputer, wherein data can be captured and updated immediately", says Vinay Deshpande, CEO. Encore Technology, which is spearheading the Simputer drive in the country.

With the land record containing details of crops grown in specific areas, it is expected that companies to whom such information is critical would pay money to obtain the database – thus, more revenue streams from a simple Bhoomi Project.

Source: *Times of India*: September 26, 2002.

(b) E. Seva, for the payment of utility bills, purchase of travel tickets, issue of birth/death certificates, etc., initiated by Andhra Pradesh has been received well by consumers in urban and semi-urban areas.

(c) Very attractive schemes are offered by mobile operators for semi-urban and rural consumers.

(d) A key factor that has inhibited the development of rural India has been lack of access to critical information and services. Project I Shakti, an IT-based rural information service has been developed to provide information and services to meet the rural needs. I Shakti kiosk is operated by Shakti entrepreneur and provide information on health, hygiene, legal, veterinary, agriculture, education and employment.

Indian Village Uploads Itself onto the Internet

An Indian village has uploaded itself onto the internet, giving the outside world a glimpse of life in rural India. Visitors to Hansdehar village's Website (www.smartvillages.org) can see the names, jobs and other details of its 1,753 residents, browse photographs of their shops and read detailed specifications about their drainage and electricity facilities.

Most of the residents can't yet surf the Hansdehar Website as the village is not yet connected to the internet. But the villagers hope the site and their imminent first internet connection — will put them in touch with the world beyond the flooded rice fields surrounding Hansdehar, located in Haryana. But younger villagers — most of whom have yet to send their first e-mail plan to use the internet to help hasten their exit by searching on — line for college places and jobs in big cities. There are few jobs available in Hansdehar beyond farming or running small shops supplying goods to farmers.

Kanwal Singh, who long ago left to work as a Website developer for the local Government in Chandigarh, said, "Some of the young people here have a lot of potential and they just aren't reaching it," he said. Which is why he set about convincing the village council of the benefits a Website and an internet connection would bring.

Carpenters and masons will tout their services on line. Others will upload their resumes to job hunting Websites when the village's first internet point is hooked up in Kanwal Singh's mother's house in the coming weeks. Now Hansdehar farmers hope they will be able to get better prices for their crops by trading online through the National Commodity and Derivatives Exchange, cutting out middlemen.

But the grand aim is to encourage India's villages to upload themselves and unite in online networks to advance the cause of rural India.

Source: *DNA*: August 18, 2006.

6. Private Initiatives

Private agencies have contributed to growth and development of rural areas through village level programmes.

Examples:

(a) Companies like HUL and Colgate have highlighted the importance of health and hygiene among villagers through school teachers, village meetings and film shows.

(b) Parry Corner, internet access centre initiated by Murugappa group in Tamil Nadu, provides information on farming techniques, bank loans, insurance, availability of agricultural inputs, Government schemes, etc., to rural population.

(c) Seeds, fertiliser and pesticide companies have created awareness among farmers about modern methods of cultivation by conducting extension activities such as farm-to-farm visits, group meetings, demonstrations and film shows.

(d) Launched in 2000 by ITC, e-Choupal has become the largest initiative among all the internet-based interventions in rural India. The farmers can sell their produce, buy a variety of products, receive all the information needed to improve their yields and get a better price for the produce through e-Choupal.

(e) Around 40 per cent of Bharti Airtel's Wireless subscribed base resides in rural areas and for Vodafone, the rural use base is around 50 per cent (2012).

(f) Rural naukari.com provides employment opportunities by creating database of rural human resources.

(g) About 53 per cent of HDFC Bank's branches are in rural and semiurban areas.

Shuttlecock Industry

Uluberia, located 40 kms. from Kolkata has about 80 Shuttlecock manufacturing units. Shuttlecock is an old Industry started as early as in 1920. There are about eight merchants who supply duck feathers. These duck feathers are procured from Murshidabad, Malda, Birbhum and South Dinajpur. Indian badminton players play with shuttlecocks made from duck feathers. The industry provides employment to about 5,000 people and generates business of ₹ 200 crore. The major brands produced from Uluberia are Skylark, Parrot fly, Albatross and Adventures.

Source: *Economic Times:* December 28, 2012.

7. Growth in Income

Number of households (in million) coming under very rich and well-off categories are high in rural areas, as shown below:

Table 2.3: Rural Rich and Well-off Categories

Classification	Urban	Rural	Total
Very rich, i.e., > ₹ 10 lakh per annum	4.84	1.32	6.16
Well-off, i.e., > ₹ 5 lakh per annum	29.45	27.36	56.81
Total	34.29	28.68	62.97
Per cent of Total	54 per cent	46 per cent	100 per cent

The average income level has improved due to modern farming practices, industrialisation of rural area, growth of service sector, migration of rural people into cities and remittance of their money, remittance of money by family members settled abroad. Rural income (farm and non-farm) contributes to over 50 per cent of the total income of the country. The farm wages have been rising and increased from ₹ 110 per day in 2006-2007 to ₹ 154 per day in 2011-2012.

Rural Prosperity
Killa Raipur, situated near Ludhiana town in Punjab is one of the most prosperous villages in the country. The village has a population of about 25,000 and owes its prosperity to modern agriculture. The village owns around 250 cars, 300 tractors, a washing machine and a TV set in every home. Also one out of two homes has a member living abroad.

Source: *Business Today*, February 11, 2007.

8. Growing Rural Market

Rural markets are growing fast and in many states they contribute to substantial sale of FMCG products. Rural contribution to FMCG sales is high in states that have significant rural population as shown below:

Table 2.4: State-wise Contribution of Rural Market to FMCG Sales

State	Contribution (per cent)
Bihar	62
Kerala	55
Assam	51
Chhattisgarh	50
Uttaranchal	49
Odisha	47
Jharkhand	41
Andhra Pradesh	40
UP	39
Punjab	38
West Bengal	37
Madhya Pradesh	35
Rajasthan	34
Maharashtra	28
Gujarat	27
Karnataka	24
Haryana	23
Tamil Nadu	22

Source: Nielson Retail Audit (2011).

NEED FOR EXPLORING THE RURAL MARKETS

Many companies having good manufacturing facilities and marketing expertise are focusing on rural markets as there are opportunities to market consumer goods and services in rural areas and also market agricultural products in urban markets.

1. Growing Rural Rarket: Apart from agricultural inputs, there is a growing market for consumer goods in rural areas. According to NCAER, the rural consumers represent more than 50 per cent of India's "consuming classes" and form the target group for consumer goods and services.

2. Severe Competition in Major Urban Markets: Intensive competition in urban market has resulted in increase in costs but not high market share and profits. Many companies have taken a lead in establishing their products in rural markets.

Example: HUL, Colgate, Marico, Nirma, LG Electronics.

3. To Change the Attitude of the Farmers so that they will Treat Agriculture as a Business: Traditionally, farmers have treated agriculture as a way of living and they produced just enough quantities to meet their family requirements. Many progressive farmers have increased the yields of crops by following modern agricultural practices. Even small farmers will be encouraged to increase production. When agriculture is well developed, the income of farmers will go up as a result of high marketable surplus. This provides good demand for industrial and consumer goods.

"Polyhouse Cultivation of Flowers"

4. Rural Marketing Creates Employment Opportunities: Diversification of agriculture, development of village level industries and marketing of modern goods and services, provide employment opportunities.

Examples:

(a) As insurance companies go more and more rural in search of business, there will be opportunities in the rural sector. Those who understand rural India will be in demand.

(b) Due to high attrition rate and growing cost of human resources, many BPO companies are moving to hinterland in search of cheaper and loyal talent pools. Even software firms are setting up centres in smaller towns. In rural areas, salaries will be up to 50 per cent lower than cities and real estate about five times less expensive, resulting in cost competitiveness.

(c) The Government is planning to set up a chain of professional institutes in rural areas on public-private partnership basis to produce skilled workers for the automobile industry. The Ministry of Rural Development has also favoured the proposal and has offered to extend financial and other support. The institutes may be similar to the existing Industrial Training Institutes.

Dy. General Manager – Rural Marketing
The incumbent should be an MBA in marketing, having strong marketing acumen and business development skills with 5-15 years experience of successfully and profitably launching and marketing a portfolio of ethical brands with top ranking Pharma Companies. The ability to analyse marketing trends, conceptualise brand strategies and ensure profitable operations as well as to motivate and lead successfully a team of managers and field personnel is essential. Duties and responsibilities include formulating policies, developing and maintaining marketing strategies, evaluation of research data on customers, markets and competitors so as to meet the organisational objectives.

Source: Advertisement released by "Franco-Indian Pharamaceuticals Private Limited, Mumbai" in *DNA*.

5. **Rural Tourism** includes a range of activities, services and amenities provided by rural people to tourists. The broad areas covered are cultural and farm tourism, nature holidays and touring in rural areas. Village lifestyle and traditional hospitality are other attractions for tourists. Many urban people would opt for rural tourism since it provides an opportunity to go back to roots (villages) and be away from the pressure of urban life. Rural tourism generates employment opportunities and increase in income for villagers. In addition, rural holidays enables the young urban population to experience rural life.

Examples:

(a) Kushti (Wrestling) Carnival in Kundal (Sangli District, Maharashtra) attracts close to two lakh people.

(b) Winers in Maharashtra have initiated wine tourism. The idea of having wine tourism is to have visitors stay in winery, see the vineyard and get a feel of wine-making process. This will also allow to relish the drink.

(c) Jallikattu (taming of the bull) conducted during harvest festival of Pongal has become a part of the tourism package of Tamil Nadu.

(d) Rajasthan has been presented as a destination with forts, palaces, sandstones, paintings, pottery, village crafts and community entertainment.

"Kushti (Wrestling) Carnival in Maharashtra"

"Nature Holidays"

(d) Purushwadi, a village situated at 180 kms. from Mumbai has become a tourist centre due to the efforts of "Grass Routes" an organisation that is promoting village tourism. Started in 2006, over 60 households welcome guests to stay with them and experience village life and visiting hill temple, trekking, working in farm, bathing in the river, etc.

"Jallikattu (Taming of the Bull)"

6. Over 70 Per Cent of Country's Population Live in Rural Areas: With a very large consumer base, rural markets have tremendous potential and companies foresee the rural markets as the markets of tomorrow.

The middle-class segment is urban India, is already well serviced. However, the rural markets are poorly serviced with regard to banking, insurance, basic health care, education and housing. In addition the penetration of four-wheelers, refrigerators, Colour TV, etc., is low in rural areas and there are huge opportunities for creative marketers.

7. Brand Loyalty: Due to low income, majority of the rural consumers are price-conscious. However, they will continue to patronise a brand once they are satisfied with the product.

Example: Parle Biscuits continue to be popular over local brands.

8. Foreign Competition: Foreign companies who are entering the Indian market, normally, focus on urban consumers. Therefore, there is less competition in rural markets.

9. Development of Regional TV Network: Has enabled the marketers to pass on the messages about products and services to rural population.

Examples:

(a) The younger village generation have a considerable exposure to various media over the earlier generation and they like to emulate their urban counterparts. Children play a major role in influencing purchase decision in rural areas.

(b) In the category of biscuits, Britannia launched the Tiger brand with children in mind. The biscuits targeted children with the tagline *'Tiger Khao, kuch banke dikhao'.*

(10) Life Cycle Advantage: Many products reach a maturity/decline stage in urban areas while in the rural areas they are still in the growth phase.

Table 2.5: Stages in Product Life Cycle

Product	Urban	Market growth rate (per cent)	Rural	Market growth rate (per cent)
Popular soaps	Maturity	2	Growth	40
Premium sops	Late growth	11	Early growth	60
Washing powders	Late growth	6	Early growth	60

Source: ORG Database.

PROFILE OF RURAL DEMAND

Modern cultivation practices have increased the yields of crops. Favourable trade terms for agricultural produce have led to rising agricultural income. Income tax exemption makes a family with moderate income wealthy in relation to its urban counterpart. Low cost of living in rural areas creates a higher disposable income with rural consumer. Expansion of TV network and developments in packaging has exposed the rural population to a variety of consumer goods.

I. Rural Markets — Classification of Goods and Services

Depending upon the tangibility and durability, the market for products and services could be broadly classified into six categories.

1. **Market for Consumer Goods**
   - (a) **Consumer Food Items:** Cooking oils, tea, coffee, health drinks, biscuits, chocolates.
   - (b) **Consumer Non-food Items:** Toilet articles, dress materials.
   - (c) **Consumer Durable:** Fans, electric irons, and sewing machines.
   - (d) **High Value Consumer Durables:** TV, VCR, and refrigerators.
2. **Market for Agricultural Inputs and Machinery**
   - (a) **Seeds:** High yielding and hybrid seeds of paddy, cotton, vegetables, etc.
   - (b) **Fertilisers:** Inorganic fertilisers (***Example:*** Urea, Ammonium Sulphate) and Organic fertilisers (***Example:*** Oil cake, Bone meal).
   - (c) **Pesticides:** Chemical pesticides (***Example:*** Ekalux, Actara) and Botanical pesticides (***Example:*** Neem Products).
   - (d) **Agricultural Machinery:** Tractors, motors, oil engines, harvesters.
3. **Market for Services**
   - (a) Insurance
   - (b) Banking
   - (c) Health.
4. Market for **Agricultural Products** like grains, pulses, vegetables, fruits, etc.
5. Market for **Construction Materials** for farms and village level industries.
6. **Transportation Equipments** such as carts, jeeps, commerical vehicles, cycles, mopeds, motor cycles.

II. Rural vs. Urban Demand

Considering the unique nature of rural markets, there is a need to understand the salient features of rural demand and the details are given in Fig. 2.1.

No.	Features	Rural	Urban
1.	Literacy	Low	High
2.	Per Capita Income	Low	High
3.	Demand	Seasonal	Uniform
4.	Sources of Information	Word-of-Mouth	Any Media
5.	Product Knowledge	Not Known	Known
6.	Product as Status Symbol	Mostly No	Mostly Yes
7.	Consumer Protection Available	Rarely	Easily Available
8.	After-sales Service Availability	Inadequate	Adequate
9.	Timeliness of Supply	Untimely	Timely
10.	Physical Communication Facilities	Poor	Very Good

Fig. 2.1: Demand: Rural vs. Urban

III. Size of Rural Demand

The rural population is nearly three times of the urban and marketers are targeting rural market for consumer goods, durables, electronic, electrical, automobiles, insurance and banking services. The rural market has been growing steadily since 1980s and is now bigger than the urban market for both FMCGs and Durables with 53 per cent and 59 per cent respectively of the total market.

A few examples about developments in rural sector are given below:

(a) According to National Accounts Statistics (2010) and National Sample Survey (2009-2010), nearly 70 per cent of India's population, 48 per cent of income, 56 per cent of expenditure and 33 per cent of savings come from Rural India.

(g) About 80 per cent of the villages are electrified though only 55 per cent of rural homes have electric connection.

(e) Out of about 63 million households having annual income of more than ₹ 5 lakh, 46 per cent are in rural areas.

(d) Out of the 6 lakh villages, 5.20 lakh villages have Public Call Offices.

(f) 42 million rural household are availing banking services compared to 27 million urban households.

(c) 41 million Kisan Credit Cards issued in rural areas exceeds the 22 million credit plus debit cards issued in the urban India.

(b) 327 million mobile connections (2011).

(h) Rural areas account for about 21 per cent of the total Pharma market, estimated at about ₹ 40,000 crore (2010). Pharma companies like Glaxo, Piramal, Pfizer, Novartis, Ranbaxy, Cipla, Roche, Novo Nordisk, Sanofi Aventis, Eli Lilly have already taken initiatives to tap the rural health care market.

(i) GlaxoSmithKline (GSK) has introduced "Asha" a variant of Horlicks, close to half the price of original product in rural market. The company plans to cover 50,000 villages by 2016 from 10,000 in 2017.

(g) Reliance Communications have launched Bharat Net Plan, a high speed internet service in rural market.

(k) Toyota Kirloskar Motors, which till date focused mainly in metros and major towns have drawn up plans to sell about 40 per cent of automobiles in rural market by 2012.

Many companies dealing with consumer goods and pharma products have achieved a high percentage of sales in rural markets as shown below:

Table 2.6: Company-wise Sales (2010-2011)

Company	Rural Sales (in per cent)
Hero	50
Colgate	50
HUL	45
LG	40
Dabur	40
Cavin Kare	40
Dish TV	33
Godrej	30
Kinetic	30
Cadbury	25
Glaxo	25
Marico	25
Ranbaxy	17
Cipla	18

IV. Consumption of Goods — Rural vs. Urban

It is seen that rural purchases are significant for a variety of products and at the same time, there is tremendous scope for increasing the sale of some of the consumer durables and cosmetics as per details given in Table 2.7.

Table 2.7: Rural Contribution to Product-wise Sales (2010-2011)

Products	Rural	Urban
Mechanical Watches	83	17
Radios/Transistors	81	19
Bicycles	78	22
Toothpowder	78	22
Washing Cakes	76	24
Tailoring Machines	74	36
Qartz Watches	59	41
Motor Cycles	48	52
Toothpaste	47	53
Washing Powder	46	54
Plucked Tea	44	56
Biscuit	41	59
Hair Oil	37	63
Colour TV	37	63
Shampoo	35	65
Face Cream	28	72
Refrigerators	28	72
Cars/Jeeps	11	89
Nail Polish	24	76
Washing Machine	17	83

CONSTRAINTS IN RURAL MARKETING

Rural India lives in villages with varying customs, languages, culture, education and prosperity and most marketers are not ready to face the same. There are many reasons why companies are reluctant to explore the rural markets.

(a) **Resources:** The companies require resources in terms of men, money and materials to enter the rural markets.

(b) **Long-term Plan:** Even if they have the resources, it may not be possible to increase the sales, market share and profits within a short period and therefore companies have to treat such expenses as investment for business development in rural areas.

(c) **Management Support:** While the top management may be committed to development of rural markets, many of the junior level staff may not have the knowledge, skills, attitude to explore the rural markets and they continue to focus on urban marketing.

Adi Godrej, Chairman of Godrej has rightly observed — "The rural consumer is discerning and the rural market is vibrant. At the current rate of growth, it will soon outstrip the urban market. The rural market is no longer sleeping but we are."

Industry Survey (2010) of over 100 companies shows that half of the senior executives are keen to tap the rural market. However, they are concerned about lack of infrastructure facilities like road connectivity, teledensity, availability of skilled manpower and seasonal demand.

While rural markets offer tremendous opportunities for the marketers, it is not possible to take a sizeable share of the market in the short run due to the following reasons.

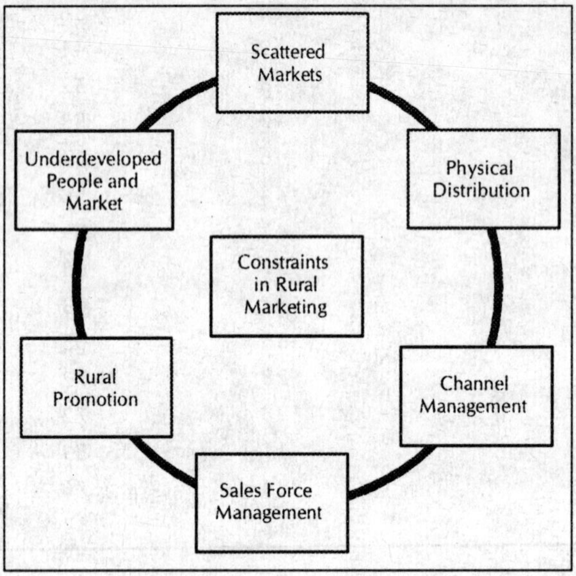

Fig. 2.2: Constraints in Rural Marketing

1. Scattered Markets

The rural market consists of about 6 lakh villages and 833 million consumers. The urban population of 377 million is concentrated in about 7,000 towns and cities. Reaching such a widely scattered consumers and retailers over a large geographical area is a challenging job indeed.

2. Physical Distribution

(a) Transportation: It involves moving goods from one place to another. The infrastructure is very poor in our country. The roads are in bad condition and 20 per cent of the villages are not connected by road. In interior villages, animal carts are used to carry goods. This type of transport is slow and inadequate. Other problems are non-availability of rail transport, poor bus/lorry services in villages.

"An Overcrowded Bus"

(b) Warehousing: Warehousing includes receiving the goods, despatching small consignments and documentation. No 'pucca' godown facilities are available in rural areas.

(c) Communication: We have 1,40,000 post offices in rural and semi-urban areas. Post and telegraph system is not well developed in interior rural areas. Even today 20 per cent of the villages are without telephone facility.

3. Channel Management

(a) **Multi-tier System** is required to service rural customers.

Example: Company depot/C&F Agent in the city, distributor in town, stockist at Mandi/Taluka level, wholesaler in feeder market and retailer in the village result in increase in cost of distribution.

(b) **No Scope for Manufacturer Owned Outlets:** Low volumes do not justify own showrooms.

(c) **Limited Availability Retailers:** It is uneconomical to run retail shops due to low sales turnover in rural areas. In many markets, retailers are not just available. Practically, there are no shops in the villages having less than 500 population and there are about 2 lakh villages under this category.

Table 2.8: Rural Retailer – Average Daily Turnover

Zone	Average daily turnover (2009-2010)
- South	₹ 650
- West	₹ 470
- East	₹ 430
- North	₹ 328

(d) **Fewer Brands:** Studies conducted have shown that the rural retailer keeps less number of brands of products due to limited sales in villages.

Table 2.9: Brand Choices – Rural/Urban

Category	Average no. of brands per dealer	
	Rural	Urban
- Toothpaste	3	7
- Toothbrush	3	6
- Biscuits	3	9
- Hair Oils	3	7

Source: ORG, 2002.

(e) Inadequate Banking and Credit Facility: Banking facilities are inadequate in rural areas. There are no banks in villages having less than 2,000 population. Marketers find it difficult to collect funds through bank. Further, the consumers and merchants are not able to avail credit facilities.

4. Sales Force Management

The salesperson plays an important role in promoting the products through direct contacts with the customers.

Requirements of a rural salesperson are given below:

- Fluency in local languages.
- Capacity to work for extended hours.
- Ability to undertake long journeys.
- Has to put up with inadequate boarding/lodging facilities.
- Knowledge of values, beliefs and perceptions that influence the behaviour of consumers.
- Preferably from local area.
- Knowledge of different types of rural customers.
- Selling skills.
- Knowledge of competition.
- General knowledge about agriculture.

Considering communication facilities, location of personnel in small towns and the large number of salesmen required to service rural market, sales force management is a very challenging for marketers.

5. Rural Promotion

Rural marketing requires special promotion efforts, such as AVP van, demonstrations, group meetings due to the unique characteristics of the market. The media and the methods have to be formulated accordingly.

Example: In urban markets, print media has become very popular. The same is not very suitable for rural markets due to low literacy level. There are 18 recognised languages and 850 different dialects. Communicating with these rural consumers hence becomes very difficult.

6. Underdeveloped People and Market

The rural markets are highly scattered and there are barriers in reaching the rural consumers due to the following:

- Low literacy
- Low income
- Seasonal demand
- Price sensitivity
- Low quality-consciousness
- Traditional practices
- Low reach of mass media.

METHODS OF MOTIVATING RURAL CONSUMERS

The general awareness about products and services is very low in rural areas and different methods of motivating rural consumers are given below:

1. Products: In order to attract the attention of first-time users, the product could be made available in small packing.

Example: Sachet pack for shampoos, coconut oil, toothpaste, etc.

'LIC Wooing Villagers Through 'Bima Grams'

The Life Insurance Corporation (LIC) of India has started developing 'Bima Gram', indicative of its social commitment under which the organisation ploughs back a portion of the premium collected from the villagers for the development of respective villages.

LIC pays back 25 per cent of the premium collected from the village or ₹ 25,000, whichever is less, for undertaking development work. The norms for identifying a village as 'Bima Gram' includes a population of over 1,000 but below 5,000, and acquisition of 100 new policies in a single year. The customer-friendly measures introduced by the LIC in the last few years have helped to face the challenge from the private sector and also improve business effectively.

2. Price: The marketer has to consider the following to increase the sales.

- Making the product available in small unit packing,
- Use of refill/reusable packaging,

- Extension of credit facilities, and
- Promotional schemes.

3. Rural Communication: The marketer has to pass on the messages about products and services through rural specific promotion media and methods.

Examples: Use of audiovisual van, group meetings, participation in haats and melas, wall paintings, and direct mailers in regional languages. TV and radio could be used depending upon the reach in rural areas.

4. Sales Force: The salesperson plays an important role in promoting the products in rural markets. He has to identify most potential markets and carry-out field activities such as house-to-house visit/farm-to-farm visit, group meeting of consumers, film shows and product demonstrations and service the demand through a network of retailers.

5. Opinion Leaders: The salesperson should establish rapport with opinion leaders to promote the products in rural areas.

6. Distribution: The most important objective is to make the products available in rural markets through an effective distribution system. The company has to establish an appropriate channel of distribution consisting of wholesalers, stockists and village level retailers and ensure that the products are available with village merchants. Rural income is highly seasonal and therefore rural consumer avails credit facilities from the merchants. The company could consider extending credit facilities to rural distributors and retailers to motivate them to stock and sell the products in rural areas. The statement **"Jo Dikhta Hai, Wo Bikta Hai"** (What is seen, sells) particularly holds good in the case of rural market.

Example: HUL is covering one lakh villages and servicing about ten lakh retail outlets.

7. Brand Promotion through Rural Youth: Considering the rural environment and dynamics of the rural markets, there are opportunities to select the local village youth and train them to promote the products and act as the local ambassador for the company. The local youths have the advantage of knowing the language, local customs and the psyche of the villagers. Being from the local area, they have access to the people and can meet them in the village without time constraints. The local youth takes pride in working for large corporations and they are able to develop a good image about the company and products among villagers. Since the cost of living in villages is low, the rural youth would be willing to work for a lower compensation.

The rural youth could be trained to undertake activities such as meeting key consumers and influencers like teachers, village president, Gramsevak, conducting demonstrations with the products, arrange for display of promotion materials, participation in melas, liquidation of stocks from dealers and distributors and assist in organising village meetings and publicity programme. Further, they could be trained to prepare database of consumer durables like TV, refrigerator, two-wheelers, etc.

CONCLUSION

Favourable Government policies and private initiatives have contributed to growth of rural market. The rural market offers lot of opportunities and challenges at the same time. The consumer base is large and therefore even a small growth leads to substantial increase in sales. Many creative marketers have already established their products in rural market. However, the market also poses problems with regard to distribution and communication. The companies have to prepare long-term plans to explore the rural market.

QUESTIONS

1. 'Nowadays many companies are announcing their intentions to go rural'. Why?
2. As a marketer, how will you go about motivating the rural consumers?
3. Elaborate on various problems faced by companies in rural market.

✿ ✿ ✿

3 RURAL CONSUMER BEHAVIOUR

INTRODUCTION

All business operations revolve around understanding consumer needs, desires, likes, dislikes and preferences and offering products and services that will give the desired satisfaction to the consumers. There has been considerable amount of data on the buying behaviour of urban consumers. On the other hand, efforts have started only recently to understand rural consumer behaviour. The following factors influence cosumer behaviour.

FACTORS INFLUENCING CONSUMER BEHAVIOUR

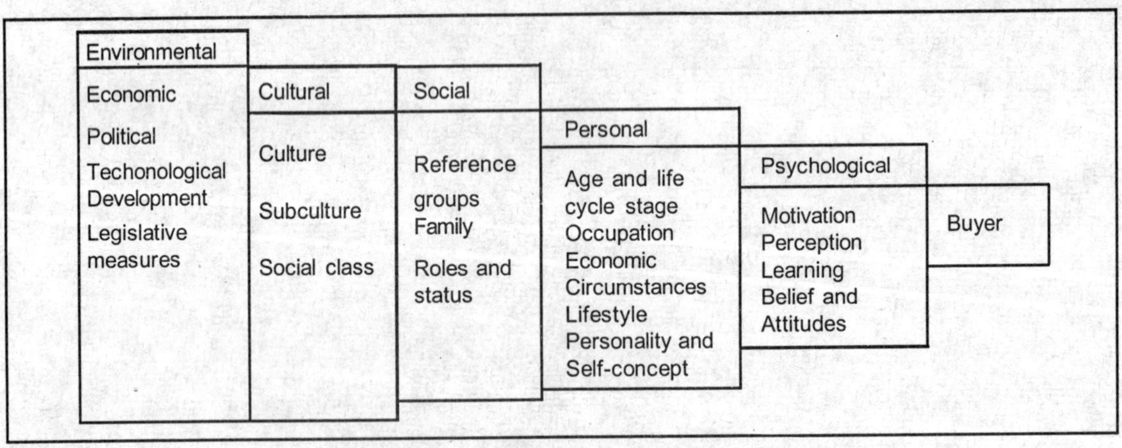

Fig. 3.1: Factors Influencing Consumer Behaviour

ENVIRONMENTAL FACTORS

(a) Economic Factors: The thrust on agriculture and rural development have enabled our country to achieve self-sufficiency in food production and we are now exporting a variety of agricultural commodities to foreign countries. Favourable monsoons during the last ten years have led to increase in crop yields and rural income. In addition, diversification of agriculture, development of village industries, village crafts, migration of rural people into cities and remittance of their money, remittance of money family members settled abroad have increased income level and buying power of villagers. Development of infrastructure facilities, expansions of TV network and packaging revolution have contributed to the growth of rural markets. The rise in income coupled with increased awareness and need for possessing modern goods have influenced the rural market environment in our country.

(b) Political Factors: The Government has taken the initiative for economic development of rural areas and have invested heavily in agriculture, animal husbandry, irrigation, electricity, dairy, khadi and village industries and infrastructure facilities such as roads, transportation, communication, hospitals, schools and banking services. While one may attribute some of these measures to win rural votes, these initiatives have certainly led to rural prosperity and opportunities for the marketers.

Example: Under One Laptop per Child Pilot Study, village school children are given an opportunity to use computers.

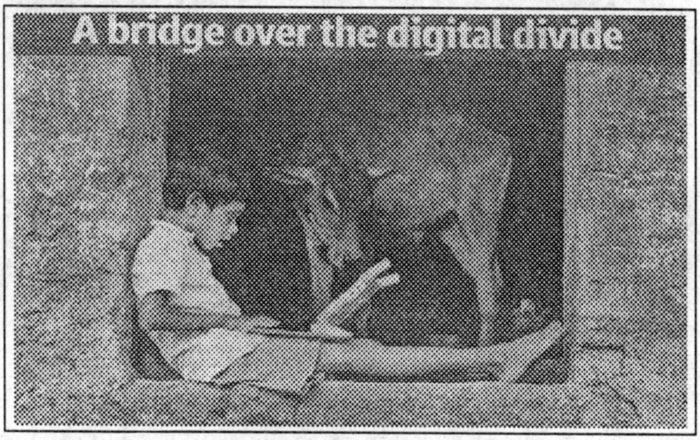

"Rural Kid with Laptop"

(c) Technological Developments: The rapid expansion of telecommunication facilities through subscriber trunk dialling (STD) system and public call office (PCO) and mobile phone have provided opportunities for rural people to keep in touch with men and markets. Development of TV network and more regional channels have enabled the marketers to pass on message about products and services to rural people. As a result of the rapid expansion of land line, mobile telephone services and internet facilities, the rural consumer is exposed to the global village. The Information and Communication Technology is changing the marketing landscape of India. Out of all India mobile subscriber base of 929 million (2011), rural India contributed around 327 million or 35 per cent. Today about 60 million villagers are aware of internet. In rural areas, especially in large villages and villages near to towns and cities, children and youth have access to information such as job opportunities, national news, weather conditions, bank loans, examination results, etc. The way television has revolutionised brand communication, IT and internet are sure to speed up exchange of information in rural India though at a slower rate compared to urban market.

The Roads are Bad, but Not Connectivity

65-year-old Y.C. Anjappa, a farmer from Maadikeri village used to spend ₹ 20 every week to visit the local market to obtain the rates for silk cocoon. In late 2006, he obtained a Reliance mobile set and uses the same to get the latest information from Chinthamani market. Salesmen from Reliance sales outlets have been able to add about 100 new subscribers in Maadikeri village. With a population of about 1,200 the village is situated about 100 kms. from Bengaluru. The roads are bad but mobile phones have become popular in the village.

Source: *Business Today*, February 2007.

Example: Gyandoot launched in the year 2000, covers about 600 villages in Dhar district in Madhya Pradesh. There are forty rural cyber cafes known as Soochanalayas operating in the district. Each kiosk costs about ₹ 75,000 and provide value-added services such as prices of commodities, land records, loans forms, examination results, community certificates, birth certificates, online registration of application, etc. E-mail in Hindi is sent to the concerned authorities and the reply is received normally within 10 days.

"Mobile Phones have Become Popular in Villages"

(d) Legal: The Government has come out with legislative measures to protect the interest of consumers. Some of the important ones are given below:

(i) Moneylenders: One of the important sources of rural credit is the moneylenders and they charge exorbitant interest compared to financial institutions. They deduct the interest portion in advance from the loan amount. They advance long-term loans against security of land and over a period of time manipulate the records and seize the land. Measures taken for regulating the activities of moneylenders include licensing of moneylenders, act to protect the assets of farmers from passing to the hands of non-agricultural moneylenders, exempting ancestral property and standing crops from attachment, restoration of mortgaged land on payment of nominal compensation.

(ii) Consumer Protection Act provides for protecting the rights and interest of consumers and we have a quasi-judicial machinery operating at three levels, i.e., consumer disputes redress forum at the district, state and national levels. In the case of unfair trade practices by any trader, supply of defective goods, or charging prices in excess of the MRP, the consumer can approach the forum for redressal of his grievances.

(iii) **Agricultural Inputs:** Modern farming involves use of high yielding varieties of seeds, adequate fertilisers and pesticides. These inputs are covered under Fertiliser Control Order, Insecticides Act and Seeds Act and manufactures, traders and consumers are covered under the Act.

(iv) **Essential Commodities Act** has been formed in the interest of the public to ensure essential commodities are made available to the general public at fair prices. The main objective of the Act is preventing business malpractices like profiteering, black marketing and hoarding by creating artificial scarcity of essential goods like foodgrains and fertilisers.

(v) **Regulated Markets:** These markets have been established to protect the farmers from the clutches of commission agents and dalals and price, quality and trade terms are regulated under legal framework. The objective is to ensure fair price to the producer through open auction and open agreement system in the marketplace.

(v) **Cold Storage Act (1964):** Deals with scientific storage of commodities.

CULTURAL FACTORS

(a) Culture and Subculture: Culture represents an overall social heritage, a distinctive form of environmental adaptation by a whole society of people. Culture is a system of shared beliefs, perceptions and customs that influence the behaviour of consumers. There are different groups based on caste, occupation, income, age, education and politics and each group exert influence on the behaviour of the people in the village. Traditional life, traditional occupation, traditional beliefs are name of the features of rural life.

"Protector of the Village"

(Each village has a deity considered as the village "Protector" and villagers worship the deity for the prosperity of the village.)

Example: While a section of the population is wiling to move ahead with the times, there also exists an equally significant traditional population that oppose the urbanisation and subsequent westernisation of their culture. Many people feel that large corporations are trying to change their food habits by promoting Western products such as Cola drinks, Burger, Pizza, etc., in place of Lime Juice, Vada pav, Roti, etc. In rural market Coca-Cola in competing not only with Pepsi and local soft drinks but also Nimbupani, Jaljira and butter milk.

Culture provides people with a sense of identity and an understanding of acceptable behaviour within a society. Our cultural institutions like family, school, temple, customs, traditions, etc., provide guideline to marketers. Technological advances, education and travel can have considerable influence on culture and change the rural lifestyle. Culture offers direction and guidance to the members of a society in all phases of life. It provides methods of satisfying physiological, personal and social needs.

Examples:

(a) The toothpowder usage is in line with rural mouthwashing habits. The person applies the toothpowder to his index finger and rubs it on the teeth. Hence, the reason for the popularity of toothpowder in rural areas. Dabur Red Toothpowder is a ₹ 100 crore brand and has about 30 per cent share in toothpowder segment. 50 per cent of the sales of the company is from rural and semi-urban market.

(b) Colgate Active Salt is mainly targeted at the rural consumers, as they are habituated to using common salt as one of the items for cleaning teeth.

(c) Many companies have come out with religious calendars with illustrations of their products and such calendars are preserved for a long time in rural areas.

(d) Culture provides standards of rule about appropriate item to eat for breakfast, lunch and dinner. Though bread as breakfast food is becoming popular in cities and major towns, it has not been accepted in rural areas.

Some of the more important attitudes and behaviours influenced by culture are the following.

(i) Traditional Life: Village life is governed by customs and traditions. They do not easily adopt new practices. Even rich people do not go for branded shoes/shirts and new models of cars. Most of the women still prefer soap nut (Shikakai), Green gram, Bengal gram powder for hair wash. Village lifestyle is in tune with nature, not the calendar or the clock. Sunday is a not a holiday in the village. Bus stops, temple premises and tea shops are the meeting places for villagers.

(ii) Traditional Occupation: They follow traditional occupation. In many cases, children of farmers continue to do farming. Apart from farming, the other traditional occupations are priest, blacksmith, washerman, barber, cobbler, carpenter, potter, village nurse, vaidya, grocer, mechanic for cycles, sprayers and pumpsets and cattle rearing.

In most cases, these occupations are carried forward to the next generation. The situation is changing, as educated youngsters are moving to towns and cities in search of employment opportunities.

"The Author with Shepherds – Rearing of Sheep is a Traditional Occupation"

(iii) Traditional Belief: There is a belief that experience is more important than education. The belief that certain diseases like jaundice, chickenpox and snake bite can be cured by mantras and tantras still continues. Very often, people depend on fate than any other thing. Many people do not buy Life Insurance Policies and the reasons are: Death — a taboo topic for discussions, it is quite bad talking about death and belief in Karma and Destiny.

Family Values: Joint families are more common in rural areas and they are useful in agricultural operations. The members of the family carry-out different operations to avoid using hired labour. The women, apart from looking after household work, also performs activities such as weeding the crops, transplanting of seedlings, milking of animals, carry agricultural produce from the field, etc.

Great stress is laid on fulfilment of the family obligations and responsibilities and the family influences the needs and wants of individual members. Buying decision may be taken by the head of the family in consultation with members of the family. Elders play a major role in the selection of bride or bridegroom. Marriages are settled by elders. In a large family, the young, strong and hard working members look after the old and the children.

During the last ten years, the number of members (per cent) in rural household has come down as shown below.

Table 3.1: Shrinking Family (Household Size)

Household Size	Total (per cent)	Rural (per cent)	Urban (per cent)
4 or less	2001: 41.90 2011: 49.70	39.80 47.10	47.00 55.40
5-8	2001.46.80 2011:43.70	48.10 45.80	43.60 39.10
9 Plus	2001:11'30 2011:6.60	12.10 7.10	9.40 5.50

It is seen that 49.70 per cent of all India households have four or less members compared to 47.10 per cent in rural and 55.40 per cent in urban areas. From the traditional joint family system, rural people are moving towards nuclear family due to pressure on land, education, migration to cities, etc.

Subculture Exists within the dominant culture, with its own set of values, belief and attitudes and behaviour pattern. We have subculture such as caste, religion and region. Thus, the pattern of behaviour would vary between North and South, Brahmins, Vaishyas, Muslims and Jains. Even in rural areas, Brahmins prefer to go for higher education and take up employment and Vaishyas are engaged in trading activities.

Religion and Caste play a major role in the life of villagers and there is hierarchical gradation of people based on caste and other considerations. Brahmin castes, landlords and affluent farmers occupy relatively high position in the rural hierarchy. Caste determines a person's status and political power in the society. During elections, the candidates depend upon the support of the people belonging to the same caste. However, during certain occasions like marriages, birth, death, etc., the people belonging to different caste participate in the functions in the village. Caste, very often decide the occupation of a villager. Apart from the hereditary occupation, most of the people are engaged in agricultural activities. A grocery merchant takes up farming in his land during rainy season and derives income from two sides.

(b) Social Class: Consumer behaviour is determined by the social class to which they belong and is determined by a combination of factors like education, occupation, income and assets. The structure of rural society consist of hierarchy of five classes of consumers as shown below.

Table 3.2: Hierarchy of Consumers

Class	Ownership of Products	1995-96	2006-07
The Affluent	Four-wheelers like jeep/car	1.6%	5.6%
The Well-off	Motor cycle, colour TV	2.7%	5.8%
The Climbers	Moped, B/W TV, sewing machines, geysers and mixies	8.3%	22.6%
The Aspirants	Bicycles, electric fan, electric iron	26%	44.6%
The Destitutes	Owning none of these items, i.e., wristwatches, transistors/radios	61.4%	21.40%

Source: NCAER IMD REPORT.

It is seen that over a period of ten years, there has been considerable reduction in the percentage of destitutes and increase in other social classes in rural areas. This is a positive indication of the growing rural market in our country.

Example: *"Thanda Matlab Coca-Cola"* is targeted specifically at the rural market and the lower socio-economic category (SEC) The "Thanda..." campaign is intended to add muscle to this initiative. The idea came up during a brainstorming session "Thanda" (cold) is the term for soft drinks in local parlance, and the brand has been positioned as a synonym for Thanda.

About 30 per cent of the company's sales come from the rural market and this is the market where the potential for growth is still high compared with the relatively staturated urban market. In the cities, the availability factor is very high and so the effort there is to get people to drink more Coca-Cola. In the rural areas and the smaller socio-economic categories, on the other hand, the effort is behind getting people to try it in the first place. The company has used the Thanda commercial to push its 200 ml pack priced at ₹ 5 in the rural markets.

SOCIAL FACTORS

(a) Family: Family is a group of persons related by blood, marriage or adoption who reside together. It is the basic social group and consists of individuals known as members. There are three types of families, i.e., the married couple — husband and wife, a nuclear family – husband, wife and at least one child and extended family — the nuclear family together with at least one grandparent. The three generation family is very common in rural areas. The head of the family provides economic security to family members. The members of the family play different roles such as Influencer, Decider and Purchaser in the buying process.

Example: The young daughter or the daughter-in-law wish to use a new brand of shampoo, soap or face powder. The buyer, on the other hand, is either the head of the family or the elder son.

Personal values, attitudes and buying habits have been shaped by family influences. Family life cycle also influences consumption pattern.

Example: Young adults are receptive to changes than their elders. They value material comforts and therefore companies dealing in two-wheelers, cosmetics are targeting this segment.

(b) Reference Groups includes family and friends with whom an individual interacts on a face-to-face basis and sportsmen, film stars, etc., with whom the individual does not have face-to-face interactions. Word-of-mouth communication is the process by which the messages are passed within group from one member to another member. The consumer develops positive opinion towards a product or service based on admiration (cricket players), aspiration (film stars) or empathy. The consumers think that if he uses it, it must be good, if I use it, I will be like him.

Example: In South, rural people are crazy about films. Many marketers have used film stars to promote consumer goods and agricultural inputs.

(c) Roles and Status are factors which influence decision making process. Roles are the activities of a person in a group. Each role carries status. People will choose products that will communicate their status in the society.

Example: Many affluent farmers/landlords buy high Horse Power tractors/expensive cars as status symbol.

PERSONAL FACTORS

(a) Age and Life Cycle: Life cycle of a person begins with child birth, move to infancy, adolescence, teenage, adult, middle age, old and then ends with death. Under each stage, buying behaviour is different. Over 50 per cent of our population is young (below 35 years) and are the target audience for consumer goods and durables.

Examples:

(a) With exposure to television and other media, school-going children even in rural areas have started influencing buying decisions with regard to consumer goods like biscuits, chocolates, toys and marketers are targeting this segment.

(b) Rural youth is exposed to mobile, internet and motor cycles.

(b) Occupation: About 500 million of the population depends upon agriculture for a living. Income from agriculture is seasonal and therefore demand particularly for consumer durables is high during post-harvest period and festivals. Of late, many farmers have diversified into poultry, dairy, fish culture and small-scale industries in order to reduce their dependence on farming and to ensure regular income. There have been an expansion of manufacturing and service sectors in our country leading to employment opportunities in rural and semi-urban areas. This is a welcome development as it is bound to increase the demand for consumer durables.

(c) Economic Circumstances refer to the spendable income, assets and savings and attitude towards spending and savings. Rural income is seasonal compared to an urban consumer who receives regular income. Regarding savings habits, traditionally rural people prefer to invest in jewellery and fixed deposits in post offices. A farmer would like to invest his funds for development of agriculture and buying lands. Another interesting observation is that for the same income level, a rural consumer has relatively high disposable income since he does not have to incur expenses on house rent, milk, vegetables, and grains as compared to urban consumer.

(d) Lifestyle studies show as to how people spend their time and money in day-to-day activities. The lifestyle dimensions are Activities, Interest and Opinions (AI0) and demographic features such as age, gender, education, occupation and income. Very often consumers buy products to enhance their lifestyle. Rural consumers prefer to spend spare time in activities such as playing cards, discussing politics, viewing films and visiting melas, i.e., commodity and religious fairs. Companies can use such meeting places for product promotion. Rural women prefer to buy jewellery out of family savings. Over a period of time, the lifestyle of rural consumers has been changing with increase in income and exposure to television. The rural youth wants to replicate the lifestyle of urban counterpart. Studies conducted show that rural consumers aspire for the same products that urban consumers buy and are willing to buy them as long as they are available at prices that suit them.

(e) Personality and Self-concept (Self-image): Personality is a unique combination of different individual characteristics. We find that many individuals are similar in terms of one or more characteristics, but they are not alike in all characteristics. Personality is a combination of factors such as sociability, self-confidence and dominance. Personality influences consumer behaviour in many ways.

Examples:

(a) Rural youth may buy tea and namkeen and urban youth popcorn and soft drinks. Self-image is what a person feels about himself and it relates to traits, habits, relationship and behaviours. The self-image has immense influence on consumer behaviour. He buys products and services that reflect his image.

(b) Bullet motor cycle continues to be popular in rural areas due to its ruggedness and the unique engine sound. It creates a macho image among villagers.

PSYCHOLOGICAL FACTORS

(a) Motivation: When a buyer purchases a product or service, he has a reason for the same. Motive is a strong feeling, urge, desire or emotion that makes the buyer to take decision to buy. Every human activity is a result of motivation. Each person is motivated by his needs and satisfaction of one need results in the creation of another need. A study of Maslow's theory of hierarchy of needs shows that rural consumers by and large are satisfied by meeting the last two needs in the pyramid, i.e., physical and security needs, whereas urban consumers would like to satisfy social and esteem needs, if not self-actualisation needs. Motives are of two types, i.e., product motives and patronage motives.

Product Motives may be classified as emotional product motives and rational product motives. Emotional motives are impulses which persuades the consumer on the basis of emotion. The buyer does not reason out or logically analyse the need for the purchases. The motives could be pride, ego, sex, romance or the desire to be distinct. *Desh ka Namak* aims at emotional bonding of Tata Salt with nation. Rational product motives are those impulses which arise on the basis of logical analysis and proper evaluation. High quality, low price, long shelf-life, ease of use, etc., are examples of rational product motives. The consumer takes a decision based on costs and benefits.

Motives can also be classified as physiological and psychogenic motives. Physiological motives are oriented towards satisfying basic needs such as thirst, hunger and psychogenic motives are focussed on achievement, recognition, etc. In rural areas, there exists a large population consisting of agricultural labourers, small and marginal farmers, petty traders who have very limited income and their needs are very basic, i.e., food, clothing and shelter. They spend very less on non-food items. However, the landlords and affluent farmers are looking for satisfying social and esteem needs.

Patronage Motives: Convenience of location, service offered, reputation of the outlet, friendly salesmen are the examples of patronage motives. Marketers are interested in patronage motives such as store loyalty and brand loyalty.

Examples:

(a) A rural person may not be able to read but would ask for Parle Glucose biscuit, and he recognises the brand by yellow stripes and Parle baby.

(b) It has been observed that the rural consumer very often buys from the same shop. They have running account with the shopkeeper. Making products available with the rural shopkeeper is an important aspect of rural distribution.

(b) Perception: All consumers are not alike. They see the world in their own special ways. For instance, all the members of the family have viewed a particular product advertisement in the television. The members may interpret the same advertisement in quiet different ways. This is because needs, wants, values, attitudes and personal experience vary from person-to-person. Similarly, consumers' perception means what he thinks about the product, producer or the brand. Consumers action, buying habits, consumption habits are based on perceptions and therefore the marketer should have good understanding of perception of consumers.

Example:

Many rural consumers prefer to deal with Government institutions such as Nationalised banks, LIC as they feel that private institutions are not reliable in the long run.

(c) Learning is the process of acquiring knowledge about products, product benefits, method of usage, maintenance and also disposal of the products. Considering low literacy, low awareness and low reach of mass media in interior areas, the marketers have to educate the consumers through rural-specific promotion media and methods.

Example:

Product demonstration is a very effective method to convince the consumers since it is based on the principle *"Seeing is believing"*. Product leaflets should be in regional language and contain more of pictures and local phrases.

(d) Belief and Attitude: In general, an attitude is a state of mind or feeling. Attitude indicates our feeling about a product, service, brand or shop and whether we are positively or negatively disposed towards the object or class of objects. Predisposition may be based on previous experience. Consumer attitudes are composed of beliefs, feelings and behaviour intentions towards a product, brand or store.

Belief may be positive, negative or neutral. The belief that consumer hold need not be scientifically correct. Consumer also hold certain feelings towards products and these feelings are based on the beliefs.

Examples:

(a) Many rural consumers believe that Cola drinks are harmful and they prefer Nimbupani (Lime juice), butter milk, etc. Change of attitudes and belief is very low in the case of rural consumers. Once he is convinced, he will continue to use the product and become a loyal customer.

(b) A majority of the lower and middle income group continue to use Lifebuoy soap and about 70 per cent of sales of Lifebuoy is in rural and semi-urban areas.

SHOPPING HABITS

A rural consumer visits different markets for buying different products as shown below:

(a) Village Markets

- **Panshops in small villages:** Match box, cigarette, beedi, supari, tobacco, local soft drink, soap, biscuit, candies.
- **Grocery shops in large villages:** Foodgrains, edible oil, kerosene, minor electrical items, over-the-counter medicines, etc.

(b) Shandies/Haats/Weekly Markets

Agricultural implements, cloth, herbal medicines, local sweets, toys, jaggery, bamboo baskets, cheap cosmetic items, grains, vegetables and fruits.

(c) Mandi Towns, Taluka and District Headquarters

Agricultural inputs, watches, cycles, ready-made garments, cement, books, electrical items, vessels, transistors, jewellery, two-wheelers, sewing machines and TV.

Considering shopping habits of villagers, the distribution set up should extend to villages and weekly markets for fast-moving consumer goods and to mandi towns, taluka and district headquarters for consumer durables.

"A Dealer for Consumer Durables in Taluka Headquarters"

TRADITIONAL AND NEW PRODUCTS

Over a period of time, the rural consumer is moving from traditional to new products as shown below:

Needs	Traditional Products	New Products
Brushing Teeth	Neem stick, Burnt husk, Common salt, Charcoal powder	Toothpowder, toothpaste
Washing Vessels	Coconut fibre, Ash, Brick powder, Tamarind	Washing cake, powder and liquid
Transport	Bullock cart, Horse cart, Cycle	Scooter, Motor Cycle, Tractors
Irrigation	Canals, Wells, Ponds	Borewells, Motor/Pumpset, Generators
Hair Wash	Green gram, Tur dhal, Shikakai powder	Shampoo

Fig. 3.2: Traditional and New Products

CONSUMER BUYING PROCESS

It is necessary for the marketers to understand as to how the rural consumer makes his buying decisions, who makes the buying decisions, the type of decisions involved and the steps in the buying process. A rural buyer has free time and therefore he spends lot of time before making purchases. He cannot be easily coaxed to buy a new product. Rural consumers buy durables during post-harvest season and festivals.

Buying roles consist of the following:

(a) **Initiator:** A person who first suggests the idea of purchasing anything.

(b) **Influencer:** A person who influences the purchase decisions.

(c) **Decider:** One who takes final purchase decision.

(d) **Buyer:** One who actually makes purchase.

(e) **User:** Person who uses the product.

Examples:

(a) The idea to buy a television set might come from the child studying in the school. The opinion leader in the village might advise on the model of TV the family should buy. The husband might make the final decision and children will be seeing the television most.

(b) When the product is expensive, bought infrequently (Motor cycle or Moped), the consumer takes a longer time to make a decision to buy the product. The consumer will first learn about the product before making thoughtful purchase choice.

(c) As regards insurance in rural market, the head of the family is the decision maker and he decides after consulting many people in the village.

(d) There are cases where rural consumers have purchased premium models of colour television designed for urban markets and also made cash down payments though they were not richer than their urban counterparts. The fact being that a joint family system calls for a wider screen so that a large number of members can watch TV.

PURCHASE DECISION MAKING PROCESS FOR NEW PRODUCT

Buying decisions of consumers differ from rural to urban areas. Rural consumers are relatively traditional and urban consumers are moving towards Western culture. Awareness about new products and brands is less among rural consumers. Languages vary from state-to-state and we do not have a common language understood by all. A rural consumer passes through the following stages in the course of adoption of a product.

(a) **Awareness:** The consumer becomes aware of the new product/service, but does not have information.

(b) **Interest:** He seeks information.

(c) **Evaluation:** He evaluates the new products, compares with existing one, if any.

(d) **Trial:** He tries the new product on a small-scale.

(e) **Adoption:** He decides to use it regularly.

ADOPTER GROUPS

Innovation adoption depends on the willingness to try out new products/new services/ new ideas. Of course, the features of the product such as affordability, social approval, easy to use will influence the adoption process. It has been observed that consumers differ considerably in their readiness to adopt new product and there are five adopter groups, as given below.

(a) **Innovators** are venturesome and opinion leaders and they try new products even at some risk.

(b) **Early Adopters** are also opinion leaders and adopt a new idea early but carefully.

(c) **The Eary Majority** adopt a new idea/product before an average person.

(d) **Late Majority** adopt only after a majority has tried it.

(e) **Laggards** adopt only when it has become a tradition.

Example: Rural youth exposed to urban life, the students, landlords, progressive farmers are the innovators and early adopter groups in rural markets.

Examples of rural consumer behaviour with respect to some of the fast-moving consumer goods are given below:

(1) Tea

(a) Tea is an essential commodity and is consumed at least twice a day. It is a part of the daily diet.

(b) Its purchase is done along with the weekly groceries and the actual purchase is done by men in rural areas.

(c) Generally, the rural consumers prefer strong brands of tea.

(d) Most of the rural households go in for loose or unbranded tea.

(e) Attractive packaging and use of bright colours plays an important role in influencing consumers to buy.

(f) Among low-income rural consumers, the tea consumption is growing at 6 per cent a year, twice the urban rate.

(2) Shampoo

(a) The decision makers are often the young wife or daughter-in-law or the daughter of the family.

(b) The buyer, on the other hand, is either the head of the family or the elder son.

(c) The retailer influences the buyers, he tries to sell the brand that gives him best margins. Though the wife or daughter-in-law may have many a times recommended a particular brand, another brand is bought under the influence of the retailer.

(d) People identify with herbal products, rely on traditional remedies.

(e) Many use soaps.

(f) There is a Friday ritual (oil bath) unique in Tamil Nadu.

(g) The small pack of low unit price is quite effective in developing brand loyalty.

(h) Some even perceive it to be product used during festivals.

(3) Soft Drinks

(a) The consumption of soft drinks seems to be a planned activity for a majority of rural buyers as compared to impulse purchase of urban consumers.

(b) When rural consumers visit the village retailer for purchasing groceries, they already have an idea of how much they have to spend. Hence, only if they have some extra cash on them after having made the household purchases, then they would buy a soft drink.

(c) Thus, purchase also depends on how recently they had their last soft drink, and so they try to bring a periodicity to their purchases by postponing their consumption. The frequency of soft drinks' consumption varies from once in a fortnight to once in a month.

(d) Soft drinks are consumed in large quantities during: 1. festive occasion — Dasara, Diwali, etc., 2. marriages in the village, when soft drinks are purchased in bulk, 3. when going to the city for the weekly/fortnightly shopping or 4. going out to a movie.

OPINION LEADERS

Villagers attach more importance to the experience of others who have used the product for making a purchase decision. Opinion leader is a person who is considered to be knowledgeable and is consulted by others and his advice is normally followed. Opinion leaders are remarkably effective at influencing the buying behaviour of other persons due to the following reasons; In rural areas, caste and profession plays important roles in deciding the social status of an individual. Priest, landlord, doctors have higher status in the village and their suggestions are followed by other villagers.

(a) Credibility: Opinion leaders are highly credible source of product-related information because they are neutral concerning the information they provide. The information they provide is in the best interest of the recipient since there is no monetary gain and the advice is based on the firsthand experience of the opinion leader.

	Opinion Leaders	Products
(a)	Agricultural officers/Agricultural scientists/Progressive farmers	Pesticides, Fertilisers, Seeds
(b)	Medical practitioners/Veterinary doctors	Pharma/Animal health products
(c)	Successful farmers/bankers	High value farm machinery like Tractors
(d)	Village President/Painters	Paints
(e)	Electricians	Fans, Electric Iron
(f)	Teachers	Soap, Toothpaste, Iodised salt
(g)	Mistry (Mason)	Cement
(h)	Village President/Progressive farmers	Banking service
(i)	Educated Village Youth	Cosmetics, soft drinks, TV, Two-wheelers

Fig. 3.3: Opinion Leaders

(b) Positive and Negative Product Information: Information provided by a marketer about a product is invariably favourable to the product. But the opinion or advice given by an opinion leader may be positive or negative, because he has no interest in the purchase. It adds to his credibility.

(c) Information and Advice: Opinion leaders are the source of both information and advice. The opinion leaders may simply tell what they know by their experience and advice what to buy or to avoid.

(d) Opinion Leadership is Category-specific: It is a fact that opinion leadership tends to be category-specific. The opinion leaders offer advice or opinion only about a specific category of product or service. When other product categories are concerned, they are no more opinion leaders. Thus, opinion leaders are not opinion leaders for all product categories.

Example: A progressive farmer may advice on what brand of pesticide is effective for controlling a particular pest. The same farmer may take the advice of another person for buying a colour television.

COMPOSITION OF RURAL DEMAND

The rise in income, increased reach of mass media and rising aspirations of people have influenced the consumer behaviour leading to changes in the type of products purchased and consumed in rural areas.

Examples: Lime juice and butter milk to aerated soft drinks, neemstick and charcoal powder to toothpowder and toothpaste, loose tea to packaged tea, bicycle to motor cycle and so on.

(a) Products that are Well Established in Rural Market:

Examples: Bicycles, motor cycles, agricultural inputs and machinery such as fertilisers, pesticides, seeds, tractors and farm implements, radios, non-alcoholic beverages such as coffee, tea, tobacco products, cooking utensils, bathing and washing soaps and textiles.

(b) Products that have Entered the Rural Market in Recent Years:

Examples: Ready-made garments, baby care products, packaged foodstuffs, modern consumer durables, cosmetics and toiletries.

(c) Products where Rural Consumption is More than Urban:

Examples: Bicycles, mechanical watches and tailoring machines.

(d) Products where Rural Consumption Growth Rate is Higher than Urban Markets:

Examples: Packaged tea, bathing and washing cake.

(e) Hierarchy of Needs:

The type of product, which a rural consumer intends to buy, depends upon factors such as (a) General level of awareness, (b) Purchasing capacity, (c) Utility of the product, (d) Cost-benefit analysis done by him, (e) His attitude towards the product, (f) Feedback from opinion leaders, and (g) Social values governing the society.

Based on the hierarchy of needs of rural consumers, consumer products could be classified into three categories.

Category I	Category II	Category III
Bicycles	Sewing machines	
Wristwatches	Mixies	DVD
Radio/Transistors	Mobile phones	Moped
Electric fans	TV	Motor cycles
Pressure cookers	Water heaters	Refrigerators

Fig. 3.4: Hierarchy of Needs (2010)

The first group is fairly well established and is slowly growing. The second category of goods is modestly penetrated and is showing healthy growth. The third group consisting of high-priced high involvement products like colour TVs, refrigerators is growing fast. Most products under Category I are of immediate use to the family. Category II includes products that break the monotony of household work or a source of entertainment. Category III includes a combination of products that help to supplement income, source of entertainment or comfortable household working. The hierarchy of needs also gives an indication of the socio-economic condition of the buyers.

CONCLUSION

Rural consumer behaviour is influenced by a number of factors. There are differences in the response of rural people to a particular stimulus even in the same village. The marketers have to understand attitudes, beliefs and aspirations of rural people and buying process to explore the rural market.

QUESTIONS

1. Do you think that an understanding of consumer behaviour is required for preparing marketing strategy? Explain.
2. Discuss the role of opinion leaders in new product introduction.
3. Describe briefly the shopping habits of rural people.
4. Do you think that the profile of rural demand is changing? Discuss.

CASE STUDY

Rural Buyer Behaviour

"It is the youngsters who decide what to buy. And it is not the urban markets one is referring to."

So you think that the village elder is the most influential decision maker in the rural household today. Surprise, surprise. It is not. "Decision making is shifting towards the younger population," says Pradeep Lokhande, Director, Rural Relations. There are many shopkeepers who come to know of new products from these young children and then stock them up in their shops. "The wide reach that television has is one major reason for this shift," adds Lokhande.

This shift has triggered many changes and has affected the buyers as well as the sellers. A couple of years ago, typically, shops in the rural areas offered goods and brands that the shopkeeper was aware of. The choice was limited, but the buyers' market syndrome has hit rural households too. The young probing and thinking minds have triggered many changes on this front. No longer can the shopkeeper pass on what he has, he has to stock brands and products that are being asked for now.

So what will be the effect of this shift? The immediate effect is being felt in the way these children and growing population is targeted, there are many promotional activities that are carried out in the schools. "We did a promotional activity for Lifebuoy in the schools and the results were amazing," comments Lokhande. This is just the beginning, there are many marketers who are targeting the younger lot to reach out and increase their market share in these regions. "The shift had to happen with more village children going to schools and improvement in infrastructure facilities in these regions," says Lokhande.

The advertising front too is experiencing a shift and focusing on the younger generation. Remember the Pepsi ad with Sachin Tendulkar in a rural background sometime back? "The shift had to take place to attract the right audience," comments Lokhande. Today, there are many versions of advertisements that are aired to suit the appropriate target in the rural areas and the vernacular advertisements are well received. It is becoming evident that the marketing-mix is focusing itself towards the new rural decision makers.

The shopkeepers on their part are finding it equally difficult to cope with the ever-changing demands of the young ones, this has made them more competitive in the way they approach the buyers. The increasing number of regional cable channels too are playing a major role and provide the young decision makers with a medium to know about new products and brands that are fast evolving.

The new scenario is making the markets very competitive for the consumer as it offers him a wide range to choose from. "The exposure has helped people to look at products differently," says Lokhande who has come up with the idea to supply computers for school children in the interiors offering them the seamless scope to explore and probe new trends and market situations existing in the urban areas.

With computer education spreading to the rural regions and the wide reach that the internet offers, the coming days could just break all the myths that surround decision making in rural markets and the potential that these markets have. Already, Lokhande has come up with the idea to supply computer for school children in the interiors offering them the seamless scope to explore and probe new trends and market situations existing in the urban areas.

In the days to come, rural consumers are going to be younger and far more choosy when it comes to making purchases. It will, thus, become imperative for marketers to focus on these new young target audience.

QUESTIONS

1. Do you agree that likes, preferences and wants of rural consumers are changing?
2. Give some promotional strategies for young rural consumers.

✿ ✿ ✿

4 RURAL MARKETING RESEARCH

INTRODUCTION

All business decisions are based on information. Such information may be based on experience, intuition or formal marketing research studies. Learning more about consumers, dealers and about marketing-mix is the heart of marketing research. As business grows, marketing management has to rely more on marketing research as a tool for solving any problem in the field of marketing. It is an invaluable tool in decision making based on scientific investigation and analysis of marketing problems. The producers have to get updated information about the needs, expectations, likes and dislikes of consumers. They have to understand the changes in consumers' preferences and consumption pattern. Rural markets and consumers are highly scattered and spread over a wide geographical area. Rising aspirations of rural people and the need for possessing modern goods has influenced the marketing environment in our country. Marketing Research (MR) finds out who are the customers, where are the customers, what do they want, when and where they want and how much they are willing to pay. This information will enable them to formulate an appropriate marketing strategy to explore the rural market.

Example: Attractive and convenient packaging may not be enough to motivate the rural consumer. The challenge is to convince the consumer to buy the product. The issue is not spending power; they have to be given a tangible reason to buy the product like soft drink when they have options to quench their thirst such as water, butter milk, marble soda, nimbupani, neera, etc.

NEED FOR MARKETING RESEARCH (MR)

Market research is of great help to those firms who intend to enter the rural market. It is also useful for firms who are interested in expanding the activities in rural market.

- (MR) provides valuable information on rural markets, rural consumers, problems and prospects in rural marketing.

- Newer and better products are being introduced in the market and consumer prefers new products in the place of old one. MR provides useful information about changing pattern of product demand.
- Rural distribution requires a large number of intermediaries and MR helps the manager to find out the most effective distribution channel considering cost and service requirements.
- The marketing manager has to take quick decisions with regard to product promotion schemes, extension of credit facilities, appointment of dealers, etc., and MR provides reliable data and updated information for the same.
- MR find out for middlemen (wholesalers and retailers) what goods to purchase, when to purchase and at what price, how to display the goods, how much to charge and what service to provide to consumers.
- MR helps the advertiser in designing most effective promotion media and methods to reach the rural audience.
- Products competing in rural markets are National brands, Regional brands, Local brands and Spurious products. Apart from price factor, other factors such as packaging and after-sales service contribute to market competition. MR provides valuable information to the marketing manager in designing marketing strategy to face competition in rural market.

SCOPE OF MARKETING RESEARCH

MR is used essentially for solving marketing problems of a business enterprise and is primarily concerned with "4 Ps" of marketing-mix. MR is a subject with wide scope and main areas of marketing research are given below.

1. Consumer Research: Consumer needs, wants, preferences, buying motives, buying behaviour, changes in demand, consumer response to competitors' sales promotion and advertising.

2. Market Research: Market demand, market share, market competition, market segmentation.

3. Product Research: Design, development and introduction of new products, testing of existing products, product usage study, product modification, product positioning, product life cycle research, packaging research and brand image surveys.

4. Pricing Research: Evaluation of pricing strategy of company/competitors, study of price-demand relationship, evaluation of schemes such as discounts and allowances.

5. Distribution Research: Effectiveness of distribution channel and modes of transportation, dealer support for the company and products, warehousing efficiency, insurance, cost of distribution, use of delivery vans, syndicate distribution.

6. Competition Research: Key competitors and their products, prices, promotion, distribution.

7. Sales Promotion and Advertising Research: Effectiveness of media, sales promotion and campaigns.

8. Sales Analysis and Research: Performance of sales territory, effectiveness of field force, sales targets and achievements, incentives, problems in personal selling, training of sales force.

SOURCES OF DATA

The sources of data are broadly classified into primary and secondary sources. When the information is collected directly from the consumers, dealers, distributors and opinion leaders, it is termed as primary data. When it is collected from published reports it is treated as secondary data. However, not much data is available on rural market and manufacturers have to collect information either directly or through market research agencies. Secondary data can be obtained from the following sources.

- Census of India Reports
- National Council of Applied Economic Research
- National Sample Survey
- District Statistical Reports
- Panchayat Office
- Central Statistical Organisation

DESIGNING QUESTIONNAIRE

A questionnaire is a set of questions for recording answers. Utmost care has to be taken in the structure (number and type of questions), wording and sequencing of questions. Considering low literacy level and low awareness of rural consumers, the following points to be considered in designing questionnaire.

- Every questionnaire must explain the purpose of inquiry so as to stimulate interest and request the respondents to offer full cooperation in giving answers to the questions.
- Questionnaire should be short, simple, easily understandable, well-phrased and have one interpretation or meaning. The meaning of all questions should be obvious to all the respondents. Avoid questions making excessive demand on memory.
- Women do not like to disclose their age. People do not like questions probing their finances. No question on personal and intimate subjects should be asked as it encroaches upon the privacy of the individuals.

- It would be preferable to pre-test the questionnaire on a sample of respondents before it is used for wider use.

PERSONAL INTERVIEW OR FIELD SURVEY

In the questionnaire method, we can collect information through mail, telephone or personal interview. Experience shows that personal interview with respondents gives the required information. It offers a sense of participation and it is more flexible for data collection. Rate of refusal is low. Depth interview is possible. Complex questions can be asked. Visual aids in the form of picture, advertisements, exhibits, etc., can be used to get views, opinions, and attitudes of respondents.

Examples:

(a) Faces for rating which shows the happiest face on the left side and saddest face on the right side and other faces in between.

(b) Wheels with different colours such as green (luxurious crop, good harvest), red (danger, risk) and black (inauspicious, sadness).

(c) Playing Cards (King, Queen, 10, 9) can be used for rating the trends.

A sample of the questionnaire for consumer survey is given below:

RURAL MARKETING RESEARCH

Consumer Survey

Product Television (TV)

Sample Questionnaire

1. Name:
2. Address:
3. Occupation: Farmer, Trader, Service, Artisan, Others (please mention)
4. Age: 18-20, 21-30, 31-4-, 41-5-, 51-60, 61 and above
5. Education: Primary School (I-V), Upper Primary School (VI-VII), High School (VIII-X) and Higher Secondary (XI-XII), College Education
6. Do you own a TV?
7. If yes, please tell us the model/make.
8. What are the factors you considered while buying a TV: A. Very important, B. Important C. Desirable D. Not Important E. Least Important

	A	B	C	D	E
(a) Design					
(b) Colour of the cabinet					
(c) Size					
(d) Number of channels					

(e) Withstand voltage fluctuations

(f) Remote facility

(g) After-sales service

(h) Reputation of the dealer

9. How do you rate the price of the TV purchased by you: High, Medium, and Low?
10. Do you buy on cash or credit basis?
11. If on credit, who provided loan to you and terms and conditions of loan?
12. Who took the decision to the buy the TV? (Rate the following people based on their importance – 1-5)

Head of the family	( )
Earning member	( )
Wife	( )
Husband	( )
Son	( )
Daughter	( )

13. Have you consulted anybody before buying the TV? If so, give details.
14. Have you seen any advertisement for TV in newspaper, television or other medium (Please mention the medium).
15. Did it influence your buying decision?

Note: The questionnaire has to be in regional language and could be modified as per local requirement.

Fig. 4.1: Consumer Survey

LOCATIONS SUITABLE FOR CONDUCTING INTERVIEWS

The following locations are suitable for conducting interviews with rural consumers.

- Tea shop
- Grocery shop
- School playground
- Temple/Gurdwara premises
- Village meeting place
- Panchayat office
- Cooperative society
- Bus stop

- Milk collection centre
- Block development office
- Primary health centre

"Temple Premises — A Meeting Place in the Village"

CHALLENGES IN RURAL MARKETING RESEARCH

- The rural population and the markets are highly scattered over a wide geographical area. Collecting information on all-India basis is laborious, time-consuming and costly process. Therefore, the companies conduct research only on selected market segments. However, such findings cannot be extrapolated to the entire market.
- There are wide variations in the secondary data provided by different agencies about rural market.
- Lack of infrastructure facilities such as all-weather roads, telephone connection, postal services, transportation, etc.
- Due to low literacy, the market researcher has to use visuals to get the views, opinions of rural people. A rural person is not at all fluent in English and the researcher should be able to speak to the respondents in the local language.
- Traits such as honesty, high level of energy and empathy will make a positive impression with the villagers.

TRAINING OF INTERVIEWERS

The interviewers should be imparted proper training to handle the interviews with rural consumers. They should know: (a) How to establish rapport with rural consumers (b) How to phrase the questions, and (c) How to record answers properly. Further, they should have a good understanding of the cultural factors that influence rural consumer behaviour and the dynamics of rural markets.

- Life in rural areas is still governed by customs and traditions. Rural people are generally suspicious of strangers. The interviewer should learn to say *Namaskar, Namaste, Ram Ram, Vanakkam* while meeting the villagers so that he can easily build rapport with them.
- There is a belief among rural people that experience is more important than formal education and therefore he should consider this point during interviews.
- A typical rural person has lot of free time and therefore the person should have tremendous patience while conducting interviews.
- Greeting visitors with folded hands, abstaining from smoking in front of elders in the villages, removing footwear while entering the houses, respecting women irrespective of their social status, sitting on the floor along with villagers during interviews are normal courtesies expected in the village life.

RURAL MARKET RESEARCH AGENCIES

Many Market Research Agencies such as IMRB, NIELSON, MART are offering services to companies engaged in sales and marketing of FMCGs, durables, insurance and financial services. With a view to offer integrated services in the field of rural marketing, leading Market Research Agencies have formed Rural Marketing Association of India (RMAI). The Founder Members of the Association are Anugrah Madison, MART, Rural Relations, Sampark, Ogilvy Activation, Linterland, RC&M, Impact Communications, Kripa Outdoor Publicity, Indian Agri-business Systems and Rural Right. The association publishes a quarterly journal, i,e., "Rural Marketing Journal".

Rural Marketing Journal

CONCLUSION

Rural markets and consumers are highly scattered and spread over a wide geographical area. Rise in income and aspirations of rural people for possessing modern goods and services have influenced the rural marketing environment in our country. Marketing Research would help the company in knowing "who are the most important consumers, where are these customers, what do they want, when and where they want and how much they are willingness to pay". This in-depth understanding of consumers is important to successfully market products and services in rural market.

QUESTIONS

1. Discuss the importance of Rural Marketing Research with special reference to consumer goods and durables.
2. What are the qualities required for a Rural Marketing Research worker?
3. A company wants to introduce a suitable model of Mobile Phone in Rural Market. Prepare a questionnaire for collecting data from rural consumers.

✿ ✿ ✿

5 RURAL MARKET SEGMENTATION

INTRODUCTION

Rural market consists of individuals and groups of people and their needs, resources, preferences and buying habits differ. The rural market is heterogeneous as seen below:

- All consumers do not share the same purchasing power in villages. The landlords and the rich farmers have already started using mobile phones. On the other hand, the agricultural labourers and very small farmers are struggling to meet both ends.
- Literacy is an important factor in developing awareness and knowledge about technological changes and there are wide variations in literacy level among states. For example, rural literacy is very high in Kerala compared to Odisha, Bihar and Himachal Pradesh.
- There are variations in population size and density of population in villages. There are about two lakh villages having population of less than 500 each and there are practically no shops in such villages.
- There are different groups based on religion, caste, occupation, income, age, education and politics and each group exerts influence on the behaviour of people in the villages.

Marketers have recognised the importance of heterogeneous nature of rural markets. They are keenly interested in subdividing or segmenting the market. Each segment consists of a group of people with similar or homogeneous demand, so that the marketer can offer tailor-made marketing-mix for each market segment or subdivision. In a sense, market segmentation is the strategy of divide and conquer, i.e., dividing the market to conquer them by formulating different sets of marketing strategies to different groups of consumers. Segmentation provides answers to two important questions, i.e., who are our target customers and what should we sell to them?

Example: Cavin Kare studied the shampoo market and came out with Chik shampoo priced at 50 paise per sachet and the brand became an instant hit in rural areas.

Market segmentation has three components, i.e.,

1. **Market:** People or organisation with needs or wants and the ability and willingness to pay.
2. **Market Segment:** A group of people or organisation having one or more characteristics that lead to them to have similar product needs.
3. **Market Segmentation:** The process of dividing a market into meaningful, relatively similar identifiable segments and groups.

There are many ways to group consumers in segmenting the market. Broadly speaking, we have two main approaches to identify market segments as given below.

PEOPLE-ORIENTED APPROACH (CUSTOMER PERSONAL CHARACTERISTICS)

We can classify the customers by customer dimensions such as geographic location, demography, socio-economic characteristics and psychographic characteristics. These are variables and they are independent of any product or service and the particular situation encountered by the buyer in making buying decisions. We try to find out the type of customer who will buy our products.

1. Geographic Location is the usual and popular basis for market segmentation. The market could be divided into urban and rural markets. While urban population is highly concentrated, rural population is scattered over a wide geographical area. Since 1980s, many companies are targeting rural consumers due to growing purchasing power. About 50 per cent of the rural population lives in about one lakh villages having a population of over 2,000 each and companies like HUL have been able to cover this segment by establishing retail network in these villages.

We have four regions, i.e., South, West, East and North. It has been observed that consumers in South, by and large, are conscious about cleanliness, health, education and culture. Due to hot weather conditions, there is increased use of talcum powder in South and Ponds has a high market share in this region. The demand for woollen dress materials is high in North during winter season compared to other regions in the country.

2. Demographic Segmentation: In rural areas, the husband provides economic security to the members of the family and he makes purchase decisions. Nowadays, school-going children have high awareness about new products and they are influencing buying decisions in the family. Therefore, the marketers are targeting the younger lot for products like biscuits, chocolates, shampoos and soft drinks.

3. Socio-economic Segmentation: Major income still comes from agriculture though the share of non-farm income has gone up in recent years. Based on occupation, there are four important groups, who form the target population for consumer durables like colour TV, refrigerator and two-wheelers.

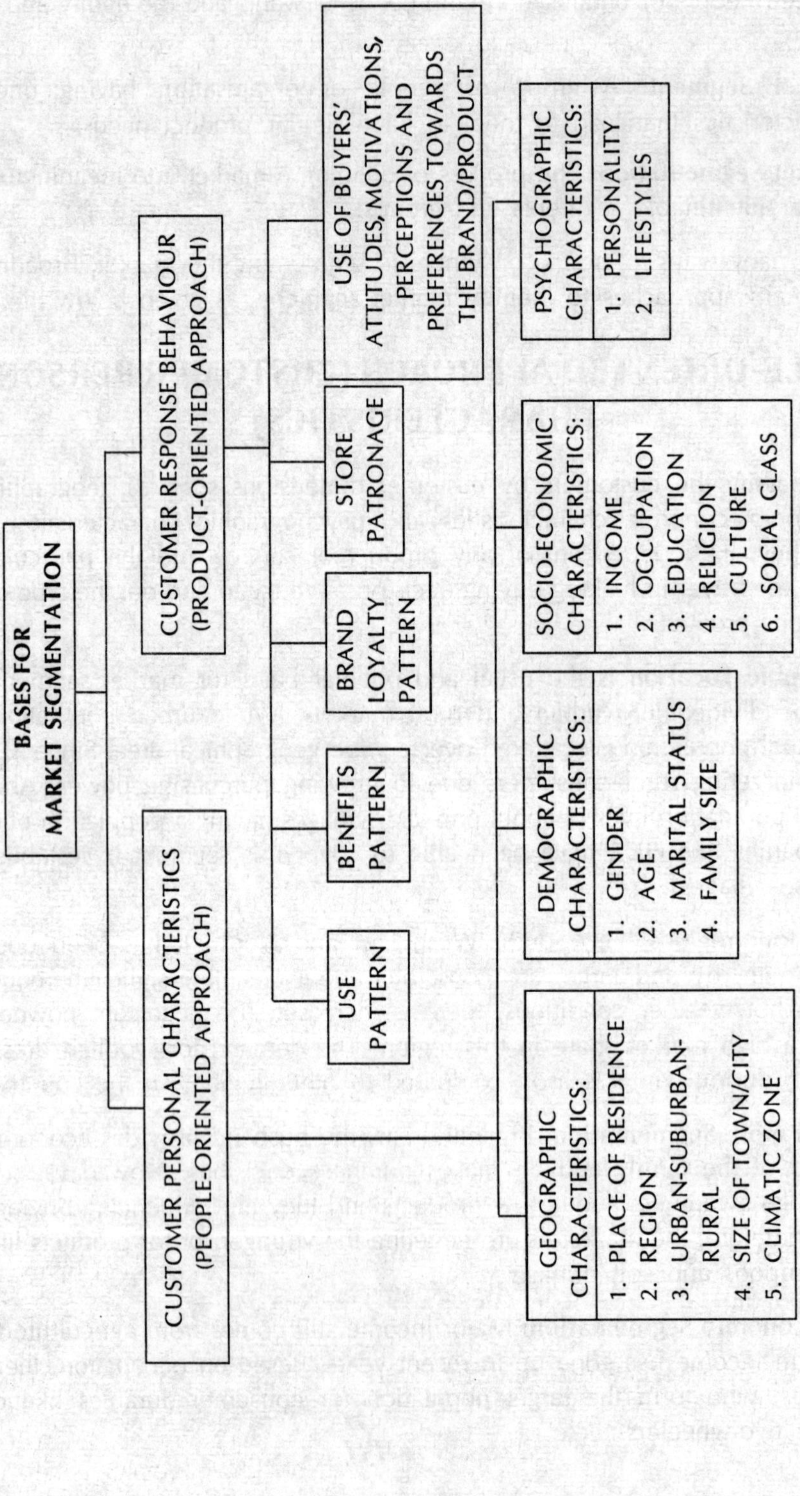

Fig. 5.1: Bases for Market Segmentation

(A) PEOPLE-ORIENTED APPROACH

(1) Geographical Characteristics·

Region:	South, West, East and North
Density of population:	Urban, rural, semi-urban
Size of the village:	Very small (< 1,000), Small (1,000 – 2,000) Medium (2,000 – 5,000) and Large (> 5,000).
Climate:	Hot, Humid, Cold, Rainy

(2) Demographic Characteristics:

Gender:	Male/Female
Age:	(Under 6, 6-11, 12-19, 20-34, 35-49, 50-64).
Marital Status:	
Family Size:	1-2, 3-4, 5 plus

(3) Socio-economic Characteristics·

Income Annual	Destitute< ₹ 90,000
	Aspirants: ₹ 90,000 to ₹ 2 Lakh
	Climbers: ₹ 2 Lakh to ₹ 5 Lakh
	Well-off: ₹ 5 Lakh to ₹ 10 Lakh
	Affluent: > ₹ 10 Lakh
Occupation:	Agriculture and non-agriculture
Education:	Literate, Illiterate
Religion/Caste:	Upper caste and lower caste
Culture:	Traditional Life, Family Values
Belief and Attitude:	Positive, Negative, Neutral
Social Status:	High, medium and low

(4) Psychographic Characteristics:

Personality:	Ambitious, team player, dominant
Lifestyle:	Opinion Leader, follower

(B) PRODUCT-ORIENTED APPROACH

Use pattern:	Ex-user, non-user, potential user, first time user and regular user
Benefits pattern:	Quality, price sensitive, service
Brand loyalty pattern:	Nil, low, medium and high
Store patronage:	Nil, low, medium and high
Use of buyers' attitude	Positive, negative, neutral, hostile

Fig. 5.2: Segmentation Variables

1. **Farmers:**

(a) The landlords which include Zamindars/Mitadars/Thakurs, traders and local moneylenders. They possess large acres of land and have spacious houses in the village. They have high disposable income. Their lifestyle can be compared to that of upper income group of urban areas. They have relatives staying in cities and in many cases abroad also. Their children go to urban schools.

"House of a Landlord"

(b) Affluent farmers who live in villages and follow modern methods of cultivation. They occupy a high position in the society that is above the normal population with respect to social and economic status in the village. They are hard working and aspire for better living conditions. They have high disposable income and try to maintain their status in the village. The owner farmers who constitute 34 per cent of households, own about 30 per cent of durables.

The small and marginal farmers occupy low rank in the rural social hierarchy and their needs are basic, i.e., food, clothing and shelter.

2. **Traders:** The traders constitute about 8 per cent of the rural households and own between15-20 per cent of the durables.
3. **Service Class:** The service class who includes teachers, clerks, mechanics, electricians in the villages and office and factory workers, who work outside the village, constitute about 13 per cent of rural households and own 30-40 per cent of durables.

Rural income is highly seasonal as it is dependent on agricultural activities. Therefore, most of the purchases of durables, jewellery and clothes takes place during post-harvest season and during festivals like Onam, Pongal, Diwali, Idd, Gudipadwa and Baisakhi.

Family life cycle exercises definite influence on consumer behaviour with regard to purchase of consumer goods.

Example: In rural areas, the users of shampoo are the young daughter or the daughter-in-law and the elderly women continue to use natural products like shikakai powder.

"Baisakhi: The Harvest Festival in Punjab"

4. **Rural Youth:** The rural youth in the age group of 20-25 years, play a major role in the purchase decisions of the family. They view television and cinema and enjoy seeing cricket matches and action movies. They are the target group for products like toothpaste, shampoo, soft drink, deodorant, television model, audio system, mobile phone, etc. They are moving from bicycles to motor cycles. Even branded clothes and shoes have entered rural homes, though the sales volumes are low at present. Marketing researchers can meet them at telephone booth, playground, retailer shop and village square. However all decisions regarding agriculture and inputs are taken by the head of the family in most of the cases.

(4) Psychographic Segmentation: Personality traits such as dominance, aggressiveness, achievement orientation, motivation, etc., may influence buyer behaviour. Lifestyle can be measured by the products the person uses and the person's activities, interests, opinions and values. In a rural society, there are grades of people based on income, occupation and wealth. The educated youth, innovative farmers, village president are the important opinion leaders and marketers are targeting this group for promoting products and services.

PRODUCT-ORIENTED APPROACH (CUSTOMER RESPONSE BEHAVIOUR)

The customer response or buyer behaviour may be considered in relation to product benefits, product usage, store patronage and brand loyalty. We want to know why consumer buys a certain product. ***Example:*** Bullet Motor Cycle is considered as a sturdy vehicle (product benefits) and creates a 'Macho Image'.

1. Use Pattern: A buyer may be classified as heavy, medium, light user and non-user. The use of consumer products such as shampoo, hair oil, toothpaste, talcum powder is low in rural areas due to poor affordability and many marketers have introduced small unit packs of these products to meet the requirements of lower and middle class rural consumers. In agriculture, cotton farmers are heavy users of pesticides and the marketers have come out with large packs (20/25 litres) of the products to meet their special requirements.

2. Benefits Pattern: Consumers buy products primarily to secure expected benefits. Rural buyers look for value for money while purchasing products. They look for quality but cannot afford high prices. They are concerned with utility of the products rather than mere good looks and frills. The rural consumers particularly the lower/middle income group are budget-conscious unlike urban consumers who are comparatively more status-seeking. The difference in the preference of the attributes is shown in Fig. 5.3.

Status-seeking Consumer	Budget-conscious Consumer
Brand name ↓ Model ↓ Technology ↓ Image ↓ Budget	Budget ↓ Warranty ↓ After-sales service ↓ Brand name ↓ Model

Fig. 5.3: Preference of the Attributes

Examples:

1. Bullet motor cycle is popular in villages due to its ruggedness.
2. HMT watches are seen on many a wrists for its utility value.
3. Rural consumers prefer strong tea (*Kadak Chai*).
4. Titan has introduced Sonata brand watches; priced between ₹ 350 and ₹ 800 to meet the requirements of price-sensitive rural and semi-urban consumers.

3. Brand Loyalty: A rural consumer is price sensitive due to low purchasing power and lack of awareness about the quality of products available in the market. However, they will continue to patronise a brand once they are satisfied with the product.

Example: A few of the popular brands are Lifebuoy, Parle, Ponds, Nirma, Tata Salt, Colgate, Philips, etc.

4. Store Patronage: It has been observed that rural consumer buys from the same shop. The retailer extends credit to the consumers and many have running credit account with the same retailer. He influences buying decisions of the consumers. Therefore, the marketers have to identify key retailers in rural markets and ensure product availability for success of business.

5. Predispositions Towards Products and Brands: The attitudes, perceptions, values, beliefs, intentions and preferences are the constituents of predisposition, indicating the consumers state of mind, predisposing the consumer to behave in a particular way towards a product, brand, dealer and the company. Segmentation studies based on buying motives, attitudes, perceptions and preferences give much better results regarding buyer behaviour than those obtained by demographic, socio-economic variables or determinants. While age, gender, usage, income can be measured objectively, personality traits, lifestyles, motives, attitudes, values and beliefs have to be inferred as they are subjective phenomena and cannot be objectively measured.

"A Shop in a Mandi"

SEGMENTATION BASED ON MULTIPLE ATTRIBUTES

Market research agencies such as Hindustan Thompson Associates Limited, MICA have tried to segment the rural markets based on multiple attributes as per details given below:

1. Thompson Rural Market Index

Hindustan Thompson Associates Limited have developed the Rural Market Index for 355 districts in our country. They have considered the following factors for developing the Rural Market Index.

1. Area of the district in sq. km.

Demographics

2. Population: (a) Number of males, (b) Number of females
3. Density per sq. km.
4. Number of villages
5. Percentage of literacy
6. Literate: (a) Males — Numbers, (b) Females — Numbers

Occupation Pattern

7. (a) Number of cultivators, (b) Number of agricultural labours, (c) Number of non-agricultural labourers.

Agriculture Related Data

8. (a) Gross cropped area in hectares, (b) Gross irrigated area in hectares
9. Area under non-food crops in hectares
10. Average size of operational holdings in hectares

Agricultural Inputs Data

11. (a) Pumpsets and tubewells — Numbers, (b) Fertiliser consumption in metric tonnes, (c) Number of tractors

Rural Electrification Data

12. Percentage of villages electrified

Commercial Banks Data

13. Number of rural branches
14. Deposits in ₹ lakh
15. Advances in ₹ lakh.

Based on the index numbers, the districts have been classified as A, B, C, D and E class markets as given below:

Table 5.1: Classification of Potential Markets

Class of Markets	Index Range	No. of Districts	Percentage of Market
A	60.00 to 100.00	22	17.80
B	40.00 to 59.99	39	20.50
C	30.00 to 39.99	54	20.40
D	20.00 to 29.99	86	23.00
E	Below 20.00	154	18.30
Total		**355**	**100.00**

From the above table, it is clear that out of 355 districts, about 60 districts have high potential as they are coming under A and B class of markets. To start with, the marketer could focus on A and B class markets. 54 districts have medium potential as they are coming under C segment and 86 districts are coming under D segment which needs more time to develop.

2. Mica Rural Market Ratings

The ratings give the relative potential of districts in India, based on the following parameters:

(a) Fertiliser consumption

(b) Irrigated area

(c) Cropped area

(d) Bank advances

(e) Value of agricultural produce.

Table 5.2: MICA Rural Market Ratings

Class of Market	Development Index Points	No. of Districts
A	60-100	33
B	40-59	75
C	30-39	76
D	20-29	89
E	Below 20	172
Total		445

3. R.K. Swamy Guide to Market Planning — 2008

The guide gives the details of top ten districts and top ten rural markets in the country, as shown below and the same is useful to rural marketers.

(a) Top Ten Districts (based on the Size of the rural market as per centage of Total District Market)

Kolhapur (62 per cent), Belgaum (69 per cent), Ahmednagar (72 per cent), Pune (26 per cent), Ernakulam (40 per cent), Kottayam (79 per cent), Trissur (61 per cent), Satara (81 per cent), Kollam (72 per cent).

(b) Top Ten Rural markets on Absolute Market Size

Medinapur, 24 South Paragnas, Barddhaman, Ahmednagar, Murshidabad, Belgaum 24 North Paragnas, Pune, East Godawari, Kolhapur.

MARKET SEGMENTATION STRATEGIES

A firm should identify the most potential and convenient segment of the total market and make effective use of the marketing-mix, i.e., product, price, place (distribution) and promotion to achieve the marketing objectives. Marketer has three strategic options.

1. Undifferentiated Marketing (Mass Market Strategy): The marketers may not prefer the idea of market segmentation and follow one marketing-mix for many market segments. This helps the company to target maximum number of consumers.

Examples:

(a) Most of the local marketers of bread, biscuits, namkeens, etc., follow mass marketing approach.

(b) Medimix is marketed as an aurvedic soap for all types of consumers.

(c) Even giant like Coca-Cola followed such an approach for a very long time — one product, one brand, one bottle for all markets — of course, today the company has a wide range of products.

2. Differentiated Marketing (Market Segmentation Strategy): A firm under differentiated marketing strategy enters many market segments but has a unique marketing-mix appropriate for each segment.

Examples:

(a) Mahindra and Mahindra market different types of tractors (based on horsepower) to meet the requirements of farmers.

(b) Indian Railways run passenger trains which halt at each and every station. The passenger trains are patronised by rural people as they can carry agricultural produce and personal luggage and it is cheap compared to bus service.

(c) Hindustan Unilever has one brand of soap for each segment of the market, i.e., Lifebuoy for lower income and Lux/Rexona/Dove for higher income groups.

3. Concentrated Marketing: A firm may decide to concentrate on one chosen segment of the total market. It selects an area where there is no strong competition and it can do best in that area. This is also known as niche marketing. Niche market is relatively a small market segment having distinctive features and requirements and with focused working provides higher returns to the marketers.

Example: Pesticides market on hybrid vegetables and flowers. The growers have distinctive requirements and they want solutions to the field problems, control of pests and diseases and correcting nutritional deficiencies. They are willing to use even expensive branded products once they are convinced.

PRODUCT POSITIONING

In simple words, product positioning refers to the position or image which a product enjoys in the present or potential customers. The core thought behind positioning is the idea that your brand must occupy a particular space continuously in the consumer's mind.

It is called renting mind space, i.e., finding a suitable space in the mind and sit on it, do not let someone else (rival) to dislodge you. Positioning is based on Unique Selling Proposition (USP). It may be unique feature of the product or brand, market or competition, which becomes the core idea and around that feature, the product is placed in the market.

Examples:

(a) LG Electronics launched Sampoorna, India's first TV with Devanagari script on the screen display. The word Sampoorna meaning "Wholesome" cuts across all linguistic barriers in our country. It is affordable can withstand voltage fluctations and aimed at rural and semi-urban consumers.

(b) Hero Honda bikes have been positioned as fuel efficient two-wheelers in the market-place.

(c) Films stars are used to influence rural consumers. Lux soap campaign based on "Beauty soap of film stars".

(d) Billy wali cell (Eveready batteries — battery with cat as symbol).

1. SEGMENTATION SUCCESS CRITERIA

Since the company cannot cover the entire market, it aims at selecting a few market segments most suited for its products. The conditions essential for successful market segmentation are given below.

1. Measurability: Demographic and socio-economic characteristics are measurable but personality, life cycle, psychological factors such as motivation, perception, attitude are subjective and non-measurable attributes. Unfortunately, the availability of data about rural markets and consumers is very limited and therefore projecting sales, market share are difficult while preparing business plan for the company.

2. Accessibility: As we have seen, the rural markets are highly scattered and spread over a wide geographical area and therefore even if a segment is identified, the marketers are finding it difficult to reach the segment through distribution and communication media and methods. Companies like HUL, Colgate, Marico, Britannia are making use of haats, melas, van delivery service, audiovisual publicity programme to reach the villagers.

3. Effective Demand: The segment must have sufficient buying power and should be profitable enough. Large villages and villages situated close to towns and cities have high level of urban orientation and are potential markets in rural areas.

4. Market Responsiveness: The market should respond favourably to the marketing efforts. The marketer should have good understanding of buying motives and buying behaviour of rural consumers.

Example: Income from agriculture is seasonal and therefore the consumers avail credit facilities from traders. These traders in turn require credit from distributors/manufacturers. Many manufacturers/distributors extend credit facilities to persuade the traders to stock their products.

CONCLUSION

Considering the heterogeneous nature of the markets, there is a need to undertake further studies both by market research agencies and the organisations to develop effective segmentation of rural markets and position products/services in the minds of the target consumers in rural markets.

QUESTIONS

1. Discuss with examples the bases for market segmentation.
2. A leading industrial house has plans to establish a chain of stores for selling consumer goods and agricultural produce in semi-urban markets. Suggest appropriate market segmentation, targeting and positioning strategies.

✿ ✿ ✿

6 RURAL MARKETING-MIX

INTRODUCTION

The rural market with its vast size and demand offers lot of opportunities to the creative marketers. However, rural markets and rural marketing have special features as compared to urban markets.

- Life in rural areas is still governed by customs and traditions and people do not adopt new practices. Even rich and educated farmers do not wear jeans or branded shoes in most of the rural areas.
- A villager would prefer a sturdy metal bucket compared to a plastic one.
- New year is celebrated with great fanfare in cities and not in villages.
- Crop cultivation is a seasonal activity. The sales interview with a rural customer extends for a longer duration, since he has free time.
- Rural people believe that experience in relatively more important than formal education.

Therefore, the marketing manager has to use his knowledge, skills and experience for developing an appropriate marketing strategy. Marketing strategy basically involves effective use of the marketing-mix to explore the rural markets. Marketing-mix indicates appropriate combination of four Ps for achieving marketing objectives. The components are also known as marketing-mix variables or controllable variables as they can be used as per business requirements. These four Ps are Product, Price, Place and Promotion. Marketing experts have included several Ps such as packaging, positioning, pace, passion, people, public and politics as a part of marketing-mix.

FEATURES OF MARKETING-MIX

1. Marketing Variables are Interdependent: Any change in one variable will have an impact on the other.

Example: A company marketing expensive branded footwear (product) wants to enter rural markets. The product (the footwear) will have to be designed to suit the needs (sturdiness, price, etc.), of rural consumer. With the change in product, the other elements such as price, place and promotion have to be adjusted to achieve the marketing objectives.

2. Flexible and Dynamic Concept: It is necessary to adjust the variables as per changes in the marketing environment.

Example: TV reach is very high in urban areas and low in rural markets. Therefore, the company has to focus on rural specific promotion media to reach rural markets.

3. Customer is the Focus Point: The marketing-mix has to be adjusted to meet the requirements of the consumer.

Example: Literacy in English is very low in rural areas compared to metros and therefore there is a need to release advertisements in local newspapers to reach the rural consumer.

4. Consumer-oriented Activity: The main purpose is to give satisfaction to consumers and therefore the marketing-mix gives special attention to consumer needs and wants.

Example: Prompt settlement of customer complaints.

4 As IN RURAL MARKETING

The rural market with its vast size and consumer base form an important part of the total Indian market. The urban markets are becoming complex and competitive and the market environment is forcing marketers to go rural. However, rural market is highly heterogeneous and this is due to geographical characteristics, varied income levels and cultural differences. Awareness about products and services is relatively low due to low level of education and low reach of mass media. Further, the products have to be made available across six lakh villages spread over three million square kilometres. The problem is further compounded when we find that there are 36 lakh retail outlets in the country. Most of these outlets are small and marketers have to reach them only through a chain of distributors and wholesalers which add to the cost of distribution.

Marketing-mix indicates an appropriate combination of 4 Ps from the marketers' point of view. Considering dynamics of rural market and the challenges in exploring the rural markets, a practical approach would be to use the model based on 4 As since it is more oriented towards consumers. The 4 As are Acceptability, Affordability, Availability, and Awareness. ***Examples:*** Action Shoes at affordable prices have been well received in rural market against premium brand of Nike shoes. Ujala in liquid form has been preferred against Robin blue in powder form.

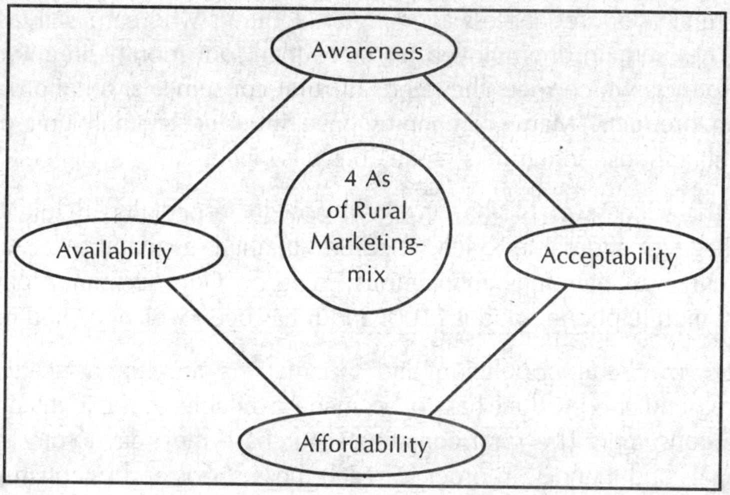

Fig. 6.1: 4 As of Rural Marketing-mix

Acceptability: Rural people are concerned with the utility of the product rather than appearance or show and companies have designed sturdy and utility products.

Examples: Philips free power radio, LG Sampoorna TV, HMT mechanical watches and Bullet motor cycles are still popular in rural areas due to these reasons. Cavin Kare studied rural consumer behaviour and introduced small pack of Chik shampoo and it was an instant hit in the market. Instead of buying large packs, they prefer to buy what they require for a short period time. Parle Biscuit continues to be preferred over local brand by villagers even though it is priced higher than local brands.

Parle G – ₹ 5,000 Crore Brand

Parle G is the most penetrated FMCG brand in the country. The largest selling biscuit brand in the world, Parle G biscuit is integral part of the lives of rural Indians for the last 75 years. The company did not increase the price for about fifteen ears since 1995. Affordable price has been the major factor for the dominance of the brand. Parle G has increased its market share from 67 per cent in 2002 to 79 per cent in 2012 while Tiger market share fell to 9 per cent from 26 per cent during the same period. Parle has ten manufacturing facilities owned by the company and seventy-five contract units and this has helped to beat its rivals in distribution efficiency and cost. Parle G has been able to grow its sales with a simple white and yellow stripped wrapper with a picture of a baby on it. Rivals such as Britannia, ITC feel that it is difficult to match Parle G in pricing. It has economies of scale which others cannot match. Parle G has grown at over 15 per cent compounded annual growth rate in the past five years. Parle G continues to be preferred by villagers over local brands.

Affordability: While rural income level has gone up in recent years, the lower income group constitutes about 65 per cent of the rural population. Major income still comes from agriculture and agriculture related activities. Income from agriculture is seasonal and depends upon monsoon rains. About 75 per cent of landholders are small and marginal farmers.

Majority of the rural poor are landless agricultural labourers who earn daily wage ranging from ₹ 60 to ₹ 150. They remain unemployed for more than four months in an year. The marketer has to design products which meet the needs of rural consumer at an affordable price. It does not mean cheap products. Many companies have introduced small unit pack of consumer goods such as shampoos, soft drinks, soap, biscuits, etc.

Example: The success of Nirma detergent powder especially in rural market is due to pedestrian packaging, affordable price, medium quality, availability at village shops and promotion through wall paintings and famous jingle on Doordarshan. Nokia came out with a basic model of mobile phone (model 1100) and it has been well accepted in the rural market.

Availability: The rural population and the markets are highly scattered over a wide geographical area and the product has to be made available at the right place as and when required by the consumer. The rural consumers purchase their day-to-day requirements from village shops, haats and mandis. In order to reach these shops and establish product presence, companies need substantial amounts of working capital and a large dedicated sales force.

Example: Companies like HUL Britannia, Marico, Colgate, Parle have built up a strong distributing system which helps the products to reach interiors of the rural market. Once the product is made available with the retailer, it is bound to be sold due to the influence of the retailer.

Awareness: Reach of mass media is rather low in rural areas and the marketer has to use rural-specific media and methods such as melas, haats, audio visual publicity units, and group meeting of consumer and opinion leaders to reach the consumers. The packs should have more visuals and colours to attract the attention of the people and create a lasting impression in the minds of people.

Example: Dabur's Lal Dant Manjan is known as Sivapu Pal Podi in Tamil Nadu. A brand must associate itself with the lifestyle of rural people. Putting stickers on hand pumps, walls of wells, tin plate on trees, painting on tractors, posters on the walls of wells are some of the innovative methods used by companies. The idea is to advertise at the point of consumption apart from point of sales.

Converting the Problem into An Opportunity

Eveready Industries, India's largest battery maker has introduced LED (Light emitting diode) under the brand name Nu Lite as a substitute to kerosene lanterns in power deficient states, like Uttar Pradesh, Bihar, West Bengal and Assam. At two-three hours' use per day, the LED lanterns cost 50 paise per hour, marginally lower than kerosene lanterns. Introduced in April 2009, the company sells at an average 3,50,000 units per month. The product has been well accepted by rural consumers. The LED lanterns are priced between ₹ 150 and ₹ 450 and two sets of batteries are given free along with the lanterns. The factors that have contributed to the success of Nu Lite are: Understanding the problems faced by villagers in electricity deficit states, affordability, manufacturing capacity, promotion through local newspapers, wall paintings and distribution might.

Source: *Businessworld*, December 2009.

CONCLUSION

Marketing-mix indicates an appropriate combination of 4 Ps from the marketers' point of view. However, the 4 As model takes into consideration the needs and lifestyle of rural people and looks at marketing-mix from consumers' point of view. Considering the challenges and opportunities, we can say that the future is very promising for those who can approach the rural market through 4 As model and explore them to their advantage.

QUESTIONS

1. Discuss the need for customising the marketing-mix for the rural market.
2. Explain the 4 As model of marketing-mix. Is it different from the conventional 4 Ps model?

✿ ✿ ✿

7 PRODUCT AND PRICING

INTRODUCTION

Product is the most tangible and important single component of the marketing programme. Without a product, there is nothing to distribute, nothing to promote and nothing to price. Product is the vehicle by which a company provides consumer satisfaction. It is the engine that pulls the rest of the marketing programme. A product is a bundle of benefits assembled in an identifiable form. In simple terms, a product is anything that satisfies human wants. The product-mix includes product quality, features, benefits, design, style, colours, brand, packaging, labelling, services and warranties. Price is the amount of money needed to acquire a product. It is the cost that has to be incurred by the buyer to acquire a product or service.

PRODUCT MARKET STRATEGIES

Marketers have the following alternatives to increase the market share and profits:

	Existing Products	New Products
Existing Markets →	(1) Market Penetration	(2) Product Development or Product Differentiation
New Markets →	(3) Market Development	(4) Diversification

Fig. 7.1: Product Market Strategies (Four Types of Sales Growth Strategies)

1. Market Penetration: It involves expansion of sales of existing products in existing markets by selling more to present customers or gaining new customers in existing markets. The firm can market its present products to existing markets. This is done through a more aggressive marketing-mix. Customers from rivals or potential buyers can also be attracted. Existing buyers may be induced to increase their rate of use. We may have temporary price cut to raise the volume of sales and penetrate the market.

2. Market Development: In market development, a present product is introduced to a new market or segment. Market development is the creation of new markets by discovering new applications for existing goods. This is another alternative to expand market opportunity, prolong product life cycles, profitability and survival.

Example: Many companies are extending their activities to rural market to increase sales volumes of products like mineral water, chocolate, potato wafer, mobile phone.

3. Product Development: Product development occurs when a firm introduces new products to a market in which it is well established. Product development is the introduction of new products in the present market.

Example: New synthetic fibres for known textile products. The firm may decide to create new products for existing market. Established firms with high customer patronage may have new product additions upon existing market successes. The firm by offering new or improved products to present markets can satisfy better the present customers.

4. Diversification: Diversification occurs when a firm seeks to enter a new market with a completely new product. The firm may adopt a daring strategy by creating new products for entirely new markets. The innovations are introduced for the first time in the new markets. Only innovating marketers venture to go in for diversification of products. The strategy is risky but the innovator can have spectacular results.

PRODUCT STRATEGIES

Product strategies used by companies in rural markets are given below:

(1) Sturdy Products: Most of the rural consumers believe that heavier the item, higher the power and durability. They prefer tough and long lasting product.

Examples:

(a) Bullet motor cycle continues to be popular in villages due its ruggedness. Royal Enfield sells about 65 per cent of two-wheelers in semi-urban and rural areas.

(b) Escort has positioned their mobike, Rajdoot as a tough vehicle. The advertisement shows Dharmendra riding Escort motor cycle.

(c) Ambassador car continues to be popular in rural areas due to sturdiness, roomier rear seat and luggage space.

(2) Designing Products: The companies can come out with new products or promote existing products to suit field conditions in rural areas.

Examples:

(a) LG Electronics came out with a unique product for rural market. It launched 'Sampoorna', India's first TV with a Devanagari script on screen display. The word Sampoorna meaning 'Wholesome' cuts across all linguistic barrier in our country. It is affordable and aimed at semi-urban and rural areas. It can withstand power fluctuations and has sold over one lakh of 20″ TV in towns with a population of over 10,000.

(b) Voltas has introduced a refrigerator for rural areas. The interior is sturdy to accommodate items like milk pots, has tough insulation and built in stabilisers to absorb voltage fluctuations. Direct cool technology keeps the refrigerator cool for several hours in case of long power cut as against frost-free refrigerators.

(c) Nokia's basic model is dust resistant and has mini-ouch light for use in rural areas.

(d) Micromax launched a mobile phone with 30 days battery backup and it was instant hit in electricity starved rural areas.

(e) Tata Swach priced at less than ₹ 1,000 provides safe drinking water to rural households. It does not require electricity or running water.

(3) Small Unit Packing has been used for many consumer products. Small unit packing provides an opportunity for the consumers to try the product and help the company to reach consumers like daily wage earners.

Examples:

(a) HULs Pepsodent is available in small pack at ₹ 5.

(b) Ponds has gained market share over the past few years by focusing on rural market and it has introduced 20 gm talcum powder.

(c) Cavin Kare studied rural buyer behaviour and introduced Chik shampoo in small sachet of 4 ml at low price of 50 paise.

(d) Rasna is now available in sachet pack priced at one rupee each and one sachet will make two glasses of soft drink. The product is available in a variety of flavours such as mango, lemon, etc.

(e) Godrej Sara Lee has single coiled sachet of Good Knight coil for rural markets.

(4) Utility Products: The rural people are concerned with the utility of the items rather than appearance/show.

Examples:

(a) Philips has introduced FreePower Radio RL 117 priced at ₹ 995 for the first time in India. The radio requires no external batteries or electricity for operation. A one-minute winding of the lever runs the radio for about 30 minutes.

(b) HMT watches are popular for utility value.

(c) Exide has introduced JAI KISAN batteries to cater to the replacement market in the tractor industry. The objective is to convert users of local battery to loyal customers. The company promotes the product through local electricians who are the influencers in the rural areas.

BRANDING

Branding is the practice of giving specified name to a product or group of products. The specified name creates individuality in the product and it can be easily recognised from rival product.

The term brand is broadly applied to all identifying marks such as trade names, trade-marks, trade symbols, picture, design of the package, distinctive colouring or lettering with or without some attractive slogan. The owner of a registered brand personally stands behind the branded product and offers personal guarantee for maintaining the quality and standards of the product as per advertisement. The pronounceable part of the brand is the brand name.

Examples: Pepsi, Lifebuoy are brand names. The part of the brand that appears as symbol, design or distinctive lettering is brand mark or logo. It is recognisable by sight but is not normally pronounceable.

Trademark is a legal term. It is a brand duly registered under the Trade Names and Trademarks Act. It is a brand enjoying legal protection. A registered brand is the exclusive property of the seller. Others cannot use it and legal action can be taken if they adopt it. The letter in a circle on each package will indicate that the brand is duly registered and cannot be used by any other producer.

A brand is more than just a product. It is a contract between the customer and the creator. It embodies a meaning, gives direction and defines unique identity in time and space. Brands are not merely symbols on a product or a graphic and cosmetic exercise. A product is what the company makes. A brand is what a customer buys — hopes/expectations/service. The rural consumer likes to stick to brands that give value for money.

Villagers are Brand-conscious

About 70 kms. from Hyderabad lies Tangadapalli village in Nalgonda District of Andhra Pradesh. Among the 3,000 odd residents of the village, the wife of the village Post master stocks and sells HUL products worth ₹ 12,000-15,000 and earns around ₹ 1,500 per month. HULs Project Shakti targets small villages with a population of less than 2,000 people. HUL hopes to have 50,000 Shakti entrepreneurs by 2007. Mangamma finds that villagers are brand-conscious and they no longer ask for "Red Soap" but for Lifebuoy.

Source: *Business Today*, February 11, 2007.

Importance of Branding

1. The marketer can build up a bright image of his organisation around the brand. It enables national advertisement of a specific product and it is pre-sold through advertising. Branded product can be easily recognised by the customer in the retail shop. It offers protection to the consumer as it identifies the firm behind the product.

2. Branding enables the firm assured control over the market. Repeat sales are stimulated and product substitution is not possible. It creates an exclusive market for the product. When brands are successfully and effectively promoted, the very existence of the middleman depends upon a continued supply of each brand.

3. Branding by differentiating a product from its rivals enables the brand owner to establish his own price which cannot be easily compared with prices for competing goods. Price comparison is very difficult and the firm has independence in price fixing. Branding also reduces price flexibility. Price rigidity, however, may not be socially desirable. Of course, price competition is never completely eliminated.

4. If a firm has one or more lines of branded goods, it can add a new item to its list easily and the new item can enjoy all the advantages of branding immediately.

The Brand Tata Shaktee

Tata Shaketee (TS) is the brand name for Galvanised Corrugated Sheet (GCS) produced by Tata Industries. It is the leader with a market share of 27 per cent. GCS is known as Chaddar, Patra and Tina. The competitive products are tiles, asbestos, thatched roof and local GC sheets. Retailers located in feeder markets with a population of 20,000 sell a variety of construction materials. The head of the family is the decision makers and the opinion leader is the Mistry. Sales promotion includes wall paintings, distribution of leaflets in Haats, display of product in dealer shops and one-to-one meeting with dealers in feeder markets.

Reasons for Branding

In the days gone by, when the demand was greater than the supply, branding was not necessary. Earlier, people wanted a product and because not enough of it was available, they bought it. Now, when the supply is more than the demand, companies not only need to create customers, but also keep them; and to keep customers, one needs to create customer loyalty. To create customer loyalty, one needs to project a personality of a brand to which the customer will be loyal. This personality is what is called a 'brand'.

Branding is the most powerful instrument of sales promotion due to the following reasons:

1. Ever-increasing competition.

2. Importance of packaging as a distinct marketing function. Branding and packaging go hand-in-hand.

3. Need for advertising and publicity. Branding alone enables advertising.

4. Development of consumer brand-consciousness as a brand image in his mind. Not only branding gives separate identity and easy recognition to the product but it also creates special consumer preference and the consumer enters the shop to demand and insist upon specific brand of the product.

5. The dealer is merely a distributing agency of the branded as product. Branding constitutes the basis for successful activity of demand creation.

6. Brands such as Vim, Parle, Lifebuoy, Sunlight, Lux and Colgate have such a great pulling power that the retail Nirma, shops draw customer to their stores on the strength of these brands even in rural market.

Essentials of Good Brand

Brand name selection is a very critical issue for new products, more so for global brands. Right brand name gets you through more than one-fourth work required for management of a successful brand.

1. A brand should suggest something about a product's benefits — its use, quality, product's nature, purpose, performance or action, e.g., Frigidaire, Lijjat Papad, Tiger locks, Vicco Vajradanti, Snowcem are popular in rural market.

2. The name should be short, simple easy to pronounce, to spell and remember, easy to identify and explain. It should lend itself to visual interpretation.

3. It should be capable of being registered and protected legally under the legislation.

4. It should have a stable life and be unaffected by time. It should not depend upon fashions and styles as they have a short life.

5. It should create pleasant associations.

6. It should not be used as a general or common name for all products. Examples of brand names which have become general names are Linoleum, Aspirin, Cellophone, Band-aid, Nylon, Dalda, Xerox, Kodak, Eveready. These were originally brand names but now they have become public names for the products.

7. It should be unique, attractive and distinctive, e.g., Sunlight, Lifebuoy, Nirma, Scissors, Philips, Bhoomiputra tractors.

Types of Brands

1. Individual Brand Name: Each product has a special and unique brand name, such as Surf, Cinthol, Chick Shampoo, Aspro, etc. The manufacturer has to promote each individual brand in the market separately. This creates a practical difficulty in promotion. Otherwise, it is the best marketing strategy.

2. Family Brand Name: Family name is limited to one line of a product, i.e., products which complete the sales cycles, 'Amul' for milk products, 'Ponds' for cosmetics, etc. Family brand name can help combined advertising and sales promotion. However, if one member of the family brand is rejected by consumers, the prestige of all other products under the family brand may be adversely affected. The manufacturers have to take extraordinary care to guard against this danger. This method of branding assumes that end-users of all products under a family brand are similar and the products are not dissimilar. If 'Kissan' food manufacturers manufacture tractors or agricultural machinery, they should not use the same 'Kissan' brand name for these goods. Similarly, products exclusively for men and those specially for women should not be sold under the same family brand name, as these two classes of customers who demand them are different. Family brand name enables creation of strong shelf display. It helps to secure quick popularity. It is preferable to have separate brands for each product.

3. Umbrella Brand: We may have for all products the name of the company or the manufacturer. All products such as chemicals, engineering goods, automobiles, etc., manufactured by the Tata concerns will have the "Tata's" as one umbrella brand. Such a device will also obtain low promotion cost and minimise marketing effort. The pulling effect for all products will be considerable when the company's name or the name of the business house is outstanding and shining in the market. However, a single bad experience in any one of the line of products, a solitary failure, may be very dangerous to the rest of the products sold by a particular business house under the umbrella brand.

4. Combination Device: Tata House is using a combination device. Each product has an individual name but it also has the umbrella brand to indicate the business house producing the product, e.g., Tata Indica. Under this method, side-by-side with the product image, we have the image of the organisation also. Many companies use this device profitably.

5. Private or Middleman's Brands: Branding can be done by manufacturers or distributors such as wholesalers, large retailers. In India, this practice is popular in the woollen, hosiery, sport goods and such other industries. It helps small manufacturers who have to rely on the middleman for marketing. It is also used by big manufacturers. The manufacturer merely produces goods as per specifications and requirements of distributors and he need not worry about marketing. Middlemen enjoy more freedom in pricing products sold under their own brands. They have more control over distribution.

Manufacturers make both national and private or middleman brands. Brand label points out either the name of the manufacturer or the name of the distributor but not both. Consumer rarely knows who is the manufacturer of the private or dealer's brand.

Branding and Marketing Programme

A product strategy ignoring the problem of product identification and differentiation through branding omits a most important element in the marketing-mix. Branding is a powerful instrument of advertising and sales promotion in order to secure consumer loyalty towards the brand. The reasons for granting unique importance to branding in the marketing programme are given below:

1. Product Differentiation: Product differentiation by branding enables manufacturer to establish his own price and eliminate price competition to some extent. A branded product enjoys a separate individuality.

2. Brand Image: is a mental picture of the product in the mind of the consumers. Consumers make their buying decisions on the basis of the images they form of the different brands offered to them. When a consumer says that the product is good, he means that he has a good image of the product. The seller can build up a bright image of his product around the brand. A brand image is built up through the years by the quality of product produced, services offered, and the company's reputation, policies and marketing efforts. It is very difficult to estimate a brand image.

3. Brand Personality: Marketers try to personify the brand as if they are persons, so that the target consumers may associate the product with such a personality.

Example: Brand personality of Lux soap is that of an urban woman (Age: 17-24 years), upper middle-class with college education and concern for beauty.

4. Creation of Market: Ever-increasing competition leads to branding of the product by a manufacturer to face competition and create exclusive market for the product.

5. Brand Preference: Branding not only gives separate identity and easy recognition to the product but it also creates special brand preference. Popular brands such as Lux, Liril, Vim, Colgate, Sunlight have very great pulling power in the market. Brand preference indicates that the customer regards the brand favourably, but will accept a substitute if the said brand is not available in the shop.

6. Brand Patronage: Development of loyal customers, acting as talking advertisements and repeat buyers is the greatest reason in favour of branding. Such customers will always insist on buying their favourite brand.

7. Brand Loyalty: A satisfied customer continues to use the brand, even when competing products are available in the market. Satisfaction of customers lead to brand loyalty.

8. Brand Associations: Customers value certain brands based on the associations linked or to it.

Example: Ganga soap with holy river Ganga, Hero Honda with fuel efficiency.

9. Brand Equity: For a company, brands are valuable assets.

Example: Brands like Colgate, Coke, Lifebuoy, Horlicks have high brand equity.

Benefits of Brand equity are: (a) trade support, (b) loyal customers, and (c) Premium price. Therefore brand equity is the intrinsic value or worth of the brand in terms of the kind of money a consumer is willing to pay for it, in preference to its rivals. There are three ways to get brand equity: (a) build it, (b) borrow it, and (c) buy it, i.e., acquire the company and its brand.

Examples:

(1) Dabur India acquired Balsara products for ₹ 143 crore in 2005. Balsara products' turnover for the year 2004 was ₹ 200 crore. The benefits to Dabur are: (a) Addition of household care products — Odomos, Odonil, Sanifresh and Odopic (total sales ₹ 80 crore (b) Balsara's distribution strength in South and West, and (c) Strong position in oral core segments with additional brands, Promise, Babool and Mesvak (total sales ₹ 100 crore).

(2) Coca-Cola paid ₹ 180 crore for Parle's soft drink brands.

(3) Colgate paid ₹ 130 crore for acquiring Ciba-Geigy range of toothpaste and brushes.

10. Expanding the Product-mix: Many successful multi-product firms today began with a single product whose success created an umbrella under which additional products could be launched with less risk. Customers remember the familiar and the successful. After winning the battle of customer recognition, they have simply to win market acceptance for their new offerings. All products in their product-mix are sold under one blanket or family brand. A new product associated with respected brand is willingly received by consumers and dealers.

Asian Paints

50,000 litres of chuna is sold every year. Most of the rural users prefer chuna over paint due to its low rate. Asian Paints identified chuna as a competitor and launched a campaign in the year 2004 with an aim to get chuna users to switch to Utsav synthetic distemper. The company identified people who were termed as TCUPS — television owing chuna using pukka-semi pukka households. These people belonged to the rural area as well as the lower income group in urban areas. The campaign was launched in Dharavi in Mumbai and rural areas of Uttar Pradesh.

The company designed flipcharts which displayed the costing of chuna vs. Utsav synthetic distemper. The cost of using chuna was displayed as: chuna ₹ 4 + stainer (for adding colour) ₹ 8 + Glue (to hold the chuna together) ₹ 8 = ₹ 20. Cost of one tin of Utsav synthetic distemper is ₹ 30.

Even though Utsav cost ₹ 10 more it held an advantage over chuna as it did not need any other ingredient for application. One coat of the distemper was enough and repainting was not needed. The team tried to explain to the consumers that by paying an excess of only ₹ 10 they would get good quality paint and would be released from the evil of chuna. Charts showing the harmful effects of chuna were displayed. The contents were: (a) Chuna when mixed with water has an acidic reaction which produces substances harmful to the skin and eyes. (b) Chuna also rubs of easily on clothes or skin. This can be very embarrassing if chuna rubs of on guests.

The embarrassment factor was used widely to convince the users to switch to Utsav. An advertisement displaying the embarrassment faced by a family when a boy's family comes to their house to ask for their daughter's hand in marriage but she is unable to serve them properly as chuna has rubbed off on her clothes. This TV ad was broadcasted all over the country.

Brand Future in India

A strong brand will always be the best protection for a manufacturer and he has to protect his franchise.

The ever-increasing number of consumers, who are making India and many other developing countries the faster growing markets, want brands, not anonymous products. The branding phenomenon has taken the Indian market by storm. Many non-branded products, for example, salt, water, essentials like pulses, rice, wheat flour, etc., have taken branding route and have joined the "brandwagon".

Examples: Bisleri, Tata Salt, Ashirwad atta, etc., are popular in rural and semi-urban markets.

Indian consumers are living in an age of brands. Brand has become a vital tool and the most important element of the total product personality. Launching a brand name in India today involves ₹ 10 to ₹ 15 crore and even more.

BRANDING AND CONSUMERS

Consumers while buying pre-packed branded goods use the following guidelines to measure quality in relation to price: (1) tips from friend, (2) advertising, (3) slogans, (4) brands and trademarks, (5) labels, and (6) comments from salesman. Generally, price is used as a measure of quality. There is a firm belief in the minds of many consumers that high price is an indication of quality. The sellers fully capitalise this consumer belief. Lack of confidence and lack of precise knowledge compel consumers to rely heavily on the familiar, heavily advertised, and generally high-priced goods. Repetitive advertisement tells consumers that advertised brands assure high quality, but consumers are rarely given facts and figures or factual evidence to prove higher quality. Price is no reliable indication of quality.

Comparative testing conducted by consumer organisations has led to the conclusion that there is no dependable correlation among brand, price and quality. Though the goods sold under the manufacturer's brand and dealer's brand are produced by one producer in the same factory, the price spread between these two brands is quite appreciable. Manufacturer's brand is a national brand and it is heavily advertised, hence, sold at a higher price. Branding process may be against public interest. It needs attractive packaging, heavy advertising and promotional expenditure. These raise the retail prices of branded goods even by 20 per cent to 25 per cent. When goods are sold under a brand name, they *appear to be different* from each other even though *basically* they may not be really different. For example, detergents are sold under 6 to 10 brands. All are practically *alike*. We are deceived into believing that each brand is unique from the other. Consumers get similar experience in different brands of detergents.

As long as branding is considered desirable and as long as we do not have overflow of branded goods, consumers in India may have the following benefits of branding.

1. Right kind of brand advertising and personal selling provide ample information to the consumer about the branded products.

2. Branded goods have uniform and standardised quality as the owner of the registered brand is personally responsible to maintain the quality. There is no need of personal inspection and no danger of adulteration.

3. Rapid sales' turnover assures fresher product due to frequent replacement of stock with the retailer.

4. There is considerable saving in time in the selection of goods and also in the making up of orders. The consumer demands the product by quoting the special brand name, e.g., Usha Fans, Brooke Bond Coffee. Retailer is saved from the botheration of separate weighing, measuring, packing, etc. He merely displays the brands and takes money acting only as a distributing agent.

Popular Brand Names in Rural Market

1. Some of the brands that have created a lasting impact on rural consumers are Billy wali cell (Eveready batteries — battery with cat as symbol), Lal saboon (Lifebuoy), Ladkawala paint (Gattu — Asian Paints Mascot), Rishi (Dabur Chawanprakash), Parle baby (Parle biscuits), Coconut tree (Parachute), Amul (From Sanskrit word 'Amoolya' meaning Priceless), Peedhari Balm (Zandu Balm), Desh Ka Namak (Tata Salt), Peela Powder (Nirma), Neeli Tikki (Rin), Lal Dant Manjan.
2. Tata Steel has branded its galvanised corrugated sheets as Tata Shaktee, a sign of power. Similarly, the galvanised corrugated sheet produced by Ispat Industries has been named as Ispat Kavach. The brand name conveys strength, durability and toughness.

PACKAGING

Once the decision is taken on the brand, we have to consider the design and the make-up of the package and the labelling of the package. Branding, packaging and labelling are distinctly specialised activities, demanding the services of advertising experts. In reality, it is not the product which is displayed and sold but it is the brand together with the package and the label which are sold or which enable to sell the product. In a sense, your brand, package and label represent the product personality. Branding, packaging, labelling, the product warranty, and service after sale are the product-related strategies and they are responsible to make the marketing programme effective. They also are the best means of promotion. They project the product in the most favourable way. Package is critically important to the buyer's recognition of the product. Aesthetically pleasing package can secure higher sales and profit.

Packaging may be defined as formulating a design of the package and producing an appropriate and attractive container or wrapper for a product. The container itself can act a forceful though silent and colourful salesman at the point of purchase or an effective medium of advertisement encouraging impulse buying. Many a time, package design itself can act as a registered brand. Almost every article has to be packed to make a trip to the ultimate consumer. It is essential to maintain freshness and quality, e.g., ghee, sauce, etc. It can prevent the danger of adulteration, e.g., butter, cheese, spices, edible oil, etc.

However, packaging is much more than mere packing. Packaging is a marketing necessity. The public does not want just the product. They want explanation, assurance, encouragement, confidence and praise, i.e., pat-on-the-back, all integrated or combined with a pleasant and eye-catching get-up appearance on the top to gain action, i.e., close the sale. Thus, a good package ensures ultimate success of the product as a commercial venture. Under keen competition, the consumer needs an effective means to recognise a difference and establish preference that will ensure repeated repurchases. Packaging does this job in a competitive market. That is why crore of rupees are spent on packaging and branding. Such huge expenditure is made for the simple reason that packaging and branding alone can sell your products. Packaging completes the sales cycle triggered by advertising, and secures a meaningful market share.

In the present age of consumer-oriented marketing approach (i.e., Buyers' Market), packaging has gained unique importance. The utility reasons for packaging, *viz.*, protection, identification and convenience are themselves exploited in selling and some features of the package may serve as a sales appeal, e.g., reusable jar. Message on the label is a constant reminder to the user of the product. Packaging decorates and beautifies the product so as to lead the consumer impulsive buying. Thus, the package serves in most cases as a vehicle by which the brand of the product is carried through to the consumers. In modern self-service stores, with mass display, well-designed packages attract attention, and through silent sales talk increase the sales volume. Packaging itself is a device of sales promotion. A customer will pay more just to get the special package — even though the increase in price exceeds the additional cost of the package, e.g., Supreme Lux Soap sold in an attractive reusable box for lunch. It demands the services of experts. It has assumed a specialised status in the process of marketing.

Attributes of a Good Package: A package should: 1. Protect the contents from breakage or spoilage, 2. Be easy to open, dispense from and close, 3. Be safe to use, 4. Keep the product from deteriorating, 5. Be of proper size and shape, 6. Be reusable, able to be recycled or be biodegradable, 7. Be economical, 8. Be available in the sizes appropriate to the market segments served, 9. Be attractive, 10. Project a favourable image of the product, 11. Play the role of silent salesman, 12. Be readily identifiable in a shopping situation, 13. Act as a unique selling proposition, 14. Have a clearly readable description of the contents, 15. Offer information on assembly, preparation and use, 16. Communicate the benefits of the product to the targeted market segment, 17. Not be deceptive or misleading in size, contents, etc., and 18. Should be distinct and stand out in the shelf agaist competitive products.

Package Design

Modern package acts as a multi-purpose arrangement. It must fulfil utility functions such as protection, identification and convenience, when it serves as a container or wrapper of a product. In addition, it is also called upon to play the role of a colourful salesman. Self-service and self-selection have developed and are gaining importance in retail trade. Customers are always in a hurry. The package must have informative labelling. The headlines, illustrations, guidelines and selling points on the package must be clear and prominent so that the matter is readable by every shopper at a glance. Pictures should help to tell the story faster and more effectively. Visibility of the product in the package helps to sell the product better. Hence, glass, cellophone and plastic packages have become very popular.

Truth-in-packaging is absolutely necessary while designing the package. Package label should not misrepresent the realities to make a sale. Information given on the label should be attractive but not bogus or imaginary. *Tell the truth more attractively.* Then only we shall have fair trade practices regarding packaging and labelling. The deceptions in packaging must be eliminated either through self-regulation or if necessary through legislation. In short, packages must be honest and helpful to the consumers.

Innovative Packaging (Value-added Package)

With product competition getting to be increasingly difficult in the marketplace marketers are now turning to innovative packaging to establish the distinctive edge. There is now a thin dividing line between value-added package and promotions for a marketer. There has been a spate of packaging innovations that go beyond mere shelf visibility (for impulse purchase) and excitement. Marketers are coordinating innovative packaging with brand equity and brand loyalty. Packaging innovations based on consumer needs can help in retaining loyalty to the brand. The innovation of a neat plastic bag with a zipper lock that could be carried in the pocket, containing five strips of Band-Aid of Johnson and Johnson is a fine example of a shift in packaging thinking to satisfy a consumer need.

Modern package provides more value addition to products and more benefits during usage. Harpic liquid toilet cleaner with its directing nozzle. Reusable mug-cum-jar pack, Surf in jar pack are examples of innovative packaging capable of becoming a very effective tool of sales promotion gaining competitive advantage for the brand. In many cases, such packaging can turnout to be a promotional campaign in itself to gain quick short-term market share, to boost sales and retain brand loyalty. The Hindustan Lever's Le Sancy soap with its unique bean shape was sold in transparent plastic soap box moulded to the same colour, shape and appearance (package identical with the soap). Within a few months of launching this package, the marketer won 20 per cent market share in the most premium soap markets. It seems we are coming to a time when packaging itself will be treated as a product worked upon with the same care that goes into developing a consumer product.

Revolutionising the Packaging System

The various types of plastics have not only helped conserve or utilise the depleted natural resources but also revolutionised the concept of packaging. Plastics have proved to be much better substitutes to wood, cotton, metal, cardboard, paper, glass and so on.

The new rigid PVC now manufactured by modern, computerised and automatic process both in the normal and non-toxic grade with printability and metallising property is going to revolutionise the packaging systems for medical and food sectors and for consumer and industrial usage by thermoforming and twist-wrapping process. In the food processing industry, the new plastic package offers strength, protection, presentation and consumer appeal. The recycling process of plastics right from collection of the garbage to segregation and conversion in prime form for reprocess and reuse has solved the problem of pollution. In India, rag pickers contribute enormously to the estimated 40 per cent of plastic which is recycled. The 'reuse' culture is more prevalent in India, where plastic containers are reused several times before they are discarded. If environmentalists believe that less plastics would mean less waste, a German study indicates that without plastics the weight of packing materials would be 300 per cent higher, the volume of waste 150 per cent higher and energy consumed by packaging at least 100 per cent higher. Plastic recycling has reduced substantially problem of waste disposal and environmental degradation due to packaging.

Social View of Packaging

Significance of societal view of packaging is summarised below:

1. Pollution control is a burning issue in packaging particularly in Western countries. Broken bottles, crushed cartons, and bent cans litter the streets and choke municipal dumps. This has created the solid waste problem in those countries. All packaging programmes must weigh environmental and ecological issues.

2. Resource scarcity is another problem. The same precious natural resources that are being wasted on non-returnable (disposable) containers, e.g., soft drink bottles and beer bottles, later create litter and pollution problem. Such a consumption pattern cannot be tolerated now.

3. Among the resources which are being wasted, energy sources are the most critical at present. Throw-away bottles use three times the energy of returnable bottles. The efficient, energy-saving, returnable bottles must be introduced.

Consumer Problems with Packaging

1. Unless the package is transparent, the buyer cannot judge the contents by appearance. If quality information on the package label is absent, the buyer has to purchase almost blindly.

2. If the consumer wants a specific quantity, he may not have that amount when goods are sold in packages.

3. There is no feasible way to check weight and volume of the contents unless a buyer opens the package to ascertain the weight volume. Pre-packaged shortages amount to about 10 per cent.

4. Package sizes and designs inflate the contents. 'One Rupee off' labels proclaim price reduction which may not be real.

5. Deceptive packages have several room-mates in trade practices. They are hidden declaration of contents, fine print, glorified illustrations, unexplainable fractions of weight, etc. Consumers think that they are getting more when in fact they may be getting less due to the cunning package design.

6. Packages are same, contents are reduced and apparently same prices are charged. This method is popular in a period of rising prices.

7. Packages may create health hazards for consumers. Certain plastic food packaging has been shown to cause cancer (vinyl chloride inhaled by humans). Packages stored in godowns are susceptible to infection by insects.

The Total Product Image: A product image is the sum total of: 1. Inner value of the product, 2. Its ability to perform and give service and safety to user, 3. Packaging, 4. Branding, 5. Labelling, 6. Product warranty, and 7. Product services. The product image also indicates the goodwill of the product and its producer. In the product planning and development, we have to consider branding, packaging, labelling, warranty and services as these constitute the vital parts of marketing programme and these are closely interconnected in building up a bright product image in the market.

LABELLING

Packaging, branding and labelling go together and constitute an integral part of product planning and development. Label is a part of a product. It gives verbal information about the product and the seller. The purpose of labelling, like the purpose of branding, is to give the consumer information about the product he is buying and what it will and will not do for him. A label is also a part of a package or it may be attached directly to the product. Label provide the following information: 1. Brand name, 2. Name and address of producer, 3. Weight, measure, count, 4. Ingredients by percentages where possible, 5. Directions for the proper use of the product, 6. Cautionary measures concerning the product and its use, 7. Special care of the product, if necessary, 8. Recipes on food products, 9. Nutritional guidelines, 10. Date of packing and date of expiry, 11. Retail price, and 12. Unit price for comparison.

PRICING

Economist defines price as the exchange value of a product or service always expressed in money. Price is the amount charged for the product or service including any warranties or guarantees, delivery, discounts, services or other items that are part of the conditions of sale and are not paid for separately. To the buyer, price is a package of expectations and satisfactions. Thus, price must be equal to the total amount of benefits (physical, economic, social, ecological and psychological benefits). However, to the seller, price is a source of revenue and a main determinant of profit. Price mix includes maximum retail price, discounts, credit, terms of delivery, handling charges and maintenance charges.

Importance of Pricing

Price is a matter of vital importance to both the seller and the buyer in the marketplace. In money economy, without prices there cannot be marketing. Price denotes the value of a product or service expressed in money. Only when a buyer and a seller agree on price, we can have exchange of goods and services leading to transfer of ownership. In a competitive market economy, price is determined by free play of demand and supply. The price will move forward or backward with changing supply and demand conditions. The going market price acts as basis for fixing the sale price. Thus, price is the prime regulator of production, distribution and consumption of goods. Pricing decisions influence the following marketing variables:

1. Sales volume,
2. Profit margins,
3. Rate of return on investment,
4. Trade margins,
5. Advertising and sales promotion,
6. Product image, and
7. New product development.

Typical Pricing Objectives

1. Growth in Sales: A low price can achieve the objective of increase in sales volume. A low price is not always necessary. Competitive price, if used wisely, can secure faster increase in sales than any other marketing weapon.

2. Market Share: Price is typically one of those factors that carries the heaviest responsibility for improving or maintaining market share — a sensitive indicator of customer and trade acceptance.

3. Predetermined Profit Level: Return on Investment, say 20 to 25 per cent is a common decision in marketing. Pricing for profit is the most logical of all pricing objectives.

4. Counter Competition: Many firms follow a flexible pricing policy to counter competition. Prices are to be varied depending upon market condition.

5. Control Cash Flow: A principal pricing objective is to return cash as much as possible (the funds invested) within a given period. Investment in research and development, market development, promotion, etc., should payback within a specified period. Capital expenditure on any project must be recovered within 5 to 10 years. Payback or cash flow objectives fits in easily with other corporate objectives.

While determining objectives of a pricing policy, marketers must take into account reactions of a number parties such as customers, competition, resellers or dealers, Government, public opinion, and so on. For instance, there may be a conflict between sales maximisation objective and a return on investment or profit objective. However, it should be noted that maxmium market penetration in the short run (in the early phase of the product life cycle) is the key to maximum ROI in the long run.

6. To Penetrate the Market: Many firms enter the market by charging a very low price for the product.

Example: Lowly priced Chinese toys have flooded the market.

Price as a Measure of Value

1. Economic theory of price has a few simple assumptions regarding products and buyer behaviour. Buyer's tastes and preferences are considered as given (constant). Buyer is considered essentially a rational human being. The marketing concepts like brand image, brand loyalty and benefit segmentation 'emotional motivation' are outside the scope of price theory. Hence, in practice, the classical price theory, saying price determines value of the product, is not true.

2. Price is the most handy (but rough) available indicator of product quality and value for many customers. Buyers believe in the statement "You get what you pay for", "If it costs more, it must be better". Marketers are bound to exploit buyer's emotions, preferences and habits. Price-quality relationship applies to products whose quality is difficult to judge and whose brands vary widely in quality.

Example: Cosmetics jewellery, clothing, wine, floor wax, etc.

A rural cosumer with limited income and low awareness has an important question in his mind while making purchase decisions, i.e., "Is it worth it". The equation is satisfaction = benefit – cost and price is the cost part of the equation.

Factors Influencing Pricing Decisions

1. Objectives: Many companies have established marketing goals or objectives such as growth in sales, profits, market share and pricing plays a major role in achieving the objectives.

2. Cost of Production: The most decisive factor in pricing is the cost of production. In the past, fixing of price was a simple affair: just add up all the costs incurred and divide the final figure by the number of units produced. Adding necessary profits with the cost of production would give the price.

The main defect with this approach is that it disregards the external factors, particularly demand and the value placed on goods by the ultimate consumer. Again under this approach, the manufacturer believes that whatever may be the price, the consumer will buy. Furthermore, today, on account of the various lines of production as well as distributing, the overhead costs finding the cost of production is not so simple.

3. Demand: In consumer-oriented marketing, the consumers influence the price. Every product has some utility for the buyer. It gives the buyer service, satisfaction, pleasure, the consumer would continue to buy the product. Higher the demand for a product, lesser the need for giving additional discounts, credit, etc., to the distributors and dealers. This leads to higher price realisation.

4. Competition: Another factor that influences pricing is competition. No manufacturer is free to fix his price without considering competition, unless he has a monopoly.

To avoid competitive pricing, a firm may decide that its product may be sufficiently different from that of the others. This is achieved through methods of advertising, branding, etc. Sometimes, a higher price may itself differentiate the product. This is known as prestige pricing. But this is possible only when the product is backed by perfect quality. Sometimes, the opposite also takes place. It is seen that many products are sold at low prices, mostly in the initial stages. This is referred to as "Mark-down Prices" or price cutting.

5. Distribution Channels: Distribution channels also sometimes affect the price. There are many middlemen working in the channel of distribution between the manufacturer and the consumer. Each one of them has to be compensated for the services rendered. This compensation must be included in the ultimate price which the consumer pays. Because of these costs, sometimes it happens that the price of products becomes so high that the consumer rejects it.

6. Supply of the Product: If the supply is less than demand, then the price of the product will be more.

7. Achieve Planned Return on Investment: While fixing the expected rate of return, the cost of the product, inflation rate, profits desired, etc., are taken into account.

8. Availability of Raw Materials in the domestic market will generally enable the firm to bring down cost of production. The firm can fix a low selling price.

9. Profit Expectations: If the firm expects higher price per unit of the product, they may charge a higher price for the product.

10. Trade Barriers: Trade restrictions such as duties, taxes, quotas would increase the price of the product and the firm fixes a higher price to recover the taxes and duties.

11. If the **brand** is very popular among consumers, then the manufacturer can charge a higher price for the product.

12. If the Purchasing Power of the consumers is high, then the company can charge a higher price for the product.

13. Promotion Cost would normally increase the selling price as the company would like to recover the cost from the consumers.

14. Research and Development: Many large organisations spent millions of rupees in developing new products and new processes and would like to recover the cost of research by increasing the price of the products.

15. Legal Constraints, Government Interference such as control of prices, levying of taxes, etc., are other considerations which also affect the pricing of the products.

Kinds of Pricing

A firm may choose various kinds of pricing for their products. A few, important one are explained below:

1. Odd Pricing: Odd price may be a price ending in an odd number or a price just under a round number. Such a pricing is adopted generally by the sellers of speciality or convenience goods. For example, Bata shoes are priced at say ₹ 999.95. Odd prices may bring more sales. An article priced at ₹ 9.95 will have more sales than when it is priced at ₹ 10. Under odd pricing, buyers may feel that it is a 'mark-down price'.

2. Psychological Pricing: It is stated that there are certain critical price points such as 1, 2, 4, 5 and 10 are psychologically appealing to consumers.

Example: Products such as shampoo, chocolate, biscuit, toothpaste, ballpoint pen are sold at certain price points to attract the consumers.

3. Prestige Pricing: Prestige price is one that is fixed at a higher price than the producer's near-perfect substitute. Prestige pricing is adopted because many customers feel that high price means high quality. They feel that at the low price the product cannot be of good quality. Moreover, the customers feel a high status at high price. At high prices, the customers buy more. If prices are dropped a little bit, then customers may bargain a little. But if the prices begin to appear cheap, they start worrying about the quality and may stop buying.

4. Consumer Expectations: Such prices are fixed by consumers. Consumers are familiar with the rates and market condition and expect a particular price to be charged for certain products. Mostly such products are standardised ones, e.g., soft drinks and shampoo packets.

5. Geographic Pricing: The distance between the seller and the buyer is considered in geographical pricing. When there is a lot of distance between the production centre and consumption centre, the producer or marketer can adopt different prices in each area without creating any ill-will among customers. For example, petrol is priced in this way, depending upon the distance from the storage area to the retail outlet. In other words, due to geographical distance, the prices will differ. There are three ways of charging transit costs, *viz.*,

(a) **FOB Pricing:** FOB (Free On Board) may be of two types — FOB origin and FOB destination. In the first case, the buyers will have to incur the cost of transit apart from the price quoted and in the latter, the price quoted is inclusive of transit charges.

(b) **Zone Pricing:** In zone pricing, price is equal in the same zone. Market for a product is divided into various zones say south zone, north zone, etc., and the price quoted will be the same in a particular zone irrespective of the differences in the distances in the same zone. In other words, prices are uniform within a zone.

(c) **Basic/Base Point Pricing:** Under base point pricing, one or more cities are selected as base points and transport cost is collected from the base point to the buyer's location.

6. Price Lining: Price lining is found more commonly among retailers than among wholesalers or producers. This system consists of selecting a limited number of prices at which the store will sell its goods. It is the policy of setting a few price levels for a given class or line of goods.

The main benefit of price lining is that it simplifies the buying decision of the consumer. For example, a buyer of a shirt can go into a shop where shirts are retailed at ₹ 250, 300, 350 and 400. It also helps the shopkeeper to plan his purchases.

7. Dual Pricing: When a manufacturer sells the same product at two different prices, it is dual pricing. Under dual pricing system, a producer is required compulsorily to sell a part of his production to the Government or its authorised agency at a substantially low price. The rest of the product may be sold in the open market at a price fixed by the producer, e.g., sugar.

8. Company Policy: The price is fixed not on the basis of cost or competitive pressures or the laws of demand and supply, but fixed purely on the basis of the policy decisions of the company. In theory, this would mean that the company disregards all other considerations except his own desire for maximising profits.

9. Monopoly Pricing: Monopolistic conditions exist where a product is sold exclusively by one producer or a seller. When a brand new product moves to the market, its price will be a monopoly price. Under monopoly, competition is absent and there is no substitute. Hence, a seller has a free hand in fixing the price. Monopoly price will normally maximise the profits.

10. Penetration Pricing: Penetration pricing is intended to help the product penetrate into markets to hold a position. In other words, penetration pricing is intended to capture the market. This can be done only by adopting a low price in the initial period or till such time the product is finally accepted by customers. Penetration pricing is adopted when substitute product is marketed. Low starting prices sacrifice short run profits for long run profits and therefore, discourage potential competitors.

11. Negotiated Pricing: It is also known as variable pricing. This method is invariably adopted by industrial suppliers. In certain cases, the product may be prepared on the basis of specification or design by the buyer. In such cases, the price has to be negotiated and then fixed.

12. Mark-up Pricing: This method is adopted by wholesalers and retailers in establishing a sale price. When the retailers or wholesalers fix the selling price, they add a certain percentage to their cost price. For example, an item that costs ₹ 20 may be sold for ₹ 25. Here, the "mark-up price" is ₹ 5 or 25 per cent.

13. Sealed Bid Pricing/Competitive Bidding: This method is followed in the case of specific job works. Big firms or Governments normally get the work done through contractors. The contractors work out the probable expenditure and give their price offers in a sealed cover. The lowest bidder gets the work.

14. Skimming Pricing/Skim-the-cream Pricing: This method is followed while launching a totally new product into the market. Under this policy, a high price is initially fixed to skim-the-cream of the market and the price moves downwards step-by-step until the right price is reached. The idea is that when the marketer is not sure about what price he has to charge, it is advantageous to begin with high initial price and move systematically downwards. It is easier to start with a high price and then reduce it, than to start with a low price and then try to raise it.

The skimming price policy will produce more income in the early stages of a product life cycle (PLC) only when the top of the market is insensitive to price and willing to pay what is asked.

Example: In the case of books, this method is followed by having a high price for the first/deluxe edition and lesser prices for subsequent editions.

Advantages of Skimming Pricing

1. First, demand is likely to be less elastic in the early stages of a product life cycle. In the early stages, price is less important, competition is at a minimum.
2. A high initial price can often generate more income/funds for expansion into new markets and for repaying research and development costs quickly.
3. The high initial prices can be used to keep demand within the limits of a company's production capacity.

PRICING STRATEGIES

The marketing manager has to formulate an appropriate pricing strategy to achieve the marketing objectives.

1. Low Price: A rural consumer in general is price-sensitive mainly because of his/her relatively low level of income and unit price of a product will have an impact on sales. Once he is satisfied with the brand, he will continue to patronise the same. Pricing the product at a lower price really attracts rural population for trying the products. Though rural incomes have grown in the past decades, the money earned by the average rural consumer is still much lower than that of his urban counterpart. A large part of the income is spent on the basic necessities, leaving a smaller portion for other consumer goods. Further marketers have to study the target audience, their income levels, frequency income (daily, weakly, post-harvest) and how they spend the money on food and non-food items.

For many FMCG companies, ₹ 5 is an appropriate price point to draw new customers and increase consumption. It has been observed that pens, razors, biscuit packs, toothpaste, washing soaps, soft drinks costing around ₹ 5 have slowly started selling in villages. The presence of such a wide array of products at ₹ 5 is linked to consumers buying behaviour.

Examples:

(a) Bharat Petroleum has introduced five kg gas cylinders to reduce initial deposit and refill cost for rural consumers. The deposit for 5 kg. cylinder is ₹ 350 against ₹ 700 for 14 kg. cylinder and refill cost is ₹ 90 against ₹ 250 for 14 kg. cylinders.

(b) Lifebuoy soap in 60 gms @ ₹ 4.50 — sells primarily in rural areas; urban sales to rural sales ratio is 40:60.

(c) Tata has introduced Samundar salt in the economic category.

2. No Frills Product: The production cost can be lowered by using less sophistication and rather concentrating on sturdiness and utility of the product.

Examples:

1. Maharaja Appliances Ltd., sells a sturdy Bonus washing machine, without a drier for rural market at ₹ 2,990.
2. The rural markets operate on a price-value proposition. LG Electronics has knocked off some of the frills in the products. The idea is to give features that are absolutely indispensable. The rural consumer does not require Golden Eye feature and therefore base models do not have this feature. Again not all consumers need 200 channels and therefore they have provided 100 channels in the base model. Everybody may not require a sound output of 350 watts and therefore they have given an output of 200 watts in base sets. The rural consumer is value-conscious. He will buy the product that gives value for money.

3. Refill/Reusable Packaging: By giving refill packaging, marketers can add value to the pricing of the product.

Examples: Bournvita available in refill pack and detergents made available in reusable packaging.

4. Credit Facilities: Income from agriculture continues to be the major source income in rural areas. Success or failure of crop depends upon climatic conditions. Favourable conditions give bumper yields and unfavourable conditions result in very low yields, and therefore rural income is seasonal in nature. The farmer requires credit for meeting cultivation expenses as well as running the family between marketing of produce and the harvest of next crop. He avails credit facilities from the village merchant for buying household necessities. The rural retailer in turn requires credit facilities from the distributors of consumer goods. Many companies extend credit to the village retailers to persuade them to stock the company's products and push it in the market. The decision to extend credit is based on the volume of business and creditworthiness of the retailers. The credit extended by company depends upon the nature of the product and market situation. The credit period varies between 7-30 days in the case of fast-moving consumer goods. The demand for agricultural inputs like pesticides is highly seasonal in nature and therefore companies normally allow a longer credit period of 60-90 days to persuade the retailer to stock the product well in advance of the season.

5. Discounts: Income from agriculture is continuing to be the major source of income in rural areas. In these days of cut-throat competition, the marketers offer a variety of discounts to the consumers and dealers to increase the sales. The common forms of discounts and allowances are:

(a) **Trade discount** is a form of functional discount and it is given to buyers, who are buying for resale, i.e., wholesaler or retailer, in payment for the marketing functions which these traders are expected to form. Normally, a wholesaler receives a trade discount of 3-5 per cent and retailer 7½ to 10 per cent in the case of consume products like soaps, toothpaste, biscuits, hair care products.

(b) **Cash discount** is a rebate or concession given to the trader to speed up payment. Against a credit period of 30 days, the company may offer cash discount to encourage the dealer to pay in full by cash, draft or current cheque.

(c) **Quantity discount**. In order to encourage the trader to make bulk purchases, quantity discount is offered. Such discount may be offered on the total volume of purchase during a certain period also.

(d) **Off-season discount** is offered to traders to stock products during slack season.

Example: Agricultural pesticides business is highly seasonal and depends upon monsoon rains. Therefore companies like Rallis, Syngenta and others offer attractive season discount to enable the dealers to buy the product well in advance of season. Considering that agricultural season starts in June, off season discount, at the rate of 2-3 per cent per month is offered for making advance purchases in February, March, April and May months.

(e) **Promotion allowances** for advertising, delivery van operation, display of products, employing salesmen for retailer coverage, etc., are offered to promote the sales in rural areas.

(f) **Promotional schemes:** Normally, villagers purchase consumer durable items after the harvest of crops. Similarly, Diwali, Pongal, Onam, Dassera, Idd and Christmas are the festivals for buying household articles. Special promotion schemes such as new product introduction scheme, festival offer by way of special discounts, exchange offer, i.e., taking back used consumer durables are offered during harvesting and festival seasons in rural areas for increasing sales of the products.

Example: Companies like HUL, Colgate offer discounts/allowances such as quantity discount, introductory offer, free goods offer, etc., to increase the sales in rural markets.

(f) **Value engineering:** This is an internationally used technique, which helps organisations not only lower costs but enhance value to customer. The concept has been implemented by a few firms in tapping the rural markets.

Example: Nirma detergent powder, over a period of ten years has become the largest selling brand in rural India. The success of Nirma is due to affordable price, medium quality, availability at village shops and use of rural-specific mass media.

CONCLUSION

A product is any tangible offering that satisfies the need or aspiration of a consumer. The product-mix includes product quality, features, benefits, design, style, colours, brand, packaging, labelling, services and warranties. The rural consumer is generally concerned with utility of the product rather than appearance or show. While rural income level has gone up in recent years, the lower income group constitutes about 65 per cent of the rural population. Price is an important component of marketing-mix. A rural consumer with limited income and low awareness is concerned with the price of the product while taking purchase decisions. The marketers have to consider the dynamics of the rural market while formulating product and pricing strategies.

QUESTIONS

1. Elaborate with suitable examples the product and pricing strategies followed by consumer companies in rural market.
2. Discuss the importance of branding in rural market.
3. Many marketers feel that rural consumers are price-sensitive and not brand-conscious. Discuss.

CASE STUDY

Marketing of Branded Tea

The Sapat Group of Companies consist of diversified businesses in tea. The various Indian manufacturing units are located in and around Nasik, with its marketing office and IT facilities located at Mumbai. Sapat has been one of the very first companies to launch the rural marketing van scheme. It was also the first to introduce a low unit pack (LUP) range as well as the flavoured tea range in India. With innovation strategies over the last decades, the company has grown five times touching a turnover of almost ₹ 100 crore, making it the largest packet tea company in the ₹ 500 crore tea market of Maharashtra. Currently, Sapat has over 250 distributors in Maharashtra and plans to expand to other tea drinking states. When Parivar Tea was being developed, the Maharashtra tea market was mainly dust tea and leaf tea. (After tea leaves are picked, they are dried and fermented to make granules. The bigger granules are packed as leaf tea while smaller granules are passed off as dust tea). Say around 1,800 tonnes of dust and similar volume of leaf. Also, there were many competitors who had products in both these categories. When the Sapat Company did a Price Sensitivity Analysis, they found that the dust tea users were willing to pay lot more for getting a leaf tea if it was strong and also, the products available as leaf were not strong. So Parivar Tea was created.

Tea Industry

The overall tea market in India consists of premium tea which are the top end which are mostly in tea bags, etc. Then there are the popular tea at two levels, one is the higher popular that is Society, Taj Mahal and then you have Red Label, Double Diamond or Sapat Parivar. Below that is the economy segment where there are a number of brands, which are like Goodricke and a whole lot of regional/local players in that market. Whereas the dust tea market, has a premium dust and a low dust segment.

The Sapat Company launched its new brand of leaf tea, Parivar, in 1999-2000. The Sapat Parivar Family Blend is a unique 'marriage' of large and small grain CTC teas for exceptional flavour and strength. Its fast-moving brand, Parivar, has helped the company shoot up the rankings, making it one of the fastest-growing top 10 tea companies in India in 2004. While the industry grew by 1 per cent in volume in 2004, Sapat grew by 41 per cent.

Distribution

One of the most difficult tasks for any company working in the rural areas is the distribution. The Sapat Company knew that the villagers wouldn't take likely to a company salesman and so the company made a research and found that each village had a population of youth with spare time on their hands. Sapat recruited these young men, all of whom met one simple precondition — they had to pass their twelfth grade and possess decent communication skills. The youth called CAs (Communication Agents) played the role of brand ambassadors in their villages. The company used its brand name, Parivar, which means family, to good effect. The CAs visited every house and welcomed residents to be a part of the Parivar. To supervise the efforts of its CA network, the company established a team of auditors who verified the work of the CAs. These auditors were village elders.

Promotion

The company knew that television gives little reach in the rural regions. Products advertised on outdoor hoardings are perceived as costly in the rural areas. So Sapat created Parivar-branded nameplates on which the CAs wrote the household's name. Families who agreed to fix this nameplate on their doors were given a free sample pack of tea. Soon, most families in a village wanted to have their names written on Parivar's metal nameplate. The company contacted close to 5,00,000 households across 1,600 villages in Maharashtra through this programme. Sapat executives claimed that this initiative earned them some brownie points. Villagers began to look at Parivar as a bonding factor, as the entire village started showing off uniform nameplates.

Having put its name on the doors, the company decided to get into the mind of rural consumers. This was best done through village schools, given that teachers and principals are largely appreciated by the community. The CAs contacted school principals and handed them quiz sheets that were distributed to students. The questions covered subjects ranging from politics, mathematics and tea habits. Students were given erasers and sample packets of tea when they returned these questionnaires. At the same time, the company vans visited villages distributing discount coupons.

Sapat also enlisted the support of its stockist and retailers with extra incentives. In all household deliveries, retailers were asked to deliver only Parivar Tea packs. With Parivar Tea, the company hit on an insight: that the Indian tea drinker loved to slurp when drinking tea. So the company produced advertising using the *'Surr ke piyo'* line, which gave consumers the social sanction to enjoy their tea while slurping it. The company, in a bid to tackle the problem of consumer resistance (which is often seen in the rural areas) offered a money-back guarantee to dissatisfied customers. It backed this offer with a complimentary packet of Britannia's Tiger biscuits, as tea with biscuits is a perfect fit across the country. To ensure repeat purchases, used packs of Parivar tea could be redeemed at retail shops, for discounts on the subsequent purchase.

Straight

As said earlier the largest selling variety of tea in the rural markets (60%) is 'dust' tea, as it was considered to be cheaper and stronger. Sapat, however, felt the time was ripe to convert the markets to 'leaf tea'. Hence, the real challenge was now to take on the dust brands which were cheaper than leaf tea, and to not only convert and upgrade, but also get consumers to pay extra for it. Each 1 kg. pack of Parivar tea is priced at ₹ 159 as compared to the other brands which are priced at ₹ 125 per kilo. Even though the Parivar tea brand was priced much higher than the other brands, it was not only accepted but was also more preferred because of its uniqueness. The taste was catered, keeping in mind the customer's needs (the rural Indian consumer likes his leaf tea to be strong and so Sapat created such a tea).

Conclusion

At present, Sapat earns 60 per cent of its revenue from Parivar. In 2004, the company entered the markets of Madhya Pradesh also. For Sapat, the eighth largest tea-maker in the country, gunning for the top slot might be a distant dream. But for now, the villages in Maharashtra have given it enough reason to throw a tea party. Parivar Tea is one of those products which show that only pricing is not an important factor. In spite of being costlier than the other products, its effective marketing and distribution strategies helped this unique product to reach the position it is enjoying now.

QUESTIONS

1. Discuss the marketing strategies followed by the company in the rural market.
2. Do you think that we can follow similar strategies in the case of other consumer goods?

✿ ✿ ✿

8 DISTRIBUTION IN RURAL MARKET

INTRODUCTION

The rural consumers normally purchase their household requirements from village shops, haats and mandi towns. There are 18.5 million lakh outlets, both in urban and rural markets in India. Out of this, 7.8 million lakh retail outlets (2010) are spread over six lakh villages and making the products available in the store shelves is a challenge for the marketer. Even if a company has a product that meets the requirements of rural consumers, it will succeed only if it is made available as and when by the consumer. Most of these outlets are small and marketers have to reach them only through a chain of distributors and wholesalers which add to the cost of distribution. Of course, in order to reach these shops and establish the products, the companies need substantial amount of working capital and large dedicated sales force.

OBSTACLES TO REACH THE RURAL CONSUMERS

1. The distribution chain requires a large number of intermediaries and this increases the cost of distribution.
2. Non-availability of dealers.
3. Poor viability of retail outlets due to low business volume.
4. Inadequate banking facilities.
5. Only about 80 per cent of the markets are connected by roads.
6. Interior village roads get flooded during monsoon.
7. Transport and communication facilities are generally poor in villages.
8. Credit requirement of channel members.

Distribution system has two subdivisions, i.e., (1) Channels of distribution, and (2) Physical distribution.

CHANNELS OF DISTRIBUTION

Marketing channel is the route taken by the title to the product as it moves from the producer to the ultimate consumer. Every marketing channel starts with the producer and ends with the consumer. It's a two-way communication. Consumers purchase goods through such channels and producers reach the consumers through marketing channels. The channel members consist of wholesalers and retailers who are middlemen in distribution and they perform all marketing functions. These middlemen facilitate the process of exchange of goods; create time, place and possession utilities. Therefore, channels are useful to producers as well as consumers. There are many channels used for the distribution of goods in rural areas and details are given below:

0 level	1 level	2 level	3 level	4 level
Manufacturer	Manufacturer	Manufacturer	Manufacturer	Manufacturer
Consumer	Retailer	Distributor	C&F Agent	C&F Agent
	Consumer	Retailer	Distributor	Rural Distributor
		Consumer	Retailer	Wholesaler
			Consumer	Retailer
				Consumer

Fig. 8.1: Rural Distribution Channel

1. Manufacturer-Consumer (Direct Sale): In this case, the stocks are directly supplied to the ultimate consumer avoiding middlemen and their commission. This benefits the consumer as well as the seller.

Examples:

(a) In many States, the Government has encouraged farmers to sell vegetables directly to urban consumers by setting up "Farmers' market". These markets are known as Rythu Bazzars (Andhra Pradesh) and Vivasayigal Santhai (Tamil Nadu). These markets are run by Government and only farmers are allowed to sell the agricultural produce to the consumers in the market. The market works both in the morning and evening hours. The market committee in consultation with farmers fixes the rates for different commodities. The farmers come from about 25 villages surrounding the city and are allotted stalls by the market committee. The market committee also provides cold storage facilities for perishable commodities.

(b) An innovative concept 'Apni Mandi' has been introduced in Northern states. In Apni Mandi, there is a direct contact between the farmer (producer) and the consumer. The prices in Apni Mandi are low, since there are no involvement of middlemen. The first Apni Mandi was started in Chandigarh in 1987, followed by Apni Mandi in Karnal in 1988. Subsequently, such Mandis have been established in Rajasthan also.

(c) Village artisans sell their goods directly to rural consumers.

2. Manufacturer-Retailer-Consumer: Here, the stocks are sold to the consumers through a network of retailers.

Examples:

(a) Mahindra and Mahindra Tractors have appointed dealers in important rural markets. A dealer either covers one district or two-three tehsils. The company arrange for supply of tractors to these retailers from their manufacturing unit. The dealer looks after sale and service of tractors. The company has transformed tractor dealers into "Samriddhi Centres" to provide farmers with information on weather, crops, pests, commodity prices, soil testing facilities, etc.

(b) Philips has direct dealers in high demand market.

(c) Royal Enfield has about 250 direct dealers spread across the country and they undertake sales and service of two-wheelers.

3. Manufacturer-Distributor-Retailer-Consumer: The manufacturer appoint distributors in key rural markets and these distributors cater to the needs of retailers in villages. This is a popular channel option used by manufacturers.

Examples:

(a) Manufacturers of tea, coffee and branded oil, appoint distributors in district/taluka headquarters and these distributors service the retailers in villages.

(b) Distribution of seeds in rural areas.

4. Manufacturer-Company-Depot/C&F Agent-Distributor-Retailer-Consumer: In this case, the manufacturer moves the stocks to company depot/depot operated by a C&F agent and from these depots, stocks are supplied directly to distributors, who in turn service the retailers.

Example: Agro-chemical companies like Syngenta, are using two/three intermediaries to reach the farmers in remote villages.

5. Manufacturer-Company Depot/C&F Agent-Rural Distributor-Wholesaler-Retailer-Consumer: The manufacturer opens his own depots or appoints C&F agents in state capital or in key cities in each state. The C&F agent, supply stocks to rural distributors. From the rural distributors, the stocks move through wholesalers and retailers to reach the ultimate consumers.

Example: Distribution of consumer products by companies like HUL, Dabur, Nirma, Parle, Marico in rural market.

Sellers

Broadly, there are two categories of sellers in the rural market.

(a) Distributors or Wholesalers: They buy in bulk with the main objective of resale to retailers or other traders after breaking down the bulk into smaller quantities. They offer special services such as collection of orders, despatch of stocks, follow-up of outstanding, after-sales service and market information.

(b) Retailers/Dealers: The village shopkeepers deal in a variety of consumer goods. They keep in touch with the wholesalers in town and collect first-hand information about new products and services. They have a direct contact with consumers and extend credit facilities. The village retailers can provide valuable information about rural markets and customers. The companies should build up excellent rapport with the village dealers for improving the business, since about 70 per cent of groceries and other daily needs are purchased from village shops.

"A Village Grocery Shop"

Examples:

Retailers	Products
(a) Fertiliser dealers	Fertilisers, pesticides, seeds, cement
(b) Grocery shops	Consumer goods (food and non-food items)
(c) Electrical shops	Motors, electric irons, lights, fans, electrical accessories
(d) High value consumer durable shops	TV, stereo system, transistors
(e) General stores	Toilet articles, medicines
(f) Cloth shops	Ready-made garments, clothing materials
(g) Hardware stores	Iron/cement pipes, pumpset parts, building materials.

Fig. 8.2: Rural Retailers

DISTRIBUTION MODELS

Companies like HUL, Marico have developed a separate channel of distribution for rural market. The C&F agent, supply stocks to two categories of distributors, i.e., urban and rural distributors. From the rural distributors, the stocks move through stockists, wholesalers and retailers to reach the ultimate consumer. A few examples are given below:

1. Star Sellers (HUL)

The company appoints 1-2 rural distributors in each district. Under each rural distributor, there are 25-30 wholesalers known as Star Sellers. They invest money and stock the products of HUL. Each wholesaler covers about 60-100 sales outlets, i.e., Grocery Merchants, General stores, etc. The wholesaler may also supply to Shakti enterpreneurs, who in turn cover villages having less than 2,000 population. HUL reaches 60 lakh retail outlets straight and out of this, rural outlets are 7.5 lakh.

2. Project Shakti

In many states, women self-help groups (SHGs) have been formed through initiative of DWCRA (Development of Women and Children in Rural Areas). The group's financial resources consist of savings, Government assistance and bank loans. Normally, members use the loan out of the group corpus for their personal needs. Such loans are also used for income generating activities. HUL has come out with a new distribution model with the main objective to develop income-creating capabilities of underprivileged rural women by providing a sustainable enterprise opportunity and to improve rural living standards through health and hygiene awareness.

Typically, a woman from the SHG is selected as a Shakti entrepreneur (Shakti Amma) and receives stocks of Lifebuoy, Wheel, Pepsodent, Annapurna salt, Clinic Plus, Ponds, Lux, Nihar, 3 Roses tea, etc., at her doorstep from the HUL rural distributor. She sells directly to consumers as well as to small merchants in the village. Each Shakti entrepreneur services 6-10 villages in the population range of 1,000-2,000 people. With training and handholding by the company for the first three months, she begins her door-to-door journey selling the products. Normally, the entrepreneur has a turnover of ₹ 10,000 to ₹ 20,000 per month and earns a profit of ₹ 700 to ₹ 1,400 a month. She also sells non-competing brands such as edible oil, sugar, matchboxes, bangles, etc. Under Project Shakti, events such as Health day, Sakthi day, film shows are organized to promote the products. The project was started in Nalgonda district in AP. There are about 45,000 Shakti entrepreneurs covering one lakh villages. The most powerful aspect of this model is that it creates a win-win partnership between HUL and the women entrepreneur. Annual turnover through Project Shakti is about ₹ 1,000 crore. The company has initiated "Shakti Vani" programme to empower rural women by educating them on health and hygiene and provide income generating activities.

Project Shakti is a win-win model for Government, Bank, HUL and Shakti Entrepreneur (SE) as shown below:

(a) **Government:** Provides income generating activities for rural women.

(b) **Bank:** Microcredit for business and social responsibility.

(c) **HUL:** Better product reach in interior villages and corporate social responsibility.

(d) **SE:** Income opportunity, increased awareness, access to urban markets.

3. Hub and Spokes Method

In the rural areas, Coca-Cola has developed Hub and Spokes method of distribution. In this method, the manufacturer in the area appoints main distributors (Hub) in important markets. These distributors in turn appoint sub-distributors (Spokes) to handle smaller markets within the territory. The sub-distributor supplies to the retailers and these retailers finally deliver it to consumers.

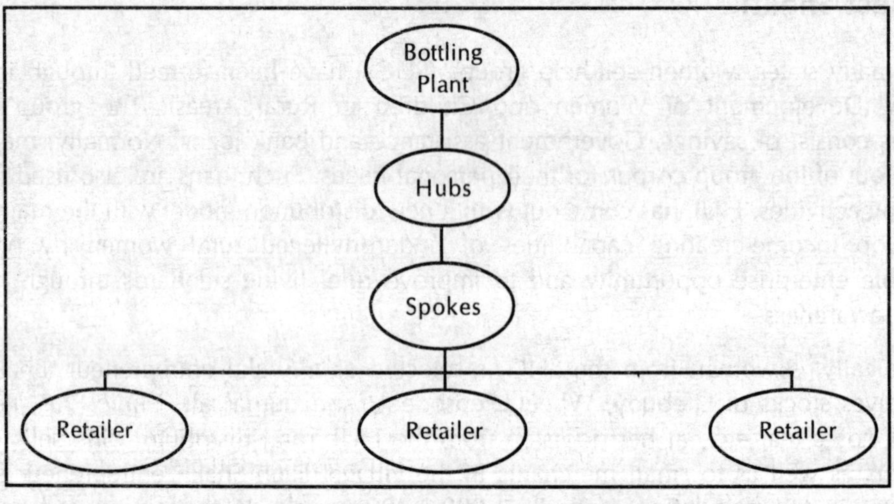

Fig. 8.3: "Hub and Spokes Distribution Method (Coca-Cola)"

4. LPG Distribution (HPCL)

Considering the problems in reaching bulky cylinders to the houses of villagers, the company has taken the following initiatives:

(a) Distributors have opened extension counters in feeder markets, so that villagers can come and take delivery of the refilled cylinders.

(b) Stocking LPG cylinders in HPCL fuel stations in highways and agricultural centres. The farmers who come for filling diesel for tractors, can carry the cylinders home in their vehicles.

(c) Operating filling van in haats and large villages for refilling empty cylinders with LPG.

5. The Bicycle Distribution Model

This model developed by MART, the specialist rural marketing and research agency Delhi, provides a sustainable business opportunity for educated village youth in the age group of 18-35 years. The selected candidates receive adequate training and are provided bicycle, inbuilt storage box, a colourful umbrella, T-shirts and cap.

The promoter buys the stocks of FMCG products from the authorised stockist of the company and sells in interior village shops and nearby haats. He is paid a monthly stipend of ₹ 1,500 and also earns margin on selling the products. His total earning is about ₹ 3,000 per month. The promoter is also equipped with public address system to communicate the message about products and attract audience to the bicycle stall. Companies like Colgate, Eveready have already tried this model with success.

Example: HUL has initiated 'Shaktiman' — a male member from Shakti entrepreneur family, to reach villages with a population of less than 2,000. Each Shaktiman earns about ₹ 3,000 per month by selling HUL products, like Lifebuoy, Ponds talc, 3 Roses, Wheel detergent, etc.

6. Satellite Distribution

We have usually a group of villages around a town which is a regular trading centre, enjoying fair infrastructural facilities. The villages are satellites dependent on the town nearest to them. The feeder town plays the role of distribution as well as collecting centre. The farmers sell their farm produce to the town traders and expect to fulfil their needs of consumer products from the town market through the village shops.

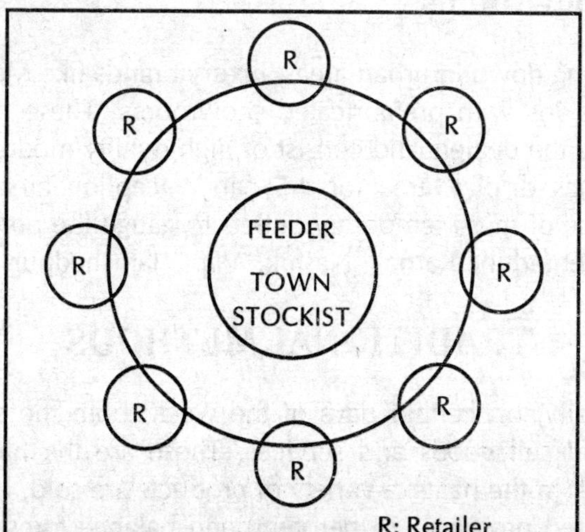

Fig. 8.4: Satellite Distribution

In this system, the company appoints stockists in important towns. These stockists are responsible for placing orders with the company, receiving the stocks, sorting of stocks and supply the goods in small lots to the retailers and merchants situated in rural areas and in and around the towns. The stockist is given 7-30 days credit by the company. Over a period of time along with increase in business, some of the good retailers will be elevated as stockists. Therefore, many retailers hover around a particular stockist. The advantage of this system is, it enables the organisation to penetrate interior markets.

Examples:

(a) Eveready batteries has appointed van operator in each district, who supplies the product to retail stockists (RS). These stockists supply the product to all retailers (R) and merchants (M) in rural areas.

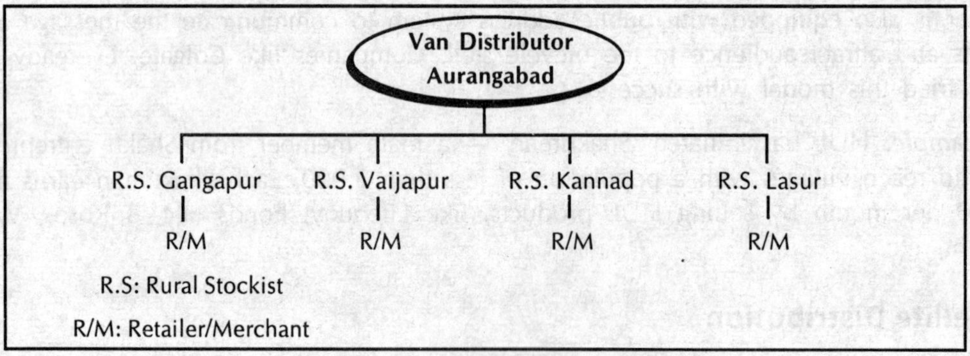

Fig 8.5: Satellite Distribution

(b) HUL, Nestle, Marico have appointed stockists to service the village merchants and the merchants are met at fortnightly/monthly intervals through van operations.

7. Pre-fabricated Showrooms

With the sales slowing down in urban areas, luxury brands like Mercedes, Audi and BMW are moving to smaller towns with prefabricated showrooms. These mobile shownrooms are set up with the support of the dealers and consist of high quality modular structure-water proof and air-conditioned. It has display area for 4-5 cars, reception area, and VIP lounge. The companies are making use of these temporary outlets to gauge the potential in new territories, i.e., small towns like Dehradun, Karnal, Nashik, Vapi, Jamshedpur.

TRADITIONAL METHODS

1. Haats: Traditionally, on certain days of the week, both the sellers and buyers meet in the village to buy and sell goods and services. These are the haats that are being held regularly in all rural areas. In the haats, a variety of products are sold, i.e., agricultural products (40 per cent), manufactured products (25 per cent) and balance forests' produce, handlooms, processed foods, dress materials, meat, etc. By participating in haats, the company can not only promote the products but also understand the shared values, beliefs and perceptions of rural consumers that influence buying behaviour. Out of about 40,000 haats, about 5,000 haats are held in + 5,000 population villages and another 10,000 haats in villages having population between 2,000-5,000. Each large haat covers about 20 villages and by making products available in these haats, the company can cover about 50 per cent of the rural population. It has been estimated that out of the total sale of FMCG products, 30 per cent are branded products.

Example: Parachute Oil, Tiger Brand Biscuits are promoted through haats.

2. Melas: Melas are of different types, i.e., commodity fairs, cattle fairs and religious fairs and may be held only for a day or may extend over a week. Many companies have come out with creative ideas for participating in such melas. It has been estimated that out of the total sale of FMCG products, 30 per cent are branded products.

Examples:

(a) Kisan Mela in Ludhiana is an annual feature and companies like Maruti have been able to book orders for cars by participating in this mela.

(b) Companies like HUL, Colgate, Britannia promote their product through melas.

3. Mobile Traders known as Pheriwaalas, are able to service interior markets which conventional distribution channels do not touch. They are also able to reach rural households especially women who do not leave their homes. They move from house-to-house on bicyle or on foot, selling a variety of goods like bangles, artificial jewellery, perfumes, toothpowder, face cream, vessels, clothes, etc. They cover two villages per-day and visit about 30 houses. These traders have been calling on the same home for years and their association with rural customers is a good example for relationship marketing.

"A Mobile Trader"

DEVELOPMENT OF RETAILERS IN RURAL MARKET

One of the important challenges faced by the marketer is the development of a chain of retailers in rural markets. The marketer could consider some of the existing retail outlets in rural areas.

1. Cooperative Societies: There are about 3 lakh cooperative societies operating in rural areas. Many of these societies distribute consumer goods and low value consumer durables.

2. Public Distribution System: Essential commodities such as sugar, kerosene, edible oils are made available to the consumers at reasonable prices through fair price shops. Such shops are run by state civil supplies department, cooperatives or by private parties. There are about 4.50 lakh public distribution shops in rural market and marketers could explore the possibility of selling goods.

Example: In Gujarat the public distribution shops have been converted into rural malls, selling a variety of products and services apart from essential commodities.

3. Agricultural Input Dealers: There are about three lakh dealers selling fertilisers. Since the demand for fertilisers, seeds and pesticides is highly seasonal, many of these dealers deal in other goods also. The marketers could approach these dealers and find out the possibility of selling electrical products, consumers durables, hardware items in rural areas.

"A Fertiliser/Pesticide Shop"

4. Potential Villages: It is seen that there are about two lakh villages having a population of less than 500 each and there are hardly any shops in these villages. There are limited number of small shops in villages having population between 500-2,000 in this category. However, sales per outlet is low and it becomes uneconomical to service these shops.

About 50 per cent of the rural population lives in about one lakh villages with a population of +2,000 each. These villages are connected by roads and account for about 50 per cent of the wealth generated in rural areas. Therefore, marketers of fast-moving consumer goods could look at villages having +2,000 population and try to cover retailers in these villages.

Examples:

(a) HUL is focusing on villages with more than 2,000 population and they are covering about one lakh villages. Villages with less than 2,000 population would be covered under Project Shakti Scheme.

(b) Hero Honda, the two-wheeler market leader plans to cover about one lakh villages under a special campaign *"Har Gaon Har Aangan"* (Every Village, Every Household). The company has collected basic information about rural households through 3,000 rural dealers, i.e., Touch Points. The sales executive meets the opinion leaders in the village and highlights product benefits; loan scheme for purchase of two-wheelers, etc., and the rural dealer plays an important role in the sales and service of two-wheelers to the villagers.

(c) Coco-Cola has started training programme for women retailers in rural areas. The programme known as "Parivartan" deals with managing stocks, receivables, display of products, finance and customer service. The retailer receives a certificate after successful completion of the programme. In addition, they are also provided with Solar coolers called eKoCool which can keep fifty bottles. This move has created opportunities for rural people to take up income generating activities in. There are more than one lakh retailers who sell Coco Cola beverages in rural areas.

5. Feeder Markets/Mandis: The villagers visit nearby Mandis for selling agricultural produce and buying consumer durables. There are about 7000 Mandis in India and states like Maharashtra (860) Bihar (810) Punjab (675), (UP (645), MP (600), and West Bengal (590) have large number of Mandis. These Mandis are mainly situated in agricultural centres and Taluka/District Headquarters. Dealers/wholesalers could be appointed in such Mandis to meet the requirements of surrounding villages.

"A Dealer for Consumer Durables"

6. Post Offices and Bank Branches: There are 1,40,000 post offices in rural and semi-urban areas and 32,000 bank branches. The domain knowledge of the postman is far superior to any other organisation. The department has entered into host of tie-ups with Government, public sector and private sector players. Some of these are given below:

- Reservation of railway tickets, especially in far-off places.
- Acceptance of passport applications.
- Inward money remittance from abroad through Western Union.
- Acceptance of bills, premia and other periodic payments for electricity, telecom, insurance, financial companies, etc.
- Non-life Insurance in collaboration with Oriental Insurance Company.
- Retailing of mutual funds for UTI, SBI, Reliance, Franklin Templeton, etc.
- Sale of gold coins and distribution of coins for Reserve Bank of India.
- Sale of application forms and acceptance of forms for UPSC, MBA, MCA, examination, etc.
- Sale of recharge vouchers for telecom companies.
- Address verification for telecom, credit cards and other companies and issue of identity cards.

Marketers could consider using the services of postal department for promoting products and services especially in rural areas.

7. Small Towns: There are about 7,000 small towns having population of less than ten lakh and they act as consuming and distribution centres for FMCG brands, durables, construction materials, transportation equipment, banking and insurance products, pharmaceutical products, agricultural inputs, etc. These small towns account for about 18 per cent of the total population and 25 per cent of the total consumption of products and services. These small towns offer health, education, banking, insurance and entertainment facilities for the villagers. Marketers could appoint dealers in these towns for increasing the sale of consumer goods and other products. Further wholesales/distributors/preferred dealers could be appointed in these towns to service the village retailers.

Table 8.1: Classification Towns in India

Town Class	Population
1	>40 lakh
2	10 to 40 Lakh
3	5 to 1o lakh
4	1 to 5 lakh
5	50,000 to 1 lakh
6	10,000 to 50,000

Source: Media Research Users Council (It is a registered not for profit body of members drawn from major advertisers, advertising agencies, publishers and broadcast/other media

Note: Total number of towns 7,935 (2011) against 5,161(2001).

PHYSICAL DISTRIBUTION

Physical distribution activities include order processing, handling of goods, packaging, warehousing, transportation, inventory control, banking and customer service. Considering the constraints in physical distribution of stocks in rural areas, many companies have come out with innovative solutions.

1. Company Owned Delivery Vans: The van may be owned by the company or by distributor. The delivery van takes the product to the retail shops in villages. The distributor's salesperson travels in the van and he delivers the stocks to the retailer and collects the money too.

Example: Bharat Petroleum has introduced Rural Marketing Vehicle (RMV) way back in 1999 in Punjab. The vehicle moves from village-to-village and fills LPG cylinders on the spot to rural customers.

2. Hired Vans: In this case, the wholesaler uses a hired vehicle to cover the retailers in villages. Normally, the cost of operation of the hired vehicle is shared between the wholesaler and the company.

Examples:

(a) HUL distributors use hired vehicles to reach the rural retailers.

(b) Syngenta distributors use hired vehicles for delivery of pesticides as well as for collections.

3. Bullock Cart or Camels are used for covering remote villages with no motorable road. In certain parts of Kerala, AP, and West Bengal, boats are also used to cover villages that are not connected by roads.

4. Syndicate Van Distribution: In this case, the firms/distributors selling non-competitive consumer goods come together to service the rural retailers. The delivery van carries the product of both the companies.

Example: A firm manufacturing edible oils and another local firm dealing in biscuits, Namkeen and Atta could jointly service rural retailers, through van operation.

COMPETITION IN RURAL MARKETS

There are four types of products competing in rural markets, i.e.,

1. National brands
2. Regional brands
3. Local brands
4. Spurious products

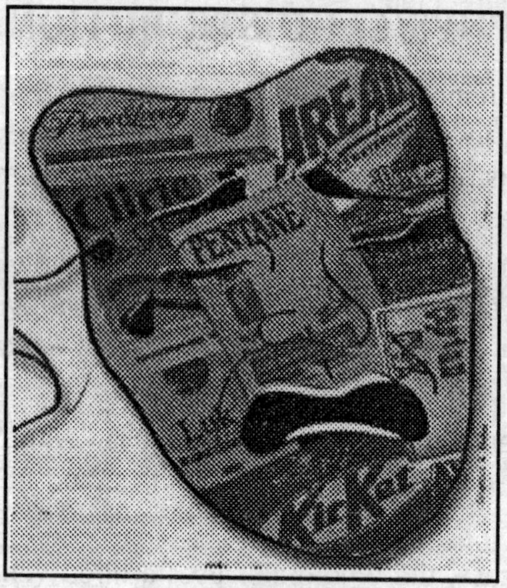

"Spurious Products"

The rural consumers in interior villages may not always ask for specific brands but ask for **'laal wala sabun dena' or 'paanch rupaiya waali chai dena'.** Therefore, the brand becomes servient to the retailer and he sells those products that give him higher returns.

There is a proliferation of spurious products. Rural people identify a product by its packaging, i.e., colour, visuals, size and it becomes easy for spurious proudcts to eat into the market share of established reputed brands. The retailer gets a larger margin and therefore promotes such products.

Spurious products consists of the following:

(a) Duplicates are exact replica of original brands in design, name, etc.

(b) In the case of look-alikes, the packaging is similar to original brand, but the name is different.

Example: Gandhi No. 1 (Godrej No. 1).

(c) While packaging is similar to original brand, the names are misspelt in the case of spell-alikes.

Examples: Teta Salt, Lucky boy, Pure and Lovely, Luk, Pentane, Cliric all clear, Kir ket, etc.

While it is practically impossible to eliminate spurious products in the market, the manufacturers have to take remedial measures. Mass awareness progamme highlighting the distinguishing features of the original product pack *vis-a-vis* spurious products has to be conducted in identified villages. Legal measures have to be initiated depending upon the situation.

CONCLUSION

The rural markets and the consumers are scattered over a wide geographical area. Considering low income of consumers, low density of population, poor condition of roads, it becomes difficult and uneconomical to individually service all the villages. The marketers have to follow a selective approach, based on market potential in developing a network of distributors and retailers in rural markets.

QUESTIONS

1. What are the constraints in distribution in rural areas?
2. "Distribution is the key factor in tapping the rural market." Explain with examples, the distribution strategies adopted by companies in rural markets.

CASE STUDY

Computerisation of Rural Distributors' Accounts

Glenmorgan and Company Limited is a fast-moving consumer product company. The company is in a business for the past 15 years. Due to saturation of the urban market, they had planned in the beginning of 2009 to expand their business in the rural areas. To set up the basic infrastructure, they decided to computerise their distributors in the rural areas. The total number of distributors were approx. 200. The implementation was to be completed by middle of 2010.

The purpose of computerisation was to get information from distributors regarding product sales, collections, outstandings, etc., on a more frequent basis. The information was to be uploaded into the ERP package for consolidation and analysis and then proposed to be sent twice a week to the head office through e-mail. This major initiative was headed by Mr. Krishnan, the Finance Head and Mr. Mehta, the Logistics Head. The programme was to be developed by the IT department along with the Logistics department.

The internal needs of the organisation were assessed and the programme developed for implementation at the distributors. The distributors were informed by means of a letter about the implementation schedule and asked to purchase the computer printer and get an e-mail connection. The zonal sales managers were similarly informed.

The big distributors in the rural area were also dealing with other products. Many of them had a computer which was used for financial accounting and keeping track of all their businesses. Some of the small distributors had a computer but it was not compatible for the implementation of the new software. The distributors also complained about lack of back-up support and infrastructural problems. Software had bugs which were not noticed before. The project was delayed and distributors resentment was growing. At the end of 2010, the heads of concerned departments sat down to get the project back on stream.

QUESTIONS

1. Do the SWOT analysis of the project?
2. Where did the team go wrong?
3. Was there a better way to implement the initiative?

CASE STUDY

India Post

The universal dakiya (postman), the permanent symbol of rural India laboriously traversing miles to deliver a postcard or money order may now become the mascot of a new-look India Post. As the largest retail network in the country faces up to multi-pronged competition from internet, IT, mobile telephony, banks and couriers/logistics companies, local more lenders and more, change is a must.

Despite the telecom revolution, the large areas of rural India, post offices remain the only connect with larger world, as a bank, Public Call Office (PCO) and retail outlet rolled in one. Now, this countrywide network of 1.54 lakh Post Offices (POs) — almost 90 per cent of them in Rural areas — aims to deliver more than just the mail. The new focus cover financial services, telecom services and retail in a resurgent rural India. The Department of Posts has commissioned KPMG to workout the modalities to enable the Indian Posts make rural POs the one-stop shop for range of services including banking. Says, IT and Communications Minister, "We have already initiated talks with Ministry of Finance and other authorities to get the required approvals. There is no reason why POs cannot offer banking services as they are already collecting deposits and repaying them on maturity. It's time to re-orient and become financially strong.

As an introduction, ICICI Bank has begun to sell tractor loan through POs. Now FMCG companies want to use POs to increase rural penetration. For starters, Emami products are being already sold in rural POs in Maharashtra's 8 districts and other companies plan to follow suit. India Post has also tied up with IDBI Capital Markets Services Limited to retail government securities (G-secs). IDBI Capital will provide quotes for purchase/sale to select POs in Tamil Nadu, Andhra Pradesh, Mumbai and Delhi.

India Post, set up in 1855 by the British as the telegraph department, employs 5.5 lakh people and delivers 53 million pieces of mail daily. It has also provided parcels, money order, banking, insurance and mutual fund services down the years. But in the past decades, private courier firm, e-mail, short messaging services and e-commerce have eaten into its revenues. According to World Bank Survey conducted two years ago, though the ₹ 2,490 crore domestic courier industry was growing at a feverish pace, India's Post share was a meagre 10 per cent.

QUESTIONS

1. Do you think it is good idea to promote goods and services of other companies through POs?
2. As a marketing consultant, what strategies would you recommend to India Post to counter the competition of couriers, e-mails, SMSs and e-commerce?
3. Explain your views – Can postman perform the role of a opinion leader?

✿ ✿ ✿

9 ORGANISED RURAL RETAILING

INTRODUCTION

The word 'retail' is derived from the French word 'retailier' meaning to cut a piece off or to break bulk and involves direct interface with the customer. Retailing involves all activities directly related to the sales of goods and services to the ultimate consumer for personal and non-business use. Retailer is a person, agent, agency, company or organisation engaged in reaching goods or services to the end-user or ultimate consumer.

Retailing is one of the fastest-growing sectors in the country. It employs about 7 per cent of the workforce and contributes 14 per cent to the national GDP. Indian middle-class population is expected to grow from 30 crore to 60 crore by 2010 and this makes retailing scenario much more attractive to the marketers. Middle income group is highly value-conscious, looks for bargains. Organised retailing provides variety, convenience, service and value for money and therefore appeals to middle income consumers. Further, consumers can directly look at the products, labels, prices and discuss with family and friends before making purchase decisions. Growing number of nuclear families, increase in middle-class income, working women, pressure of work, commuting time and convenience are contributing to the growth of organised retailing in our country.

The retail sector can be broadly classified as Unorganised (Grocery shops, Kirana stores) and Organised Retail Sector (Malls, Hypermarket and Supermarket). Organised retail sector has large format stores and provides a variety of goods in many locations. In an unorganised sector, there are large numbers of small retail outlets with limited variety of goods. In countries like USA, the share of organised retail sales is about 80 per cent, whereas in our country organised retail contributes only to 4 per cent of total sales. With over 12 million retail outlets, we have the largest number of retail stores in the world. There are 9 outlets per 1,000 people and about 96 per cent of these outlets are less than 500 square feet in size. Retailing is going through a transition phase in our country from the corner stores to independent formats. Currently, the growth of retail is mainly confined to cities and towns. A few retail chains like Pantaloon, Reliance, RPG Retail, Shoppers' Stop, Westside (Tata Group), Aditya Birla Group are already active in the organised sector.

Rural market offers opportunities for growth and development of organised retailing and companies like ITC, DCM, and Godrej, Future Group have already established large format branded stores. These organised retail stores have to overcome the problems connected with the traditional grocery stores by offering value-added facilities to the rural consumers.

LIMITATIONS OF THE TRADITIONAL RETAIL OUTLETS IN RURAL MARKET

Rural retailer is the connecting link between the consumer and the company and he plays a major role in distribution. Some of the limitations of retailers are given below:

1. Shop Loyalty: In rural markets, loyalty to the shop is relatively high and therefore, the retailers are able to influence the buying decisions of consumers.

2. Availability of Products: The retailer visits the wholesaler/stockist once in a week/ fortnight. In case, stock of one brand is not available, he may substitute it with another brand. He keeps a smaller number of Stock Keeping Units (SKUs) of a product, as he has limited working capital.

3. Credit Facilities: The retailer extends credit to his customers and many rural people have running account with retailers. Many companies extend 7-30 days credit to rural retailers to persuade them to stock the products.

4. Constraints: The retailer has to put up with a number of constraints such as low sales volumes, less retail space, power fluctuations, inadequate funds, seasonal demand and poor transportation facilities. If the marketers can arrange to deliver the products at his premises, he will save on travel time and transportation costs and will be motivated to buy and sell such products.

5. Display of Products: In rural shops, the products are not displayed properly. Therefore, the marketers have to focus on display of products in village shops.

6. Free Gift Offer: It has been observed that retailers do not pass on the gifts to consumers and the marketer has to create awareness among consumers for successful implementation of free gift scheme.

7. Retail Sale Price: In rural markets, the sales per retailer is low, the competition is less and the product is sold at MRP or above MRP.

8. Seasonal Demand: Normally, the retailers stock more varieties of products during harvesting period and festivals, since demand is high during this period. The marketers should come out with innovative schemes to promote the products during this period.

9. Profit Margin: The retailer pushes the products that give higher margin.

10. Spurious Products: There is a proliferation of spurious products in the rural market. Villagers identify a product by its packaging, i.e., colour, visuals, size and it becomes easy for spurious products to eat into the market of share of established brands. The retailer gets a larger margin and therefore he may promote such products.

OPPORTUNITIES IN ORGANISED RURAL RETAILING

The following factors have contributed to the growth and development of rural retailing.

1. **Growth in Income:** The average income level has improved due to modern farming practices, industrialisation of rural area, growth of service sector, migration of rural people into cities and remittance of their money, remittance of money by family members settled abroad. Rural income contributes to over 50 per cent of the total income of the country.

2. **Rising Aspirations of Rural People and Attraction for High Standard of Living:** The rise in income coupled with increased awareness and the need for possessing modern goods have influenced the rural marketing environment in our country. The mobility towards higher income group has in fact been much higher in rural areas than urban. The aspirations of rural people and attraction for high standard of living have contributed to the growth of rural market. The young affluent farmers, traders, rural youth, service class for a distinct segment of the population. They are modern, knowledgeable and receptive to changes. They value material comforts and would like to go in for two-wheelers, ready-made garments, soft drinks, cosmetics, etc. Even premium brands like Denim Talc, and Pantene have entered the market, though in current volumes are very low. A rural person wants to replicate the lifestyle of urban counterpart.

   Example: Moving from B&W TV to Colour TV, Cycles to Motor Cycles.

3. **Urban Shopping Experience in Rural Areas:** Large format branded stores provide pleasant shopping experience for the people in villages. Some of the attractions are:
   - Long, clean brightly lit aisles lined with deep plastic bins full of products.
   - Each product is displayed and clearly labelled with price.
   - Recreation, restaurant, juice bar, banking, etc.
   - Touch and feel experience.
   - Outing for family members.
   - Fulfils the need of women, children, parents and even grandparents.

4. **High Quality Products are Available at MRP and Very Often Below MRP:** There is no discrimination in pricing, product or service.

5. **Availability of a Wide Range of Products Under One Roof:** The consumer has the choice of buying all his requirements such as consumer goods, durables, agricultural produce, medicines, agricultural inputs, etc., from corporate retail stores.

6. **Retailing is a Labour-intensive Activity and Creates Job Opportunities to Educated Rural Youth:** Normally, the staff density for a store is one per 100-400 square feet depending upon the store format. Many urban youth feel that front line job involves standing in a store and it is a low status job compared to jobs in business process outsourcing operations. Most of the front line employees are undergraduates and organised retail outlets provide an attractive career for rural youth who are otherwise unemployed.

PROGRESS OF ORGANISED RURAL RETAILING

Many companies are attempting to establish systems to procure agricultural produce of desired quality from farmers and offer remunerative price for the produce. The consumer goods and agricultural produce are sold through retail outlets, criss-crossing the country.

1. Choupal Sagar promoted by ITC is the first organised retail outlet in the rural market. The rural mall serves as a shopping and information centre. Spread over an area of 8 acres at Sehore in MP, the Mall sells everything — sarees, footwear, groceries, cosmetics, television, agricultural inputs, motor cycles, scooters and even tractors. Banking, ATM, restaurant, post office, fuel pump, health care centre are the other facilities offered by Choupal Sagar. The farmers can log on to internet and find out modern methods of cultivation of crops and prices of agricultural commodities.

"Choupal Sagar"

ITC purchases agricultural produce through e-Choupal and sells consumer goods, durables, etc., through its own Choupal Sagar outlets. At present there are 24 outlets covering UP and MP.

2. Haryali Kisan Bazaar: DCM Shriram Limited, founded in 1889 is a large business house with interest in sugar, chemicals, fertilisers, seeds and plant protection chemicals. The group turnover is over ₹ 4,000 crore. DCM has opened Haryali Kisan Bazaar in 2002 in Hardoi in UP. At present there are about 200 stores operating in UP, Punjab, Haryana, Rajasthan and MP and each store caters to the needs of about 15,000 villagers. There are two types of outlets, i.e., large format stores over 10,000 to 15,000 square feet and company owned and small format stores on leased premises. Large stores spread over 3-4 acres of land offer a variety of products and services to villages. There are qualified agronomists who provide technical advice to farmers on modern cultivation practices. Since agricultural input business is seasonal, the company has added other items such as kitchen ware, LPG, FMCGs, durables, banking and insurance services. It has tied with ICICI, HDFC, Bharti, and Motorola to offer comprehensive services to villagers. The company has taken initiative to build computerised data of customers and membership cards are issued to them. Various promotion schemes are offered to attract and retain customers.

"Haryali Kisan Bazaar"

3. Godrej Agrovet has launched rural retail outlets known as Godrej Aadhar in Maharashtra. The stores offer agricultural inputs, consumer goods, banking, postal and pharmacy services. The first store was started in Manchar, near Pune, in 2003. There are 30 Aadhar centres and each centre services 15-25 villagers. The Aadhar outlets have taken supermarket concept to rural areas.

The Aadhar outlets also source fruits, vegetables for Godrej urban outlets, i.e., "Natures Basket". In 2009, Kishore Biyanis Future Group bought Aadhar outlets from Godrej and has launched a pilot project at Shrirampur in Ahmednagar district of Maharashtra. Christened Aadhaar Shopping Mall, the company has made changes in terms of the looks of the store, communication line, offerings and interiors of the store. The objective is to create an image of urban goods provider in rural markets. It is reaching out to consumers more directly using communication tools such as rallies, auto advertising and banners. The company plans to add more Aadhar retail stores in other locations covering 100 towns by 2014.

"Aadhar Outlet"

4. Tata Kisan Sansar, promoted by Tata Chemicals, offers solutions to field problems right from sowing to harvesting and also supply agricultural inputs such as seeds, fertilisers and plant protection chemicals to farmers. There are about 500 franchise run stores covering 16,000 villages in Punjab, Haryana, UP, Bihar and West Bengal.

"Tata Kisan Sansar"

5. Aditya Birla Group deals in viscose yarn, carbon black, branded garments, fertilisers, textiles, insulators, insurance and telecommunication. The company offers consultation services through its **Birla Shaktiman Kisan Seva Kendras** in UP, Bihar, Jharkand and West Bengal.

6. Warna Bazaar: The super stores are located in Kolhapur and Sangli town. In addition, they have over 25 small stores in key villages in Western Maharashtra. Kasti Society has set up a large rural retail centre near Ahmednagar in Maharashtra.

7. Indian Oil and Bharath Petroleum have set up large number of retail outlets along with fuel stations in prosperous rural and semi-urban markets. These outlets sell consumer goods and agricultural inputs. There are about 3,000 Kisan Seva Kendras attached to fuel stations in rural areas.

8. Mahindra Shublabh Services Limited (MSSL) is a subsidiary of Mahindra and Mahindra Ltd. The main objective is to optimise agricultural production by integrating availability of quality agriculture inputs, scientific farming techniques, mechanisation, farm finance and providing consultancy services to the farmers to improve yields. MSSL aims to be a One-stop Shop catering to various farming requirements ranging from sowing to marketing of agricultural produce including finance for farming operations.

Note: The progress of large format stores in rural areas, has not been satisfactory. DCM Shriram (Haryali Kisan Bazaar) and Triveni (Khushali Bazaar outlets) have closed down unprofitable outlets. The reasons are many, i.e., fluctuating demand due to monsoon, diverse buying habits and difficulty in competing with Kirana stores. Even ITC has not expanded since 2007.

CHALLENGES

While rural market offers lot of opportunities to the creative marketers, they have to face the following challenges:

- It is feared that with the entry of corporate retails, a large number of small traditional retailers will lose business and may have to close down the shops and many State Governments are objecting the entry of corporate retailers.
- Kirana stores have advantages over malls. Close relationship with rural consumers and extension of credit facilities are the differentiating factors which go in favour of Kirana stores. Shop loyalty is high in rural areas and the rural consumer may not immediately change his shopping habits.
- Real estate costs will go up with the entry of corporate retailers. It is preferable to opt for leased property.
- Selling third party brands will not yield high margins to cover initial fixed costs.
- He may have to travel long distances to reach the mega stores.
- He may be even uncomfortable with the ultra modern environment also.
- Rural income is seasonal and purchases of consumer durables are done during post-harvest season and during festivals.
- Infrastructure facilities like all-weather roads, transport facilities are generally lacking in rural areas.
- Lack of trained manpower in rural areas.
- The rural consumer may feel that the prices are higher in such stores.

GUIDELINES FOR ACHIEVING EFFICIENCY IN RURAL RETAIL OPERATIONS

- Provide clean and hygienic but functional surrounding. Corporate retailers have to assess whether there is a need for central air-conditioning, soft lighting and glass and chromium fixtures in the premises. The consumer should feel that he is in a familiar and comfortable environment and will get a good deal.

- Must adapt strategies to local needs and demands.

  Example: Free transport facilities to the villages based on a minimum value of billing, create loyal customers and issue of membership cards, extend credit facilities on a case-by-case basis based on assessment of creditworthiness of the buyers.

- Make use of ruralspecific promotion media and methods such as audiovisual publicity van, village opinion leaders, advertisement films in rural cinema theatres, Mandis, Haats to create awareness among villagers.
- Prices affordable to middle and lower income groups.
- Educate consumers about products and services.
- Employ local staff so that they can easily connect to the rural consumer.
- Provide adequate training to the staff on customer service.

CONCLUSION

The organised rural retail formats offer goods quality products at competitive rates and provide pleasant shopping experience for the people in villages. A few companies have already entered the rural market with retail formats. Corporates have to find out ways and means to improve the efficiency of retail operations and also resolve the conflict with the existing distribution channel.

QUESTIONS

1. Discuss the progress of organised rural retailing in our country.
2. Do you think that organised retail stores will be successful in the long run in rural market?

CASE STUDY

Modernising Sales Outlets

Mr. Harish Panjwani, a refugee started a grocery business, about 40 years ago. Over a period of time he expanded the business and now owns shops dealing in consumer durables, dairy products, a general store and a medical shop. He is emotionally attached to his original grocery business and continues to operate it with enthusiasm. His sober temperament, reliable dealings and amiable nature won him many friends and his shop has become a meeting place for people belonging to his generation. His eldest son, Rajesh has completed his management education from abroad and is assisting his father in the business. He feels that his father's way of dealing with people is traditional and outdated. He feels irritated when his father's old friends drop in at the shops and spend time talking to him. Rajesh feels that this type of casual get together is a waste of time. He would like to be more business like and serve the customers a methodical manner. Left to himself he would like to start a supermarket, selling all categories of products under one roof. This will provide a pleasant shopping experience for local people and outing for the whole family. He has broached his feelings in an indirect way to his father and found that his father believes in maintaining close personal relations with customers. Unlike his father, his approach is more professional and the customers have lately started taking notice of his behaviour. They feel that the old warmth is missing and they are less welcome at the shop. A few of them have started purchasing from other shops too.

QUESTIONS

(a) State at least two assumptions.

(b) What do you think is the contribution of personal relationship in such a business?

(c) Do you agree with the approach adopted by Rajesh in dealing with customers and his preference for a supermarket?

(d) Do you have any suggestions to make?

✿ ✿ ✿

10 RURAL PROMOTION

INTRODUCTION

Promotion is the process of marketing communication to inform, persuade, remind and influence consumers or users in favour of your product or service and has three specific objectives:

(a) It communicates marketing information to consumers, users and sellers.

(b) Promotion persuades and convinces the buyer and influences his behaviour to take desired action.

(c) It stimulates demand, capture demand from competition and maintain demand for the company's products even in a competitive market situation.

Essentially, promotion is persuasive communication to inform potential customers of the existence of products, to persuade and convince them that those products have want satisfying capitabilities.

PROMOTION-MIX

The promotion-mix includes four ingredients.

1. Advertising is a paid form of non-personal presentation and promotion of ideas, goods and services by an identified sponsor and is a method of mass communication. Regional TV channels, radio, cinema, regional newspapers and magazines are being used by marketers to pass on the message about products and services to rural audience.

2. Publicity involves stimulating demand for a product or service by placing commercially significant news about it in a publication or obtaining favourable opinion through radio, television or stage without making payment by the sponsor.

Example: Many local newspapers and magazines carry reports of the field activities conducted by companies, creating awareness about the products among the villagers.

3. Personal Selling: It is one of the most effective methods of promotion and involves face-to-face communication with the prospect for the purpose of making sale.

Example: Personal selling plays a major role in selling high involvement products such as tractors, two-wheelers, pesticides, insurance policies, etc.

(4) Sales Promotion covers those activities other than advertising, publicity and personal selling that stimulate consumer purchasing and dealer effectiveness.

Example: Many marketers offer attractive schemes to promote the sale of television in rural markets during post-harvest season and festivals.

PROMOTION STRATEGY

Promotion strategy lays down the broad principles by which a company hopes to secure an advantage over competition, exhibit attractiveness to buyers and lead to full use of company's resources.When marketers resort to promotion in marketplace, we have a kind of promotion square. It has four sides of equal importance, i.e., the product, the buyer, the company and the channel.

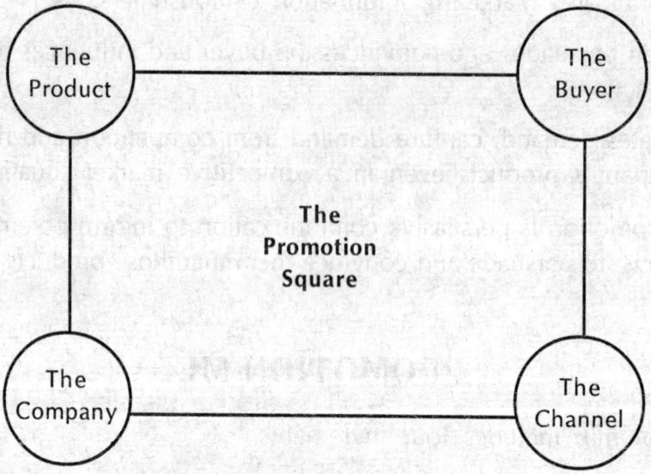

Fig. 10.1: Promotion Square

1. The Product is one of the factors determining the form of promotion. Toys are effectively shown on television. Press advertisements are unsuitable for children. Mass selling products can be easily promoted through radio and television advertising. Agricultural inputs could be promoted through personal selling and rural-specific activities like AVP van, group meeting, etc.

2. The Buyer: The marketer must know their customers, their needs, desires, attitude, values, aspirations and expectations. Marketers should have updated information about consumer demand and consumer behaviour.

3. The Firm has a unique image in the market. Source credibility in promotion plays a very important role in making promotion believable to the receiver. Effectiveness of communication depends upon the firms' image in the market. When the perceived risk of buying a product is high, the source credibility becomes important in making purchase decisions.

4. The Channel Choice: The promotion strategy also depends on the channel or route through which the products of the firm flow to consumers.

Example: India today is a mix of developed and developing markets. There is a large upper class population having lifestyle similar to developed West. At the same time, there is the emerging middle class and bottom of the pyramid where there are lot of opportunities for creative marketers. We have two good examples of communication targeted at both ends of the pyramid. Vodafone's *Zoo Zoos* and HULs *Khushiyon Ki Dole* to reach villagers. This shows that marketers have to understand the profile of the market before coming out with marketing strategies.

PULL AND PUSH STRATEGIES IN PROMOTION

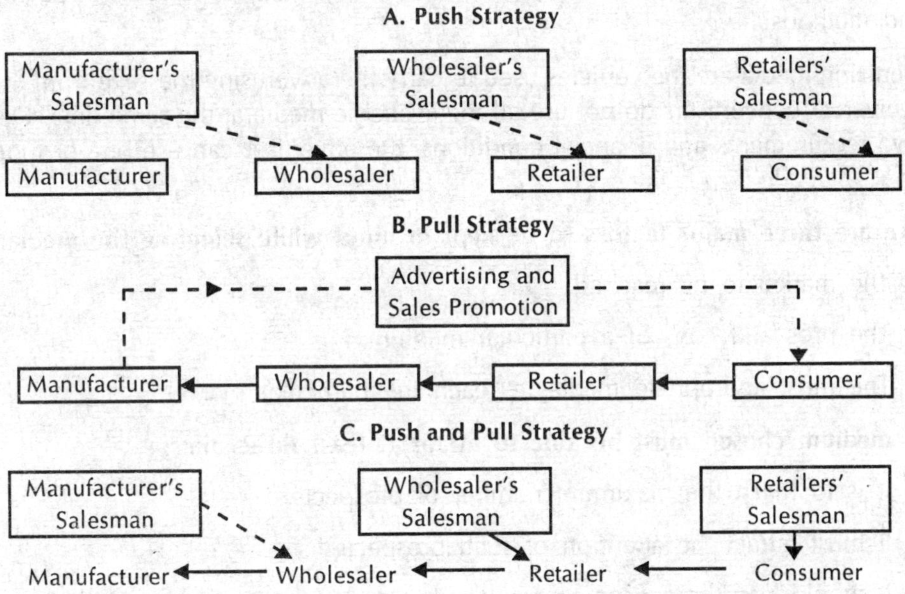

Fig. 10.2: "Pull and Push Strategies in Promotion"

In a pull strategy, the product is pulled through the channel by creating end-user demand. Consumer demand forces the retailer to stock the promoted products. In turn, retailer demands the product from wholesalers and wholesalers are forced to stock those products by placing orders with the manufacturer. The firms having well known brands can exercise control over channels through pull promotion strategies. Retailer margins are relatively low in pull promotion. Extensive and heavy use of advertising and sales promotion would be required to generate consumer demand. Under push strategy, the manufacturer, direct all promotional efforts mainly on distributors, wholesalers and retailers. Product is pushed through the channel by offering financial incentives to middlemen. In rural markets, most consumer goods and agri-business companies generally employ a pull and push strategy to sell their products. The ratio of pull to push may differ according to market requirements. The salespersons are used to push the goods through marketing channel. Advertising and sales promotion supports personal selling to increase sales. Thus, all the tools of promotion works together.

REACHING THE RURAL CONSUMER

Though the rural markets offer big attractions to the marketers, one of the most important questions frequently asked is "How do we reach the large rural population through different media and methods?"

Advertising media are the vehicles used to carry the advertising message from the sender to the receiver. All advertisers do not use all the available media at the same time. Depending on his own requirements and financial conditions, the advertiser can use one or more of the media.

There are three major factors to be kept in mind while selecting the media:

1. The market to be reached.
2. The pros and cons of a particular medium.
3. The most appropriate media to reach the particular market.

Any medium chosen must be able to attain at least three aims:

1. It is to reach the maximum number of prospects.
2. It must attract the attention of such prospects.
3. It should lead the consumers from unawareness to action as per AICDA method of communication, i.e., awareness — interest — conviction — desire — action.

Allahabad Kumbh Mela (2013)

Known as the biggest spiritual carnival on earth, Allahabad Maha Kumbh Mela attracts ten crore devotees. Many marketers have come out with out of the box ideas to connect with pilgrims and praying for a space in pilgrims' mind space. Kolkata based Emami launched a talent hunt programme for women at the Kumbh for Boroplus antiseptic cream. The talent hunt called Meleka Big Star has three rounds-general knowledge, singing or dancing and a task such as how many vegetables a contestant can chop in one minute. There were daily winners and overall winner chosen from the nearly two-month campaign and the same was telecast live on CBS channels. The company has also hired stilt walkers in and around Mela venue to attract consumers.

Coca-Cola sold its flagship Cola in 150 ml cups (₹ five per cup) through 15 exclusive outlets supported by 140 coolers. Amul ice cream proved to be one of the best sellers at the Mela in spite of harsher winter. Dabur tied up with several restaurants at the Mela venue to serve Hajimoola digestive candy free. It has also gave free sample of mosquito repellent Odomos at the Mela.

HUL launched one the most over eye catching promotions with Roti Reminder. The company tied up with over 100 eateries at Kumbh to serve Rotis stamped with the message "Lifebuoy se haath dhoye kya (Have you washed your hands with Lifebuoy?)

The leading telecom brand Vodafone embedded devotional music into the earmuffs and got them branded with Vodafone logo and message that instructed people to dial 123 to listen to devotional songs.

Source: *The Economic Times*: February 11, 2013.

INTEGRATED MARKETING COMMUNICATION (IMC)

Marketing communication mix consists of advertising, sales promotion, personal selling, public relations and publicity. All these tools have one common objective, i.e., communicating a message to the consumer. For communication to be effective, the receiver has to understand the contents of the message. The message is based on unique features of the product, features that are appealing to the consumers, comparison of brands, competition and the position of the product in the minds of the customer.

Very often, companies make use of different promotion media and methods to pass on the message about products and services to consumers. Lack of clarity and consistency in the message from different sources may lead to confusion in the mind of the target audience. To avoid such a problem, companies are now following the concept of integrated marketing communication.

Integrated Marketing Communication (IMC) combines the various communication media and methods to produce clarity, consistency and create maximum impact on the target audience. The purpose of IMC is to combine the brand positioning and messages and communicate a common theme to build a strong brand identity in the marketplace.

PROMOTION MESSAGES

The messages transmitted through all forms of promotion must describe the product features and benefits in terms of customer wants and desires. The problem solving/need-satisfaction approach is better while transmitting the message. For effective communication, sender and receiver must have a common background of experience, i.e., a common culture, common language so that they will be able to create messages that will be easily understood. Creativity is the main function of advertising messages. The message claims that the advertised product will satisfy consumer needs and wants. The facts and figures relating to the product are to be highlighted to assure them that they will be satisfied by using the advertised product.

Unfortunately, we do come across misleading advertisements. The rural consumer relying on the advertisement, purchases the product. He soon finds out that the product performance does not match the claims made by the marketers. This leads to adverse publicity through word-of-mouth communication.

Think Global and Act Local should be the focus of rural communication as well as other marketing activities. The rural markets and the consumers are scattered over a wide geographical areas. There are certain features like simple living, high personal relations, speaking through the heart, traditional lifestyle in tune with nature, family values, traditional belief, hard working nature, aspirations of rural youth, etc., which have to be considered for effective rural communication. The advertisement message should revolve around family, affection, love, success, welfare of the society. It should also focus on solving the problems of the villagers.

With regard to message form, we have spoken and written words, picture and music. A picture communicates a message very easily. Spoken word is also an effective communication tool. Use of local phrases, idioms will strengthen the message. The message should be simple and easy to understand. Music contributes to effective communication. An audio visual is an effective advertising medium.

Examples:

(a) Tata Motors introduced sturdy four-wheeler commercial vehicle — ACE in semi-urban and rural market. Roadshows were conducted in selected villages. ACE was called "Baby Elephant" compared to Tata Truck that represents "Mother Elephant".

(b) Vim Khar Khar Challenge TV commercial features ladies struggling to scrub and clean utensils making a rough noise (*Khar khar* in Hindi language denotes noise) with an ordinary washing bar and Vim bar is shown as a solution to the problem.

(c) TV advertisement "Thanda Matlab Coca-Cola" continues to be a big hit in rural areas.

(d) Mera Gaon, Mera Desh, Mera Mahindra (My Village, My Country and My Mahindra)

(e) Keedon Ka Maha-Kaal, Phasal Ka Pehredaar (Great enemy of insects and great protector of crops) – Syngenta Karate Insecticide.

The promotion media and methods could be broadly classified into formal and informal/ rural specific media. The effectiveness of different media and methods depend upon the products, profile of the consumer and market environment. Studies conducted have shown that mass media such as TV, radio, printed materials are very useful in creating awareness and interest, whereas product demonstrations, farm-to-farm visit and opinion leaders would stimulate action among consumers.

FORMAL MEDIA

It includes press, print, TV, cinema, radio, point of purchase and outdoor advertisement. Reach of mass media is low in rural households as shown in Table in 10.1.

Table 10.1: Media Reach in Rural Households

All India	Press (per cent)	TV (per cent)	Satellite (per cent)	Radio (per cent)	Cinema (per cent)	Internet (per cent)
All India	38	57	40	20	9	2
Urban	57	82	69	23	16	6
Rural	14	47	31	18	6	1

Source: Indian Readership Survey (2010).

There are wide variations with regard to reach of Mass Media in villages.

Example: TV reach is high (55 per cent) in larger villages having + 5,000 population compared to small villages with less than 1,000 population (TV reach 35 per cent).

1. Newspapers and Magazines: Press reach is low in rural areas and varies from 6 per cent (Assam) to 65 per cent (Kerala). English newspapers and magazines have negligible circulation in rural areas. However, local language newspapers and magazines are becoming popular among educated families.

Examples: Newspapers such as Eenadu (AP), Dina Thanthi (Tamil Nadu), Punjab Kesari (North), Loksatta (Maharashtra), Rajasthan Patrica, Anand Bazaar Patrica (West Bengal), Dainik Baskar, Dainik Jagron (North), and Magazines like Grihashoba, Anandalok, Taranga, Vanitha, Kumudam, Annadata, Chitralekha are popular in rural areas.

2. Television has made a great impact and large audience has been exposed to this medium. However, rural reach differs from state-to-state, i.e., Rajasthan: 14 per cent, Bihar: 17 per cent, Maharashtra: 45 per cent, Punjab: 48 per cent, Tamil Nadu: 54 per cent and Kerala: 63 per cent. Regional TV channels have become very popular especially in rural areas as shown in Table 10.2.

Examples: Sun TV (Tamil Nadu), Asianet (Kerala), Eenadu (AP), Alpha Punjabi (North), and Alpha Mararthi (Maharashtra). Dabur promotes Vatika brand of shampoo through local TV channels such as Alpha Marathi and Surya TV. Satellite television is becoming popular with rural consumers and the reach is low in Bihar and Uttar Pradesh, (1 per cent each) and high in Andhra Pradesh (15 per cent). The advertisement rates on regional channel are about one-tenth the rates on a Hindi channel. Their total share of the total TV advertising revenues is 25 per cent compared with their viewership share of 37 per cent.

Table 10.2: Key Regional Television Advertisement Market Size

State	Market Size (in Crore)	Key Players
Tamil	1,000	Sun TV, Raj TV, Vijaya TV, Jaya TV, Kalaignar TV
Telugu	700	Gemini TV, Eenadu, Maa Telegu, Zee Telegu
Malayalam	500	Asianet, Surya TV
Kannada	500	Udaya, ETV Kannada, Zee Kannada
Bengalli	700	Zee Bangla, ETV Bangla, Star Jaisa, Aakash Bangla
Marathi	350	Zee Marathi, ETV Marathi, Mi Marathi

Source: Industry estimate (2012).

3. Radio: Radio is a cost-effective medium to reach rural people. It has advantages and the message can be prepared in local languages. Illiterate people can understand and it can be carried to the fields. However, the progress has been slow due to restrictive policies of the Government. Now that private operators have been given licences, radio, as a medium is bound to become more popular with rural audience. Radio reach is the highest in Kerala (62 per cent) followed by Tamil Nadu (40 per cent) and Karnataka (35 per cent). Radio reaches large population in rural areas at a relatively low cost.

Example: Colgate, Jyoti Labs, Zandu Balm, Zuari Industries are some of the companies using radio communication programme.

There are specific programmes for farmers like Farm and Home/Krishi Darshan in regional languages. The farmers have a habit of listening to Regional news/Agricultural news in the morning and late evening. The advertisement has to be released during this time to get maximum coverage in rural areas. Another advantage is that the radio commercial can be prepared at short notice to meet the changing needs of the rural market.

Example: *Aya Naya Ujjala, Char Boondan Wala* (Here comes Ujjala, only four drops are required). A ten seconds spot in a regional station would cost only about ₹ 5,000.

All-India Radio has a network of 215 broadcasting centres with 144 medium frequency, 54 high frequency and 139 FM Transmitters. Social responsibility and public service broadcasting continue to be the hallmark of AIR. The share of Indian Radio in the ₹ 12,000 crore advertising market is around 3 per cent. In March 2000, the Government invited private sector into FM radio broadcasting by opening up frequencies in the FM Band. The share of Radio will jump to about 8 per cent once the 300 plus commercial FM stations start operating. Some of the private companies involved in FM broadcasting are: 1. Reliance Adlabs, 2. Dainik Bhaskar Group, 3. Zee, 4. The Times of India Group, 5. The India Today Group.

The Government is taking up e-auction of phase 111 of FM Radio that envisages setting up 840 FM Radio channels. The plan is provide all cities with a population of more than one lakh with private radio services. The project will generate an additional revenue of ₹ 1,500 crore.

4. Cinema attracts large audience especially in rural areas. In cities, its popularity has come down due to TV and VCD players. Film viewing habit is high in southern states and the reach of this media is highest in Andhra Pradesh (43 per cent) closely followed by Tamil Nadu (41 per cent), Karnataka (40 per cent) and Kerala (31 per cent). About 65 per cent of the earnings from cinema are from rural markets. Village theatres do roaring business during festivals by having four shows per day. The monthly charge for showing an ad film is about ₹ 600. Local distributor or dealer who has good contacts with cinema houses in villages can easily monitor this activity.

Examples:

(a) Films on products like Vicks, Lifebuoy, Colgate and Shampoos are shown in rural cinema halls. Apart from films, Ad slides can also be screened in village theatres.

(b) LIC and Private sector insurance companies have been showing short movies in rural theatres to create awareness about life insurance.

"A Cinema Theatre"

5. Outdoor Advertisements: This form of media which includes signboards, hoardings, bus boards, dealer boards, product display boards, etc., are cost-effective in rural areas. Symbols, pictures and colours should be used in outdoor advertisements so that the consumers can easily identify the products. Generally, rural people prefer bright colours and the marketer should utilise such cues.

"A Hoarding for Pesticide"

6. Point of Purchase: Display of hangings, festoons and product packs in the shops will catch the attention of prospective buyers. However, a clutter of such POP materials of competing companies will not have the desired effect and is to be avoided.

Examples:

(a) Tata Salt highlights features such as high purity, iodised and vacuum evaporation through POPs.

(b) HUL has been promoting lifebuoy soap at the point of consumption by putting stickers, posters, tin boards on the walls of wells, tanks and trees near rivers.

7. Direct Mail Advertising: It is a way of passing on information relating to goods or services for sale, directly to potential customers through the medium of post. It is a medium employed by the advertiser to bring in a personal touch. In cities, lot of junk mail is received by all of us and very often such mails are thrown into the dustbin, whereas a villager gets very few letters and he is receptive to such mailers. Some of the important points to be remembered while preparing a direct mail are:

- The mailing list is to be updated at least on a year-to-year basis.
- The name of the recipient together with the father's name has to be included in the address.
- The message should be in regional language and should contain pictures and local phrases. Word-by-word translations of English write-up may not convey the exact message.
- It is preferable to mention the address of the local dealers/distributors to increase their involvement in the business.
- The mailing is to be timely.
- The company representative/local dealer could meet the recipient of such letters at random to gauge the response for such circulars.

Examples:

(a) Direct mailers on consumer durables to be sent during the harvesting season so that the farmers will have money for purchasing the same.

(b) Mailers for seeds and pesticides to be sent as per agricultural season.

8. Wall Painting is an effective and economical medium for communication in rural areas, since it stays there for a long time depending upon the weather conditions. The cost of painting one square foot area is about ₹ 45. Retailers welcome painting of their shops so that the shop will look better. Walls of farm houses, shops and schools are ideal places for painting and the company need not have to pay any rent for the same. The walls have to be painted at least one or two feet from ground level. It is better to take permission of the owner. Very often, the owner takes responsibility for taking care of the wall painting. Painting to be avoided during election time and rainy season.

"A Bus Shelter Painting"

The matter should be in the form of pictures, slogans for catching the attention of people. A wall painting of 100 square feet is quite adequate to convey the message about a product or service. The local distributor/dealer who knows the market and people could be involved in selection of spots and for arranging wall painting.

Examples:

(a) Companies marketing TV, fans, branded coffee/tea, soap, toothpaste, pesticides, fertilisers, etc., use wall painting as a promotion medium in rural areas.

(b) Insurance companies have also put up wall paintings in prosperous rural markets.

"A Farm House Painting"

9. Tree Boards are painted boards of about two square feet in dimension having the picture or name or slogan of the product painted on it. The cost of such a painted board is about ₹ 200. These boards are fixed to the trees on both sides of the village road at a height of about 10 feet from ground level. These boards attract the attention of slow moving vehicles like cycles, bullock carts and tractors and people walking on the roads. Considering the poor condition of roads, even the buses move at slow speed through village roads. Tree boards are low-priced promotion items and can be used for consumer goods like tea, soap, toothpowder and toothpaste.

"A Tree Board"

10. Information and Communication Technology (ICT): Information and Communication Technology has been found to be an effective tool in rural communication and it is sure to speed up exchange of information in rural India in the coming years. A few examples are given below:

Fig. 10.3: ICT and Rural Communication

Initiatives	Remarks
1. Agricultural Technology Information Centre by Indian Council of Agricultural Research, New Delhi	Call Centres, Researchers and farmers linkages on cultivation practices, technological developments and use of inputs.
2. Accessing Rural India by Govt. of India, IIT Chennai, MIT and Harvard University	Internet kiosk, wireless local loop for access caste, birth and death certificate, voice mail, e-mail service, etc.
3. Inforthela by IIT, Kanpur, BSNL, Kanpur	IT kiosk, internet for information on education, health and weather conditions.
4. Digital Smart cards by Chatrapathi Shahu Cooperative Sugar Factory, Kagal in Kolhapur	Smart cards-details on shares, deposits, sugarcane weighing, billing, etc.
5. e-Choupal by ITC	e-Choupal for market price, weather and cultivation practices.
6. I-Kisan Portal by Nagarjuna Group (Andhra Pradesh)	Portal in regional languages on agricultural practices, plant protection, weather and animal husbandry.
7. Apollo Telemedicine by Apollo Hospitals	Telemedicine software, videoconferencing for doctors opinion and interpretation and patient data.
8. Village Knowledge Centre by MS Swami Nathan Foundation, Chennai	Knowledge centre for agricultural practices, Govt. schemes on agriculture, weather conditions, etc.
9. Jal Chitra by Ajit Foundation	Jal Chitra software for water mapping, water quality testing, water source, etc.
10. Vogram by Indian Institute of Science, Bangalore	Voice telegram for illiterate masses.

Source: Dhanraj A Patil (2012) Communication for Rural Development in India, Serial Publications, New Delhi.

Online and Mobile Advertising: Online advertising market was estimated at ₹ 1,000 crore in 2010. Due to low internet penetration, there is some reluctance by companies to spend on online medium. However in the coming years the market is expected to grow. It can be customised to target rural audience. Similarly, Indian mobile advertising market is estimated at ₹ 400 crore in 2010. Companies like Nokia have already entered the market by providing information on weather conditions, output prices, etc., to the farmers.

INFORMAL/RURAL SPECIFIC MEDIA

The rural consumer participates in local fairs, melas, haats, social gatherings such as card sessions, etc. The need for unconventional media arises as the mass media is too glamorous, and impersonal for a rural consumer. The traditional media with its powerful input and personalised communication has an effective reach in rural areas. We are the biggest users of traditional media and development programmes. While formal media develop awareness and interest among consumers, rural-specific media and methods such as demonstrations, farm-to-farm visits could persuade the consumers to buy the product.

1. Farm-to-Farm/House-to-House Visit: Rural people prefer face-to-face communication and farm visits facilitate two-way communication. The advantage is that the salesperson can understand the needs and wants of the rural customer by directly discussing with him and answer his queries on products and services. Potential customers in the village are identified and the company's representative/distributor's representative makes farm-to-farm visits and highlight the benefits of the products. The person carries with him literature in local language and also samples of products. The person does not sell the product but only promotes the use of the product. Very often, the local dealer also joins the representative in making farm-to-farm visits. The dealer clarifies the terms and conditions of sale and also makes independent follow-up visits for securing orders.

"A Farm House"

Examples:

(a) Many LIC agents and companies dealing with high value consumer durables have tried this approach with success in rich rural areas.

(b) ACC representatives/retailers make house-to-house visit and give information about product stability.

(c) This approach has been found to be very effective for agricultural machinery, animal health products and agricultural inputs.

2. Group Meeting of rural consumers is an important part of interpersonal media. The company is able to pass on the message regarding benefits of the products to a large number of consumers through such meetings. The salesperson should focus on the following for successful conductance of meetings:

- Potential village and the group of consumers to be identified.
- The date, time and place of meeting to be informed to the farmers.
- The salesperson should have good knowledge of the products, needs and wants of the customers and also be fluent in the local language. He should explain in simple language using local idioms and proverbs.
- Question and answer session will make the programme very interactive.
- Early morning hours, i.e., before farmers leave for their farms or late evening hours, i.e., after they return from their farms are ideal for conducting meetings.
- The meeting could last about 2 hours and therefore, light refreshments could be served to ensure continuous attention of the participants.
- Local dealers and opinion leaders such as progressive farmers, panchayat president, school teachers, bank officials, Government officials, etc., should be invited for the meeting and could be requested to share their experience with the consumers.

"A Group Meeting of Rural Consumers"

- Posters, product packs to be displayed and handbills in local languages to be distributed after meeting to serve as a reminder.
- Film shows could be conducted during the meeting to reinforce the sales messages.
- Follow-up visits to be made to the same village to assess the impact of such meetings.

Examples:

(a) The bankers, once in a week visit a village, get the villagers in school hall or panachyat office and explain to the villagers the various financial facilities offered by the bank.

(b) Insurance companies have been conducting group meetings to promote life insurance among villagers.

(c) MRF conduct tractor owners meet in association with local distributors. They identify pockets having high number of tractors and send invitation to all tractor owners. The meeting is held in a common place and field activities such as film shows, demos, discussions, tractor maintenance, damages to tyres and identifying defect-free tyres are conducted by the company representatives.

(d) Group meeting of key customers are conducted by agricultural input and machinery companies in rural areas.

(e) TTK Prestige organises group meeting of women for popularising pressure cookers.

3. Opinion Leaders: Villagers place more emphasis on the opinion of others who have used a product/brand to make purchase decision. Such opinion leaders could be big landlords, bank official, panchayat president, teachers, extension workers, etc.

Examples:

(a) Asian Paints promoted its Utsav brand of paint by painting the Village Sarpanch's house a few months prior to the launch to demonstrate that the paint does not peel off and is an ideal replacement for Chuna.

(b) Mahindra Tractors use bankers as opinion leaders for their product.

(c) The health development assistant of HUL regularly meets school teachers to promote Lifebuoy soap in villages.

(d) ACC Limited, conduct field meetings with the group of masons and local building contractors to highlight the superiority of Suraksha Cement.

(e) Tata Motor Company has introduced the new referral programme known as "Motor Dada" which engages village people such as teachers, mechanics, village influencers. They are provided with a product manual and board "Motor Dada", which they can hang outside their homes. They recommend new and used vehicles purchases.

Painters Meet

Asian Paints have identified the dealers and painters as opinion leaders in a rural market. That's the reason why the company pays close attention to them. The company organises a meet where all the painters of the town are invited. The company outsources the responsibility of organising the event. A company is hired to make arrangements for booking the venue, hotel reservations, food and sending invitations. The painters are given information about the product, Utsav. Details are given by means of verbal explanations and distributed literature. The painters are informed about how to use the product and where to procure it. The event moves from town-to-town or may be held in a feeder town and painters from neighbouring villages are invited. This event is extremely important for the company as it helps strengthen the relationship with the painters and helps in promotion of Utsav.

4. Melas: Ours is a country of melas and it is estimated that over 20,000 melas are conducted every year. Melas are different types, i.e., commodity fairs, cattle fairs, religious fairs and exhibitions and may be held only for a day or may extend over a week. The number of visitors to melas is very high. The melas can be successfully used to give information about products among villagers and also to make spot sales. One of the significant points is that about 40 per cent of the stalls sell manufactured goods in Melas. ***Example:*** The month long Sonepur Mela (Bihar), Asia's largest cattle fair is held in the month of November and goats, horses, dogs, ponies, rabbits and even elephants are sold during the fair. The Mela has its origin in ancient times when Emperor Chandragupta Maurya used to buy horses and elephants from across Ganges. Some of the important Melas in our country are:

State	Melas
Bihar	Sonepur Mela, Vaisakh Purnima Mela, Budgaya
Gujarat	Navaratri Fair, Ambaji
UP	Nauchandi Mela, Meerut, Ramlila Mela, Varanasi
West Bengal	Gokulanda Mela in Midnapur
Himachal Pradesh	Minjar Fair, Chamba
Haryana	Kisan Mela, Karnal
Madhya Pradesh	Kartik Mela, Gwaliar Trade Fair
Odisha	Rathayatra, Puri
Punjab	Rural Olympics, Baisakhi
Rajasthan	Pushkar Mela
Karnataka	Mahadeswara Mela
Tamil Nadu	Deepam (Thiruvannamalai), Jallikkattu (Madurai), Tai Poosum (Palani)

Many marketers have come out with creative ideas for participating in such Melas.

Examples:

(a) Paint companies supporting Pola fair in Maharashtra by painting the horns of the bulls.

(b) Screening of popular films along with advertisements by pesticides companies during the Pongal festival.

(c) Companies sponsoring boat races in Alleppey.

"A Horse Dances at Pushkar Fair"

"A Company Stall in an Agricultural Fair"

A few points to be considered for participating in Melas are:

- Preparation of a list of Melas where the company wants to participate based on location, number of visitors, profile of visitors, product under promotion and prospects for the company's products.
- A large number of stalls sell snacks and the villagers spend time in these stalls. It is better to put the stall near these food stalls. The stall has to be properly decorated.

- Women and children are the prime customers for the fast-moving consumer goods and therefore product display and demonstrations would go a long way in keeping the attention of this group.
- It is better to keep generators since electric supply is very erratic in villages.
- Decorate the stall with posters, cutouts banners.
- The salesmen in the stalls have to be properly dressed and should be thoroughly trained to be courteous and answer queries about products and services.
- Lucky draws/surprise gifts/scratch cards can be organised to attract the people to the stall.
- Microphone publicity can be arranged in the surrounding villages that will serve as a reminder to the villagers.
- The local distributor who understand the rural psyche well and the company representative should play an active role for successful participation in Melas.

Haridwar Maha Kumbh Mela (2010)

Lakh of pilgrims head towards Haridwar for holy dip during Maha Kumbh. During this year, more than twenty-five companies promoted their products. Messages such as Kumbh snan aaj, dettol snan har roj, Baccho ka hath pakdo, Everest ka saat pakdo were put up on Welcome Gates.

"Dettol Promotion at Maha Kumbh"

Melas and Haats are closely linked to the lifestyle of rural population and can serve as an ideal platform for the creative marketer, not only to promote and sell the products but also understand the shared values, beliefs, and perceptions of rural customers that influence his buying behaviour.

"Temple Chariot Procession"

5. Haats: Traditionally, on certain days of the week, both the sellers and buyers meet in the village to buy and sell goods and services. These are the haats (Shandies, Hatwari, Chandies, Angadi, Peta) that are being held regularly in all rural areas. The haat is held in a commonplace in the village, has thatched/tiled sheds for the sellers to keep their goods in an open ground. A small amount is collected as rent from the sellers by the local agency. The sellers in haats are mobile. The sellers arrive in the morning in the haat and remain till late in the evening. Next day, they move to another haat. The reason being that in villages, the wages are paid on weekly basis and haat is conducted on the day when the villagers get their wages. In the haat, agricultural products, processed foods, garments, groceries, stationery and packed consumer goods are sold. Each haat caters to the needs of about 5-25 villages, Since large number of villagers visit the Haat, the local merchants also do good business on the days when haat is held in the village. It has been observed that many village retailers and mini-wholesalers buy goods from Haats. Another attraction is that about 80% of the sales in haat is on cash-and-carry basis.

Example: The haat in Pollachi (Sandai in Tamil) is very popular in Tamil Nadu and a large number of villagers as well as village merchants from the bordering Kerala state visit the haat for buying agricultural products as well as consumer goods.

"A Weekly Bazaar (Haat)"

For the marketer, the haat can be an ideal platform for advertising and selling products. Display of posters, dangers, banners, film shows and mike publicity could be carried out in the haats. Further, product display, demonstrations, sampling and actual counter sales are possible. By participating in haats and melas, the company can not only promote the products but also understand the shared values, beliefs and perceptions of rural customers that influence his buying behaviour.

About 40,000 haats are held in rural areas in our country. The highest number of haats is in UP, (10,000), followed by Bihar (5,000), West Bengal (4,000), Maharashtra (3,700), Odisha (3,500), and Assam (3,200), Southern states have less number of haats, i.e., Tamil Nadu (1,100), Karnataka (1,200), AP (500) and Kerala (650). It is not possible for any company to invest resources and participate in all the haats. Therefore, the marketer has to identify the haats based on total sales, type of products sold, distance from the nearest town; number of visitors to the haats and their wants and needs, probable sales expected for the company's products including cost and benefits and prepare an action plan. It is better to start with biggest haats in each territory. The involvement of company staff as well as the local distributor is crucial for successful implementation of the plan.

Examples:

1. Tata Steel has promoted GI Roofing sheet (Tata Shakti).
2. Parachute oil, Nirma washing powder and Tiger brand biscuits have been promoted through haats.

6. Rural Entertainment Programmes: There are a number of well-appreciated forms of entertainment available to the rural people.

Examples:

(a) Tamasha is an extremely lively form of folk theatre of Maharashtra.

(b) Dashavatar is a re-enactment of the ten incarnations of Vishnu and is popular in Konkan region of Maharashtra.

(c) Nautanki (named after the charming Rani Nautanki of Multan) is a North Indian folk drama performed on an open and bare stage.

(d) Puppetry has proved popular in different parts of the country.

(e) Keertana is a kind of drama in which a gifted actor performs a whole series of characters and moods.

(f) The folk dance "Kuravan Kurathi" is popular in Tamil Nadu. The troupe consists of dancers, drummers and musicians and they move in a well-decorated van from one village to another village singing and dancing. In a day, the troupe covers about 8-10 villages. As soon as the van reaches a village, film songs are played to attract the attention of the villages. This is followed by folk dances. Mike announcement is made about the company's products and leaflets are distributed. After the dance

"Folk Dance"

programme, queries, if any, about the products are answered by the salesperson. Folk dance programme costs about ₹ 5,000 per day and therefore these programmes are conducted during the peak season in selected villages.

(g) Jhadi Patti Ranghbhumi — the theatre of the jungle deals with social problems in Vidharba region of Maharashtra.

Examples:

(a) Companies like FACT, SPIC, Syngenta are using Kuravan Kurathi dance programme to promote fertilisers and pesticides.

(b) Folk dance programme known as **Thumsup chowfula** is based on the concept of Marathi folk dance — Lavni. The programme provides wholesome entertainment to the rural folk. Guest appearance of film stars helps to attract the crowd.

(c) Brook Bond/Lipton India Limited have started an All India Campaign to promote its Kadak Chhap tea through magic shows and skits. A local magician delivers the message under the garb of a skit. One of the boys plays the role of Nathoo who kills the evil guys after he had a strong cup of Kadak Chhap. At the end of the show, everybody is given a sample pack.

(d) Marico has used folk theatre groups to promote Parachute in rural areas in West Bengal.

LIC is Getting Street Smart

It has taken to the streets, literally, and is all set to speak the language of the masses of rural India through the street plays. It has been organising for the rural folk. **Street plays** with local people performing skits with overtones on the importance of insurance and the disadvantages of not being covered adequately will hit the right chord. But for a mammoth 44-year-old organisation as huge as LIC, it is even more easier to initiate brand recall and find takers for its products considering the brand equity it already enjoys — an asset be it in urban or rural India.

7 Audio-visual Publicity Van (AVP Van) Video Van: AVP Van is one of the effective tools for rural communication. The van is a mobile promotion station having facilities for screening films, slides and mike publicity. Portable exhibition kit can be carried in the van and an exhibition of the products could be put up as and when required. The van can also be used for product demonstrations, sampling and retail sales. Tata 407 or Bajaj Matador is used for AVP programme.

A few points to be considered for effective AVP unit operations are:

- Preparation of a route plan covering key villages/markets.
- Giving advance information regarding films shows in the selected villages.
- Involvement of local distributors/dealers in publicity campaign.
- Thorough training to the mechanic to take care of the instruments.
- Availability of generator in the van.
- Experienced salesperson who is fluent in the local language and can answer queries from the customers.

During day-time, the unit is used for mike publicity, pasting of posters and distribution of literature. In the evening, with the help of local dealer/distributor and opinion leaders, film shows are organised in two/three different villages. As per the plan, the van reaches the first village in the evening. A suitable place such as village ground, school, and panchayat hall is selected for the meeting as well as film screening. A few film songs are played to attract the attention of the villagers. The salesperson makes a brief talk about situation in the village, the products and the benefits. The ad film is screened along with some popular film shots and this continues for about 30 minutes. At the end of the film show, he distributes handbills and answers queries of the customers. The whole operation takes about 1-2 hours depending upon the products under promotion, number of participants in the meeting and time taken for question and answers. The van moves to the next village for the second film show. The company representative visits the villages at random meeting dealers and key consumers to

"An AVP Van"

know the impact of the AVP unit operation. The cost of running a fully equipped AVP Unit is about ₹ 3,000 per day and an AVP van operation has to be considered as an investment for business development in rural areas.

Examples:

(a) Nippo promotes batteries through specially designed vans called melavans. The vans are equipped with TV/VCR for showing product awareness films.

(b) Agricultural input companies regularly use AVP vans for promoting their products.

(c) Audio-visual units are used for promoting Exide batteries in rural areas.

(d) Colgate India makes extensive use of AVP units.

(e) ITC's Mobile Vans take the message of e-Choupal to new villages.

(f) Cavin Kare organises AV unit programmes by showing popular films interpersed with chilk commercials to develop awareness among villagers.

(g) Marico launched van campaigns to create awareness for Parachute Coconut Oil Pouches in villages with less than 20,000 population. The campaigns aimed at rural women and were conducted by women volunteers.

(h) The internet van launched by Google covers small towns highlighting internet services such as e-mail, networking maps, etc.

8. Syndicate Van: In this case, companies selling non-competitive products come together and operate AVP van to promote their products and the expenses are shared.

Example: A fertiliser company joins with pesticides company to run AVP van in rural areas.

9. Product Display Contest: Package is an integral part of the product. Its main purpose is to protect the product during transit, to preserve the quality and to avoid any loss in quality and quantity. Nowadays, companies are making lot of efforts to produce good quality packages as the package is the face of the brand and carry advertising value. The product pack should have more visuals and colour scheme to attract the attention and create a lasting impression in the mind of the people. Regional language plays a major role in communication.

"Display of Products in a Village Shop"

The objectives of Product Display Contest are:

- Create awareness among consumers.
- To remind the customer to buy the product as soon as he enters the shop.
- Influence the dealer to stock the product and support the company in increasing sales.
- Develop relations with dealers.

The display contest has to be announced well in advance and promotional materials to be distributed to all the selected dealers in a geographical area. Prizes for best displays are announced to motivate the dealers and the contest lasts for about a month. Dealer incentives based on the counter sales of the products to be announced to increase sales. A well-planned product display contest not only increases the involvement of dealers in the company's products but also increases the sales during the contest period. Product display contests could be organised successfully in prosperous rural markets for promoting consumer goods such as shampoos, soaps, toothpaste and paints.

Asian Paints Display Contest
The company selects 3-4 towns where a display contest is announced. About 20-30 dealers take part in this contest. The dealer has to set up display stands for Asian Paints featuring its products. The dealers are given a target of improving sales by 100 per cent. The contest is a month long and the dealers are judged on innovation, POPs (point on purchase), creativity, etc. The first round is judged by the area manager, second by the group brand manager and so on. 6-8 dealers are awarded for the display stands. The prizes range from 29 inch colour TVs to scooters. These contests generate enthusiasm in the dealers and help generate a lot on the spot sales as consumers get attracted to the displays and get enticed into trying the product.

10. Product Demonstration is based on the extension principle *"Seeing is believing"* and is one of the most effective methods to show the superiority of the company's products to the customers. A progressive villager who is an opinion leader is selected and the demonstration is conducted in his field/house/or common place in the presence of a group of consumers in the village. The consumers observe the results and the local dealer persuades them to buy the particular brand or the product.

Examples:

(a) Hawkins Pressure Cooker have demonstration representatives who carry-out demos in rural households. The representatives receives 1per cent commission for every customer who approaches the dealer via demonstrations.

(b) Effectiveness of detergents, vacuum cleaners, and shampoos could be shown by demonstrations in selected markets.

(c) Asiant Paints conduct demonstrations with Utsav Acrylic distemper to prove the durability over competitive brands.

(d) The field team of HUL organises Germ-glow demonstration among school children to highlight the need for washing hands with soap (lifebuoy) to eradicate germs since visual clean is not safe clean.

(e) Demonstrating the use of tractor/implements for different agricultural operations.

(f) Application of urea fertiliser in paddy fields to show the luxurious growth of the crop.

(g) Spraying a particular brand of an insecticide against insect pests and showing the farmer how effectively the insects are controlled.

(h) MRF, manufactures of tyres, focused on educating the farmers about the advantage of using Nylon tyres for bullock carts. They conducted what is known Nylon Cord breaking Contest with Pahalwans. The bullock cart tyres became the brand leader in this segment within three years of the launch of the campaign.

11. Information Centres: They provide latest information, products, services and availability of loan facilities. The companies sponsor such centres. Many consumer goods companies have opened showrooms in prosperous rural areas.

Examples:

(a) Hero Honda has opened Extension Counters with showroom facilities in major rural markets.

(b) Bank of Maharashtra has initiated field information, centres manned by agricultural field officers. The vans loaded with touch screen computers provides information on good agricultural practices and also details about crop loan, kisan credit card and other schemes to farmers in Maharashtra.

(c) Agri-input companies operate Kisan Seva Kendras in villages.

(d) The farmers bring sugarcane in their tractors and they have to wait for a long time in the queue for delivering the sugarcane to the factory. Taking advantage of the situation, Hero Honda dealers put up stalls near sugar mills during harvesting season in UP.

12. Village Meeting Places: There are meeting places such as temple premises, banyan trees where people assemble for social interaction. The marketers can use this opportunity to interact with the villagers and: (a) understand the needs and wants of rural consumers, (b) pass on the message about products and services, and (c) obtain feedback.

"A Meeting Place in a Village"

13. Tom-tom: is the traditional way of spreading formation through a communicator or messenger. It involves beating the Tom-tom at village meeting points and making announcements about collection of land revenue, visit of Government officials, public tender etc. Messages about birth and marriages are also conveyed through Tom-tom.

14. Lifestyle Marketing: Lifestyle reflects as to how a person lives and spends time and money. Lifestyle can be determined by the product a person consumes, his activities (shopping, hobbies), interests (food, recreation, fashion) and opinion about business, society and the Government. Each rural market segment has certain special features, i.e., they share common lifestyle traits. They include village sports, religious events, prominent personalities and role models.

"Buffalo Fight"

Example: Over 100 rural sports festivals are held in Punjab every year. During such festivals, exhibitions on the latest farm practices, agricultural implements, handicrafts, and other things are organised. Bullock cart races, camel races, races of horses are some of the attractions of the rural sports festivals in Punjab.

Lifestyle Marketing

The Annual Rural Olympics held in Grewal stadium in Killa Raipur, a prosperous village near Ludhiana attracts around 4,500 participants and five lakh spectators. The majority of the participants came from Punjab, apart from the Punjabis living in Canada, USA and UK. Athletics, volleyball, kabbadi, wrestling, gymnastics, dog race, tug-of-war are some of the main disciplines in the three days event. The bullock cart race and Nihang warrior astride two speeding horses are the most popular events. Rural Olympics is a solid event and enjoys mass support and companies like Parle, Ambuja Cement, Idea Cellular, Zusuki have been promoting the Killa Raipur Games.

The company can initiate certain activities like supporting melas and local festivals, village sports, community garden maintenance, scholarship, yield contest, health care programmes, village adoption, etc., that gel with the pattern of life in villages. Through these activities, the company can create long-term relationship with the rural consumers for mutual benefits.

Examples:

(a) Mineral water companies supplying clean drinking water during summer festivals in villages.

(b) Consumer goods companies sponsoring Kabbadi.

(c) Agri-business Companies sponsoring film shows during village festivals.

Media Innovation

Taking Tips from Ramayana

Bihar has a very low mass media reach. Local player Maxo dominated the mosquito repellent market with 51.3 per cent share, whereas Mortein, the No. 1 national brand had only 28 per cent share. Mortein had to outwit Maxo by connecting with the consumer using what would attract the locals. The route was to break traditional media formats in the most traditional part of people's lives — The Sonepur Mela. In a market dominated by low-priced, unorganised local players, Mortein strategically chose its higher end "10 hours" variant to demonstrate its powerful protection platform.

Sonepur Fair is the largest cattle fair in Asia. More than 1 million people visit the mela every year. The month long fair also coincides with Dassara. The company chose an adaptation of the great Indian epic — Ramayana, which is enacted at the Dassara Fair. Ramayana is a classic story of the victory of good (Lord Rama) over evil (Ravana). This fitted in well with the brand platform of the Strength of Mortein (the savior) over Mosquitoes (the evil).

What they did?: A 50 feet high effigy of Louie (the king of pests) was created. For the entire month, a huge publicity was given in the form of a 'Rath yatra' (chariot procession) taken through the mela. On the D-day (Dassara), Mortein hexagonal coil (the protector against the menace of pests) shot lasers to burn down the effigy of Louie, in the same way that the effigy of Ravana is burnt by the arrows of Rama in Ramayana. This year, in place of the traditional Ravana, Louis the mosquito was the cynosure of all eyes.

An emotional chord was established through the use of an epic legend with more than 1 million people who visited the fair. The support media of radio, posters, cinema and rath yatra kept the momentum going, paving the way for the grand finale of the burning of the Louie Ravan effigy. The value share of Mortein 10-hour coil in Bihar showed a huge jump post the activity. The usage of this innovative targeted medium ensured a growth of 49 per cent, moving its share from 28 per cent in September 2005 to an average of 46 per cent during December 2005 to March 2006. The halo effect also resulted in 8 per cent increase in share value of other Mortein variants.

Source: *DNA* June 6, 2006.

CONCLUSION

Rural markets have special features as compared to urban markets. Considering the uniqueness of rural consumers and infrastructure facilities, the marketer has to design rural-specific promotion media and methods to reach the rural population. Further, companies have to consider promotion expenses as investment for business development in rural areas.

QUESTIONS

1. What are the constraints in rural marketing communication?
2. Explain briefly the rural-specific communication media and methods that can be used in the case of life insurance, two-wheelers and shampoos in rural market.
3. Discuss the importance of Haats, Melas, Mandis in rural distribution and promotion.

✿ ✿ ✿

11 DEVELOPING THE SALES FORCE FOR RURAL MARKET

INTRODUCTION

Every organisation has people who are entrusted with the responsibility of dealing with prospects and customers for selling their products or services. These people form the sales force in an organisation. Salespersons are the backbone of the organisation and success of the organisation depends upon how effectively they are able to sell goods and services to meet the changing needs of the customers. The salesperson has to educate the customers on products and services, sell the same with benefit to the customer and profit to the seller. In many cases, he has to even create the need for the product and services. ***Example:*** Life Insurance. Therefore, the rural salesperson is not merely an order taker, he is the "carrier" of developmental messages to the less informed rural population.

THE JOB OF A RURAL SALESPERSON

1. Increase Sales: Rural markets are highly heterogeneous and therefore depending upon the products and services offered by the company, he has to identify the most potential area and call on progressive consumers, village retailers/merchants and opinion leaders.

It has been observed that a rural consumer buys from the same shop. The retailer extends credit facilities to consumers and many have running credit account with the same retailer. He is the carrier of messages about new products and services. In short, he is the connecting link between the consumer and the company.

In making a purchase decision, rural consumers are influenced by the opinion of other persons in the village. The opinion leader may be a teacher, bank manager, leading farmer, gramsevak or panchayat president. Based on their opinion, the consumer takes a decision regarding purchase of the product or service.

During the active season, he has to organise campaigns with special emphasis on group meeting of villagers, film shows and make publicity. He has to identify the most important Melas and Haats in his territory and promote the products in rural areas. Building a good rapport with distributors and retailers and motivating them would enable him to improve trade sales. Further, he has to train the distributors promotion staff or sales assistants on product knowledge and basic selling skills.

"A Farm House Meeting in Progress"

2. Managing Credit: A sale is completed only when the money is collected and therefore the salesperson should not resort to dumping of stocks with dealers and distributors to achieve the sales targets and ensure that stocking of goods is proportional to the expected sales. This will enable him to collect the dues as per company's credit policy.

3. Effective Use of Resources: The salesperson has to prepare tour programme considering sales targets, product under promotion and inventory at dealer and distributor level. He should be able to present product promotion schemes to the distribution chain in an effective way. Sales promotion materials such as posters, leaflets and samples have to be used judiciously.

4. Developing the Market for Future: The salesperson has to keep in touch with changes in the marketplace — climatic conditions, cropping pattern, competition, Government policy, local practices, etc. He has to increase the use of the products in new geographical area. Identification of new markets, developing distribution system including a network of dealers and undertaking demand generation activities are essential for developing market for future.

5. Company's Image: A salesperson is the link between the customer and company. The business is highly seasonal and transactions are based on trust with the salesperson and the company. Village merchants very often make payment by cash and therefore salesperson should possess unquestionable integrity while dealing with rural customers. He should avoid discussing controversial issues connected with caste, religion and politics. He has to create a positive impression with customers by his conduct in personal and professional life.

6. Self-development: Many salespeople feel that they have no time for reading, as they are preoccupied with sales and collections in the field. These days lot of development is taking place and progressive consumers would like to know the developments in products and services. They respect the salesperson who can disseminate such information. Selling has become a specialised function and one has to seek knowledge in all relevant subjects and apply the same day-to-day work. This is possible by developing regular reading habits to improve technical knowledge, managerial and selling skills. He has to improve skills on communication, public speaking and presentations.

The management has to take a decision on the following aspects of sales force management.

OBJECTIVE OF THE SALES FORCE

In many consumer goods companies, the salesperson calls on village merchants, wholesalers and distributors and obtains orders by high pressure selling techniques, slick presentation and on the spot order booking. Such order booking activities require good commercial acumen and persuasive power on the part of the salesperson.

Example: Selling of soaps, biscuits, toothpowder, etc. In Agri-business companies, the salesperson tries to understand the field problems of the farmers and offer solutions. Further, the salesperson concentrates on field activities such as group meeting of villagers, farm-to-farm visit, demonstrations and film shows and the demand generated is serviced through a network of dealers in the market.

The ideal would be to strike a balance between demand generation and bazaar selling, since both activities are essential for establishing the products.

SELECTION

The job of a rural salesperson involves creative selling and therefore he should have sound technical and commercial knowledge to provide solutions to customer's problems. Most rural customers say that they want the salesperson to be honest, reliable, helpful and knowledgeable. The company should look for the following while selecting candidates:

1. Educational Background: As regards salesperson dealing with consumer goods, he should have a basic degree with additional qualifications in management/marketing and good commercial acumen and persuasive power. For positions in sales and marketing of agricultural inputs like seeds, fertilisers and pesticides, a degree in agriculture preferably with postgraduate qualifications in management is preferred by the companies, since the job involves offering solutions to the problems faced by farmers in increasing yields.

2. Fluency in Local Languages: In our country, as many as 18 major languages are spoken. The rural consumer is not at all fluent in English and therefore depending upon the place of posting, the person should be able to speak in the local language.

Example: In Western and Northern parts of India, proficiency in the local languages (Marathi, Gujarati, Punjabi) or at least Hindi is essential for working in rural markets. Similarly, knowledge of Tamil is essential for working in Tamil Nadu, as majority of the people do not speak Hindi in the state.

3. Knowledge of the Market, Products and Competition: He should have thorough knowledge of his products and competition. With his superior knowledge, he can answer the queries of the customers and convince them to buy or use the product.

Examples:

(a) The television salesman should possess sufficient knowledge of the different brands/ models of televisions and necessary selling skills to convince the buyer to go in for a particular model of television.

(b) A fertiliser salesperson should have sufficient knowledge on modern cultivation practices of crops, so that he can guide the farmer in increasing yields of crops by using fertilisers.

4. Basic Knowledge in Agriculture: Agriculture and agriculture-related activities are the main source of income to people in villages. Irrigated areas are more prosperous than rainfed areas. Farmers cultivating cash crops such as chillies, fruits and vegetables have higher income than farmers growing jowar and maize. Farmers make purchases after the harvest of crops. The demand for goods and services is seasonal in nature. Diwali, Pongal, Onam, Dassara, Idd and X-mas are the festivals for buying household articles. Therefore, a rural salesperson should have a general knowledge about the dynamics of agriculture so that he can implement appropriate marketing strategies to meet the needs of the market.

5. Knowledge of Cultural Factors: Culture is a system of shared values, beliefs and perceptions that influence the behaviour of consumers. There are different groups based on religion, caste, occupation, income, age, education and politics and each group exerts influence on the behaviour of people in the villages. The rural salesperson should have good understanding of rural buyer behaviour and the dynamics of rural markets.

- Life in rural areas is still governed by customs and traditions and people do not easily adapt new practices.

  Example: Even rich and educated classes of farmers do not wear jeans or branded shoes in most of the rural areas.

- Rural buyers look for value for money while purchasing products and don't make impulse purchases. They look for quality but cannot afford high prices. They are concerned with utility of the products rather than mere good looks and frills.

  Examples:

  (a) Bullet motor cycle is still preferred in rural markets due its ruggedness.

  (b) HMT watches are seen on many a wrists for its utility value.

- With regard to consumer goods, it has been observed that husband dominates the decision making in rural areas, while wife is the decision maker in urban environment.
- Studies by market research agencies have revealed that rural consumers are price-sensitive. Once he is persuaded to buy a particular brand and he is satisfied with

the brand, he remains as a loyal customer and continue to use the brand. The brand name spreads in the local community by word-of-mouth. Apart from established brands such as Lifebuoy, Lux soap, Colgate, Lipton tea, Scissors cigarettes, Bullet motor cycles, many of the recent brands have also established in rural markets. These brands include Nirma, Rasna, Velvettee shampoo, Paan Parag, and Parachute.

- Greeting visitors with folded hands, abstaining from smoking in front of elders in the villages, removing footwear while entering the houses, respecting women irrespective of their social status, sitting on the floor along with villagers during village meetings are normal courtesies expected in village life. The sales executive should learn to say *Namaskar, Namaste, Ram Ram, Vanakkam* while meeting customers so that he can easily build up rapport with them.

It is desirable that the salespersons especially those who have been brought up in cities are given a thorough training consisting of both theory and practical aspects of village life so that they can align themselves with the market realities and settle down smoothly in their jobs.

6. Knowledge of Different Types of Customers: The approach of a salesperson will depend upon the type of customer he is meeting. There are friendly, talkative, silent, argumentative and suspicious customers. A typical rural customer has lot of free time for making purchases. A salesperson should have tremendous patience while dealing with such customers. He should answer all the queries and convince him about the benefit of the products.

7. Sales Personality: Traits such as honesty, reliability, self-confidence, high level of energy, empathy will make a positive impression with customers.

8. Selling Skills: It is not enough a person has good technical and product knowledge. He should be able to understand the needs and wants of the customer and highlight those specific benefits that will appeal to the customer. He has to demonstrate the product so that the customer is convinced that he has the best choice. He should answer the queries of the customers and book an order or obtain commitment for buying or using at a later date.

9. Capacity to Work Extended Hours: Rural markets are highly scattered and spread over wide geographical area. The salesperson has to undertake long journeys moving from one market to another market and meeting various categories of customers. During the season, many shops are kept opened till late in the night and the person has to spend long hours in the market to generate business for the company.

10. Ability to Put up with Inadequate Boarding and Lodging Facilities: The salesperson has to stay in small hotels and has to put up with problems like salt water, mosquitoes in the rooms, dirty linen, unclean toilets and rooms.

11. Experience: There is a belief among rural people that experience is more important than formal education and they respect salesperson who can offer practical solutions to their problems.

12. Matching Men and Markets: Another important point is that the market requirements and capabilities of the candidate should match. Normally, experienced persons are posted to competitive markets with high sales turnover and fresh people to markets with lower turnover. It is evident that rural marketing requires a dedicated mindset which many management graduates brought up in cities do not possess. Recruiting from rural institutes or from second level institutes in smaller towns could be considered by corporates. With proper training and career prospects, these recruits would certainly contribute to the growth and development of the organisation.

TRAINING

Sales training consists of planned programmes undertaken to develop knowledge, skills, attitudes, and social behaviour so that the performance of sales force and organisation improves considerably. A few of the important sales training programmes conducted in the organisations are given below:

1. Induction Programme: After the selection of the salesperson, the next important function is their induction or orientation. The key objectives here are familiarising the sales force with the internal and external environment of the company. History of the company, organisational structure, nature of the business, policies and procedures, product range, technical and selling skills are covered in the programme. In order to get an overall picture of the functioning of the organisation, heads of departments such as sales, marketing, finance, IT, HR, materials make presentation about departmental activities to the participants. Apart from classroom teaching, the persons also visit the manufacturing unit to understand and appreciate the good manufacturing and quality assurance practices followed in the factory.

The duration of the programme depends upon the nature of business, product range, competition and experience of the candidates and lasts for about five days. During induction programme, special emphasis is laid on learning rural buyer behaviour, product profile, buying benefits and product detailing by role-plays.

2. Role-plays allow participants to learn and strengthen their selling skills by calling on different types of customers and testing the responses in the classroom atmosphere.

For each role-play, background scenario, salesperson and customer briefs are prepared and detailed guidance is given to all participants. One of the participants plays the role of a salesman and other that of a rural customer. The salesperson has to sell a product or service or obtain a commitment from the customer by making use of product knowledge and selling skills. Other trainees in the group serve as observers. The trainer observes the sales interview and give instant feedback to the salesperson and the customer. In the subsequent interview, the roles are changed and each person gets the opportunity to play the role of a salesperson and customer. The participants learn by each other's experience. Role-plays are extensively used during induction and refresher programmes in pharma, consumer durable and agricultural input companies.

3. Workshop on Territory Management: A salesperson is the manager of the assigned territory and he has to increase sales volumes, profits and market share. He has to effectively manage the resources such as promotional materials, product promotion schemes and distribution network. He has to identify the most important customers, make regular calls, generate demand for the range of products and service the demand through a network of dealers.

The subjects covered are identification and classification of consumers, dealers and influencers, tour programme and routing, making effective sales calls, conducting effective meeting of villagers, visit to dealers and distributors, running campaigns, market segmentation, market intelligence and maintenance of records and reporting. The programme runs for 3-4 days and the output will be a territory file containing all relevant information and sales plan for the territory.

4. Selling Skills Course: The programme on selling skills is normally conducted for three days and deals with buying motives, preparing for a sales call, different stages of sales interview, product detailing, overcoming objections and methods of closing of sales. Role-plays, practical sessions on product detailing, assignments, etc., make the programme very informative and interesting to the participants.

5. On-the-Job Coaching: In this method, the superior travels with the salesperson in the marketplace and meets different types of customers. He closely observes the sales interviews and gives feedback after every sales call. He answers the tough questions from the customers and guides the salesperson in making effective sales call. During infield working, other aspects of the job such as identification of important customers, tour programme, frequency of calls, progress of sales and collections, etc., are also discussed. Theoretical knowledge of selling skills is of little use unless an individual can apply them in a live sales situation and on-the-job coaching is an effective method of training sales force.

6. Apart from the above, training programmes on Time Management, Presentation and Group communication skills are also conducted by many organisations for the benefit of the sales force.

SUPERVISION

One of the important responsibilities of a manager is to supervise the activities of his salesperson who operates in isolation, facing day-to-day challenges. The manager should focus on-the-job coaching by undertaking joint tours, meeting key customers in rural markets and solve the problems faced by the salesperson. The manager has to play the role of boss, friend and guide and develop the salesperson to become a high performer in the organisation.

COMPENSATION

The compensation plan should provide for a regular and steady income to the salesperson and also provide adequate incentive to increase sales volume and achieve sales targets. The objective should be to attract, retain and develop sales force in an organisation. Therefore, apart from monthly salary, there should be handsome sales incentives for achieving sales volumes of products together with timely collection of outstanding.

PERFORMANCE EVALUATION

Performance of the salesperson is assessed by comparing achievement of sales against sales targets together with collection. Since business in rural areas depends upon a number of uncontrollable factors such as timely and uniform rainfall, crop yields and prices of agricultural produce, his performance can also be indirectly judged by activities undertaken.

Examples: Number of villages/markets covered, number of orders booked, size of the orders, addition of new dealers, number of demonstrations, film shows and village meetings conducted.

The salesperson can be rated on the extent of his knowledge of the products, customers, competition and territory. Personal qualities such as communication ability, initiative, and working under tough conditions, temperament, interpersonal skills and customer focus can also be rated. Evaluation also helps the person to understand his strengths and areas for improvement assess training needs and plans for improving future performance. Evaluation has a beneficial effect on salesperson since it confers rewards on good performers.

CAREER GROWTH

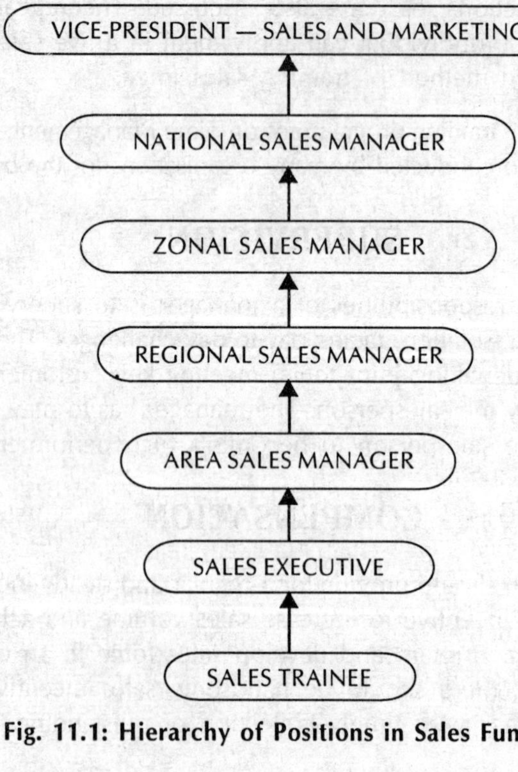

Fig. 11.1: Hierarchy of Positions in Sales Function

A salesperson joins an organisation as a trainee or sales executive depending on his qualification and experience. Consistently good performers, over a period of about five years can become Area managers or District managers covering a larger geographical area and supervising the work of a few sales executives. Further, promotion to positions like Regional manager/Zonal manager is based on performance and managerial skills of a person. A good performer can reach all-India position in sales, marketing, distribution or/and sales training over a period of about 20 years.

Opportunity to Live Close to the Nature: Apart from the rewards and awards a person receives for consistently good performance, rural marketing offers a few more personal benefits to the individual. The person gets an opportunity to live close to the nature, free from pollution and its problems facing growing cities in our country. He is able to see the flora and fauna during his working in rural markets.

Examples:

(a) A salesperson working in Sourashtra will be able to see places of tourist importance, i.e., temples, forts and wildlife sanctuary, while covering rural markets.

(b) The sales executive can enjoy the fine weather while working in Himachal Pradesh, during summer months.

(c) Selling fertilisers in Kuttanad paddy (Kerala) market involves travel by boat in the backwaters.

There are many such places a person can visit while working in rural areas. Such opportunities will enable a person to harmonise the demands of work with a pleasurable lifestyle, which very few careers can offer in a typical urban environment.

INDIAN RETAIL INDUSTRY

The retail sector is developing very fast and is proving a major boost to career opportunities. The jobs are opening up at entry level functions such as front sales, retail store management, visual merchandising, supply chain and warehousing. Many companies like Reliance, Pantaloon, Godrej, ITC and Tata have ambitious plans to retail agricultural produce like fruits, vegetables, agricultural inputs and consumer goods in important agricultural centres and semi-urban centres. At present, there is shortage of trained manpower in this field and a few educational institutions are offering courses in retail management. There will be job opportunities for trained rural youth in areas like contract farming, procurement, grading of agricultural produce, supply chain management to ensure that high quality produce is made available in the outlets as per demand.

DISTRIBUTORS' PROMOTION STAFF

Rural people prefer face-to-face communication and personal selling plays a major role in rural areas. However, the younger generation who are brought up and educated in cities are not comfortable to work in rural areas. Infrastructure facilities such as schools, hospitals, housing, transport, communication, entertainment centres are relatively poor in rural areas. Due to wide variations in urban and rural life, they are not able to adjust to rural realities and settle down in the job. Some of the other reasons are:

- Rural markets are highly scattered and spread over wide geographical area. The salesperson has to undertake long journeys moving from one market to another market and meeting various categories of customers. The public transport facilities are poor in rural areas and therefore the salesperson spends a lot of time in travel.
- Most of the village roads are in bad condition and driving a vehicle is a strenuous activity.
- The salesperson has to stay in small hotels with inadequate facilities.
- During the post-harvest and festival season, many shops are kept open till late in the night and the person has to spend long hours in the market to generate business for the company.
- Further, a typical rural customer is not in a hurry to buy things and therefore the sales call takes a longer time.
- The work schedule also results in irregular intake of meals. At times, he may have to forego lunch/dinner.
- The farmer leaves for the field early morning and returns home late in the evening. Therefore, the salesperson has to reach the village early in the morning and remain till late evening hours to meet the farmers. But the salesperson who is based in towns reaches the rural market late in the morning and also returns early to his base town in the evening. In this process, he misses the target customers during morning and evening hours.

Considering the rural environment and dynamics of the rural markets, there are opportunities to select the local village youth and train them to promote the products for the company. The local youth have the advantage of knowing the language, local customs and the behaviour of the villagers. They have access to the people and can meet them in the village without time constraints. The local youth take pride in working for large corporations and they are able to develop a good image about the company and products among villagers. Since the cost of living in villages is low, the rural youth would be willing to work for a lower compensation.

They are designated as Field Assistant, Promotion Assistant, Sales Assistant, Pilot Representative, etc. Normally, their expenses are shared between the company and the distributors. The rural youth could be trained to undertake activities such as meeting key consumers like landlords, affluent farmers, and influencers like teachers, village president, gramsevak, conducting demonstrations with the products, arrange for display of promotion materials, participation in Melas, liquidation of stocks from dealers and distributors and assist in organising village meetings and publicity programme. Further, they could be trained to collect data on consumer durables like TV, refrigerator, two-wheelers, etc.

The marketers have to consider the following in selection, training and development of village youth.

1. Selection criteria would include:

(a) Age 20-35 years

(b) Family background — preferably from agricultural family

(c) Command over local language

(d) Does not want to move to bigger towns/cities

(e) High School education.

(f) Interested in meeting people and communicating to them about products and services

2. Training

Classroom

(a) Product knowledge — company's products and competition

(b) Product buying benefits

(c) Handling objections

On-the-job coaching

(a) Detailing the products to consumers

(b) Conducting product demonstrations

(c) Organising meetings of villagers

(d) Village level retailer calls

3. Work plan

(a) Area of operation

(b) Targets in terms of number of villages, number of consumers and retailers to be met and promotion activities to be carried out

(c) Liquidation of stocks from retailers/distributors

Compensation includes monthly salary and reimbursement of travel expenses. There should be an incentive scheme for completing all field activities as per plan and achievement of sales targets.

Examples:

(a) HUL has embarked on a massive rural campaign using the concept of hygiene as a platform to reposition its leading brand, Lifebuoy. The objective is to spread awareness about invisible germs and good health and hygiene practices among children, the carriers of change. The targeted audience includes primary school and middle school children, parents and key influencers like teachers, retailers and registered medical practitioners. A Development Officer and Health Development Assistant cover 72 villages in a quarter.

The main criteria for selection are:

- Age group of 20-30 with college education.
- Must have roots in the village and willing to remain in their home town.
- Ability to communicate with key consumers and influencers.

The remuneration includes insurance cover, cash incentive for achieving the targets and monthly payment during the campaign period of one year. Their expenses are reimbursed through distribution channel.

(b) **Marico** uses the services of pilot sales representatives under the control of super distributors for meeting the village merchants, key influencers and promotional activities. Their expenses are shared between the company and the distributors.

(c) **Agricultural Input Companies** dealing in seeds, fertilisers and pesticides make extensive use of local youth to promote their products at village level. Most of these people have farming background and have college education. They have good understanding of a rural buyer behaviour and are able to build up rapport with villagers even during the first visit. They prepare a list of key farmers and key retailers and meet them at frequent intervals during the crop season. They highlight product benefits and conduct demos to convince the farmers about the efficacy of these products. They are paid monthly salary and travel expenses and are eligible for sales incentives for achieving the targets. They work under the control of distributors/C&F agents.

(d) **Colgate** has launched Hero No.1 programme to motivate the salesmen attached to distributors. Over 5,000 salesmen will be covered under this programme.

(e) **OM KOTAK** life insurance has set up a separate rural business division. They have selected rural youth and trained them to become effective life insurance agents.

(f) As a part of recent rural initiatives, **Dabur** has started "Astra", i.e., Advanced Sales Training for Retailer Ascendance. The company has recruited about 75 sales executives who will educate over 2,000 distributors/wholesalers about complexities of sales and distribution through audio-visual medium. The module is available in six languages, i.e., Bengali, Tamil, Malayalam, Kannada, Telugu and Hindi.

The rural youth with proper training could complement the efforts of the company and distributors in exploring the rural markets and establishing the products. In addition, consumers will have the pleasure of enjoying urban facilities in rural areas.

CONCLUSION

Rural people prefer face-to-face communication and personal selling plays a major role in rural marketing. The rural salesperson should have good understanding of rural buyer behaviour and therefore both classroom and on-the-job training will go a long way in improving the performance of sales force. Further there are opportunities to make use of the services of village youth to promote the products in rural areas since they have the advantage of knowing the language, local customs and behaviour of the villagers.

QUESTIONS

1. Describe the job of a rural salesperson and how it differs from urban counterpart?
2. Do you feel that rural youth could play a major role in brand promotion?
3. "A career in rural marketing is very rewarding." Discuss.

CASE STUDY

Direct Selling to Rural Consumers

Sai Households Ltd., (SHL) is a very well established company in the field of manufacturing and selling of consumer durables like TV, washing machines and water filters since 1980. The company has achieved remarkable success in marketing of their products through direct selling method in urban areas.

The company started with a team of 100 direct selling salesmen. They have a separate sale force training and development cell now, as there are more than 1,500 well-trained salesmen. SHL conducts carefully structured training programme and prepares salesmen for different kinds of situations they might encounter. The team is trained mainly to attract the housewife as the products deal with household items. The salesmen first develop a causal conversation as they enter the house and then move to a practised sales pitch on the products to demonstrate how the product will make life better for the housewife. SHL also keeps salesmen's enthusiasm alive with seminars and discussions. It is ensured that they stay highly motivated. Achievers are also rewarded by SHL.

Now, SHL decided to go to semi-urban and rural markets instead of confining to urban markets only. SHL wants to encash in rural areas also through direct sales. So, it diverted some of its salesmen to nearby town centres and each team was given 10-15 villages of population less than 500 each. The salesmen first contacted the village heads and then made an entry into the area.

As per the earlier experience, salesmen here also tried to start with casual conversation and target the housewives. Over a period of 15 days to 1 month all the salesmen came back to parent department with no success in sales and many had very bad experiences also to share with. The CEO of SHL fired the sales force training and development cell incharge and asked his marketing department to develop a new strategy to focus on the semi-urban and rural areas.

QUESTIONS

(a) Was CEO right in firing the sales force training and development cell incharge? If so, why?

(b) When SHL was doing so well in urban market, why did the same strategy not work in rural areas?

(c) If you were the marketing manager, what is the new strategy you would develop to focus in rural markets?

Note: Relevant facts and assumptions carry due weightage.

✿ ✿ ✿

12 MARKETING OF CONSUMER GOODS AND SERVICES

INTRODUCTION

Our country with a population of over 120 crore is the second largest market in the world. NCAER study highlights that the key to growth lies in rural areas. With improvement in infrastructural facilities, organised rural retail stores are coming up in rural and semi-urban areas. Mobile phones have become popular in villages due to improved connectivity and availability of mobile phones at affordable prices. Even usage of computers is growing especially in large villages and villages close to towns and cities. In rural areas, children are influencing purchase decisions for FMCGs. Rural areas contribute to over 50 per cent of national income, but it is being shared by 70 per cent of the population. Due to relatively low income, rural consumers are price-sensitive and they spend on basic necessities and utility products.

FAST-MOVING CONSUMER GOODS (FMCGs)

Fast-moving consumer goods are essential goods and are used frequently by consumers. They are also known as consumer packaged goods. They move fast at the sales counter. Normally, consumers spend less time and effort in buying these goods. FMCG includes a variety of products such as soap, biscuit, shampoo, toothpaste, talcum powder, etc. They are relatively high volume and low value products. Normally, they are large number of stock keeping units to meet the needs of the consumers. Packaging plays a major role in attracting the attention of consumers and the product has to be made available at a price within the reach of the consumers. There are a large number of players in FMCG market and each of them competes for a share of the total market. Large volumes are required to make it profitable. However, margins are low due to intense competition and focus on high volumes. The capital investment in setting up a factory is low and major investment is in brand promotion and distribution. Launching new product requires heavy investment and the marketer has to continue to focus on 4 Ps to fight competition and achieve desired volumes, profits and market share.

About 50 per cent of the FMCG market is unorganised and a large number of local products are available in rural market. Brand differentiation is very less in the case of most of the FMCGs and therefore the rural consumer prefers to buy the product based on price.

They have to be made available with village retailers through an effective distribution set-up. Value of the order given by rural retailer during each visit by the company representative or distributor is very low and it becomes expensive to service the highly scattered rural retail outlets. In order to reach these outlets and establish brand presence, companies need substantial amount of working capital and a large dedicated sales force.

The penetration of FMCGs has been high in rural market.

Examples: Toilet soap (85 per cent), Washing cake (88 per cent), Tea (77 per cent), Salt (64 per cent), Biscuit (62 per cent) and some of the popular brands are Lifebuoy, Lux , Wheel, Lipton Taaza, Nirma, Tata Salt, Parle, Colgate toothpaste and toothpowder, etc.

However, penetration of modern FMCGs continues to be low in rural areas: ***Examples:*** Soft drinks (9.8 per cent), Mineral water (3.8 per cent), Noodles (2.2 per cent), Candies (13.8 per cent), Chocolates (3.1 per cent), Jam (1 per cent), Ketchup (1 per cent), Instant coffee (8 per cent).

1. Tea: We are the largest producers of tea in the world and it is the second biggest market after soft drinks' market. Branded tea contributes to about 60 per cent of the sale of tea in the country. HUL and Tata Tea are the major players and both put together have about 50 per cent of the market share. Some of the popular brands are Taj Mahal, Red Label, 3 Roses and Taaza (HUL) and Agni, Kannan Devan Tea, Chakra Gold, Gemini (Tata). There are other players like Wagh Bakri and Society.

Tea is an essential commodity and is consumed at least twice a day. It is a part of the daily diet among villagers. Rural consumers prefer strong brands of tea and most of the rural households go in for loose or unbranded tea. Tea consumption is growing at 6 per cent a year among rural consumers, twice the urban rate.

Advertisements in regional TV channels and local newspapers, wall paintings, introduction of small packs, dealer incentives are the major marketing activities carried out by companies to reach the rural market. Tata Tea has appointed rural distributors at district level, who in turn supply to mobile rural wholesalers. Mobile wholesalers sell to tea shops, grocery merchants, etc.

2. Carbonated Soft Drinks are mainly sold in urban markets. However, the younger population has shown liking for bottled soft drinks in rural areas. The purchase of soft drinks appears to be a planned activity for a majority of villagers compared to impulse purchase of urban consumers. Soft drinks' consumption varies from once in a fortnight to once in a month. However, soft drinks are consumed in large quantities during festivals and marriages. Considering the stiff competition in urban areas, companies are trying to enter the growing rural market.

Coca-Cola and Pepsi have over 90 per cent share of carbonated soft drink market in the country. Coca-Cola launched 200 ml coke priced at ₹ 5 to bridge the gap in prices between bottled soft drinks and local products like nimbupani, lassi, coconut water and marble soda. To reach out to rural market, Coke prepared a list of prosperous villages in important districts. They appointed large distributors (Hubs) who order out full lorry loads of the products. From

Hubs, stocks are supplied to Spokes. These small distributors undertake fixed journey plan on weekly basis to supply to dealers in rural areas. The company launched the "Thanda Matlab Coca-Cola" campaign targeted at the villagers and the lower socio-economic segment of the population. The word "Thanda" is the term used for soft drinks in local parlance and the brand has been positioned as synonym for Thanda.

3. Toilet Soap segment is one of the most competitive markets in the country. The percentage of penetration is about 85 per cent in rural market compared to over 97 per cent in urban market. In rural areas, in many households a single cake is used by all the members of the family. Similarly, toilet soap is used by bathing as well as hair wash. Most of the rural consumers do not feel that there are major differences between different brands and therefore they buy the brand based on price. Broadly, there are four categories of toilet soaps, i.e., Carbolic, Popular, Premium and Super Premium prices ranging ₹ 8 to ₹ 40 per cake of 75 gram. Some of the popular brands of soaps in rural areas are Lifebuoy, Nirma, Lux, Rexona, Hamam, Breeze, Godrej No. 1 and Cinthol. The total toilet soap market is over ₹ 12,000 crore and it is dominated by HUL (60 per cent market share), followed by Nirma, P&G and Godrej. Godrej No. 1, launched in 1922 has a market share of 6 per cent and is the fifth largest selling soap in the country. It is Grade 1 Soap, i.e., Grade 1 is the highest standard laid down by the Bureau of Indian Standards.

4. Detergents: Rural areas contribute to about 40 per cent of the sale of detergents. About 80 per cent of the sales of detergents are brands priced between ₹ 18 to ₹ 25 per kg (Nirma, Wheel, etc.). The rural consumers make use of wells, rivers, ponds, open places for washing clothes and prefer detergent cakes. However, of late, the use of detergent power is growing fast in large villages and villages close to towns and cities. Considering cut-throat competition in urban market, the marketers are now focusing on rural market for increase in sales volumes. As in the case of soaps, the consumers feel that there are no major differences between different brands of detergents. HUL, Nirma, P&G, Ghari are the major players in this segment.

Ghari is a popular detergent brand (Sales ₹ 2,000 crore) in UP, MP and Maharashtra. The company sells the product at an affordable price to consumers by keeping a low profit margin (9 per cent) compared to competitive products (30 per cent). Similarly, Wheel is the single largest detergent brand (in value) in our country and is very popular in rural areas due to affordable pricing.

5. The Shampoo market is estimated at about ₹ 1,000 crore. The shampoo penetration is low in rural market (15 per cent) compared to urban areas (40 per cent). In rural areas, the decision makers for shampoos are the young wife or daughter or the daughter-in-law, but the buyer is either the head of the family or the elder son. The retailer influences the buyers and he tries to sell the brand that gives high margins. The older generation still prefers herbal products and traditional remedies. The small packing of low unit price has been found to be effective in increasing brand loyalty. Some of the popular brands of shampoos in rural market are Chik and Nyle (Cavin Kare), Sunsilk and Clinic Plus (HUL), Vatika Henna Cream and Anmol Silky Black (Dabur). Shampoo marketing requires a lengthy distribution set-up to reach rural retailers backed by mass media such as regional television, local newspapers, use of AVP van, film shows in cinema theatres.

6. Fairness Creams: Traditionally Indian women have used home made preparations like Chandan and Haldi as skin lightening and glow products. The fairness cream market is estimated at ₹ 1,500 crore and is growing at about 15 per cent per annum. HUL launched Fair and Lovely in 1975 and today it is the leader in the fairness cream market with a market share of about 55 per cent.Other products are Fair Glow (Godrej), Fairever (Cavin Kare) and Clearacil cream (P&G).

CONSUMER DURABLES

Consumer durables are tangible goods and are used over an extended period of time. They are purchased once in few years. ***Examples:*** TV, Refrigerator, etc.

The data (Census 2011) shows how India lives – ownership of Assets – Radio/transistor, TV, Telephone, Computer and Two-wheelers in rural and urban areas.

Table 12.1: Ownership of Assets (2011) – All-India (Figures in per cent)

Ownership of Assets (per cent)	Total	Rural	Urban
Houses with Telephone (Mobile/Landline)	63.20	54.30	82.00
Houses with Television	47.20	33.40	76.70
Houses with Computer	9.40	5.10	18.70
Houses with two-wheeler	21.00	14.30	35.20

Table 12.2: Ownership of Assets (2011) – Maharashtra

Ownership of Assets (per cent)	Total	Rural	Urban
Internet	5.80	.80	11.70
Telephone	69.10	54.70	86.40
Television	56.80	37.90	79.40
Computer	13.30	4.70	23.60
Radio/Transistor	19.50	12.10	28.30

The consumer spends lot of time in collecting information about various brands and models, discusses with neighbours, friends and opinion leaders, check and re-check the prices from various outlets before making purchase decisions. The consumers are concerned about perceived risk and after-sales service. Therefore, personal selling and after-sales service play an important role in selling consumer durables.

The rural consumer durable market is growing faster at around 20 per cent annually compared to the growth rate of 7-10 per cent for urban market. Godrej has introduced Chotukool, affordable refrigerator costing about ₹ 3,250 in rural market. However, the penetration of durable is still low in rural areas as shown in table 12.3. The major reasons are low income, low infrastructural facilities, social and cultural factors and lifestyle in villages.

Example: Washing machine penetration only 0.8 per cent is low due to availability of cheap labour for washing clothes, lack of assured electricity and water supply.

Table 12.3: Ownership of Consumer Durables (per cent) in Urban and Rural Market

Product	Urban	Rural	All-India
Air-conditioner	2.80	–	.90
Air Cooler	17.00	2.90	7.10
Electric Iron	39.60	12.70	20.80
Electric Geyser	4.40	.20	1.40
Computer	5.80	.30	1.90
Pressure Cooker	71.00	23.40	40.00
LPG Stove	70.10	19.10	33.00
Ceiling Fan	84.60	43.30	53.00
Television	77.10	34.90	46.00
Refrigerator	32.90	5.40	20.00
Washing Machine	13.30	.80	8.00
Car/Van/Jeep	4.70	.60	4.00
Scooter/Motor Cycle	28.20	10.30	15.70
Music System	27.00	17.50	20.40
Vacuum Cleaner	1.50	–	.50
Electric Water Purifier	2.50	–	.80
Internet access at home	2.70	.10	.90
Camera	7.70	1.00	3.10

Source: *Business World*, Marketing White Book, 2010-2011.

1. Television forms the major portion of the durable item in rural areas. Television transmission was started in our country some forty years back but colour transmission was introduced only in 1982. Penetration of TV is high in urban areas compared to villages. With the urban markets getting saturated, the semi-urban and rural areas offer great scope for growth and development of the industry. The market for TV in rural areas is value for money-driven and highly price-sensitive. They look for brand, promotion, schemes and after-sales service. There are three categories of TV sets available in the market, i.e., low cost (Videocon, and Akai), Medium (Philips, Samsung, LG) and Premium (Sony). Companies are extending attractive schemes and credit facilities to channel members in rural market. There is also a good replacement markét since black and white television users are switching over colour TV sets in rural market. The ownership is high in south (50 per cent), compared to east (20 per cent), west (33 per cent) and north (31 per cent).

2. Mobile Phone industry has been growing very fast since 1996. Ending 2011, our country had about 929 million mobile subscribers and we are the second largest users of mobile phones in the world. Rural teledensity is still at 35 per cent and it is expected that the future growth would from rural areas.

The growth in subscriber base has mostly come from operators like Bharti, Idea Cellular, Vodafone, Reliance and Tata. Around 38 per cent of Bharti Airtel's wireless subscriber base resides in rural areas and for Vodafone, the rural base around 33 per cent (2010). Land line connectivity is low at 38 million phones and this shows a clear preference of consumers towards mobile phones. Some of the factors that have contributed to the growth of mobile phone industry are given below:

(a) Availability of low-cost mobile phones and cellphone service.

(b) Pre-paid service is suitable for lower income group of consumers.

(c) Poor service offered by land line telephone operators. The prices should be affordable to the consumers and the manufacturers have to focus on low-cost models with voice, SMS, alarm and date facility handsets to meet the specific needs of the market. Mobile phones having FM radio, music and camera have also become popular among the rural rich. Replacement market is also growing at 25-30 per cent due to introduction of new models.

Nokia offers products to meet every price segment and has models to suit the needs of rural consumers. The most popular being low end phone Nokia 1100 – the made for India phone. The company has introduced 'Showroom on Wheels' and is in operation across the country for the benefit of rural consumers. Apart from Nokia, others like Samsung, Motorola, LG, Reliance, Karbonn, Micromax are also active in rural market.

"Indian Mobile Handsets are Popular among Villagers"

3. Motor Cycles: We are the largest producers of motor cycles comprising of Moped, Scooter and Motor Cycles in the world. However, the penetration of motor cycle is relatively low (15 per cent) compared to 35 per cent in urban market (2011). Initially, scooters were preferred by consumers and the trend has changed since 1995. Today, motor cycles share is about 75 per cent of the total market. There are broadly four categories in the two-wheeler segments, i.e., Standard (up to about ₹ 40,000), Executive (₹ 40,000 to ₹ 50,000), Premium (₹ 50,000 to ₹ 65,000) and Super premium (₹ 65,000 to ₹ 75,000). At present, Hero Honda, Bajaj and TVS are the main manufacturers and marketers of two-wheelers in the country.

Hero's two-wheeler "Splendor" priced at about ₹ 45,000 has been one of the most successful models in the country. With an annual sale of about 20 lakh units, the Hero Splendor family includes Splendor Plus, Splendor Pro, Splendor NXG and Super Splendor.

Public transport facilities are poor in rural areas and the villagers are interested to own motor cycles in place of bicycles to reach the feeder market. They want two-wheelers which are affordable and reliable with low maintenance cost. Entry level (Standard) models of Bajaj, Hero Honda, TVS, Yamaha, Kinetic are popular in the villages.

Hero Honda has about 5,400 touch points, i.e., sales and service outlets in rural areas of the country (2011). The company is accelerating efforts to tap the growing rural market and has decided to start door-to-door service facility for rural customers. Called "Service Har Jaghha" this network is based on specially customised bikes with necessary equipment to provide service on wheels in the interiors. About 1,100 customised bikes servicing remote areas have been introduced. Further the company has about 600 rural support executives to contact opinion leaders in the villages to enhance bike sales. It has taken up with State Bank of India for extending loan to farmers for purchase of two-wheelers.

Bajaj is focusing on melas, weekly haats in large villages. They have started about 3,500 Rural Service Outlets to provide sales and service of two-wheelers.

4. Automobiles: There is tremendous scope for marketing automobiles as penetration in only Two car per 1,000 people against 10 cars in urban areas. Automobile major, Maruti has initiated ***"Panchayat Scheme"*** to focus on Landlords, Agriculture produce traders, Village president, Traders and Arhatias for selling Maruti 800, Alto, Wagon R and Zen. They also offer scheme for financing the purchase of cars. The company has identified about 60,000 villages in Maharashtra, Gujarat, Rajasthan and Punjab as high potential. The company, through their authorised dealers, has appointed about 3,000 rural sales executives for generating demand from the rural market. The objective is to strengthen interaction with potential customers and convert them to buyers.

Shriram City Union Finance engaged in personal finance business for over three decades, specialises in areas of Consumer Durables and Auto Finance. The company has a strong hold in rural and remote locations. The company has joined hands with Maruti Suzuki, to offer easy, transparent and hassle-free can finance to its customers particularly in semi-urban and rural markets in South India.

Reaching the Rural Consumers: The rural consumers visit nearby towns for buying consumer durables and 90 per cent of the durables are purchased from towns, having population less than 10 lakh. There are about 7,000 such towns in our country and the companies have to appoint dealers in these towns for consumer durables to cover the rural market. Considering the low reach of mass media in interior villages, the marketers have to consider rural specific media and methods such as Audio-visual Publicity Van operations, participation in haats and melas, group meeting of villagers, use of opinion leaders, product demonstrations, etc., to reach the rural market.

SERVICES

In our country, the service sector is assuming increasing importance. The service sector offers better employment opportunities as compared to others. The sectors which are showing high growth potential are travel, tourism, financial services, health services, and telecommunication and information technology.

1. Microfinance: In our country, there are millions of people who are operating small business known as Micro Enterprises.

Examples: Making sweets, papads, candles, mudpots, bamboo baskets, tailoring, selling vegetables, running grocery/tea/pan shops, rearing cattle, etc. These small enterprises require credit for purchasing raw materials and equipments but lack access to formal financial institutions. They may be forced to take loan from moneylenders and traders at exorbitant interest rates.

Micro credit refers to loans and credit needs of micro enterprises. It means providing very poor families with small loans to help them to engage in productive activities. Micro credit is offered often without security to a group of people or to an individual. Microfinance covers a wide range of financial services such as savings, insurance, housing loan, etc.

For several decades, the institutions have been offering subsidised credit to the poor, but the outcome in most of the cases has been increased in non-performing assets. Detailed studies have shown that the main issue for the poor is access to credit rather than the cost of credit. If they have access to credit, they can undertake income generating activities, earn profit and repay the loan with interest. For instance, a grocery shop with an investment of about ₹ 20,000 in rural areas is able to generate an income of about ₹ 1.50 lakh yearly and a profit of ₹ 8,000 after meeting interest charges and other expenses.

The well known example of microfinance institution is the Grameen Bank in Bangladesh. In our country, a number of lending institutions, have come up in the area of microfinance and they include NGOs, professionals and banks in private and public sector. Commercial banks consider microfinance as an excellent way to raise deposits and lending at low risk.

Examples:

(a) Among the private microfinance institutions (MFIs), SKS Microfinance Ltd., (H.O. Hyderabad) is one of the fastest growing MFIs in the world. The company has about 1,500 field branches, 15,000 employees covering about 70,000 villages and has disbursed about ₹ 9,000 crore. Apart from extending credit to micro enterprises, SKS has tied up with companies for supply of basic mobile phones, solar lights and water purifiers.

(b) Self-employed Women's Association (SEVA) has started Mahila Sewa Cooperative Bank (1974) in Gujarat. The bank has been providing banking services to poor, illiterate, self-employed women and has become a viable financial venture. Under doorstep banking, pioneered by Seva Bank, the mobile bank travels to areas of high customer concentration to collect cash from members.

Micro credit interest rates are higher due to higher administrative cost. ***Example:*** Administrative cost for processing a loan for ₹ 50 lakh is less than 1,000 loans of ₹ 5,000 each. Further micro credit borrowers are unable to provide security against loans. These people stay in interior places and cost of lending is high. Therefore commercial banks normally stay away from such customers.

2. Micro Insurance: The major focus of insurance companies has been on the urban markets due to high literacy and awareness among consumers, availability of agents and profitability of the operations. However, the lower economic segment of the population offers lot of opportunities to the insurance sector. The value of each transaction may be of low value, but the increased number of transactions can make it a profitable business. At present, the penetration of insurance in this segment is less than one per cent. The most important forms of micro insurance are life insurance and health insurance. It is an emerging market for private sector insurance companies and many agencies like microfinance institutions, cooperatives, non-government organisations, self-help groups are involved in rural insurance.

Example: SBI Life Insurance has launched a micro insurance product 'Grameen Shakti', a pure term product with return of premium in 2006-2007. The policy is highly affordable and is designed to meet the requirements of the weaker section of the rural population. Grameen Shakti is a dual benefit life insurance product that provides protection and maturity benefit at low prices. For a five-year term, the annual premium payable would be only ₹ 301 for a sum assured of ₹ 25,000. In case of death of the group member, the nominee receives the sum assured and on maturity the member receives the premium paid for a five-year term.

CONCLUSION

Indian rural market presents huge opportunities for the companies. Expansion of TV net-work, mobile phone services, internet facilities, rising aspirations of rural people and packaging revolution have contributed to the growth of rural market. There has been a shift from an agricultural economy to manufacturing and service economy and this development has resulted in increase in job opportunities, income and demand for goods, and services in rural markets. However, there are wide variations among rural consumers due to socio-economic and cultural factors. The marketers have to understand the rural realities and come out with innovative marketing programmes to establish the products in rural market.

QUESTIONS

1. Discuss the scope for marketing of insurance and banking products in rural market.
2. How can companies make use of 4 Ps to establish their products in rural market?

CASE STUDY

Self-help Group

Call it business with a good cause. A strong but silent social revolution is taking place beyond urban borders. Surpassing all targets, an overwhelming number of 18 lakh credit-linked "self-help groups" (SHGs), being predominantly women-oriented, are working wonders in rural areas and in managing microfinance matters. Cumulative bank lendings to SHGs have grown to almost ₹ 8,000 crore till November 2005. The southern states of Andhra Pradesh, Tamil Nadu and Karnataka have recorded the largest number of SHGs. Odisha follows close behind.

Interestingly, while public sector banks, regional rural banks and cooperative banks provide maximum loans to SHGs, private sector banks have begun assisting SHGs with credit facilities in recent times. And, recovery levels have by far been the highest from these SHGs, who are otherwise denied of banking facilities.

National Bank for Agriculture and Rural Development (NABARD) is spearheading all microfinance projects has, in fact, asked banks to lend more to these groups. For banks, the amount may be small in their entire loan portfolio, but these people can be customers of the future. As part of its exercise in bringing more people under microfinance, NABARD has initiated involving rural volunteers to help in creating different SHGs. While the numbers in the southern states have been the highest, NABARD is working on measures to step up activities in the northern and eastern states.

Some states like West Bengal have the highest share of credit coming from state and district central cooperative banks. The growth in credit-linked SHGs has grown very fast and has led to them to be creditworthy. Perhaps, the greatest benefit comes in the form of social change. There are distinctly less instances of school dropouts, alcohol drinkers, domestic abuse and harassment in a family. Moreover, with access to bank finance, dependence on moneylenders is minimal. The financial discipline among the SHGs has been very high. The moral strength, confidence and empowerment levels are definitely higher among women who have become confident decision makers, investors and mentors for their families.

QUESTIONS

(a) With respect to various kinds of credit required by farmers, what role microfinance and SHG can play?

(b) What are the various agencies currently involved in granting credit to agriculture community?

(c) Explain with example how companies have use SHG to distribute their products?

CASE STUDY

Marketing of Consumer Goods

Karim and Vijay were discussing the dismal performance of their company's prime products in Indian rural markets. Both were employed with Home Personal Product (HPP), a company that produced and marketed FMCG's like hair oils, shampoos, toothpaste, etc. Karim was the product manager and Vijay was the head of the Rural Sales Department.

Two of the products of HPP were not doing well across all rural segments. The first was a transparent 250 ml coconut oil in a plastic bottle branded; "Satellite Coconut Oil". On its sticker label was a picture of a dish antenna. This product was promoted, across all segments, with the help of a 15 per cent price discount on the combined purchase of two bottles. The other product was a burgundy coloured 200 ml shampoo in a plastic fibre bottle branded as "Vitality Hair Wash". This product had a printed textual label with a diagram showing improved hair growth due to the usage of the product. The promotion campaign of the "Vitality scratch card sweepstakes" that gave away music CDs.

Like all other HPP products, both of these products were also advertised on TV and Radio in 10 to 30 second slots using beautiful models and a female voice over.

Vijay thought that the products were doing in urban markets because they were developed by keeping the urban consumer in mind. Moreover, even Karim confessed that a large percentage of the urban market share was attributed to the chain of industrial buyers. While Karim thought that the problem lay in the media methods and promotion campaigns, Vijay felt that the problem lay in the branding, packaging and labelling.

QUESTIONS

(a) Who do you think is right, Karim or Vijay?

(b) If you were Karim, what would be your promotion and distribution strategy for rural India?

(c) What changes do you think Vijay has in mind with regard to Branding, Packaging and Labelling of the two products?

✿ ✿ ✿

13 CORPORATE INITIATIVES IN RURAL MARKET

INTRODUCTION

India is one of the largest consumer markets in the world and rural market presents huge opportunities for creative marketers. The rise of rural market has been one of the important marketing phenomena of the nineties. At the same time, there are wide variations among consumers due to socio-economic and cultural factors. The rural market share of FMCGs such as shampoo, toilet soaps, washing cake and washing powder and automobiles like scooter, motor cycle, jeep and car has increased over a period of fifteen years as shown below.

Table 13.1: Rural Market Share as a per cent of all-India Market

Product	1995-96	2001-02	2009-10
Shampoo	27	32	33
Toilet soap	50	53	55
Washing cake	69	71	76
Washing powder	50	51	55
Scooter	30	39	40
Motor cycle	45	47	48
Car/Jeep	2	8	11

Source: NCAER – Reproduced from the Marketing White Book, *Business World*, Kolkata.

Many companies have established their products through innovative marketing programmes and a few corporate examples are given below:

ASIAN PAINTS

Asian Paints with a wide product range and turnover of over ₹ 9,000 crore is the leader in the Indian paint industry. When the company started its operations in 1940s, it had to compete with major paint companies like ICI, Blundell Eomite, Goodlass Nerolac, Jenson and Nicholson and Shalimar Paints. These companies were focussing on urban markets.

In order to increase sales, Asian Paints (AP) concentrated on smaller towns, ignored by multinationals. In 1954, famous cartoonist R.K. Laxman created a mascot for the company and Gattu emerged as one of India's most memorable mascots and popularly known as **Ladkavala paint** in rural areas.

Product

The company caters to different segments of the population. The brand Royal in the premium segment, Apcolite in the middle segment, Tractor and Utsav in the lower segment. Keeping rural consumers in mind, the company was the first to introduce small packings of paints. It introduced oil paint in 50 ml/250 ml packings to paint the horns of livestock.

The company studied the rural markets and found that huge volumes of 'Chuna' (Lime) was used for painting the houses and walls in rural areas. Packed distempers, dry distempers and lime wash priced between ₹ 5 and ₹ 20 were sold in these markets. The consumers in general were not much satisfied with chuna, since it has to be done every year. Further, chuna affected the hands, eyes and even lungs. There are no choice of colours. Chuna tends to flake off, leaving ugly patches on the walls. However, some people in rural areas used distemper for painting the houses and walls in the place of chuna. The company developed a special brand of distemper "Utsav" priced at ₹ 25.00 per kg. Utsav was made available in one kg packing to meet the requirements of small-sized houses. The launch of the product in each state/region coincided with festivals. Supplies were made to grocery shops in villages through company dealers. Demonstrations and use of local newspapers helped in creating demand for the product. *The product 'Utsav' has been accepted in rural markets as a replacement for chuna and has been recognised as a successful marketing strategy in the paint industry.*

Distribution

The company has an extensive distribution network of over 20,000 dealers serviced through six regional distribution centres and 72 sales offices. While many paint companies deal through distributors, Asian Paints make supplies directly to dealers situated in rural and semi-urban markets with a population of 10,000. These are the feeder markets surrounding villages. The villagers have the habit of visiting towns for selling agricultural produce and buying consumer durables. Thus, the company is able to reach rural consumers through retailers in feeder markets.

Promotion

The carpenters and painters are the opinion leaders for paints and therefore the company conducts meetings to educate them on the benefits of the products. It uses mobile vans and demonstration-cum-sales method to promote Utsav brand paint in rural markets.

The company has entered into technical collaboration with US and Japanese companies for the manufacture of automotive paints to increase its share in industrial paint segment. On the IT front, all the 50 depots are connected to the manufacturing plants and head office for faster flow of information, monitoring supplies and inventories. Asian Paints is the leader in decorative paint segment with a market share of about 38 per cent.

MICROMAX

Micromax is one of the leading Indian Telecom Companies with 23 domestic offices across the country and international offices in Hong Kong, USA, Dubai and now in Nepal. With a futuristic vision and an exhaustive R&D at its helm, Micromax has successfully generated innovative technologies that have revolutionised the telecom consumer space.

In the year 2008, after delivering upon the technology of fixed wireless-powering desired products, the company forayed into telecommunication — Mobile handsets. Since then Micromax has received commendable response for its unique and interesting handsets.

Micromax has a lot of "firsts" to its credit on their versatile product portfolio. It was the first to introduce, Handsets with 30 days battery backup, Handsets with Dual SIM/Dual Standby, Handsets Switching Networks (GSM-CDMA), Aspirational Keypad Handsets, Operator Branded 3G Handsets, OMH CDMA Handsets, *etc.* One of the major aspects that contribute towards the substantial monthly growth of Micromax is its 80 per cent sales in the rural areas. It has a market share of eight per cent, behind Samsung in second position with 10 per cent market share.

GO-TO-MARKET STRATEGY — Micromax concentrated on the rural market first. Micromax launched its first phone in the rural market with a very unique USP-30 days battery standby time. The first product was a big success — Micromax XII priced at ₹ 2,150 was lapped up by rural market. Established Distribution Network-34 super distributors, 450 distributors and around 55,000 retailers. Micromax managed to make dealers pay in advance by offering them more margins. It offered higher margins of 15 per cent margin, which is higher than the industry average of 6-10 per cent. To increase penetration in the Indian telecom market, Mixcromax is bundling with telecom operators such as Aircel. For better accessibility and prominence in the market, Micromax is coming up with 150 experience zones (exclusive stores) across the nation, in addition to ensuring bigger presence at the multi-branded stores.

They introduced products with comparatively lower prices focusing mainly on adding particular innovative features. This gave them a competitive edge over the others and made Micromax a primary choice for the rural consumers.

- **30-day Battery Phones:** April 2008: ₹ 2,249; Now: ₹ 1,999 The X1i, Micromax's first phone, had a battery that could give 17 hours of talk time and go 30 days on a single charge.
- **Dual-Sim Phones:** July 2008: ₹ 1,999-2,999; For those who want two numbers but one handset.
- **Phone-Cum-Remote:** May 2010: ₹ 2,999; A mobile that can switch TV channels and even change the temperature settings on AC.

Besides the focus on product development, Micromax has invested heavily in brand building. The brand is one of the big spenders in the latest edition of IPL (2011). Micromax has centred much of its brand building exercise around cricket. The company believes that cricket promotions will prove to be a great platform to reach out to the audience and give the brand an opportunity to bond with the youth. Micromax has taken up the title sponsorship for the entire Indian cricketing season from May 2010. Micromax is also planning an innovative activation across the cricket season, breaking away from the vanilla branding that we are all used to. Activation will see some intelligent product placements, on ground-on air integrated product coverage and mentions, crowd branding and the brand will be visible on a digital platform on the ground throughout, adding to the technology stand-point.

Micromax was one of the principal sponsors of the South Africa *vs.* India ODI series in 2010. In the just concluded 'Micromax cup', as the name suggests it was the chief sponsor. Micromax, has shelled out a whopping ₹ 100 crore for its brand building initiative. It is targeting a wide base of new and existing subscribers, using a 360 degree media approach via multiple platforms. It has allotted ₹ 60 crore for ATL (above the line) advertising, of which print will take the maximum share, followed by TV and radio, another ₹ 40 crore will go into the BTL (below-the-line) initiatives. The communication has been launched in the beginning of 2010.

CAVIN KARE

Established in 1983, Cavin Kare is a ₹ 980 crore (2011-2012) company with a wide range of popular brands like Nyle and Chik Shampoo, Meera Hair Wash, Ruchi pickle, Fairever cream, Indica Hair Colourant, Spinz Talcum Powder and Raga Cool Hair Oil. The name was selected by combining CAVIN meaning beauty and grace in Tamil language and K instead of C as a tribute to founder Chinnikrishnan. Cavin Kare logo has the letters C and K well-defined in a leaflet form and gives the company a herbal orientation.

"Cavin Kare"

Chik Shampoo was targeted at rural and small town consumers and by 1990, it became a brand leading in South with about 50 per cent market share. Chik Shampoo, attempted to provide the consumers, a superior product at a relatively low price in comparison to leading brands. It came with floral fragrance shampoo, i.e., Jasmine and Rose for the first time. Considering the number of adults per family (5 members) and four hair washing per month, and ₹ 2 per sachet, the monthly bill will be ₹ 40 for hair wash alone and the rural consumer cannot afford to spend such an amount for hair wash every month. Therefore, by offering a shampoo at 50 paise, the monthly bill per person will be just ₹ 2 and for a family of five, ₹ 10.00 per month. Today, Chik Shampoo is a ₹ 200 crore brand and dominates the rural and semi-urban market.

"Display of Sachet Packs"

Many rural consumers who were using bathing soap for hair wash for generations, got an opportunity to try out inexpensive Chik Shampoo and the product became a success in the rural markets. Development of packaging enabled the company to give the brand a distinctive look and easy identification by rural consumers.

Promotion

The company makes use of traditional markets such as Haats and Melas to penetrate interior villages. Radio advertising is used as an important media to reach the rural and semi-urban population. The radio jingles had dialogues from popular films and that appealed to common masses. The company educated people by conducting "Touch and Feel Demonstration". To encourage trials, the sales team travelled extensively in rural markets, caught hold of school boys to demonstrate how to lather and wash while using shampoo. Another innovative scheme involved supply of one sachet of shampoo free for every five empty sachets presented to the retailer.

New Products

A mix of various herbs in powder form is used in South for hair wash. Cavin Kare took the opportunity to introduce herbal hair wash powders, i.e., Meera and Karthika. Cavin Kare has acquired Ruchi Pickle Brand from Ruchi Agro Foods, Andhra Pradesh. It has introduced Chinni pickles in single use sachet packing priced at 50 paise successfully. Ruchi Brand is being promoted as premium brand and Chinni caters to mass market.

Cavin Kare which began as a small player in 1980s, has emerged as a major fast-moving consumer goods company competing with major players like HUL, P&G in various product segments. The company has studied consumer lifestyle and has come out with products that meets the requirements of rural markets with regard to affordability and availability.

CHOLAYIL GROUP

Soap maker Medimix, from the Chennai-based Cholayil group, is the maverick marketer that got its product and marketing-mix just right. The company's success is reminiscent of Nirma's in the West. Its revenue rose metroically from ₹ 50 crore (1997) to ₹ 200 crore in (2001) on sales of its ayurvedic soap. Besides, it got an ORG rating of number nine, among soap categories on a national basis with minimal high decibel advertising, no sexy packaging, no glamorous film star endorsements and no compromise on its shape, perfume or colour in order to bag bulk orders from hotels.

Six plants of the Cholayil group make 1.5 crore cakes of soap, each weighing 75 gm and 30 lakh cakes of the 125 gm variety. The soaps are made manually, without the use of power and even the cutting of the bars into cakes is done by hand-operated hydraulic cutters. However, the company plans to set up a state-of-the-art unit in Goa. "Once production starts there, we will make 1,000 cases per month and establish a supply chain to serve the northern market," says K.H.S. Manian, Vice-president, of the company.

The story of Medimix is the evolution of a home-grown product, from idea to research to manufacture, packaging, distribution and marketing, all done by a family proprietary concern. Most important, the company has managed to develop a brand on its own terms. It all started with Dr. V.P.S. Sidhan (who traces his bloodline to the Cholayil Tarawad of Kerala, a family lineage of ayurvedic *vaidyans*, followers of saint Narayana Guru), who served as assistant medical officer with the Southern Railways. Sidhan had trained for his DMS at the Kilpauk Medical College and so ayurveda took a back-seat until his retirement. His medical experience showed that chronic ailments, especially skin conditions, defied allopathic remedies and post-retirement, he focused on finding cures through ayurveda. His work with Viparthy Oil (extract of wild ginger) and its efficacy in treating skin diseases yielded promising results.

Now all he needed was a better vehicle to overcome the oil mess as an applicator. So, Medimix soap was born. Sidhan's soap was made with 18 herbs in a coconut oil base in the backyard of his Chennai Choolamedu house. The firm was incorproated in the name of Sidhan's wife Sowbhagyam. She also doubled up as chief of manufacture. In 1969, Sidhan launched the Medimix brand as a total ayurvedic skin care soap with just ₹ 500 as seed capital and lots of goodwill from the medical fraternity and chemists network. Sidhan's soap and its efficacy spread through actual user endorsements. "We priced it at 85 paise at the time and today it sells for ₹ 9.50," says Manian. There are five plants, one in Pondicherry, two in Chennai, one in Tada in Andhra Pradesh, one in Bengaluru and one in Villupuram, to cater exclusively to hotel bulk orders.

According to the July-September 2001, ORG figures of volume in tonnes of the top 25 brands of soap on a national basis, Medimix at 2,625.3 tonnes is way above Mysore Sandal, Margo, Nirma, Jai, Cinthol Fresh, Pears, Lux International skin care, Liril and Dettol. In the south zone alone, it is the sixth highest seller with 1,873 tonnes.

What is the strategy that worked for Medimix in a bubble-filled soap arena in which multinational companies such as Hindustan Lever Limited tower above the rest of the market? Manian unabashedly says that his group had to run all existing and considered marketing wisdom on its head. "While FMCG (fast-moving consumer goods) products usually take off in the urban centres, and then spread through the hub format, Medimix was pitched in the villages first," says Manian. "We targeted the village *kiranawala*, our best friend and local influencer of decisions so far as buying habits go. He accepted the merits of Medimix as an ayurvedic product. When he was convinced, his customers got convinced. The only alternative was Chandrika soap, which had adopted a direct marketing approach. We used to attend numerous village *melas* and talk to the people. We went all over India only two years ago. Today, of the three lakh tonnes of soap sold, ayurvedic soap comprises 7 per cent, of which we have 3 per cent."

Medicated soap that is 100 per cent hand-made is exempt from tax and rural consumers seem to be attracted to the medical qualities of the soap far more than they are to the same qualities in a cosmetic, according to Manian. He says that when a villager visits a city he asks for Medimix soap by name. No offers, no schemes, no inducements. As Chandrika soap was following the monopoly of direct distribution. Medimix decided to woo the stockists and distributors and claims there are 25-year-old loyalties here. "From 1969 to 1990, growth was slow," says Manian. "But when S. Pradeep joined the company as managing director the firm took off in just four years."

It was Pradeep's idea to target hotels. A firm decision was taken that Medimix would aggressively market to over 3,000 small hotels all over India, even in small towns. Pradeep says, "He was pleasantly surprised to find that even foreign tourists to places such as Pondicherry were impressed by the medicated quality of Medimix. We decided that we would not compromise on the packaging or appearance or the perfume or colour of the soap to gain entry into five-star hotels. Hotels will never buy at the maximum retail price (MRP), so we supply at cost. What's more, we even manage the inventory for them."

While Medimix has done well, the company's brand extension, Vrinda Tulsi Soap failed and is being relaunched with a changed perfume and translucent appearance. Meanwhile, Manian is focusing on the Indian community in the Middle East, where he believes Medimix can command loyal customers. The product is exported to Brazil and Italy, as well. "Even in the Indian market, there is a 50 per cent untapped potential," he says. "We have plans for a sandal soap, Viha, and a herbal Ziva shave cream. People are turning to ayurveda in a big way.

"We have the research and knowledge capabilities to turnout more ayurvedic products and build on our current marketing strength. In the past five years our ad-spend has grown to ₹ 30 crore. We conducted an Ayurveda Congress in Hyderabad and got an impressive response."

Medimix has proved that it is not always glitz and glamour that sells products... a back-to-your-roots plank that espouses natural products appeals to the average Indian.

COLGATE-PALMOLIVE INDIA LIMITED (CPIL)

Colgate-Palmolive India Ltd., (CPIL) is a 51 per cent subsidiary of Colgate-Palmolive, USA and is engaged in manufacturing and marketing of oral care products, toilet soaps and shaving products. With an employee strength of about 1,200, Colgate is a ₹ 2,700 crore company (2011-2012). Colgate is a household name in India, with one out of two consumer using Colgate toothpaste. About 33 per cent of the sale of Colgate toothpaste is in the rural market.

Product

Colgate is a market leader with a market share of 51 per cent in toothpaste, 48 per cent in toothpowder and 30 per cent in toothbrush. Colgate dental cream is the largest selling toothpaste in India with 39 per cent market share. Other products are Palmolive and Protex bathing soaps, Halo and Optima hair care products, Axion for utensil cleaning, Charmis skin cream and Palmolive shaving cream.

Distribution

'Project intell', is aimed at connecting dealers and the company has undertaken various initiatives at distributor and retailer levels. The company has initiated School Dental Health Education Programme. The **"Hero No. 1"** programme wherein the stockist and salesmen are motivated with recognition and reward for outstanding achievements and the **'Dil se'** through which wholesalers are rewarded for their loyalty and consistencies in marketing of company products. Colgate's main strength lies in its wide reach. It has direct distribution link to eight lakh retail outlets and its products are available in 2.4 million outlets. The company derives about 35 per cent of the turnover from rural markets.

Promotion

Oral hygiene is neglected even today in rural India. Many rural people still clean their teeth with traditional products like neem twigs, charcoal powder, burnt paddy husk, etc. The penetration of toothpaste is low in rural India, however, toothpowder is popular.

Considering the opportunities in rural market, Colgate launched a programme called Operation Jagruti, a village contact programme designed to increase rural penetration. The programme focused on oral health awareness and availability of the products at village outlets. The products were promoted through shandies/haats and melas. The company runs Dental Health Education Programme and has tied up with Indian Dental Association and covered 18,500 dentists in towns. It has also tried syndicate distribution to increase penetration in villages with less than 2,000 population. Colgate is now available in 2.4 million outlets.

The company makes extensive use of audio-visual publicity units to reach the interior villages. The van is fitted with a large dummy colgate toothpaste on the top of the vehicle. As soon as the AVP van reaches the village, popular film songs are played to attract the attention of villagers. A thirty minute film is screened focusing on oral hygiene and the need for brushing the teeth with Colgate toothpaste. A few free samples are also distributed. The company hires about 100 AVP vans and films are screened for about nine months in an year except during monsoon season.

Competition

The company has been facing the threat of losing its market share and has followed an aggressive strategy of introducing new products and increase in marketing expenditure. The company has been targeting schools to create oral awareness among children and conversion of non-users through various sales promotion measures. The focus on distribution and promotion is continued to face the competition and maintain dominant position in the industry.

HINDUSTAN UNILEVER LIMITED (HUL)

HUL, India's largest fast-moving consumer goods company has a turnover of over ₹ 27,000 crore. The rural and semi-urban market contribute to about 50 per cent of the sales of the company.

Product

The company has launched a large number of successful brands.

Examples: Lifebuoy soap (1895), Pears (1902), Vim (1913) Sunsilk shampoo (1964), Rin, Bru (1969), Clinic Shampoo (1971), Liril soap (1974), Closeup toothpaste (1975), Fair and Lovely (1978), Breeze soap (1987), Pepsodent (1992), Vim dish wash bar (1993).

Distribution

One of the HUL's initiatives was in the form of "project streamline" that was introduced in 1998. Project streamline addressed the problems of the rural distribution system and to increase the number of retail outlets in rural areas. The project was carried out with the help of rural distributor who had 15-20 rural sub-stockists.The sub-stockist serviced the interior villages using cycles, bullock carts and tractors. As a part of the project, the company provided high quality services in terms of increased frequencies of visit to dealers, availability of full range of products and credit. The number of brands and product packs stocked by village retailers increased. This initiative helped HUL increase its reach in the rural market to about 40 per cent in 1998 from 25 per cent in 1995.

Project Shakti: In many states, women Self-Help Groups have been formed through the initiative of DWCRA (Development of Women and Children in Rural Areas). The group's financial resources consist of savings, Government assistance and bank loans. Normally, members use the loan out of the group corpus for their personal needs. Such loans are also used for income-generating activities. HUL has come out with a new distribution model with main objective to develop income-creating capabilities of underprivileged rural women by providing a sustainable enterprise opportunity and to improve rural living standards through health and hygiene awareness.

Typically, a woman from the SHG is selected as a Shakti entrepreneur and receives stocks of Lifebuoy, Wheel, Pepsodent, Annapurna Salt, Clinic Plus, Ponds, Lux, Nihar, 3 Roses tea, etc., at her doorstep from the HUL rural distributor. She sells directly to consumers as well as to small merchants in the village. Each Shakti entrepreneur services 6-10 villages in the population range of 1,000-2,000 people. With training and handholding by the company for the first three months, she begins her door-to-door journey selling the products. Normally, the entrepreneur has a turnover of ₹ 10,000 to ₹ 20,000 per month and earns a profit of ₹ 700 to ₹ 1,400 a month. She also sells non-competing brands such as edible oil, sugar, matchboxes, bangles, etc. The project was started in Nalgonda district in AP. At present, there are about 45,000 Shakti entrepreneurs in fifteen states. The plan is to have one lakh Shakti entrepreneurs. The most powerful aspect of this model is that it creates a win-win partnership between HUL and the women entrepreneur. Project Shakti is a business model that is sustainable, scalable and relevant. It empowers through enterprise and at the same time creates awareness on health and hygiene through HUL brands.

Promotion

'Project Bharath' is a direct marketing exercise undertaking to address the issues of awareness, attitude and habits of rural consumers and increase the penetration level of HUL products. The company carried out direct marketing operations in the high potential areas of the country to attract first-time users. Under 'Project Bharath', HUL van visited villages, video films were shown and sold small packs of detergent, toothpaste, face cream and talcum powder for ₹ 15.

"House-to-house Visit by a Shakti Entrepreneur"

Subsequently, the company initiated "Integrated Rural Promotion Van" to increase awareness of HUL products in villages with 2,000 population. The company covered 13 million households project.

Lifebuoy Swasthya Chetana: Lifebuoy Swasthya Chetana meaning "Health Awakening" is the single largest rural health and hygiene educational programme ever undertaken in India. Its objective is to educate people about basic hygienic habits.

It has been developed around the insight that people mistakenly believe "visible clean is safe clean". The programme establishes the existence of "invisible germs" and the associated risk of infection. In India, this is important, because diarrhoea, caused by invisible germs, is the second largest cause of death among children below the age of 5. The project will help reduce incidence of such diseases, by raising awareness of preventive hygienic practices.

The campaign has been divided into various phases. In the initial phase, a Health Development Facilitator (HDF) and an assistant initiate contact and interact with students and influencers of the community, like village community representatives, medical practitioners, school teachers, etc. A number of tools like a pictorial story in a flip chart format, a "Glow-Germ demonstration" and a quiz with attractive prizes to reinforce the message are used. The "Glow-Germ demonstration" is a unique tool to make unseen germs visible and emphasise the need to adopt hygienic practices. The first interaction with students is then replicated with the rest of the community. Subsequently, follow-up visits and communication are undertaken at periodic intervals which reinforce the message and learnings.

Started in 2002, the programme has as of now, covered about 15,000 villages in 8 states — Uttar Pradesh, Bihar, Jharkhand, West Bengal, Odisha, Madhya Pradesh, Chhattisgarh and Maharashtra; it has already touched about 70 million people, imparting hygiene education to over 25 million children. The vision of this ongoing project is to make a billion Indians feel safe and secure by focusing on their health and hygiene needs.

Maha Kumbh Mela, Allahabad (2013): HUL came out with a novel method to remind people to wash their hands before having food. Lifebuoy along with creative agency (OGILVY) designed a Roti Reminder. The Roti is a staple item served with every meal and the only way to eat it is – with your hands. Lifebuoy created a special heat stamp; with the message: Did you wash your hands with Lifebuoy? It hired over 100 promoters to stand in eateries spread across Mela and stamp the Rotis with the message. More than 25 lakh Rotis were heat stamped with this message. The product was also placed nearby the eating spaces so that people can get into the habit of washing their hands. It did create ample buzz on ground and across the nation.

"ROTI Reminder".

Community Dental Health Campaign: Community Dental Health Campaign was launched by the company in association with Indian Medical Association. As a part of the project, several infomercials were launched to increase awareness on dental hygiene and highlight dental problems and their causes. These films were relayed through national television channel. Dental health programmes were organised at public health centres. Educative demos on good brushing habits, correct use of toothpaste, toothpowder, and dental check-up were held. The campaign aimed to increase the direct reach of toothpaste in rural India to 1.25 lakh villages by 2001 from the existing 40,000 villages.

Project Millennium: In 2000, the company launched another campaign called "Project Millennium" with the objective of increasing the share in tea market. The company tapped the tea shops and provided blended tea to appeal to rural taste (Kadak Chai – strong tea).

In 2001, the company participated in a rural communication programme called "Grameen ke Beech" (amidst villages). Besides HUL, companies like Colgate, Mahindra and Parle participated in the programme. The programme covered 3,000 villages in UP, and activities included putting up exhibition stalls, demos, lucky draws, magic shows and screening of films interpersed with product films.

1. Shakti: HUL has launched an internet based rural information service called 1. Shakti in Andhra Pradesh in association with Andhra Pradesh Government's Rajiv Internet Village Programme. Desktop computer have been set-up in the homes of Shakti entrepreneurs. 1. Shakti has been developed to provide information and services to meet rural needs in medical health, hygiene, agriculture, animal husbandry, education, vocational training and employment. HUL expects that the information services provided would improve the productivity of rural community and lead to economic and social progress. Companies like Dabur, ICICI Bank, TVS Motor Company have started using 1. Shakti kiosk to promote their products. "Khushiyon ki Doli" is a rural marketing initiative and it aims to reach out to media dark villages with HUL brand messages.

LG ELECTRONICS

LG Electronics (Sales ₹ 16,000 crore in 2011) established in 1997 is the first MNC to focus on rural markets in a big way. It has launched a new CTV range by name "SAMPOORNA". The brand specially designed for rural areas, offers extra durability and can adapt itself to high voltage fluctuations in Indian rural areas. Rural India needs products at affordable prices. LG has used C&F agents for distribution. The company's logic in doing away with the distributors was that in the long run with more products it would cheaper to go directly to the dealer. LG provides financing option throughout India. The biggest customer in the village is the farmer who is dependent on the harvesting season for extra liquidity, the above option will do away with the problem.

It has launched vans to promote brand through jingles and gifts distribution in between movie shows. There are roadshows where a dealer sets up a promotion and sales outlet for 2-3 days. LG also advertises in TV network for 2-3 months. The company has set up a Lifestyle

Research Team to study the needs and preferences of consumers. Rural and semi-urban markets account for about 50 per cent of the sales of the company.

MARICO INDUSTRIES LIMITED

Marico is a leading Indian group operating in skin, hair care and healthy foods, segments with a turnover of over ₹ 3,000 crore.

Product

The important products are Parachute, Saffola, Mediker, Oil of Malabar, Meal maker, Revive, Kaya, Sundari, Hair and Care. Parachute coconut oil, is a market leader with a share of 35 per cent of the rural market.

The company has gone into sachet pack of parachute since the rural consumer may not buy a bottle. Since he may not have a separate bathroom, he takes bath in the pond, river on near open well, and would like to use the oil and throw the pack. It has launched tamper proof coconut hair oil to overcome the problems of duplicate products. The new cap for 200 ml and 500 ml bottles of parachute is promoted as 'Shuddhata seal' to educate consumer against duplicates. The rural consumer requires value for money and the offerings of Marico are priced between rupee one to ₹ 50. The USP of the product is changed according to the place. In Jharkhand, Parachute is promoted as pure coconut oil while in Rajasthan, it is promoted as a fashion product.

Marico has acquired 'Mediker', the anti-lice treatment from P&G for an amount of ₹ 10 crore and it is positioned as a shampoo-cum-rescuer from headlice, especially among school children. The company has initiated a massive programme of addressing the problem of lice among school children by organising lice check in schools and promoting the use of mediker available in 25 ml/50 ml packing.

Marico has acquired Nihar Coconut Oil from HUL in 2006. Nihar complements Maricos' strengths in coconut oil and perfumed hair oils. Nihar has a turnover of about ₹ 120 crore and has excellent reach in the east. In perfumed hair oils, Nihar Naturals is (Jasmine and Rose) the market leader. This will help Marico's growth in the coming years. Recently, Marico entered into a tie-up with P&G where Marico will handle the distribution of the products of both companies and P&G will focus on marketing and product promotion.

Distribution

Marico has a separate distribution network for rural and urban market. A selected team of Territory Sales Executives and Pilot Sales Representatives cover the market and ensure availability of products with retailers.

(a) Urban

Manufacturing plants – Depots – Distributors – Retailers – Urban consumers (Number of sales territories – 135, distributors – 850, Direct reach retailers – 3.20 lakh).

(b) Rural

Manufacturing plants – Depots – Super distributors – Stockist – Retailers – Rural consumers (Sales territories – 35, Super distributors – 120, Stockists – 2,600, Direct reach retailers – 2.80 lakh).

Promotion

The company uses many promotion media and methods to reach the consumer.

(a) Haats: For Parachute, Shanti amla, Mediker.

(b) Melas: All products.

(c) TV: Parachute.

(d) Delivery vans: To reach retailers in interior villages.

(e) Jatra: To promote Parachute uttam brand coconut oil, in West Bengal and Odisha.

"A Campaign in Progress"

The company believes that the potential is huge in rural markets and would like to expand the operations in the long run.

NIRMA CHEMICALS LIMITED

In olden days, the detergent powder category belonged to Lever's Surf. Common opinion was a quality detergent, had to be a blue powder, packed in a colourful carton. But Nirma was launched as a white coloured product, packed in pouches, sealed at the top, with no colour or design sophistication on the pack. The product was priced at around 35 per cent of Surf. Nirma's market share grew from 0 per cent in 1976 to about 60 per cent in 1987. Nirma dared to break the rule that a packaged, especially advertised brand needed the paraphernalia of branch office, area managers and sales representatives in order to carry it through wide and complicated network. Nirma went in for a "no-frills" approach in production, sales distribution and organisational arrangements. The title 'Nirma girl' going round and round on her feet makes a strong mnemonic for the brand.

Nirma shattered the myth 'economy at the cost of quality.' Nirma over a period of ten years has become the largest selling brand and the success of Nirma is due to affordable price, medium quality, distribution reach and effective use of media.

NOKIA INDIA (PRIVATE) LIMITED

Nokia is a Finnish Multinational and it is said to be one of the largest manufacturer of mobile phones in the world. Nokia was one of the first companies to realise the importance of rural market and started developing mobile phones to meet the specific requirements of rural India. Nokia 1100, the most popular handset has a rubber key pad which is dust resistant and also has a Torch. The phone is compact, sturdy and very reasonably priced. It holds the record for the highest number of mobile handsets sold in the world. The company after extensive research has launched Life Tools. Nokia Life Tool is a software suite embedded in some models of Nokia phones and provides specialised services. These services are available in handset models such as Nokia 2323, 2330, 2070 and 2730.

Examples: Nokia Life Tools Agricultural Services provide information on seeds, fertilisers, pesticides, market prices, rainfall, temperature, etc., via mobile phones. Nokia Life Tools Education Services aim to give career and education services and Nokia Life Tools Entertainment has features such as news, ringtones, astrology, etc. Nokia has launched these services in Maharashtra with great success. The service is priced at ₹ 60 per month and the farmer receives information on three crops and weather conditions.

SYNGENTA (INDIA) LIMITED

Syngenta is a leading multinational engaged in production and marketing of high quality seeds and crop protection chemicals and has an annual turnover of over ₹ 2,500 crore. The company has appointed over 100 consignment agents/distributors in key agricultural centres in the country. These distributors receive stocks directly from the factories and they in turn supply to wholesalers working at district/taluka/mandi level. The retailers obtain stocks from wholesalers. Interior markets are covered through van delivery operations.

The company uses mass media like regional television channels, local newspapers and radio for promoting their products. In addition, audiovisual publicity vans, group meeting of farmers, field demonstrations, participation in melas and haats are extensively used as a part of rural promotion. The field representatives focus on meeting the farmers, educating them on modern agricultural practices and right use of pesticides. They also regularly meet opinion leaders such as agricultural officers and research works to get recommendations for their products. The demand thus created for the products is serviced through a network of villager-level retailers.

TATA GROUP

Tata Group, one of the most respected corporates in the country, is engaged in manufacturing and marketing of a wide range of products from steel to retailing. The group has taken a number of marketing initiatives to improve the living conditions and quality of life of rural people.

Tata BP Solar: About 70 per cent of the electricity is used in towns and cities, though 70 per cent of the population lives in rural areas. Considering the basic needs of rural people, Tata BP Solar has come out with products and services.

Example: Solar home lighting, Solar lanterns, Solar cookers, Solar hot water systems, Arogya (vaccine refrigerator) and Teja electric power to computers. Sun Bank, a customised package for rural banks, consists of a power pack along with solar modules, batteries and controllers and provides power for three to six hours a day. 75 per cent of the product is sold in rural and semi-urban areas.

Tata Chemicals have set up Tata Kisan Sansar offering technical service and agricultural inputs to farmers. Tata Kisan Sansar offers soil and water testing, contract farming, credit facilities (through banks). Qualified agricultural graduates visit farmers' fields and advise them on modern farming methods. Farmers can become members of the Tata Kisan Parivar. There are about 30,000 farmers who have been trained in latest farming practices.

Tata Motors found out through field research that rural market required a product between a three-wheeler and a pick-up truck at an affordable price. They come out with Tata Ace, a sturdy vehicle that can carry a load of 1.5 metric tonnes over a distance of about 300 kms. It is a mini-Tata Truck and the utility vehicle is used to transport goods to villages and back. Roadshows were conducted in selected villages. ACE was called "Baby Elephant" compared to Tata Truck that represents "Mother Elephant". The Ace has been well received in the market.

Tata Tele Services started its operations in Andhra Pradesh. The company has started Family and Friend Programme at special calling rates and provide information services. The farmers can avail the SMS facility to find out crop prices, get weather updates and price of agricultural inputs and equipments. The cost of the service has been adapted for the rural customers.

TTK (PRESTIGE PRESSURE COOKERS)

Prestige, India's leading pressure cooker brand, over the last few years was faced with the problem of stagnant/declining sales and reduced realisations. The pressure cooker category growth rates itself were on the decline and with the menace of the underorganised sector, volumes have been under pressure for most manufacturers. Urban markets were getting saturated, in fact, markets like Mumbai were having negative growth rates. Also, Prestige Popular, in larger sizes (which sell in the South – strong hold) was launched in 1999, and since then the sales of premium offering has been on the decline. This was when the company decided that rural markets were going to be a thrust area. Traditionally, Prestige was very strong in the higher population strata markets and market share declined as one came down the population strata.

The company decided to do a pilot project in the rural Mehboobnagar district of Andhra Pradesh with the help of MART, an agency with vast expertise in the field. At this point of time, Hindustan Lever was in the process of rolling out its Project Shakti, its rural marketing initiative also with assistance from MART in AP. The Women's self-help group (SHG) movement has been very strong in AP. These are basically groups of women – around 15 a group – who save a rupee a day and the corpus so generated is loaned out to members of the group to help them in their work and not for meeting personal needs. The groups get a matching loan from the Government on soft terms. The interest earned is ploughed back into the corpus. There are over four lakh such groups in AP.

MART and the company organised meetings of the women of the SHGs explaining the concept of pressure cooking, giving them details on the company, the brand and what they stand to gain by selling Prestige pressure cookers. For enlisting dealers, the help of 'animators', who are paid a stipend by the Government for propagating/implementing developmental activities of the State Government among the rural population, was enlisted. All those who became dealers were given a demo pressure cooker. Meetings were organised by the dealers for potential customers, where the concept of pressure cooking was explained. These meetings were attended by company personnel so that the dealers got trained on the concept of pressure cookers.

Intense working of these markets for two months by a management trainee of the company along with the guidance provided by MART saw the company selling 50 pressure cookers. There were major learnings for the company on how to go rural and the problems like logistics and high price points. They realised that we needed to have a product at a much lower price point, as rural purchasing power was limited. There are now working on a 'rural' brand at a much lower price point, which should get launched in the next two months. The other crucial aspect was the need to take care of the logistics as there were no distributors, where these dealers existed. TTK is now directly supplying to these dealers from warehouses at Hyderabad/Vijaywada.

To take the initiative forward, the company got in touch with the Department of Women Empowerment. The TTK group was asked to make a proposal on how it could work with the Government on improving the lot of the rural women. After prolonged discussions with the department, TTK gave a proposal which was a three pronged strategy:

- Appointing women as dealers of 'Prestige';
- Setting up an assembly plant in AP with land and building provided by the Government using women of the rural areas;
- Setting up a ready-to-fry snacks conversion units in each of the 21 districts of AP with equipment provided by TTK and appointing dealers to sell these snacks in each

of the mandals in these 21 districts (around 1,000). The TTK group had its own brand of ready-to-eat snack. Fryums, which had been withdrawn but the group sells pellets to converters who convert it to ready-to-fry snacks and sell it. The whole proposal involved creating one lakh women work days and generating ₹ 3.42 crore of income for the rural women in the fifth year of operation.

For setting up the assembly unit, the group asked for some fiscal benefits from the State Government. The proposal was accepted in principle by the department and the company and the departments are working hand-in-hand for its implementation.

TTK Prestige has set up a four-member sales team to take the rural initiative forward. During the financial year 2003-04, 1,000 dealers are to be appointed. Dealers would be women as individuals or SHGs themselves. A woman or an SHG can become a dealer by paying around ₹ 5,000 for a lot of six pressure cookers. The company provides one free demo cooker to the dealer. The company coordinates with the department and organises a series of meetings involving SHG members in the district to enlist dealers.

Once a woman becomes a dealer, the rural promoter of the company works with her in making calls to prospective customers. When the dealer is able to get a gathering of prospects, a demo is done by the rural promoter. The AP Government has been releasing gas connections under the 'Deepam' scheme to the people in rural areas, whereby the Government pays the deposit to the oil company and the beneficiary has to pay for the cylinder, gas stove and regulator. The beneficiaries are the members of the SHGs based on seniority. The TTK group is selling its gas stoves to the SHGs, who in turn, sell to the beneficiaries making a profit. Around 16 lakh gas connections are to be released this year and the company intends to make a dent in this segment.

TTK Prestige is working on a separate sub-brand to be sold exclusively through rural women. This will be at a much lower price point. As sales from the rural initiative are incremental, margins have been kept to a bare minimum. The products will not be compromised in any way. There will be some product differentiators to prevent the product from coming into the normal channel and affecting company realisations.

The assembly unit proposed to be set up will be for pressure cookers and gas stoves which can be sold in AP, both in the regular channel and the 'rural' channel proposed to be established. The 'polishing' and 'assembly' part will be done in this plant. Both these operations are labour-intensive. The department will provide the land and building and the company the machinery and expenditure. Employment will be provided to 75 women in the first phase.

In the ready-to-fry foods project a group of around 30 women will be formed in each district. Each member of this group has to invest around ₹ 4,000. The groups are licensed to use the Yummies brand name owned by TTK. Pilot projects are underway in four districts – Chittor, Ananthapur, Kurnool and Nellore where the groups are being formed to generate the corpus.

The company intends to replicate this model in three other southern states, i.e., Tamil Nadu, Karnataka and Kerala in the near future. This initiatives shows how the corporate sector and the government can work hand-in-hand to bring about rural upliftment.

SKS MICROFINANCE

SKS Microfinance is an Indian non-governmental organisation specialising in microfinance. It was founded in 1998 by Vikram Akula in Hyderabad, to provide small loans to poor women in rural areas. It is one of the largest and fastest-growing microfinance organisations in the world, with total disbursements exceeding $500 million to about 2.2 million customers mostly women spread across 25,000 villages in 15 states of India. SKS Microfinance had a logo that is distinctive and easy to identify. It included a visual of a group of five women which is core to the business. The visual was enclosed within two concentric circles in blue with "Swayam Krishi Sangam" (the full form of SKS) written in Telugu. Of late the company is facing problems in collecting dues from villages especially in Andhra Pradesh and it has affected the profitability of the company.

From Village Selection to Loan Disbursal

SKS Microfinance follows the Joint liability model founded by Prof. Mohammed Yunus's Grameen Bank in Bangladesh. They have adapted the model to the local context, integrating best practices from the industry and adding some of their own innovations. The methodology involves lending to individual women, utilising five member groups where groups serve as the ultimate guarantor for each member.

Before starting operations, the staff of SKS conducts village surveys to evaluate local conditions like population, poverty level, road accessibility, political stability and means of livelihood. After a village is selected, SKS staff introduces the community to its mission, methodology and services. Women form self-selected five-member groups to serve as guarantors for each other. Experience has shown that a five-member group is small enough to effectively enforce group peer pressure and, if necessary, large enough to cover repayments in case a member needs assistance. Compulsory Group Training (CGT) is a four-day process consisting of hour-long sessions designed to educate clients on SKS processes and procedures and to also build a culture of credit discipline. Using innovative visual and participatory teaching methods, SKS staff introduces clients to their financial products and delivery methods. CGT also teaches clients the importance of collective responsibility, how to elect group leaders, how to affix signatures and a pledge that serves as a verbal contract between SKS and its members.

During this training period, SKS staff collects quantitative data on each client to ensure qualification requirements are met, as well as to record baseline information for future analysis.

On the fourth day, clients take a "Group Recognition Test" conducted by a different staff member than the one who trained them. If they pass, they are officially accepted as SKS members.

Technology

SKS has designed and deployed a web-based Business Intelligence Portal using state-of-the-art technology and a highly flexible and scalable platform to support the business growth and operations. The systems designed and deployed at SKS have enabled the business to grow to nearly 5.5 million customers and are providing the technology foundation to achieve the next phase of growth, reaching 15 million customers by 2015.

The Products

(a) **Income Generating Loan** is available to all SKS members who use it for setting up micro enterprises that help generate income for their families.

Examples: Vegetable vending, General store, Sweet making shop, Ice cream vending, Leasing mango trees and Farm lands, Flour mills, Tea shop, Pan shop, etc.

Members submit a loan application and based on approval receive the loan after one week. Loans are repaid in 50 equal, weekly instalments. In the first year, a member is eligible to borrow up to ₹ 16,000. After completion of a loan cycle, the client can submit a loan application for a future loan. SKS's guiding principle is to provide opportunity, not charity. SKS approach is to enable the poor to lift themselves out of poverty by providing a stream of credit rather than one-time charitable grants that are short-term solutions to long-term economic problems. The company charges an average interest rate of 24 per cent and may look high. However, the moneylenders charge anywhere between from 50 per cent to 100 per cent. The poor are earning high returns on their micro enterprises that they have no problem paying 24 per cent if their returns are averaging 100 per cent or so.

Examples:

1. Ananthamma an SKS entrepreneur live in Nakrekal village in Nalgonda district. Ananthamma learnt the art of weaving baskets from thin strips of bamboo from her husband. Together they make 15 baskets in a day and sell them in the Sathupally village market. Ananthamma came to know about SKS and its financial services in her village. She joined as a member and availed an income-generating loan of ₹ 8,000 to purchase raw materials for weaving bamboo baskets, broomsticks, etc., for their products. As the raw material is available only from December to April, they had to purchase as much as possible and preserve it for future use. A mid-term loan of ₹ 8,000 helped her to handicraft more products with new designs to sell them in the local market. They also supply few of their products in the shops of Nalgonda, Nakrekal and Suryapet. With another income-generating loan of ₹ 8,000, her husband invested in the purchase of raw materials. He undertook orders for making bamboo mandaps at marriage venues and other functions for which their charges range from ₹ 2,000 to ₹ 10,000.

2. Manju Devi, an SKS entrepreneur belongs to Chomu village near Jaipur. She got married to Lakhraj at the age of 18 and has three children who are studying in a nearby school. Lakhraj designed sarees with 'aara thaari' and 'zardosi work' to earn his living. He received orders from his neighbours and the local shops to design the sarees and earned income based on the workmanship. He wanted to set up a shop and employ few others in the village, but financial constraints restricted his growth. Manju often shared his work, in order to get more orders from the customers.

She joined SKS in 2006 and availed an income generating loan worth ₹ 10,000 and bought plain sarees from a local wholesale dealer. She also invested some amount to purchase embroidery threads and needles. Later, with a mid-term loan of ₹ 6,000, she bought two sewing machines and employed two workers for the same. With the second income-generating loan of ₹ 14,000, she purchased two more machines and bought another set of sarees from the wholesale dealer. Apart from the workers in the workshop, she employed skilled labour to undertake hand-made 'zardosi work'. All the workers are paid according to their workmanship on an hourly basis while she earns ₹ 150 per day. Her sarees range from ₹ 100 to ₹ 5,000. Meanwhile, Lakhraj developed contacts in Jaipur and visited the shops every week to take orders personally. This has helped Manju to monitor the workshop and the workmanship of her labour.

(b) Emergency Loan helps members survive during times of emergencies, such as illness, funeral expenses or maternity and health care. Very limited applicability reserved for only the most desperate situations. Level of need may be determined by seeing if member is willing to sell or pledge her jewels for money. Minimum amount granted is ₹ 500. Maximum is ₹ 2,000. No interest is charged.

(c) Abhay Loan Cover Insurance is intended to protect the member and her family from the financial burden of loan repayment in the event of death of spouse or the member, or both.

(d) Health Insurance Programme: Sum insured (maximum available limit in a year) — ₹ 10,000 per individual for single member family. Family floater ₹ 20,000 per family of 2, 3 and 4 members.

(e) Mobile Financing: In its bid to provide products and services that the members need SKS offers a mobile handset loan product which aims at improving productivity and offering connectivity for their members. SKS has tied up with Nokia, one of the world's largest maker of mobile handsets, and Airtel, India's largest mobile service provider, to help member's access mobile phones and quality phone services. SKS members can take a mobile loan after paying ₹ 175. The balance payment can be made in 25 equal weekly instalments of ₹ 70. SKS charges an interest rate of 26.14 per cent on this loan. SKS members get a Nokia handset Model 1662 at ₹ 1,798 while the market cost is ₹ 1,999. Airtel's package offers price advantage features like extra talk time.

(f) Sangam Stores Project is aimed at providing working capital finance to SKS members who own small 'kirana' stores. With credit supplied by SKS, shopkeepers can buy consumer goods and groceries through a dedicated third-party vendor. This relationship gives access to quality products at competitive prices that are delivered straight to their shops. The members of SKS save time and transport costs normally spent on buying goods from local markets. SKS is partnering with Metro, the German wholesaler, which supplies member kiranas from a special inventory of 250 SKS. Under this project, SKS generates and aggregates demand from kirana store owners, in addition to supplying credit to them. The Sangam store project currently covers 85 stores on the outskirts of Hyderabad in Andhra Pradesh. This pilot project is the first step towards creating a vibrant distribution network across sections of the society currently not serviced by manufacturers.

(g) **Housing:** Many SKS members have asked for larger loans to make improvements on their homes or build new ones. SKS has launched a housing loan project for members who have been with SKS for a minimum of three years. Members can repair their houses, such as changing a thatched or asbestos roof to RCC or make improvements such as building a latrine or adding an extra room. The loan has a repayment period of three to five years as per the repayment capacity of the members. SKS is currently carrying out a pilot programme in rural markets with support from HDFC and hopes to roll out housing loans more widely in the next financial year.

(h) **Water Purifier:** The company has partnered with Hindustan Unilever to provide Pureit water filter devices to SKS members. SKS provides the loan to make the water filter affordable and HUL provides the distribution, installation, and servicing that ensures that members have access to clean water. SKS is currently assessing the learning from the pilot branches and will determine a rollout plan to reach SKS members all over India in the coming months.

(i) **Solar Lamps:** Most of the members of SKS live in areas that have erratic power supply forcing business and normal lifestyle to come to a halt with sunset. Solar-powered lighting gives members the opportunity to be independent from unreliable, low-voltage electricity grids or to light their homes if theirs are currently unelectrified.

Beyond Microfinance

In order to provide access to quality primary education across India, SKS in 2009 registered an SKS Educational Society, which established 16 academies around Andhra Pradesh. The SKS Bodhi Academies located in 4 districts of Andhra Pradesh (Medak, Nalgonda, Warangal and Khammam) were launched on June 15th, 2009.

SKS Bodhi Academies focus on providing excellent education to children of rural villages at a low cost price. The schools only charge 160-220 rupees per month and provide children with a complete English medium education. Care is taken to ensure that the schools are run professionally and the student-teacher ratio never exceeds 1:25. Teachers are recruited from local and non-local areas and are well qualified. They are then retrained in order to absorb the concepts and methodologies that are unique to SKS Bodhi Academies.

SKS believe that the most important way to improve the lives of the poor is through economic development. At SKS, they are proud of improving the lives of more than 5 million members through microfinance, which in turn fosters economic development. Each member is able to use microfinance to make a better life for herself and her family. Microfinance enables people to earn income and build assets, which means families eat better, they can afford health care, and children are more likely to attend school. Within the microfinance sector, SKS has been able to distinguish itself through its performance. SKS have successfully applied methods from the business world, such as the use of standardisation and automation, to build an organisation that leads the microfinance industry in a number of areas, including rapid growth, high quality service to the members, streamlined delivery, transparency and innovative products.

WESTERN UNION SERVICES INDIA (PRIVATE) LIMITED

India is the largest recipient of remittances in the world and roughly 60 per cent of those go into rural areas. In 2009, the overseas remittances in to India touched 50 billion US dollars.

Western Union was founded in 1851 as the New York and Mississipi Valley Printing Telegraph Company. Today, the company has become an industry leader in global money transfer with four lakh agent locations in 200 countries. Western Union offers money order, money transfer, payment and prepaid services. In India, Western Union started operations in 1994. For the next seven years, it set up 3,000 agent locations, mostly in cities. Between 2001 and 2008, the company added 54,000 locations and about 5 per cent of them in the rural areas where there are no bank branches.

Today, Western Union is more village-centric, with almost 60 per cent of its entire network in rural India. Of the 54,000 locations, about 1,000 are sub-agents, 8,500 post offices and 20,000 bank branches. This makes the Western Union, the largest money transfer player in India in terms of reach. In order to further increase its reach, the company is looking at new channels like microfinance institutions and e-governance and IT solutions providers like CMS computers.

The rural strategy started with tie-ups with post offices and bank branches. The company found out that there are several villages with no post offices or bank penetration and therefore appointed sub-agents in remote villages. The sub-agent operates through phone and fax. The receiver gets a MTCN (Money Transfer Control Number) from the sender which he takes to the sub-agent. The sub-agent fills in a form with the transaction amount to be remitted. He then verifies the MTCN and the transaction amount with the principal agent's office. Once all the details are verified, the transaction is cleared. The sub-agents then hands over the cash against photo ID of the receiver. Typically, a sub-agent earns about ₹ 4,000 per month. The average ticket size of the transaction is between ₹ 5,000 and ₹ 10,000. The sub-agent gets a commission on each transaction, which ranges between 0.5 to 0.8 per cent of the transacted amount. The higher the value of the transaction, the higher the commission and it can go up to 1 per cent.

The biggest challenge for Western Union is the availability of cash in the villages. The company needs sub-agents who are cash-rich and are able to give money to the receiver as and when he needs. Another issue is awareness of the Western Union service which is currently low in rural India. The company is conducting awareness campaign to educate receivers.

CONCLUSION

Rural India is emerging as a large market for a number of goods and services. Many companies are actively promoting their products and have achieved a high percentage of sales in rural markets. It is evident from the above corporate examples, that to succeed in the market-place, companies should have long-term plans, high level of commitment to rural markets, effective distribution set-up coupled with promotion plans and a dedicated sales force.

QUESTIONS

1. Elaborate with examples the problems faced by companies in rural markets.
2. "Think Global and Act Local should be the focus of rural marketing initiatives." Discuss.
3. What is that we can learn from "Success stories" of companies in rural market?

CASE STUDY

Rural Marketing Strategy for Fast-moving Consumer Goods

West Coast Industries is a leading player in consumer goods industry with a turnover of over ₹ 800 crore. The company has three types of products, i.e., Health Care Products (Healthy Life sunflower oil, Mothers' Choice groundnut oil, Milky White toothpaste/tooth-powder), Natural Products (Kesavardini hair oil, Everfair Teen fairness cream, Glow 'n' Flow shampoo) and Third Party Brands (111 bar soap, Babycare diapers, Cool Spice after-shave lotion, Sun detergents).

The company, through 40 C&F agents and about 1,000 distributors, is able to reach one lakh retailers. The distributors get 3 per cent discount on health care products and 5 per cent discount on nature care products. The retailer gets 5 per cent margin on health care products and 10 per cent on nature care products. About 30 per cent of all India sales is from rural and semi-urban areas. The products are targeted towards young and middle-aged people; and middle/high income rural population. The company has also observed that loose oils are preferred in many markets and branded oils have become popular in a few states only.

The company has made use of television to reach rural population, but finds it expensive to cover all the states in the country.

The set-up of Sales and Marketing Department is given below:

Chief Executive Officer

General Manager (Sales), General Manager (Marketing) and General Manager (Supply Chain)

Regional Sales Managers — 8

Area Sales Managers — 32

Terriroty Sales Executives/Officers — 160

The company has undertaken the following initiatives in rural areas:

- The company has introduced sachet pack (100 ml/50 ml) of Kesavardini in areas of Tamil Nadu, Andhra Pradesh and Maharashtra.
- The company has 120 super distributors and 2,700 stockists to service the rural markets. The super distributors get 15-21 days' credit facilities.
- The distribution covers 20,000 villages (in comparison to Colgate — 50,000 and HLL — 80,000). The products are sold in village shandies and through company vans to retailers.

- The Territory Sales Executive spends about 70 per cent of his time in meeting retailers and key influencers, participation in village events, organising meetings and balance in planning activities.
- Under Territory Sales Executives, there are Pilot Sales Representatives (partly subsidised by the company) for meeting the village merchants. They are under the control of super distributors. Each village merchant is met once a month through van operations.

QUESTIONS

1. Do you think that there is scope for increasing sales volumes in rural market.
2. Give your specific recommendations as to how the company can improve distribution and promotion reach in rural markets.

CASE STUDY

Rural Marketing Strategy for Ready-made Garments

MFL Group is an established business house in urban market for ready-made and designer garments with the brand name of COMFORT. The company mainly targeted the middle and upper-middle-class customers in urban markets and has earned a good name in selling reasonably priced, good quality of ready-made garments for children and adults. Considering the success of India's leading denim manufacturer Arvind Mill's Ruf & Tuf Jeans and T-shirts in rural market, the management of the company decided to identify target market and work-out marketing plans for selling ready-made garments in the rural areas having a population of minimum 2,000 and above.

A market research was conducted and the study revealed:

- Pricing at ₹ 195 per piece, training to local tailors for easy accessibility and availability of product at local garment shops were some crucial factors for success of Ruf & Tuf ready to stitch jeans.
- The Western attire is catching up among rural youth. But, branded clothes and shoes have not been able to make any mark here. The male rural youth prefers sober wear and there is a huge potential for cotton and formal trousers. The role models of rural youth are elder members of the family who have been successful in big towns, cities or metros. Rural consumers are more particular about quality and value and are also brand loyal.
- During the recent past, rural women are becoming more aware of fashion and also playing influential role in buying decisions. However, the mobile traders or *pheriwallas* are major source of purchase for majority of rural women and several complained of them selling spurious products and moving on.
- The demand for garments is throughout the year but it drastically increases during the festival seasons. Social customs and community influences still play a major role in rural area.
- Alternative media and local brand ambassadors are considered more effective in generating hype about a new product or re-launch an existing one. Since the survey indicated tremendous potential waiting to be tapped in rural market, the company decided to enter the rural market with a new brand of ready-made garments tailored to suit the needs of the rural market.

QUESTION

- As a management consultant, please give your comments on strategy to be adopted by company in respect of: (a) Product (including brand names), (b) Pricing, (c) Distribution and Servicing, and (d) Promotion.

14 AGRICULTURAL MARKETING

INTRODUCTION

Agriculture continues to be a major source of income in the rural areas of our country. It provides employment to about 65 per cent of the rural population. Agriculture supplies raw materials like raw cotton, sugarcane, etc., required by the industry. However, the contribution of agriculture to GDP has come down during the recent years and there is a need to come out with an integrated approach to accelerate agricultural production in our country and improve the efficiency of agricultural marketing.

AGRICULTURAL MARKETING

According to Thomsen, "the study of agricultural marketing comprises all operations and the agencies conducting them, involved in the movement of farm produced foods, raw materials and their derivatives such as textiles from the farm to the final consumers and the effects of such operations on farmers, middlemen and consumers". This definition does not include the input side of agriculture.

Agricultural marketing comprises of all the operations involved in the movement produce of food and raw materials (For exmple, cotton and sugarcane) from the place of production to the place of consumption. It includes handling of products at the farm, initial processing, grading and packing in order to maintain and enhance the quality and avoid wastage. It is the study of all activities, agencies and policies involved in the movement of agricultural produce from the farms to the consumers. Agricultural commodities have special characteristics and therefore marketing of agricultural commodities is different from marketing of manufactured goods. One of the important objectives of agricultural marketing is to ensure that agricultural produce is brought from villages and moved to urban areas for human and industrial consumption. Agricultural produce marketing is a link between the farm and the non-farm sectors.

"Potato Harvesting"
(potato production is seasonal and agricultural marketing facilitates availability of the produce throughout the year)

FEATURES OF AGRICULTURAL COMMODITIES

1. Small and Scattered Production: About 75% of the land holdings consist of small and marginal farmers as shown below:

Table 14.1

	Size of Land Holding in Hectares	Proportion of Holding (%)
(a) Marginal farmers	(Up to one ha)	56.50
(b) Small farmers	(1-2 ha)	18.00
(c) Semi-medium farmers	(2- 4 ha)	14.00
(d) Medium farmers	(4-9 ha)	9.10
(e) Large farmers	(above 10 ha)	2.40
		100.00

Example: Kerala has maximum percentage (90 per cent) of farmers having less than one hectare of land, followed by West Bengal (80 per cent).

As the small farmers' production is very small, they cannot influence the market supply or the price of his produce. In the case of manufactured goods, the manufacturer can fix the price of the product and can influence the price of the product he sells.

2. Seasonal Production: Crop cultivation is carried out during khariff and rabi season. During harvesting season, the prices of the commodities come down in the market. The production and supply of manufactured goods can be adjusted, based on the demand and the prices can remain almost the same throughout the year.

3. Bulky and Perishable Products: Most farm products are perishable in nature. While with proper storage facilities, the agricultural commodities can be stored for a longer period;

they cannot be made non-perishable like some of the manufactured goods. Due to bulkiness of the farm products, transportation and storage become difficult and expensive. This demands greater care in storage and transportation.

4. Variation in Quality and Quantity: The production depends upon environmental factors like rainfall and pest incidence. Therefore, the products vary in quality and quantity.

5. Demand: The products are essential commodities. Hence, price changes do not bring great changes in demand. During season, the supplies are high and prices fall.

6. Unorganised Market: The markets are unorganised, unregulated and subject to manipulation by middlemen. It has been observed that the farmer gets only 40 to 60 per cent of the price paid by the consumer with the balance shared by various intermediaries.

7. Production-oriented Activity: The farmer is concerned only with production and he does not have sufficient finance, knowledge and expertise for marketing of the produce. He has no voice in fixing the ultimate price for the consumer.

VARIATION IN QUANTITY AND QUALITY

The heavy rains that hit the state have damaged the best varieties of Kashmiri apples, that were to hit markets by September-end. The recent hail storms have only added to the farmers' agony.

"Thousands of tonnes of apples have fallen prematurely. We were expecting a good harvest but the storm has left us shattered," said Bashir Ahmad Bashir, general secretary of New Kashmir Fruit Association. "Farmers had taken huge loans from banks and moneylenders, but now they are ruined," he added.

Kashmiri apples, known for their taste and juice, have already lost a huge market share to those grown in other Northern States due to the low prices of the latter variety. But planters in the state maintain that apples grown elsewhere are not as tasty as the one's grown in Kashmir.

Apple orchards cover around 72 per cent of the Kashmir Valley and the state produces 1.1 million tonnes of apples annually. Nearly 2.5 million people are directly or indirectly associated with this trade. The fruit industry, along with the tourism sector, goes a long way in sustaining the state's economy. The horticulture industry in Kashmir earns over ₹ 500 million yearly, a major share of which comes from apples.

Source: *DNA* September 23, 2006.

MARKETED AND MARKETABLE SURPLUS

One of the important objectives of agricultural marketing is to ensure that the surplus agricultural produce is brought from villages and moved to urban areas for human and industrial consumption. The marketable surplus is required for feeding the urban population and as raw materials for manufacturing and processing industries.

The importance of marketable surpluses is given below:

1. Marketable surpluses from agriculture is an important factor in the growth and development of economy. The real surpluses lead to increase in income and savings.

2. It indicate agricultural productivity in terms of input-output relations.
3. Marketable surpluses provide adequate availability of agricultural commodities to urban population.
4. Provide opportunities for growth of agro-based industries such as paddy processing, cotton ginning, oil extraction and sugar factories.
5. Increase in the purchasing power of rural people and development of consumer goods and services sector.
6. High marketable surpluses will lessen the burden on food subsidies.

Nearly 60 per cent of the area under cultivation is occupied by food crops. Farmers prefer to retain sufficient quantities of food production for own consumption and therefore only about 50 per cent of production goes to the market. In the case of manufactured products, the entire production is set aside for sale, but not so in the case of agricultural produce. The actual amount of produce sold is dependent on a large number of factors. The producer's surplus is of two types:

Manufactured Goods	Agricultural Commodities
1. Industrial manufacturers give equal attention to production and marketing of their products.	1. Farmers are concerned only with production of commodities.
2. Manufacturer has major voice in marketing and channel choice.	2. Farmer has practically no voice in marketing and channel choice.
3. Middlemen cannot exploit the manufacturer.	3. As the middlemen dominate the market, they exploit the farmer in all possible ways.
4. Assembling is not a problem.	4. Assembling is the major problem.
5. Manufacturer has effective control on the quantity of the goods to be manufactured.	5. Farmers have no effective control over quantity as well as quality of the produced commodities.
6. Marketing process is not very complicated or elaborate.	6. Most complicated, with many middlemen involved in the process.
7. Cost of transportation and storing is not excessive.	7. Transportation and storage costs are too exorbitant.
8. Tools of promotion or demand creation play a very important role in marketing.	8. As demand for agricultural goods is inelastic, continuous and regular, there is no need for demand creation activities.
9. Product differentiation, branding, advertising and sales promotion are common features.	9. Show progress in branding and product differentiation.
10. Manufacturer's reputation can indicate quality of products. Manufacturer is the creater of his brand.	10. In the absence of branding, products are bought only on the basis of real quality and not on the basis of producer's reputation.

Fig. 14.1: Difference between the marketing of agricultural commodities and manufactured goods

1. Marketable Surplus

The farmer keeps some quantity of the output to meet his requirements for family consumption, seeds, cattle feed, payment to labour, carpenter, mechanic, landlord as rent and other payments in kind. Balance quantity of the produce is made available to non-farm population.

The marketable surplus can be expressed as:

MS = P – R

Where MS = Marketable surplus, P = Total production and R = Total requirement.

2. Marketed Surplus

The quantity of farm produce actually sold irrespective of his requirements for family, farm needs and other requirements. Marketed surplus can be more than, less than or equal to marketable surplus, as per example given below:

Table 14.2

MARKETABLE AND MARKETED SURPLUS

Example: Paddy

Total production: 1,000 kgs.
Total requirement: 400 kgs.
Marketable surplus: 600 kgs.

Marketable Surplus	Marketed Surplus	Remarks
600 kgs.	700 kgs.	Farmer retains less than his requirement.
600 kgs.	500 kgs.	Farmer retains more than his requirement.
600 kgs.	600 kgs.	Farmer retains neither more nor less than his requirement.

Marketed surplus is more than marketable surplus when the farmer *retains less than his actual requirements for family and farm needs*. This is common for small and marginal farmers who are forced to sell the produce to meet immediate cash requirements. The quantity sold increases with the fall in the prices of the produce. These farmers also buy the produce from the market at a later period to meet household requirements.

Marketed surplus is less than marketable surplus when the farmer *retains some of the surplus produce*. Large farmers very often sell less than the marketable surplus anticipating a higher price at a later period.

Marketed surplus is equal to marketable surplus when the farmer *retains neither more nor less than his requirements*. This holds good for perishable commodities and of the average farmers.

FACTORS AFFECTING MARKETABLE SURPLUS

1. Intensity of Cultivation: Intensive cultivation practices such as use of high yielding seeds, fertilisers and pest management practices will lead to higher yields.

2. Consumption Habits: Northern states produce both rice and wheat but they are wheat-consuming states. Therefore, almost entire quantity of rice produced is sold.

3. Cash Requirements of Farmers Affect Marketable Surplus: If the farmer is badly in need of money to meet his household expenses or other commitments, he may sell a large quantity of the produce.

4. Size of the Farm: The production is high and more marketable surplus in the case of larger farms.

5. Nature of Crops Grown: Some farmers grow food as well as cash crops and they sell only produce from cash crops.

Example: A farmer cultivates cotton and paddy in the same farm. He keeps paddy for family consumption and sells cotton to merchants.

6. Size of the Family: will have an impact on the marketable surplus.

Example: A farmer with a large family will have to keep more quantities of paddy for family consumption and therefore the quantity available for sales will be less.

7. Non-farm Income: If the farmer has income from other sources such as poultry, animal husbandry, then he will sell less than marketable surplus.

8. Storage Capacity: If the farmer has insufficient storage capacity, he will sell more in the market.

RELATION BETWEEN PRICES AND MARKETABLE SURPLUS

There are two theories advanced to explain the relationship between prices and marketable surplus of foodgrains.

Positive Relationship: According to V.M. Dandekar and Rajkrishna, there is a positive relationship between prices and marketable surplus of foodgrains. The farmers are price-conscious and when there is an increase in the prices of foodgrains, the farmers are inclined to sell more and retain less quantity of the produce. This results in increase in marketable surplus.

Inverse Relationship: P.N. Mathur and M. Ezekiel have presented a hypothesis, which states that there is an inverse relationship between prices and the marketable surplus. The farmer's cash requirements are almost fixed and they sell that quantity of foodgrains, which meets their cash requirements. With the increase in prices of foodgrains, they sell less quantity of foodgrains to get the cash they need. Therefore, with increase in price, the farmers sell less and with the fall in price they sell more quantity.

It has been observed that in the case of small farmers, there is an inverse relationship and there is a positive relationship between price and marketable surplus in the case of large farmers.

As per latest estimates, the percentage of the marketed surplus to total output is 60 per cent in the case of wheat, 50 per cent for rice and over 80 per cent for fruits and vegetables.

CLASSIFICATION OF MARKETS

The agricultural markets are classified as per details given below:

Basis for Classification

1. Frequency of Holding: Daily, Weekly and Bi-weekly markets.

Traditionally, on certain days of the week, both the sellers and buyers meet in the village to buy and sell goods. These are the Haats or Shandies that are being held once or twice in a week in rural areas. The sellers come in the morning and remain in the haat till late in the evening. Next day, they move to another haat. Vegetables, grains, consumer goods, etc., are sold in the haats to meet the requirements of the villagers. Similarly, there are daily markets for vegetables, fruits and grains in towns.

2. Time Span: Short period markets are held mostly for highly perishable commodities like milk and fish and in long period markets foodgrains, oilseeds are traded.

3. Volume of Business:

(a) **Wholesale Market:** Commodities are brought and sold in bulk quantities. Generally, the transaction takes place between traders. They are situated in towns and cities and act as a link between producing and consuming centres.

(b) **Retail Markets:** Commodities are sold to consumers. They are located very near to consumers.

4. Commodities Traded: The markets could be classified depending upon the type of agricultural commodities traded.

Example: Grain, vegetable, fruit and cotton markets.

5. Type of Marketing Functions:

(a) **Assembling:** Collecting the produce from farmers and moving them in large quantities in wholesale markets.

(b) **Processing:** Processing adds to the utility of the produce.
Example: Milling of pulses.

(c) **Distribution:** The farm produce is taken to the consuming market. It involves selling of the produce, storage and physical movement of the produce.

6. On the Basis of the Area Coverage:

(a) **Village Markets:** Buying and selling transactions are confined to the same village or nearby villages.
Example: Milk, vegetables and fruits.

(b) **District-level Market:** Buyers and sellers are drawn from a larger geographical area.
Example: Foodgrains.

(c) **State/National Level Markets:** Here commodities like tea, jute, etc., are traded.

(d) **World Market:** Sellers and buyers from all over the world participate in such markets.
Example: Gold, coffee, tea and cotton.

We can also classify agricultural markets into Village, Primary markets, Secondary markets, Terminal markets and Seaboard markets based on the location, frequency and volume of transactions.

TYPES OF AGRICULTURAL MARKETS

(a) Village Markets are located in villages and major transactions takes place among buyers and sellers of a village.

(b) Primary Markets: The basic function of primary market is to serve as assembling centre for local produce but they also function as distribution centre for local consumption. Produce from surrounding villages are sold in these markets. These markets are located in large villages or near centres of agricultural production and transactions take place between producer (farmers) and traders. These markets are held in open space or in thatched sheds in centrally situated localities. There is inadequate space that causes congestion and there is also lack of market amenities. There are about 27,000 rural periodic market in our country.

"A Weekly Bazaar (Haat) in Progress"

In these markets, a variety of commodities like cereals, pulses, oil seeds, fruits, vegetables and consumer goods are sold. They serve a radius of about 10 kms. depending on the availability of transport and communication facilities. Such markets provide a common platform to buyers and sellers in the village. These markets are also called "Haats or Shandies".

(c) **Secondary Wholesale Markets:** These are popularly known as Mandis or Gunjs and are located at taluka, district towns, main trade centres or near railway junctions. Transactions take place between village merchants and wholesalers. These markets assemble large quantities of commodities and commission agents/brokers play a major role in linking buyers and sellers in these markets. These markets have adequate transport, communication and banking facilities. There are around 7,000 wholesale assembling markets in India.

"A Grain Mandi"

(d) **Terminal Markets:** Here, the commodities are finally disposed of to the consumer or to the processor or assembled for exports. Terminal markets are situated in big cities like Mumbai, Delhi, Kolkata, etc. They are well organised and provided with storage and warehousing facilities.

(e) **Seaboard Markets:** These markets are situated near seashore and are meant for import and export of goods. Seaboard markets exist in Chennai, Mumbai, Cochin, Mangalore and Kolkata.

METHODS OF SALE

1. Moghum Sale: Sometimes, cultivators borrow from traders before the harvest of the crop. Under this method, the cultivator is bound to deliver the produce to the buyer on a set date within a period prescribed by a verbal understanding between the two. In return, the buyer is supposed to pay the price ruling on the date of delivery. In this type of sale, trust and understanding between the buyer and seller are important.

2. Hatta Sale (Undercover): The commission agent fixes the price of the produce on behalf of the farmer. Under this system, the commission agent covers his hand with a kerchief and invites offer individually from each buyer. The buyers make these offers in a secret language, which is mostly understood only by the commission agents and the buyers. Most of this secret language is a sign language that involves pressing fingers and finger joints. The highest offer made is intimated to the seller and if he agrees, the bid is closed. Thus, a sale gets confirmed. However, there is no guarantee that the benefit of this higher price always goes to the producer, as he is unaware of the price offered. This system is popularly known as undercover or secret sale.

Example: A box containing mangoes is first displayed to a group of vendors. The vendors bid by holding the merchant's hand under a cloth. Holding two fingers means ₹ 200 for each box. To show ₹ 250, the vendor holds two fingers and then grasps the vendor's palm.

"Hatta sale in Mango Market"

3. Sale by Open Auction: Under this method, the produce is sold through an open auction by the general commission agent or the brokers or some other auctioneer in the presence of the seller or his agent and the competing traders. The offer of the highest bidder is accepted with the consent of the seller. The seller has the discretion to refuse the offer of the bidder if he considers the bid too low. The objective of the system is to create conditions of perfect competition by eliminating undercover practices and providing for the interaction of the forces of supply and demand in relation to the quantity and quality variations. This is possible as a pre-auction inspection of the graded lots is allowed and disputes regarding the quality are eliminated. The farmer who views the open auction process gets a kind of a psychological satisfaction. He feels he cannot be cheated due to the open method of price fixation (bidding). The demerits of this system are:

(a) The process is very time-consuming and requires an extensively developed system of commercial grading.

(b) The auction has to be done by lots and this results in a large number of traders in the beginning but the number thins out as the day progresses.

Three types of open auctions are seen in agricultural commodities markets:

(a) Phar System of Open Auction: Under this method, one bid is given for all the lots in a particular shop and all the lots are sold at that price.

(b) **Random Bid System:** In this method, the commission agent invites only a few buyers. He does not inform all the prospective buyers in the market. This leads to less competition in the marketplace. In addition, bidding may continue in several places to reduce competition.

(c) **Roster Bid System:** Here, the auctions takes place in a systematic manner and is prevalent in regulated markets. Bidding starts from the point as notified earlier to all the prospective buyers. After completing auction in one shop, the bidding party moves to the next shop in a clock-wise or anti-clock-wise direction and completes the auction at all shops or till the expiry of the auction time. Next day, the auction starts from the last point. This overcomes the defects existing in the previous two methods of open auction.

5. Private Negotiations: This method of sale is common in villages and the prices are fixed between the buyer and seller by mutual agreement. The individual buyer come to the shop of commission agent, inspects the sample and offer the prices for the produce. If the price is accepted, the produce is sold to the buyer after weighment.

6. Sale by Tender System: Under this system, the produce is arranged lot-wise and is open for inspection by the intending buyers. The time is stipulated (fixed) for submission of tenders. The intending buyer after examining the lots, records the bids in their tender slip supplied by the market committee. These tender slips are then deposited in a sealed box. While depositing the bid-slip, the buyer also signs a priority register. The objective of using a priority register is that in case of tie-bid; the slip deposited first, as indicated by the register is deemed as the highest. Usually, the tender box is opened and the market superintendent or secretary compares the slips. The highest quotation for the lot is recorded in the bid-declaration slip. The maximum price quoted is announced on the public address system for the benefit of the sellers and buyers. If the seller is not willing to sell at the quoted price, he has to inform the market secretary within a predefined and stipulated time limit. There is a certainty of completing the sale of all the lots by the stipulated time irrespective of the numbers involved. It is further observed that the differences in price offered by the highest bidder and the nearest competitor in many cases is just a few rupees. This clearly indicates that the prices quoted are based more on individual calculations of profit margins rather than by simply working out the parity price based on terminal prices. The tender system of sale has one definite advantage over the open auction system, as it is time-saving.

7. Dara Sale Method: In this system, the heaps of grains of different quantity/quality are sold at a flat price. The advantage is that within a short time a large number of lots (heaps) can be sold.

Example: Sale of cumin by dara sale method.

8. State Trading: Government purchases huge quantities of paddy and wheat for distribution. While the procurement price is fixed, the actual price paid depends upon the quality of the produce, i.e., moisture content, inert materials, damaged or discoloured grains, chalky grains and pest infestation.

9. Forward Sale: Under this system, the producer sells his anticipated future produce in advance to the trader directly at a price fixed at the time of striking the deal either in the village or at the business place of the trader. Very often, it is an oral contract and is not enforceable in any court of law. The trader usually enters into a contract with a speculative motive and when the price declines subsequently he may force the seller to reduce the price by refusing to lift the produce.

Under Jalap sales, the traders purchase the standing crop of the producer well in advance of the harvest at a price fixed on the date of the bargain.

Example: Many contractors approach the mango growers and normally enter into verbal agreement with them by looking at the flower setting. The price is usually quoted in lump sum for the entire crop and the seller may receive 50 per cent of the value of the sale transaction in advance. Usually, the sale goes against the agriculturalist as the price is fixed and determined by the buyer on the basis of the urgency to sell and not on the basis of the prevailing market rates. Such price quotations are in most cases abnormally low, further if the crop fails to give the expected return, the buyer may force the producer to reduce the price further.

10. Sale by Sample: It is the most convenient method of sale where the produce is systematically graded. It saves the cost of transportation and inspection. However, utmost honesty in the dealing is to be followed. The producer or the commission agent shows the sample to the trader and finalises the price.

Examples:

(a) During cardamom auction, the buyers quote the price for the produce by looking at the samples.

(b) The mills purchase cotton by examining the sample shown by the cotton merchant.

CHANNELS OF DISTRIBUTION OF AGRICULTURAL PRODUCE

A number of intermediaries are involved in buying and selling of agricultural produce as per details given below:

1. Producer-Consumer: Farmer sells directly to consumer. Since there are no middlemen, the farmer receives a high price for the produce.

Example: Government-sponsored Rytubazar, i.e., Farmers' Market in Andhra Pradesh, Hadapsar vegetable market in Pune, Shetkari Bazar in Maharashtra and Krushale Bazar in Odisha.

2. Producer-Village Shopkeeper-Wholesaler-Retailer-Consumer: Village merchant buys tamarind and foodgrains from producer. The merchant either sells the produce in the same village or in the market.

3. Producer-Itinerant Merchant-Wholesaler-Consumer: Mobile merchant buys from farmers in small lots and pays after selling the produce. Many farmers prefer to sell to these mobile merchants since they get fair price and do not have to bother about transportation of the produce.

4. Producer-Primary Wholesaler-Secondary Wholesaler-Retailer-Consumer: This is a very common marketing channel in foodgrains producing areas. The farmer sells the produce in primary wholesale markets through Kachcha Arhatias. They in turn sell the produce to the secondary wholesaler through Pucca Arhatias. The wholesalers supply to retailers in urban areas.

Paddy and Rice Distribution

1. Producer-Commission Agent-Miller-Wholesaler-Retailer-Consumer: This is the most common marketing channel for paddy in our country. Commission agents contact the farmers and arrange to sell the produce to the millers. The millers sell the rice to wholesalers in urban areas and the wholesalers to retailers.

2. Producer-Itinerant Merchant-Miller-Retailer-Consumer: Itinerant merchant replaces commission agent.

3. Producer-Village Miller-Consumer: In many cases, the rice produced in the village is consumed in the same village or in the neighbouring villages. Therefore, milling is done in small rice mills and the rice is sold directly to the consumers.

4. Producer-Miller-Wholesaler-Retailer-Consumer: In this case, the miller buys the produce directly from the farmer and after milling, sells to wholesalers in towns. The retailers buy from wholesalers and sell it to consumers.

5. Producer-Government Miller-Fair Price Shop-Consumer: Here, Government procures a very large quantity of paddy and therefore exercises control over purchase, sales and distribution.

Wheat Distribution

Wheat is collected by intermediate traders, village banias, and cooperative societies. They in turn sell to the wholesale merchants. These wholesale merchants will distribute the wheat to rural, urban and export markets.

Cotton Distribution

The cotton passes from the farmer to village dealer/travelling buyer/cooperative society. From there, cotton passes through various middlemen and ginning mills. These middlemen sell the cotton to mills or exporters or merchants.

1. **Cotton Farmer-Village Dealer-Broker-Ginning Factory-Commission Agent-Mumbai Market.**
2. **Cotton Farmer-Travelling Buyer-Middlemen/Commission Agent-Ginning Mills-Broker-Mills.**
3. **Cotton Farmer-Cooperative Society-Mills/Exporters/Merchants**

PRIMARY MARKETING FUNCTIONS

1. Assembling: Assembling means collecting and bringing together goods of the same type from various sources or places of supply at a central place. A trader dealing in agricultural produce collects the goods lying at different places from different farmers and then brings the goods at a central place for the purpose of selling. The farmers are highly scattered over a wide geographical area and they produce in small quantities. There are variations with regard to quantity and quality of the produce. Therefore, assembling is an important function and many intermediaries participate in the process.

Examples:

(a) Farmers directly bring their produce to the nearby market.

(b) Big farmers collect produce from small farmers.

(c) Mobile merchants who move from village-to-village to collect agricultural produce. Kachcha Arhatias assemble the produce in the market.

2. Processing: Activities to convert raw materials and bring the product nearer to human consumption. It involves change in the form of the commodity. It adds value to the produce.

Examples: (a) Paddy to boiled rice and raw rice, (b) Tea processing, (c) Coffee curing, (d) Cashew processing, and (e) Milling of pulses.

3. Distribution: After assembling and processing, the farm produce is taken to the market for consumption. This involves storage, change of ownership of the produce through intermediaries and physical movement of stocks.

SECONDARY MARKETING FUNCTIONS

1. Standardisation and Grading: Standardisation involves fixing certain norms for the products. The norms are established by customs and tradition or by certain authority.

Grading follows standardisation and refers to classification of produce based by standards. Standardisation and grading benefits both the producers and consumers. It helps the consumers since they are able to get goods of standard quality and helps the producers in getting better price for their products.

2. Packaging: The main objective of packaging is to preserve the quantity and quality of the produce during storage and transit. It also helps in easy handling of the produce.

Example: Cotton after ginning is pressed into bales. Fruits like apple, grapes, strawberries are packed in hardboard boxes.

3. Transportation involves moving the agricultural produce from the place of production (farms) to the place of consumption. Agricultural products are perishable and therefore quick transportation from the farm to the consumption centres is required to maintain the quality of the produce. Transportation cost and handling charges for agricultural produce are high due to long distances beween farm and market and number of middlemen between the producer and consumer.

4. Storage: While agricultural production is seasonal, the consumption takes place throughout the year.

Example: Commodities like potatoes, apples can be stored in cold storage to make them available during off-season also.

5. Financing: Agricultural production takes place in interior villages. The produce has to be moved long distances and takes long time to reach the consumers and capital remains locked up during this period. Credit and money have to be made available to meet the cost of selling the produce to the final consumer.

6. Selling involves identification of different categories of customers, understanding their needs and wants and supplying the produce to meet their requirements and collecting money for the produce sold.

AGRICULTURAL MARKETING AGENCIES

The farmer has rich experience in cultivating the crop, but does not have the knowledge of marketing of agricultural produce. He engages the services of an intermediary, i.e., commission agent or dalal for selling his produce. A number of middlemen are involved in the marketing of agricultural produce as per details given below:

I. Village Level

1. Landlords: They are big cultivators and buy surplus produce from farmers and sell the same in the mandis.

2. Village Beoparis have their small establishments in villages. They purchase produce from farmers and they also supply consumption goods to the farmers. They act as financiers to the poor farmers. They visit neighbouring markets to know the prevailing prices and they sell the produce in the nearby market or even sell it in the village itself.

3. Mobile Beoparis (Itinerant Merchants) are petty merchants who move from village-to-village and purchase the produce from farmers. They do not have shops in the village. They transport the produce to the nearby market.

II. Mandi Level

There are two types of agents operating at mandi level and they are:

1. Commission Agent is a person who offers to make a purchase or sale of agricultural produce, on behalf of another person (buyer or seller) and receives a commission. He carries out all the activities required for completing sale or purchase of the commodities. The important functions are:

- Show the produce to the buyer
- Arrange for weighing equipment
- Arrange for delivery of the produce
- Collect payment from the buyer and make payment to seller.

There are two types of commission agents, i.e., Kachcha Arhatias and Pucca Arhatias.

(a) **Kachcha Arhatias:** They are basically small commission agents and act for the sellers including farmers. They sometimes provide money to farmers on the condition that the produce will be sold to them.

(b) **Pucca Arhatias:** They are big commission agents and act on behalf of traders as well as farmers. They are processors of rice, oilseeds and dealers in cotton/jute, etc. They are wholesalers. They advance loan to farmers to enable them to meet their cultivation expenses. They often advise the farmers on the use of agricultural inputs and also supply these inputs to them. They arrange for storage facility and advance loan for the stored commodities. They arrange for transportation of the agricultural produce. Arhatias charge arhat or commission of about 2 per cent in addition to the normal rate of interest on the money they advance. In vegetable markets, the commission earned by Pucca Arhatias is about ten per cent depending upon the type of service offered to the farmers.

2. Broker/Dalal: The main function of a dalal is to bring together buyer and the seller on the same platform for negotiation and they charge brokerage from the buyer, the seller or from both. Dalals do not invest in trade. They pass on vital information such as details of arrivals, price trends to the buyers and sellers. Dalals have no regular establishments in the market. They are commonly seen in mandis/gunjs. He is not concerned with the custody of goods sold or purchased and does not take responsibility for payment. He acts as a middlemen between buyers and sellers and his brokerage is less than that of commission agent.

CONCLUSION

Indian agriculture is known for providing employment, livelihood and food securities. The situation of Indian economy is likely to remain unchanged for a long time. In order to meet the requirements of growing population, there is a need to increase food production and make the produce available to urban population. Agricultural marketing comprises of all the operations involved in the movement of food and raw materials from the place of production to the place of consumption and facilitates availability of the produce throughout the year.

QUESTIONS

1. Define agricultural marketing. What are the features of agricultural produce? How are they different from consumer goods?
2. Discuss primary and secondary marketing functions.
3. Describe the role of marketing agencies in agricultural produce marketing.
4. Discuss the concept of marketable surplus and marketed surplus and factors affecting marketable surplus. Is marketable surplus price-sensitive?
5. What are the methods of sales used in marketing of agricultural produce? Which are the methods not favourable to farmers? Which methods are practised in regulated markets and Why?
6. Distinguish between Haats, Mandis and Melas.

✿ ✿ ✿

15 DEFECTS IN THE AGRICULTURAL MARKETING SYSTEM AND LINES OF IMPROVEMENT – PART I

INTRODUCTION

Agricultural marketing includes all activities, agencies and policies involved in the movement of agricultural produce from the farms to the consumers. In our country, the markets for agricultural commodities are generally unorganised and unregulated. Very often, the farmers are forced to sell their produce at low prices due to deficiencies in the agricultural marketing system.

DEFECIENCIES IN AGRICULTURAL MARKETING SYSTEM

1. Lack of Organisation among Producers

Lack of organisation among producers is one of the basic and fundamental problems in the Indian agricultural marketing scenario. The farmers of India are small and scattered all across the country. The farmers are not united at village level and they are not able bargain and obtain a higher price for their produce. An organisational attempt at the grass root level usually fails. The progress of Cooperative Movement in India is very slow and the small farmers lack organisation.

2. Forced Sale

A majority of the farmers are forced to sell their produce in the village itself and the reasons are:

(a) A high percentage of produce is sold in the village itself due to the indebtedness of the farmer. It is this indebtedness that is responsible for low standard of living and poverty among the villagers.

Example: Village sale in about 20-50 per cent in the case of foodgrains.

(b) The farmers borrow money from moneylenders at exorbitant rates for meeting cultivation expenses or performing marriage ceremony. The farmers are forced to sell the produce to the moneylenders at low rates. The farmers are dominated by moneylenders.

(c) The presence of uneconomic holding is also responsible for rural indebtedness. When the holdings are small, the cultivation becomes unremunerative and the farmers' capacity to repay gets reduced.

(d) The farmers lead a simple life but spend lavishly during festivals and marriages. They spend money for buying ornaments and for litigations.

(e) The indebtedness is passed on from one generation to another. Thus, we find people making efforts to repay the loans taken by their fathers and forefathers. However, they are quite ignorant that if no property is inherited there is no liability to pay the debt. In their anxiety to repay the loans to one moneylender they borrow from another moneylender. Thus, the financial burden goes on increasing. It is not for nothing that the Royal Commission on agriculture remarked that the Indian peasant is born in debt, lives in debt and bequeaths debt.

(f) Inadequate transportation facilities. The marketing possibilities of perishable commodities depend very largely on the rapidity with which they can be transported to the marketplace.

(g) Lack of storage facilities.

3. Superfluous Middlemen

There are too many intermediaries between the producer and the ultimate consumers, such as village bania, itinerant merchant or beopari, dalal, kachcha and pucca Arhatias, commission agents, wholesale merchants and the retailers. They function at various stages in the process of assembling and distribution of the produce. The existence of a long chain of middlemen reduces the share of the consumer's price received by the actual cultivator.

"A Vegetable Vendor"
"There are Many Intermediaries between the Farmer and the Consumer"

4. Multiplicity of Market Charges

In the course of transacting sale or a purchase, a number of operations are involved which sellers or the buyers cannot attend to. These necessarily have to be done by the respective functionaries. In order to pay these functionaries, market charges are collected from growers or buyers at prescribed rates.

One of the main problems is "the multiplicity of market charges" in unregulated markets. In the absence of statutory regulations these charges are neither defined, nor are based on any service consideration and are recovered either in cash or in kind and often both. These charges have no sanctions except usage or the customs prevailing. They are always introduced in favour of the traders and the functionaries. On a sale of produce worth ₹ 100, as much as 15 per cent of the income of the producer goes to meet the various expenses.

The charges and deductions existing in unorganised markets are: 1. Arhat (commission), 2. Hamali (handling charges), 3. Tulai (weighment), 4. Chalani (Sewing), 5. Karad (impurities), 6. Excessive Moisture Content, 7. Sample (shared by the commission agent and the buyer), 8. Rent for storage in godowns.

Some of the charges justifiable are: 1. Arhat, 2. Hamali, 3. Tulai, and 4. Chalani. Hence, in the light of numerous unwanted deduction and high market charges, there is a need for regulating the markets.

5. Malpractices in Unregulated Markets

Some of the malpractices commonly resorted to by middlemen are as follows:

(a) Scales and weights are manipulated against the seller. This practice is rendered easier by the fact that there are no standardised weights and measures nor any provision for regular inspection.

(b) Large quantities are taken away from the produce of the cultivator, as *bangi* or sample.

(c) The broker whom the cultivator employs is more likely to favour the purchaser with whom he comes into contact almost daily than the seller whom he only sees very occasionally. This tendency becomes all the more pronounced when, as it frequently happens, the same works for both parties.

(d) When disputes arise, the cultivator has no means of safeguarding his interest.

(e) Differential prices for the same grade of product and levying unfair charges for basic services.

(f) Arbitrary deductions on account of alleged adulteration and inferior quality.

6. Lack of Grading and Standardisation

Although the Agricultural Produce (Grading and Marketing) Act was passed in 1937, even today in most unregulated markets the practice of grading is unheard of. There are no standard grades commonly accepted throughout India even for such important commodities as rice and wheat. Many State Governments have not so far specified grades and standards for many agricultural products. Number of farmers have little knowledge about grading their produce and usually mix up goods and bad quality produce into one lot which secures them a lower price in the market.

7. Inadequate Storage Facilities

In most of the villages, farmers store their produce in raceptacles (earthen cylinders) or in pits lined with mud and straw or concrete or in room like structure made up of wood or brick lined with lime or cement. The indigenous methods of storage adopted in the villages as well as in most of the upcountry markets do not adequately protect the produce from dampness and weevils. The losses due to inadequate storage have been estimated to range from 1.5 per cent (Foodgrains Investigation Committee) to 2.5 per cent (The Prices Subcommittee). This in turn is due to moisture absorption, excessive heat, insects, rodents and birds. Poor storage of produce leads to loss in quantity and quality.

(a) When wheat is harvested, it contains some moisture, which evaporates in summer and is regained during the monsoon month. Dampness raises the moisture content of the grain thereby making it soft and therefore susceptible to insects. The damage is greater when the grain is stored in kachcha underground pits where the sub-soil water table ranges from 8 to 10 feet below the surface. It has been observed that the foodgrain stocks held by grain merchants, farmers and even cooperative societies are not kept in proper conditions. Therefore, the losses are substantially larger.

(b) In addition there are crops like jowar, pulses and maize, which are infested by stored grain pests even before harvest.

(c) Losses due to rodents are also very great. It has been noticed that apart from damaging crops and foodgrains in storage, rats carry foodgrains to their nests in burrows. The rats damage 10 times the quantity of food material they eat. The small mice in the paddy fields have been found to climb up to the paddy plant and eat every grain and the big field rat usually cuts the whole plant.

8. Underdeveloped Transport System

Transport plays a very important role in the marketing of the agricultural produce. A smooth and efficient system of transport from the farmer's village to the consumer door will help the agriculturalist to bring his produce to the market without much difficulty. The transportation cost of agricultural produce depends upon mode of transportation, condition of the road, nature of the produce, risk in transportation and availability of return journey consignment.

In India, the existing means of transport are inadequate. Communications from the field to the village and from village to the mandi are often extremely poor and defective. Bad roads, lanes and tracts connecting villages with the markets not only add to the problems of transportation and aggravate the strain on bullocks but also lead to the multiplication of small dealers and intermediaries.

"A Village Mud Road"

Thus, the rural transport network is very bad. The railways have not been developed further and hence are inadequate by today's standards. Bad roads lead to delay in supply and also due to the time lag, the produce may be damaged. The bullock carts do most of the transport in rural areas. Some of the agricultural produce needs special storage systems even while being transported. Carts pulled by bullocks cannot provide these kind of facilities.

"Transportation of Vegetables from Farm to Mandi by Bullock Cart"

9. High Cost of Borrowing

The cultivator is financed by the village sahukar-cum-trader who in turn is financed by Arhatia and the indigenous banker. In the absence of warehouses and the lack of facilities for taking advances against the security of warehouse receipts, there cannot be any system of cheap finance against security of goods. The various marketing agents borrow funds at a high rate of interest. This naturally leads to a rise in the cost of marketing with the ultimate result that the share of the price received by the producer is correspondingly reduced.

Though Government has taken active measures to provide cheap institutional finance, farmers are still dependent on private moneylenders and commission agents in obtaining credit. Only about 60 per cent of credit requirements of farmers are met by institutional sources and the balance by moneylenders and traders. It may be noted here that the activities of traders and commission agents through money lending curtail the freedom of the grower-seller to dispose of their produce profitably in market yards. The official machinery has to realise the gravity of the situation and take effective steps to release the poor and innocent agriculturist from the clutches of the moneylenders-cum-commission agents.

10. Lack of Standard Weights and Measures

The Government of India has implemented the use of metric measures under Standard Weights and Measures Act – 1958, but primitive measures like stones and iron pieces are still used in many rural areas. It affords greater opportunities for cheating the ignorant cultivator and unscrupulous dealers readily avail themselves of such opportunities. For the collection of data on price movements, the relative level of prices in different regions, the volume of agricultural production, etc., lack of standard weights and measures is bound to be a great handicap and seriously affects the accuracy of statistical calculation.

11. Adulteration

Adulteration is often resorted to while marketing crops and one of the most important reasons for such deliberate adulteration of agricultural produce is the high amount of deduction allowed towards impurities in most markets and the non-mutual terms. In most of the wholesale markets, in the producing areas a deduction of about 2 per cent is made for impurities and the terms are non-mutual, i.e., a producer offering, cleaner produce receives the same price as the producer offering produce containing lot of impurities. Naturally, when this is the case, the seller whether he is the middleman or the farmer resort to adulteration of the produce to the maximum limit allowed in the market.

Examples:

(a) Damping of cotton is done by the middlemen.

(b) Small chippings of white stones have been found in rice in some localities.

(c) Most of the common salt contains large quantities of white chalk.

(d) Turmeric is adulterated with lead chromate, which has a deep yellow colour.

(e) In red chillies, many unscrupulous traders use lead oxide to brighten the colour and add weight.

12. Lack of Marketing Information

The price information if available grade-wise helps him to know the approximate returns he is likely to get for his produce. It also induces him to produce better quality crops and thus raises the standard of farming. Generally, the producer-sellers have to depend upon oral information about market conditions, market arrivals, demand conditions, ruling prices and market trends, etc., that reach them through village sahukar or commission agent or their own neighbours. The villagers have practically no contact with the outside world and they mostly depend on hearsay reports received from the village trader who is not at all interested in supplying them the correct information as to the prices prevailing in the wholesale market. Even in cases where information on prices is available, such prices are not comparable on account of:

(i) The lack of standard grades acceptable to the whole country;

(ii) Inaccuracy of information supplied by various agencies concerned;

(iii) Variation in the price quotations give by the local traders and Central Government; and

(iv) The considerable variations in weights and measures used in several markets in the absence of standardisation of weights and measures.

CONCLUSION

The farmers do not receive remunerative prices for the produce, due to defects in agricultural marketing system. Marketing infrastructural facilities are beneficial to all the agencies in agricultural produce marketing. It reduces marketing cost, helps the farmer in getting remunerative prices for the produce. At the same time, the consumer gets the produce at low price. Physical infrastructure facilities include roads, rail and road transport, warehousing facilities, cold storages, telecommunication, standardisation, grading and processing. The facilities are well developed in states like Punjab, Haryana, Kerala, Tamil Nadu, Gujarat, Goa and low in Bihar, Odisha, West Bengal, Eastern UP and Assam. Government of India has estimated that an investment of about ₹ 2,68,000 crore would be required in the next ten years for development of infrastructural facilities in rural areas.

QUESTIONS

1. What do you mean by forced sale of agricultural produce?
2. What are the malpractices in unregulated markets?

✿ ✿ ✿

16 DEFECTS IN THE AGRICULTURAL MARKETING SYSTEM AND LINES OF IMPROVEMENT – PART II

INTRODUCTION

As we have seen in earlier chapters, vagaries of monsoon, unorganised markets and superfluous middlemen are the major reasons for wide fluctuations in the prices of agricultural commodities and we have to develop an efficient system that will benefit all sections of the society, i.e., the farmers and consumers. Our farmers will be motivated to follow modern methods of cultivation and increase the yields, if they receive remunerative prices for their produce. The Government has initiated several measures to improve the system of agricultural marketing in our country.

1. Establishment of regulated markets.
2. Standardisation of weights and measures.
3. Standardisation of contracts.
4. Transportation facilities.
5. Warehousing.
6. Provision of grading and standardisation of produce.
7. Provision of marketing news.
8. State Trading (Agricultural commodities).

1. REGULATED MARKETS

Regulated markets have been established to protect the farmers from the clutches of sellers and brokers and price, quality and trade terms are regulated under legal framework. Market committee, consisting of nominees from State Government, local bodies, traders and farmers, does the management of such market. ***Example:*** APMC Market in Vashi, Mumbai. Normally, there are 15-18 members in the committee. Thus, all interests are represented in the committee. The committee formulates rules and regulations for all business transactions conducted within the market area. The committee fixes the charges, allowances and deductions that can be levied. Any dispute between the seller and buyer is settled through disputes sub-committee. The finance of the marketing committee is obtained from Government grants, market fees, license fees and rent of godowns. The market fees varies between 0.5 per cent to 2 per cent.

"Market Yard in Regulated Market"

The main functions of market committee are:

1. Maintaining and management of the market.
2. Enforcing the provisions of the Act.
3. Enforcing the conditions of licences.
4. Granting, renewing, suspending and cancelling licences.
5. Providing all facilities in the market.
6. Levying fees on the product bought or sold in the market.
7. Managing the income, expenditure and investment.
8. Preparation of budgets.
9. Maintaining a register of licensed traders, general commission agents.
10. Prescribing market charges for the services of different market functionaries.
11. Taking all possible steps to prevent adulteration of agricultural commodities in the market area.
12. Promotion, grading and standardisation of agricultural commodities.
13. Collecting and maintaining daily lists of prices of different types and grades of agricultural commodities regulated by it.
14. Issuing directions for the guidance of persons using the market.

Objectives of Regulated Markets

1. Ensure a fair price to the producers (farmers).
2. Provide congenial environment for business transactions by prohibiting malpractices in the market.
3. To stabilise the prices of agricultural produce.
4. Provide a commonplace for buyer and seller to meet and undertake buying and selling activities.

Advantages of Regulated Markets

1. Ethical practices in selling the produce through tender system, open auction and open agreement.
2. Unnecessary market charges have been removed.
3. It has removed malpractices in weighing the produce.
4. Use of certified weights and measures.
5. It has overcome adulteration.
6. Machinery for settlement of disputes.
7. Provide facilities for grading and storage.
8. Quick settlement of disputes.

Benefits to the Farmers

1. The farmers get fair price for the produce, as the intermediaries are not able to indulge in malpractices.
2. Correct weighing of the produce.
3. Storage facilities for agricultural produce.
4. Ethical practices in selling the produce, i.e., open auction and open agreement.
5. Maintenance of daily list of prices of commodities for the benefit of farmers.
6. Immediate payment after disposal of the produce.

Benefits to the Consumers

1. He gets a fair price and good quality produce.
2. Adulteration is practically nil.
3. Correct weights and measures are used.

Problems of Regulated Markets

1. **Location:** The regulated markets are situated in district/taluka headquarters and therefore they are not easily accessible to the farmers. On an average, a regulated market covers about 450 sq. km. which is high.
2. **Payment:** There are delays in receiving the payment after disposal of the produce.
3. **Presence of Middlemen:** The middlemen continue to operate in regulated markets and charge higher commission.
4. **Working Hours:** The business is done for a few hours and the farmers coming from far-off places are not able to reach the market on time.
5. **Lack of Information:** Many small and marginal farmers are not aware of the existence of regulated markets.
6. **Incentives:** Many farmers are not aware of the incentives, concessions, subsidies provided to them by Government.
7. **Expenses:** A major portion of that total revenue is being eaten away by their establishment expenses leaving little money to take up developmental projects in a big way.
8. **Grading:** No substantial progress in the field of grading has been made in many of the regulated markets. In states like Bihar, only small per cent of the goods are sold in these markets.
9. **Administration:** Many regulated markets are not administered democratically, as elections for their market committees have not be conducted for long.
10. **Market Information:** The market information collected by these have only limited use for the sellers as the information is not wide and thorough.
11. **Malpractices:** Number of these markets do not seem to have observed the financial discipline imposed on them. There is rampant corruption among their officers and employees.
12. **Management:** Management of some of these markets are unscientific and has favoured more powerful sections of the population.

Measures to remove the deficiencies in the working of regulated markets

1. **Publicity:** The farmers should be made aware of the existence of regulated markets and the benefits offered in the market through village level publicity campaign.
2. **Commission Agents:** The committee should abolish the presence of commission agents in the market.
3. **Payments:** The farmers should get immediate payment for the produce sold.

4. **Effective Supervision:** The officials should increase their involvement in the working of the regulated market and ensure effective supervision of the activities. Political interference should be avoided.
5. **Information:** The regulated market should work throughout the harvesting season and should send out details of the prices of commodities to all the villages.
6. **The Regulated Market** should consider use of IT and internet for providing cost-effective and commercially viable information to farmers.

Establishment of Terminal Markets

With a view to help the farmers sell fruits and vegetables directly to consumers, many State Governments have established terminal markets by amending Agricultural Product Market Committee Act. Such markets are functioning in Tamil Nadu and Andhra Pradesh. Maharashtra Government is establishing markets in Mumbai, Nashik and Nagpur. The model for the terminal markets would be replicated from the one existing in Bengaluru developed by National Diary Development Board.

Air-conditioned Agro Mall in Rohtak (Haryana)

Agro Mall, an initiative of Haryana State Agricultural Marketing Board, will have modern facilities for retail sale of Agro-products and other consumer goods and services and entertainment facilities in the form of Multiplex theatre complex. Salient features of the Mall are: Retail chain for vegetables and fruits, space for agri-based financial institutions, space for offices dealing in agriculture and allied products, car parking, power back up, lift, escalators and Wi-Fi connectivity.

2. STANDARDISATION OF WEIGHTS AND MEASURES AND IMPROVEMENT IN WEIGHING PRACTICES

Some of the traders resort to using unauthorised and faulty weights and scales. They also resort to very unethical practice of freely taking away of excess left in the lot after weighing. All such malpractices co-exist due to the absence of an impartial and independent agency for weighing. There is also a complete absence of uniform weighing charges.

Weighing of agricultural produce in most regulated markets is done wholly within the premises of the market yard. The produce is weighed by different licensed weighmen simultaneously at different spots in the yard. Depending upon the nature of the commodity, the procedure of weighing differs. Mostly, it is done lot-by-lot by the same weighmen; sometimes if a seller has a high amount of produce to be weighed, he engages the service of more than one weighman. The system adopted, however, depends on the availability of sufficient number of licensed weighmen, in turn it is determined by the size of the market, the frequency, the scale of the commodity arrivals and the possibility of earning sufficient daily income by way of charges collected. It is however observed, that in many regulated markets across the country the number of licensed weighmen was small. Many times it so happens that though the sale transactions are over in the morning, the growers have to wait for getting their produce weighed till late in the evening and may be even overnight. This shortage of weighmen in all the markets is due to the fact that the market committees are averse to issue more and more licenses to weighmen. Their logic is that if more weighmen are given licenses the earning of the existing set of weighmen would be adversely affected.

It is suggested that the market committees should expedite the process of issuing license to weighmen in the interest of the producer-seller. It is also suggested that the market committees should themselves provide weighing and measuring equipment as against the present practice of traders using their own equipment.

The use of standard weights and measures safeguards the interest of parties against cheating by false or underweight. The Planning Commission has recommended to adopt the metric weights and measures throughout the country because it is simple, easier to learn and remember and its use would save time and labour in calculations. The Standard of Weight and Measures Act has been passed in 1958 and enforced in all the states with a view to check fraudulent views of weights and measures.

Malpractices can be eradicated if there is an efficient supervision by authorities of the market at the time of weighing. It has been observed that the "surprise inspection" weapon provided to the market committees with respect to weighing provisions is a failure. This is because most market committee members are honorary and thus indifferent to pay such visits and invite trouble. Also the employees appointed as inspection staff by the Government are far too inadequate in number. Also these inspection staff (agricultural supervisors) are in the habit of taking bribes from the commission agents and traders for conniving at improper weighing.

It is suggested that market committees take punitive actions against offenders and check these malpractices. Further, the weighing work among the licensed weighmen should be given on a rotation basis. This will minimise the group affiliations and thus reduce the malpractices in weighing agricultural produce. The grower should be diligent and meticulous with respect to the procedure of weighing laid down by the authorities. The grower should also take the trouble of weighing the produce at his own end before bringing it to the markets.

3. STANDARDISATION OF CONTRACTS

In India, the farmers are very poor and small. They have no waiting capacity to store the harvested produce for a favourable selling time. When they bring the produce to the market their immediate goal is to sell and obtain cash. The traders take advantage of this situation. The mode of actual payment of sales proceed differ from region-to-region, market-to-market and within the same market from transaction-to-transaction. Most of these modes are exploitative. Some of these methods are:

1. Instead of prompt payment of the total value of the produce purchased, payment by instalments is forced on the seller. This happens usually after the delivery of the entire purchase lot.

2. In cases where the moneylenders are the buyers, it is seen that they make direct adjustments in the debt accounts of the sellers who have earlier borrowed funds from them. The farmers being less educated and ignorant seldom understand such adjustments.
3. Most traders insist that all transactions should be on credit and make the seller agree to this. If they cannot convince the seller for a credit transaction, they deduct exorbitant amount for cash payment.
4. Almost all marketing charges of transport, storage and weighment are pushed on to the seller. The buyer behaves as if these are traditional practices and if changed will result in something untoward happening. Thus, the seller is forced to follow such rules of thumb.

With the setting up of regulated markets, all such irregularities can be eliminated to a large extent. The market legislations have clearly provided for ensuring prompt payments, but the problem is of implementation. It is recommended that market committees play an active role in implementing such legislations. It is expected that at least this will make direct sales in the markets free and fair.

However, in the case of indirect sale, the system of payment by the buyer to the commission agents is more governed by trade convictions. The commission agent may not necessarily recover the amount from the buyer immediately on delivery of goods. There may be a time lag between the delivery of goods and the payment by the buyer, which generally varies. Further, it is seen that the commission agents in most of the markets follow the practice of calling on to get their payments. This is particularly so in the case of certain commodities like cotton and groundnut. The buyers of these commodities are generally the processing factories, which make payments at their own premises. It may be noted that due to this practice of deferred payments the commission agents demand a higher rate of commission from the producer-seller for prompt payments or resort to a system of deferred payments to the farmer.

As far as the operations of moneylenders are concerned, they are governed by the Bombay Agricultural Produce Market Rules of 1941. The rules state that licensed general commission agents or brokers could give advances either in cash or in kind to the agriculturalist on the condition that:

1. "If an agreement was entered into between the moneylender and the borrower, the lender should supply a copy of the agreement to the borrower.
2. The lender should keep an account book, recording all advances made by him to an agriculturalist and repayments affected in the manner specified by the committee in its by-laws and should supply a copy of an account book, under his signature, to the borrower, entering therein every loan transaction and its recovery".

However, the committees have practically no direct control over the credit activities of the traders, general commission agents and the brokers and coordination between the working of the market committees and the administration of the moneylenders Act should be attempted.

4. IMPROVEMENT OF TRANSPORTATION FACILITIES

It has been observed that the cost of transport directly affects the price of the agricultural produce. All involved in agricultural marketing, i.e., the farmer, the trader and the consumer are affected by the shortage of transport facilities. The market committees are under no statutory obligation to provide for transportation, but the nature of the problem is such that it is suggested that they step in. Most farmers would like to sell their product directly at secondary markets and not at village markets. However, due to bad transportation facilities, the farmers are not willing to take the risk of transportation.

It is suggested that the market committees take upon them some responsibility. They should organise some trucks or lorries for the transport of the produce of small farmers from village assembly centres to urban secondary markets. The fact is that the produce of just one farmer may not be enough to fill in an entire truck. Hence, the market committees should help co-ordinate 2-3 farmers to pool their produce together so that an entire truckload is completed. The cost of such facilities provided could be recovered from the sale of the produce.

1. The individual grower-seller may record their transport requirements with the market committee.
2. The committee after receiving such requisition pools them and contact lorry supply offices, thus arranging for the transportation.
3. As mentioned earlier, the cost of coordinating and transporting can be deducted from the sales proceeds.

Similarly, to help the traders in having adequate transport facilities, the committee officials may contact transporters as well as railway authorities in obtaining the required number of lorries or wagons. This would reduce substantially the transport bottlenecks thus benefiting both the farmers as well as the traders. The markets will also function continuously without the need for closure for want of transport facilities.

5. WAREHOUSING

Agricultural production is highly seasonal and there is a need for scientific storage facilities in rural areas to protect the quantity and quality of the produce. However, the storage facilities are quite inadequate and this results in: (a) immediate sale of the produce to avoid damage and subsequent non-remunerative prices, and (b) damage due to insects and rodents. Warehousing consist of a group of activities concerned with the storing and preserving of goods from the time of production till the time of consumption.

Importance of Warehousing

1. Storage Facilities: Warehousing facilities allow large-scale production since the excess stocks can be conveniently stored till the demand picks up and prices are high.

2. Perishable Goods and Dairy Products: Vegetables and fruits can be kept in cold storage.

3. Bank Finance: The producer can approach banks for loan against security of the goods.

4. Timely Availability of the Produce: Goods can be made available as and when required.

5. Seasonal Production: Many agricultural products like fruits and vegetables can be produced only during specific seasons. The produce can be stored so that the same can be made available throughout the year.

6. Servicing the Demand: The goods can be stored in many towns and cities to meet the needs of people.

7. Stabilisation of Prices: Warehousing helps in the stabilisation of prices by adjusting demand and supply.

8. Factory Requirements: Raw materials such as cotton, oilseeds must be stored in large quantities to feed the factories and keep them running throughout the year.

Types of Warehouses

Warehouses may be classified into three based on: (1) ownership, (2) facilities offered, and (3) the type of commodities stored.

1. On the Basis of Ownership

There are four types of warehouses on the basis of ownership:

(a) **Private Warehouses:** Private warehouses are owned by private parties and are located near the farms or near the factories.

"A private warehouse near a farm"

(b) **Public Warehouses:** Public warehouses are licensed by Government and are mostly used by manufacturers, traders, exporters and importers. There are different type of public warehouses, i.e., cold storage warehouses (vegetables, fruits, etc.), special commodity warehouses (cotton, foodgrain) and general commodity warehouses (for all types of products).

(c) **Cooperative Warehouse:** Cooperative marketing societies provide warehousing facilities for agricultural commodities.

(d) **Government or Semi-government Warehouse:** State and Central Government have established warehouses for storing agricultural produce and other goods.

Example: Central Warehousing Corporation and State Warehousing Corporation have warehouses in important agricultural and trade centres.

2. On the Basis of Facilities Offered

(a) Bonded Warehouses. These warehouses are located at seaport or airport and imported goods can be stored till payment of customs duty by the importer of goods. The goods stored in these warehouses are bonded goods. Such warehouses are licensed by Government.

(b) Duty Paid Warehouses are owned and managed by dock authorities. After duty is paid, the goods are transferred from bonded warehouses to duty paid warehouses. The importer can keep the stocks till he distributes the same in the market. This is a temporary warehousing facility and the authorities charge rent based on the space occupied and the period of storage.

3. On the Basis of Type of Commodities Stored

There are three types of warehouses on the basis of the type of commodities stored.

(a) General Warehouses are used for storing foodgrains, cement, fertilisers, etc.

(b) Special Commodity wares are specially constructed for storage of commodities like cotton and tobacco.

(c) Refrigerated Warehouses are meant for storage of vegetables, fruits, meat, etc. In cold storage, the temperature is maintained in the range of –10°C to 10°C. Potato is the main product, which is stored in cold storages. Nearly 85 per cent of the cold storage units are privately owned and these units are used for about four months in a year. There are about 4,500 cold storage units with a storage capacity of 155 lakh tonnes.

Example: South Asia's largest controlled atmosphere storage facility, i.e., Harshna Natural Agri Service Pvt. Ltd., located at Lassipora (J & K) has a capacity to store 5,000 tonnes of apples grown in the state of Jammu and Kashmir.

The following organisations provide warehousing facilities:

A. Central Warehousing Corporation: (CWC) The finance sub-committee (1945) recommended a three-tier system for scientific storage of agricultural produce, i.e., national/ state level and district level and village level. The Central Warehousing Corporation was established in 1963 and has created storage facilities in important centres in the country. Central Warehousing Corporation has warehouses at state and district level.

Objectives of Central Warehousing Corporation:

1. Maintaining warehouses for agricultural produce, other commodities and imported products.
2. Training of personnel in scientific management of warehouses.
3. Facilitate credit through the medium of warehouse receipts.
4. Consultancy services in all aspects of warehousing.
5. Extend pest control service to private warehouses, merchants, millers and other organisations.
6. Assist Government agencies in price support schemes.
7. To build warehouses at suitable places in the country.

Major activities undertaken by Central Warehousing Corporation are:

1. The corporation operates 515 warehouses with a total capacity of about 103 lakh tonnes.
2. Establishment of air-conditioned warehouses in Kolkata, Mumbai and Delhi and cold storage facilities in Hyderabad.
3. Running of customs bonded warehouses in Delhi, Kolkata, Surat, Baroda, Kochi, Bhopal, Kandla, Ludhiana, etc.
4. Handling of export-import cargo at Delhi and Amritsar airports.
5. Educating farmers on the benefits of scientific storage of agricultural produce and the benefits of public warehouses.
6. Pest Control Service: The services include anti-termite treatment, disinfestation of grains and fumigation of warehouses.
7. To overcome the problems in the movement of goods to and from the port, the CWC operates Container freight stations and Inland clearance depots and offers a comprehensive service for movement of export and import cargo.

Working of Warehouses: The person brings his produce for storage and agrees to pay the prescribed charges. Only notified commodities will be allowed to be stored in the warehouses. A receipt/warrant stating the name of the warehouse, the date of issue, type of commodities and approximate value of goods, is issued. The warehouse warrant is a negotiable instrument and can be transferred by endorsement. The warehouse receipt serves a security for the purpose of getting credit and the banks advance up to about 75 per cent of the value of the goods stored in the warehouses. The products stored in the warehouses are protected against rodents and other insects by chemical treatments. The warehouse receipt has to be surrended for taking delivery of the goods.

B. State Warehousing Corporation (SWC): The share capital is contributed by the concerned State Government and the Central Warehousing Corporation. All the State Warehousing Corporations put together are operating about 1,600 warehouses with a capacity of about 150 lakh tonnes in the country.

C. Food Corporation of India (FCI): FCI was established in 1965 to procure and store foodgrains for public distribution. FCI has created storage facilities for about 26 million tonnes of foodgrains and other agricultural produce. The facility includes 250 scientifically designed godowns as well as cement floor as the base and tarpaulin as the cover.

D. Cooperative Sector: The cooperative sector has built up storage capacity of about 14 million tonnes. They have also constructed about 200 cold storage warehouses with a capacity of about 2.50 lakh tonnes.

Utilisation of Warehouses

Studies conducted on the utilisation of the warehousing facilities have shown that the storage capacity is mostly utilised by traders and public agencies. The main reasons for low utilisation by farmers are:

1. Most of the warehouses are located in taluka/district level/near railway stations and the farmers find it difficult to transport their produce to these warehouses from villages.
2. Cumbersome procedure of depositing and removing the produce from the warehouses.
3. The marketable surplus available with farmers is small and they are forced to sell the produce to the traders to meet immediate cash requirements.

Progress of Warehousing

With the increase in the production of paddy, wheat, vegetables and fruits and the focus on projects like mushroom, tissue culture, etc., there is a need for establishing warehouses in important production centres. At present, storage facilities are inadequate in the case of perishable products like fruits, vegetables, dairy and meat products. There are three agencies in public sector, i.e., FCI, CWC and SWC which are engaged in building large-scale warehousing facilities. FCI provide storage facilities for foodgrains. Both CWC and SWC operate warehouses for storage of agricultural produce and fertilisers.

Suggestions for development of storage facilities in rural areas:

1. Construction of rural warehouses on priority basis for the benefit of farmers. This will help to avoid distress sale, loss due to rodents and pests and deterioration in the quality of the produce.
2. The cost of construction should be through subsidy from Central/State Government as well as through bank loans.

3. The warehouses have to be managed by cooperatives or the Gram Panchayat.
4. Technical guidance for construction and maintenance of these warehouses has to be provided by CWC/SWC.

6. STANDARDISATION AND GRADING

Standardisation is the process of fixing certain norms for the products. These norms are established by customs or tradition or by certain authority. It involves determination of basic characteristics of a product on the basis of which the product can be divided into various groups. It also means determining the standards of products to be produced with regard to size, colour, form, weight, shape and quality. Standards are model products, which form the basis for comparison.

Examples: Staple length in cotton, moisture and inert material content in grains, minimum germination percentage in seeds.

Advantages of Standardisation

1. **Convenience in Selling:** Facilitates marketing of the product, as the consumer prefers to buy standard goods.
2. **Increase in Demand:** The demand for standard products is high as the consumer is assured of quality of the products.
3. **Increases Goodwill:** Sales of quality products leads to customer satisfaction and goodwill in the market. This results in repeated sales of the product.
4. **Pricing:** Prices can be fixed based on size, weight, taste and purity.
5. **Elimination of Risk:** The consumer is assured of the quality of the product and eliminates the risk involved in buying non-standard products.
6. **Assurance of Quality:** Quality is assured when the product is tested and given quality certification by authorities
   Example: AGMARK for agricultural products.

Grading

Grading is a physical process and it follows standardisation. It involves division of products into classes made up of units possessing similar characteristics. Grading is mostly done for agricultural products and mineral products.

Examples:

(a) Tea graded as BOP, OP and Dust.

(b) Cardamom: Alleppy Extra Bold (Aeb), Alleppy Green Bold (Agb), Alleppy Green Superior (Ags), Alleppy Green Light (Agl).

(c) Wheat is graded into grades – 1, 2, 3, 4 based on the percentages of foreign matter, other foodgrains, damaged grains, immature grains and insect infested grains. The moisture content should not exceed 12 per cent in all cases.

Types of Grading

(a) **Mandatory Grading:** The Government of India has fixed standards and grades for agricultural commodities meant for exports.

(b) **Centralised Grading:** Subject to inspection and audit, cooperatives, private agencies, and farmers, associations can take up grading activities. Items covered are ghee, curd, milk, edible oil, jam and juices.

(c) **Variable Grading:** Depending upon the size and quality of the crop, the farmers fix their own method of standards.

Advantages of Grading

1. **Large-scale Production:** Grading helps in large-scale production and expand the market. Even sellers and buyers situated at remote and far-off places can enter into agreement for buying and selling on the basis of grades.
2. **Quality Assurance:** The buyer is assured of quality of graded products and therefore buys such products with confidence.
3. **Pricing:** Grading helps the producer to get higher price for the commodities.
4. **Facilitates Selling:** Graded products can be easily sold in the market.
5. **Future Trading:** Prices and terms of sales can be easily decided based on the grade.
6. **Bank Facilities:** The banks are willing to advance loan since the prices of graded commodities can be easily established.

Problems in Standardisation and Grading

1. **Lack of Standards:** For many products, the standards have not been developed.
2. **Poor Awareness:** The general awareness about standards and grades is very low in rural areas. The reasons are low literacy and low standard of living and low reach of information in rural areas.
3. **Poor Testing Facilities:** The testing facilities are quite inadequate and producers are facing problems in getting the product tested.
4. **Unauthorised Standards and Grades:** Many producers use certification marks without testing their products.

Table 16.1: Grade Standards for Oranges

Grade	AGMARK Label Colour	Minimum Size (inches)	Other Conditions
Special	White	3.50	1. Oranges should not be ripened so that they may not get spoiled in transportation.
Grade I	Red	3.00	2. The colour of oranges should be as per variety but should not be green.
Grade II	Blue	2.75	3. There should not be wrinkles in oranges.
Grade III	Yellow	2.50	4. Oranges should be free from cuts, infestation of insects and diseases.
Grade IV	Green	2.25	5. Tolerance limit is 10 per cent of the next lower grade.

Table 16.2: Grade Standards for Eggs (Hen)

Grade	AGMARK Label Colour	Minimum Size (inches)	Other Conditions
Special	White	2.00	1. Eggs should not have been preserved by any method.
"A" Grade	Red	1.75	2. Eggs should be spot-free and without blemishes.
"B" Grade	Blue	1.50	3. Yolk of eggs should be central.
"C" Grade	Yellow	1.25	4. Eggs should be solid.
			5. Eggs should be transparent.
			6. There must be air space of size less than 3/8".

The grading of agricultural produce has not made much progress in our country for the following reasons:

1. Some the agricultural products are perishable and even graded products, by the time they reach the consumers, deteriorate in quality resulting in customer complaints.
2. Grading agricultural products is more difficult since the producer has to examine each and every product for grading.
3. The producer does not get higher prices for graded products since the consumers are not very quality-conscious in most of the markets.
4. Commonman does not understand the grading system.
5. Grades such as C, D makes a negative impression with consumers, although the differences may be only marginal.
6. Consumer preferences vary and are based on a number of factors and are therefore very difficult to meet their individual requirements.

Suggestions for Making Grading and Standardising Popular

1. Grading and standardisation have to cover all types of agricultural commodities and be made compulsory for trading in agricultural commodities at all levels.
2. Samples of graded products should be exhibited in all markets for the benefit of traders and consumers.
3. Create awareness about the benefits of using AGMRK products among consumers.
4. Highlight the benefits of selling graded products to the producers.

Government of India has initiated the following measures for development of marketing of agricultural produce and quality-consciousness among producers and consumers.

(a) AGMARK

The Directorate of Marketing and Inspection (DMI), headed by Agricultural Marketing Advisor to the Government of India (AMA), implements agricultural marketing programmes of the Central Government, under the supervision and control of the Central Ministry of Agriculture. DMI aims at bringing integrated development of marketing of agricultural and allied produce in the country and maintains a close liaison between the Central and State Governments through its regional offices (11) and sub-offices (37) spread all over the country.

Quality control of agricultural commodities is the responsibility of the Directorate of Marketing and Inspection. The directorate has specified grade standards for various agricultural products under the Agricultural Produce Grading and Marketing Act, 1937. AGMARK stands for Agricultural Marketing. It is quality certification mark under Central Agricultural Produce (Grading and Marketing) Act, 1937. The AGMARK label indicates the quality and purity of the product based on the prescribed standards. Labels of different colours indicate the grade of the product. The labels are numbered and the marketer has to maintain records of the labels. The package bears the date of packing and expiry date of the produce. There are about 15,000 licensees who are marketing their produces under AGMARK certification marks.

At present, there are 718 approved grading/testing laboratories consisting of 111 state-owned laboratories, 549 licenced private packers, 9 labs in cooperative factor and 49 private/commercial laboratories. DMI has a network of 22 regional AGMARK Laboratories with its Central **AGMARK** Laboratory at Nagpur. DMI operates special laboratories for testing wool, cotton, tobacco, sunhemp and meat.

Thrust Areas/Functional Responsibilities of DMI:

1. Promotion of standardisation and grading of agricultural and allied produce;
2. Market research and surveys;
3. Manpower training in agricultural marketing;
   Example: Diploma course in agricultural marketing, training course in grading, analytical technology, pre-shipment inspection, quality control and market news service.

Fig. 16.3: "AGMARK"

4. Market development through regulation, planning and designing of physical markets;
5. Marketing extension to educate consumers/producers;
6. Administration of Meat Food Products Order (1973);
7. Promotion of cold storage;
8. The agricultural marketing adviser grants certificates of authorisation to organisations or individuals to grade and mark the agricultural produce. So far about 200

commodities have been covered and includes tobacco, coffee, ghee, potato, wheat, atta, eggs, cotton, butter, grains, oilcakes and vegetable oils such as lemon grass oil, sandalwood oil. AGMARK grading is compulsory for some commodities for export: ***Example:*** Ginger, cashewnuts, pepper.

(b) Bureau of Indian Standards — BIS (Previously Known as Indian Standard Institution — ISI)

ISI Act was passed in 1952. It is managed by board consisting of members from Central and State Governments, research institutes, laboratories and development boards. The activities of BIS are two-fold: (a) formulation of Indian standards, and (b) their implementation by promotion and through voluntary and third party certification system.

Major Activities are:

1. Determines standards of different products.
2. Making standards popular.
3. Determining standard marks for new products.
4. Developing healthy competition among producers to develop and promote quality products in the market.
5. Protects the interest of consumers by supplying them quality products.
6. Research and development activities in the field of standardisation.

Manufactured products are graded in accordance with the standards laid down by the Bureau of Indian Standards and bear ISI label. The ISI label is an indicator of the quality of the product. The institution has established a central laboratory at Delhi and regional labs in Chennai, Mumbai and Kolkata. It has prepared over 14,000 standards for products covering agriculture, chemicals, and civil, mechanical, electrical, electronics, textiles and many other commodities. The bureau has over 2,000 standards covering agricultural inputs such as fertilisers, pesticides and agricultural machinery. Certification has been made compulsory for certain products affecting safety and health of people. Government has made it mandatory that all products meant for export should meet the quality standard prescribed by BIS. ISI has been made compulsory for supplies under Government rate contract.

7. PROVISION OF MARKETING NEWS

The availability of prompt and reliable information about what is happening in the market, what quantities are arriving and what prices are quoted for different commodities considerably improve the decision making capability of the farmers and strengthens their bargaining power.

At present, the information is disseminated through various media like radio, newspapers, blackboard display and public address system at market yards. The information provided by these methods is stale and does not help the farmers sufficiently in taking decisions in marketing their produce. The farmers are also not able to know about the prices prevailing in other markets, as the Market Committees are able to disseminate information in respect of their own markets. The farmers are, therefore, left with no alternative but to dispose of their produce in the nearest market, even at uneconomic prices.

1. Use of IT and Internet

Information Technology and Internet play an important role in Agricultural Marketing by providing cost-effective and commercially viable information to the farmers. Major areas of use of IT in Agricultural Marketing are given in Chapter 18:

2. Development of Agricultural Marketing Information Network (AGMARKNET)

By and large, the States and Union Territories are providing some market information in one form or the other for the benefit of market users like producers, traders and consumers. However, the information is collected and disseminated by use of conventional methods, which cause delay in communicating the information to different target groups, adversely affecting its utility. Improvement in the present market information system by linking all important Agricultural Produce Markets, Agricultural Marketing Boards and Departments in the States and Union Territories is envisaged by DMI under its Agriculture Marketing Information Network (AGMARKNET) by installing computer facilities at Agricultural Produce Markets and connecting with NICNET for Internet/E-mail services.

Project Aims at

1. To establish a nationwide information network for speedy collection and dissemination of market information for its efficient utilisation.

2. To computerise data on market fee, market charges, total arrivals, arrivals by agencies, prices (variety-wise/quality-wise), storage, despatches with destination, mode of transportation, costs, sold and unsold stocks, sources of supply with destination, method of sale, payment, weighment, grading facilities, quantities graded, market personnel (trained/untrained), market functionaries, market finance, development programmes, infrastructure facilities, constitution/ composition of Market Committee, income and expenditure and other activities of the Agriculture Produce Market Committees, State Marketing Boards and Departments.

3. To ensure flow of regular and reliable data to producers, traders and consumers to derive maximum benefit of their sales and purchases.

4. To increase the efficiency in marketing by effecting improvement in the existing market information system.

NICNET based Agricultural Marketing Information Network (AGMARKNET) envisages to transmit price and market arrivals to State Agricultural Marketing Board/Directorate for analysis and local dissemination as well as for onward transmission to DMI Headquarters at Faridabad. To start with, it involves connecting 670 Agricultural Produce Markets and 40 State Agricultural Marketing Boards and Directorates. The improved communication system will enable the producers to know about probable markets where they can dispose of their produce more profitably. The traders and consumers can also derive maximum advantage out of their purchases at low communication cost. With the modernisation of existing market intelligence system, it is hoped that the efficiency of the markets and farmers participation in the markets will be increased. This will increase the income of the farmers, which in turn will activate them to increase the agricultural production.

Example: Maharashtra Government has launched Commodity Suchana Kendra (SK) a linkage of 290 agricultural produce marketing committees across Maharashtra.

e-mandis: Market of the Future

Gulbarga is known as the Tur bowl of Karnataka. After the launch of e-mandi platform around 14 lakh quintals of Tur and two lakh quintals of Bengal Gram were sold during 2012. In this process farmers have been the biggest beneficiaries. This system could also win the confidence of 700 traders who adapted this platform which immensely contributed to the success of the initiative. There are plans to cover fifty top mandis in the state under e-auction system. Delegation from more than ten states has visited the market and has in principle agreed to adopt this model popularly known as Gulbarga Model.

The process starts when the farmer reaches the Mandi Gate. The APMC issues him a unique lot number which captures various details including farmer's name, the village, quantity of the produce. Grading of the produce is done in the market. Farmers are also offered warehousing facilities along with unique number tags given to them. The farmers have to offer only half kilogram for sampling against five kilos under old system. Buyers inspect the samples and based on identification numbers, quote their bids on the computer. The quality of the produce is already certified and the highest price quoted for particular produce is identified as a successful bidder. Officials inform the farmers about the price at which the trade was executed using a public address system installed in the mandi. The farmer is also sent a message on his mobile giving all the details of the trade. Farmers are paid at the end of the day. e-Auction platform also known as e-mandi brings in transparency in the system and at the same time creates a level playing field for all the stakeholders, i.e., buyers, sellers and APMC

Source: *The Economic Times*: March 26, 2013.

8. STATE TRADING (AGRICULTURAL COMMODITIES)

State trading means Government involvement in foreign trade. The Government may operate either directly or through Government-owned organisation. It may carry on foreign trade in the place of or in addition to private traders. In India, there are a number of organisations namely, Minerals and Metal Trading Corporation (MMTC), Commodity Boards, Marketing Federations who undertake import and export of commodities. With regard to agricultural commodities, state trading has the following objectives:

(a) To ensure adequate and regular supplies at reasonable and stable prices of essential commodities to meet local demand.

(b) To effect exports and imports at more favourable prices through increased bargaining power.

(c) To stimulate production of essential agricultural and industrial commodities by means of price and other incentives.

(d) To stabilise the domestic prices of specified products by controlling their production and marketing.

(e) To explore export markets for products and to dispose of exportable surpluses of commodities.

(f) To conduct surveys and provide information to Government.

Key Activities of State Trading are given below:

1. Supply of essential commodities to consumers at fair prices.
2. To ensure fair price to farmers so that they will have incentive for increasing production.
3. To arrange for supply of fertilisers and pesticides.
4. To undertake procurement and maintenance of buffer stocks and their distribution as and when required.
5. To minimise price fluctuations as a result of seasonal variations.
6. To check hoarding, blackmarketing and profiteering.

Types of State Trading

Partial State Trading: Here, Government and private traders operate in the same market. The Government may put some restriction on their activities such as declaration of stocks. The Government procures the produce and distribute to consumers through a network of fair price shops.

Complete Shops: The purchase and sales of commodities are done by Government or their agencies. Private traders are not entertained either for purchase or for sale.

State Trading Corporation of India

The State Trading Corporation of India Ltd., is a premier International Trading House owned by Government of India. Set up in 1956, it trades with almost all the countries of the world and has achieved annual turnover of over ₹ 15,000 crore in 2006-2007. While undertaking import and export operations, the corporation renders the following services:

(a) **Overseas Buyer:** STC acts as an expert guide for buyers interested in Indian goods.

(b) **Indian Industry:** STC helps manufacturers to find out markets abroad for their products.

(c) **Indian Consumers:** STC imports essential commodities to cover shortfalls in the domestic market.

The Role of State Trading Corporation is given below:

1. To explore new markets for traditional items of export and develop new items with a view to diversifying and expanding the export trade.
2. To undertake import and/or internal distribution of commodities in short supply with a view to stabilising prices and rationalising distribution.
   Example: Edible oil, fertilisers.
3. To facilitate and organise exports of difficult-to-sell items (such as manure, meal, sodium, de-oiled linseed cake, etc.) by linking essential imports with additional exports and under special trade promotion agreements.
4. To organise production to meet export demands and to help production units in overcoming difficulties of procuring raw materials and other essential requirements.
5. To help local producers by procuring at reasonable prices and to hold stocks to maintain ultimate production at optimum level of commodities with high export potential, thus, avoiding dislocation in production, maintaining adequate availability for export and ensuring a fair price to local producers.
6. To import items which are canalised by the Government through this Corporation so as to ensure that adequate supplies at the right time and at the economical prices are made and are distributed to the industries and other users in a coordinated manner. ***Example:*** Edible oil, sugar, urea, fatty acids and pulses.
7. To undertake import of commodities where bulk purchase would give better terms. To undertake imports from state trading countries or from where monopolies are involved and to import commodities, which is in short supply in the country.
8. To undertake price support and buffer stock operations with a view to ensure fair prices to the growers of certain agricultural commodities, to stabilise internal production and sustain foreign demand.
   Example: STC had also undertaken price support operations (at the instance of the Central Government) for natural rubber in 1970 and tobacco in 1972. Growers were assured of remunerative prices and surplus quantities, mopped up by the STC, were exported.

MEASURES TO OBTAIN REMUNERATIVE PRICES FOR THE PRODUCE

1. **Impurities:** The buyers are interested in purchasing the produce free from impurities such as mud, stones and other grains. The farmers have to ensure that they bring clean produce to the market to get higher prices from the buyers
2. **Segregate Goods and Poor Quality Produce:** Many farmers bring the produce which contains both good and quality produce and get a low price for the whole consignment.

   Example: In the case of vegetables, damaged/pest infested produce could be separated before transporting the produce to the market. This will enable them to get a good price for the produce.
3. **Grading** of agricultural produce will enable the farmers to get high price for the produce. Fruits and vegetables can be graded in the farm itself immediately after the harvest of the crop.
4. **Weigh the Produce** before transporting the same to the market. This is to safeguard against malpractices in weighing.
5. **Market Information:** The farmers should take initiative to find out arrivals in the market and current prices of agricultural commodities through newspapers, TV, middlemen, progressive farmers in the village, regulated markets and internet so that they can negotiate a higher price with traders.
6. **Avoid Sale Immediately After Harvest:** The price of the produce is normally low during peak harvesting season. The farmers can store the produce in warehouses and sell the same when the prices are high.
7. **Sell Through Cooperatives/Regulated Market/Supermarket:** The farmer can get a remunerative price for the produce since he does not have to pay unnecessary market charges and commission to middlemen.

Wal-Mart Plans Direct Procurement from Farmers

Wal-Mart, the most aggressive foreign supermarket operator expects to open its first store selling directly to public by 2014. The company plans to deal with about 35,000 farmers and procure vegetables and fruits to meet retail stores requirements. At present the company operates 18 wholesale stores in the country. Fresh produce accounts for about 30 per cent of Wal-Mart sales in its wholesale outlets.

CONCLUSION

The Government has initiated several measures to improve the system of agricultural marketing. These measures include establishment of regulated markets, farmers markets, standardisation of weights and measures, warehousing, cooprative marketing, provision of marketing news, grading and standardisation of agricultural produce, electronic auction system, food processing and state trading of agricultural commodities.

QUESTIONS

1. Explain the role of regulated markets to promote agricultural marketing. What are its limitations?
2. Describe standardisation and grading. What is the perception of farmers and consumers about standardisation and grading?
3. Discuss the role of IT in Agricultural Marketing.
4. How can a farmer get remunerative price for his produce?

CASE STUDY

Marketing of Packaged Food Products

Many studies have been conducted by various Government organisations, Cooperatives and Corporate companies on changing food habits in the urban centres of the country. The major findings of these studies are as under:

- With changing profile of the middle-class and hired domestic help becoming costlier, significant number of families are switching to packaged, ready-to-cook and ready-to-eat food products.
- With increased health-consciousness, the demand for green vegetables, salad vegetables, fresh fruits, corn and potato-based products is increasing in urban centres. In addition, products like pickles, chutneys, fruit pulps, canned fruits and vegetables, dehydrated vegetables and frozen fruits and vegetables are gaining popularity.
- Due to hygienic reasons, consumers prefer fruits and vegetables, milk and milk products, fish, meat and poultry products in packaged form rather than buying loose.

Considering the huge demand, many organisations are willing to market these products as branded goods. However, due to scattered nature of production, small holding of growers, perishable nature of goods and infrastructural bottlenecks, these organisations want to ensure an economically viable marketing strategy.

QUESTION

- As a management consultant, please give your views on product-mix, marketing channels and promotional strategy to be explored for timely supply of products to meet the regular demand in various urban centres.

✿ ✿ ✿

17 CO-OPERATIVE MARKETING

INTRODUCTION

In our country, a majority of the farming community continues to be small and marginal farmers. They are forced to sell the produce at a low price to meet their cultivation and household expenses and repay the loan taken from moneylenders. The farmers are disorganised at village level, have low bargaining power and are at a disadvantage against the traders.

Agricultural marketing has to meet two broad objectives:

(a) The farmer has to get a fair return for investing labour, money and materials in farming operations.

(b) The consumer pays a fair price for the produce he buys.

Selling the produce through marketing co-operative can change this situation. Therefore co-operative marketing society is an organisation formed by the producers for the producers that aims at eliminating the chain of middlemen operating between producers and the ultimate consumer and thus securing the maximum price for their produce. It is a collective and institutional form of rural marketing.

THE NEED FOR CO-OPERATIVE MARKETING

1. Agricultural marketing in India is riddled with various malpractices such as arbitrary deduction from the price of the produce, manipulation of weights and scales, collusion between the workers and the buyers. In such circumstances, co-operative marketing helps to reduce the malpractices to a greater extent.

2. There exists a large number of middlemen who take part in collections, storage, financing, grading, sale and transportation of agricultural produce. Their charges are out of proportion to the services they render, with the result that the producers do not get their due share of the price paid by the ultimate consumer.

3. Lack of sufficient finance make the Indian farmers indebted to the moneylenders, who always try to exploit the situation by taking the produce immediately after the harvest, at a low price. Co-operatives try to eliminate this situation by providing need-based credit to the farmers.

4. Even in normal market conditions, co-operative marketing of agricultural produce has been considered necessary. But the need becomes much greater when marked conditions deviate from healthy practices and where undesirable forms of speculation are resorted to. In such cases, the profit motive on the part of the middlemen leads to price manipulations and consequent fluctuations of prices. In all these circumstances, the need for co-operative marketing of agricultural produce on a substantial scale become urgent so that it can help in stabilising prices and can save the farmers from their evergrowing problems.

OBJECTIVES

1. To sell the produce in the market and obtain fair price to the producers. The society will be the main link between the producer and the buyer eliminating middlemen in the process.
2. To provide credit to the farmers to save them from the necessity of selling the produce immediately after harvesting.

   Example: Crop loan, produce loan, at approved rates against 2-4 per cent per month charged by moneylenders.
3. To increase the bargaining power of farmers compared to merchants and intermediaries.
4. To influence the market price and obtain better prices for agricultural produce.
5. Provide agricultural inputs such as seeds, fertilisers, pesticides and consumer goods at low price to farmers.
6. To undertake processing of agricultural produce like milling of paddy, ginning and pressing of cotton and provide facilities for grading of agricultural produce.
7. To obtain updated information on market prices, demand and supply position of agricultural commodities and plan activities accordingly.
8. To provide storage facilities so that the farmers can store the produce and wait till the prices are encouraging. Further, this facility will also prevent loss of quantity and quality of the produce due to moisture, rodents and insects.
9. To extend credit facilities to the members against security of the agricultural produce. This increases the holding power of the farmers and prevents distress sales. Generally, the farmer receives about 70 per cent of the value of the produce as credit from the society. The loan amount is deducted from the sale proceeds.
10. Procurement of agricultural produce for implementation of the price support policy.

WORKING OF CO-OPERATIVE MARKETING

The members willingly agree to sell their produce to the society. After receiving the produce, the society gives them an advance to meet the expenses for cultivation of crops. The society collects the produce from all members and sells the same at the best price eliminating the large number of intermediaries operating in the mandi. The society will undertake to store the products if the prevailing market prices are not encouraging. As soon as the produce is sold, the society pays the members after deducting the advance. The society is managed by paid staff and the main objective is service to the members. Profit is a secondary objective. The profit earned by the society is distributed among members after meeting staff and welfare expenses. A part of the profit is transferred to general reserve.

GROUPING OF CO-OPERATIVE MARKETING SOCIETIES

Based on the commodities dealt, the co-operative marketing societies could be grouped as follows:

1. Single commodity co-operative marketing societies deal in one agricultural commodity. ***Example:*** Cotton co-operative marketing society and oilseed growers co-operative marketing society.
2. Multi-commodity co-operative marketing societies deal in a large number cf commodities ***Example:*** Cereals, cotton and groundnut.
3. Multi-commodity and Multipurpose co-operative marketing societies deal in a number of commodities and also extend other services.
   Example: Credit facilities to members, supply of agricultural inputs and household items.

"A Village Co-operative Society"

STRUCTURE OF CO-OPERATIVE MARKETING SOCIETIES

The co-operative marketing societies have both, two-tier and three-tier structure. In the case of two-tier structure, there is a primary society at block level and state marketing federation at apex level. In three-tier pattern, there is district level marketing society in the middle.

1. Primary co-operative marketing societies are located in primary market or at block level. Primary marketing societies buy and sell agricultural commodities and other goods for the benefit of farmers. These societies advance loans and make arrangements for sale of agricultural produce of the members.
2. Central co-operative marketing societies operate at district level and are located in secondary wholesale market. They market the produce of primary co-operative societies and co-ordinate the activities of primary societies.
3. Apex (State) co-operative societies operate at state level. They co-ordinate the activities of societies and are engaged in inter-state trade, export and import of produce, procurement and distribution of agricultural inputs and essential consumers goods.

PROGRESS OF CO-OPERATIVE MARKETING SOCIETIES

The value of agricultural commodities traded by the societies was about ₹ 8,000 crore in mid-nineties. The produce traded through these societies account for about 10 per cent of the marketed surplus. The important items are foodgrains, cotton, oilseeds and plantation crops. The value of agriculture inputs marketed through these societies is about ₹ 2,000 crore.

BUSINESS OPERATIONS OF A MARKETING CO-OPERATIVE

1. Commission Business

In this type of business, the marketing society only acts as the agent between the farmers and traders. The farmers bring their produce to the society and under its guardianship the sale of crops takes place. The commodities are sold to the highest bidder. Money got from sale is immediately paid to the grower. Farmers as individuals possess less bargaining power and small marketable surplus which prevent them from securing higher prices for their produce. With the role of the co-operative as commission agent, though the farmers are benefitted to a certain extent, it does not solve their basic problems as the crops are sold again to the local trader. The benefits to the farmers from this type of co-operative are limited when compared with the benefits that they could have got through the sale of the products in the urban markets.

2. Outright Purchases

The marketing society purchases the farmers' produce outright by making them payments immediately. This is done with a view to induce the farmers to bring their produce to the society. There is no doubt that this kind of a market practice will ensure farmers with reasonable prices. But it involves in it certain amount of risk. That is why it is suggested that only those societies which: (1) are financially sound and possess the borrowing capacity, (2) have technically qualified management, (3) have reputed credit societies affiliated to them, and (4) proper processing facilities, will have to undertake outright business operations. To minimise the risk factor, the society has to work under the following safeguards, namely,

(a) Outright purchases should be made only up to a limit, the limit being twice that of its owned funds.

(b) Should undertake outright business either in collaboration with or on behalf of the higher marketing organisation.

(c) Should not indulge in speculative transactions which might lead to lying idle of the produce bought by the society with it for a longer period.

(d) The transactions should be carefully watched which gives guidelines for future business policy.

3. Advance Against Stock

Poor farmers cannot wait for sometime in the sale of their produce even if they know that it rewards them with better prices. The marketing co-operative helps farmers by allowing them to store their product with it for which they receive advance payments up to 60-75 per cent of the total value of the produce. This provides the farmers sufficient staying power. When the market price increases, the marketing society sells the produce stored with it and pays the farmers the remaining amount (Amount received from sale less advance payments made). Here, the primary producer is benefitted in the form of higher prices for his produce. At the same time, it is safe for the co-operative also since there is no risk involved in this kind of a business operation.

4. Pooling

Pooling refers to a process by which the farmers' produce is physically assembled and sold as one lot instead of selling on an individual basis by the farmers separately. The farmers gain through this practice of the marketing co-operative as the crops are sold in large volumes.

5. Grading

The marketing co-operative engages itself in activities like grading and standardisation of agricultural produce which will reward the farmers with better returns. The society insists on farmers to produce better quality goods. After assembling the crops, the society classifies it into different grades so that the farmer producing higher quality goods does not suffer but on the other hand is motivated to raise its quality still further.

6. Processing

Commodities sold as raw materials fetch lesser price to the farmers than when they are processed and marketed. Processing implies the transformation of the commodity into a form fit for consumption. The marketing society can take up the work of processing the commodities like paddy, groundnut, cotton, etc., through which their form can be changed. To do this, the organisation of the co-operative should be broad based. Some of the marketing co-operatives of India perform processing function.

7. Procurement

On behalf of the Government, the marketing society may take up the responsibility of procuring agricultural produce from the farmers to ensure their products with the minimum support price fixed by the Government. When the prices fall to a very low level, which is not even equivalent to the cost of cultivation, then the Government resorts to the procurement operations. The task of the Government becomes easier if it allots the work to the marketing co-operatives.

8. Supply of Inputs to Agriculture

The marketing co-operatives are also engaged in supplying the members with the inputs necessary for better cultivation. Some of the marketing co-operatives provide only seeds and fertilisers. They do not possess the arrangements for the supply of farm implements and pesticides.

9. Distribution of Consumer Goods

In those areas where viable consumer co-operatives do not exist, the marketing society supplies essential goods like kerosene, controlled cloth, sugar, consumer goods and kitchen appliance at reasonable prices. But the supply of consumer goods by the marketing co-operatives is restricted to only a few commodities.

10. Services

Other services rendered by the marketing society are related to storage and transportation. For the storage of commodities, the societies maintain godowns so that the agricultural produce is well protected from sun, wind and rains. As far as possible, the marketing co-operatives maintain their own transport vehicle for the movement of goods to marketplaces.

11. Export

Marketing co-operatives extend their marketing activities even to foreign countries. If there is foreign demand for the goods produced by the members, then the society arranges for their export through its higher marketing organisation. This act helps the farmer on the one hand and the country on the other. In our country, the National Agricultural Co-operative Marketing Federation and the State Marketing Co-operatives export agricultural goods such as pulses, groundnut, tobacco, cotton, etc.

REASONS FOR POOR PERFORMANCE OF CO-OPERATIVE SOCIETIES

The progress of co-operative marketing has been rather slow and the reasons are given below:

1. The societies are not evenly distributed all over the country — States like Punjab, Haryana and Maharashtra have more number of societies.

2. The operation of societies is too small.
3. Many societies are only distributing controlled commodities such as sugar and kerosene.
4. Many societies do not distribute agricultural inputs.
5. The turnover of most of the societies is far below economically viable minimum level.
6. The co-operative societies have to follow cumbersome administrative procedures and operational regulations.
7. Farmers are in need of immediate cash after the harvest of the crop to meet their commitment. They sell the produce to local traders and do not have the time to take the produce to the nearest society.
8. The farmers are indebted to the traders and they enter into advance contracts with them for the sale of the crop.
9. The societies are located in big markets/towns and transport facilities are not available to take the produce from the villages to societies.
10. Members do not have full confidence in the societies as many of them are running at loss.
11. The societies lack trained manpower.
12. The societies suffer from political interference. The official of the societies, very often support traders to the disadvantage of the farmers.
13. The societies do not have sufficient funds to meet the credit needs of the members.
14. The co-operative societies are not able to compete with the traders due to lack of market information and business expertise.
15. Inadequate storage facilities and therefore the societies have to dispose of the stocks immediately, which result in lower prices.
16. The societies do not have facilities to provide boarding and lodging facilities to farmers when they visit the market to dispose of their produce.

SUGGESTIONS FOR IMPROVING THE WORKING OF CO-OPERATIVE SOCIETIES

1. Marketing societies should be situated at mandi level and new societies have to be formed in production centres of commercial crops.
2. Training has to be given to the society staff.
3. Co-operative societies should have warehouses for storing the produce of farmers.
4. Recovery of loan from members to be improved.

5. Greater coordination between members and the society.
6. The societies should arrange to sell the produce of small growers who are at the mercy of moneylenders.
7. Grading and processing of agricultural produce to be organised so that the grower will get higher price for the produce.
8. The societies should be free from political interference.
9. The area of operation of the society should be large enough to be economically viable.
10. The officials should have sufficient technical and commercial knowledge so that they can run the societies efficiently.
11. The societies should deal in agricultural produce, agricultural inputs and also extend credit facilities to the farmers.
12. The societies should provide boarding and lodging facilities to farmers when they come to the societies for selling their produce.
13. The societies should have transport facilities to bring the produce from the villages to the mandi.
14. Distribution of essential commodities should be routed through co-operative societies to improve their business.

NATIONAL AGRICULTURAL CO-OPERATIVE MARKETING FEDERATION (NAFED)

The National Agricultural Co-operative Marketing Federation (NAFED) is an apex body of the marketing co-operatives in our country. It was established in 1958. The State Level Marketing Federations and the National Co-operative Development Corporation are its members. NAFED with its Head office in Delhi and offices in Mumbai, Kolkata and Chennai operates throughout the country. Board of Management includes Government of India, RBI, SBI and State Trading Co-operatives. Present membership consists of 16 State-level Co-operative Marketing Federation and 5 Federations in Union territories.

Objectives of NAFED

1. NAFED facilitates the working of co-operative institutions.
2. Promote the trading/marketing activities of members in agricultural commodities.
3. Undertake supplies of agricultural inputs, agricultural implements and consumer goods in rural areas.
4. To act as an agent for the purchase, sale, storage and distribution of agricultural produce on behalf of the Government.

5. To promote the trading activities of co-operative institutions.
6. To promote international trade of agricultural commodities.

Activities of NAFED

1. Processing of Fruits and Vegetables: The main objective is to develop the fruits and vegetable processing industry in the co-operative sector and NAFED has established fruits and vegetables processing units in the country.
2. Develop Scientific Storage Facilities: NAFED has established cold storages and warehousing complexes for the benefit of the producers and traders.
3. Supply of fertilisers, pesticides, seeds and agricultural machinery.
4. Acts as an agency for undertaking price support operations for oilseeds and pulses.
5. Export of agricultural commodities such as onion, ginger, garlic, black pepper, cardamom, turmeric, processed fruits and vegetables.
6. Import of pulses, chicory seeds and fertilisers as per Government policy.
7. Inter-state trading of agricultural commodities such as foodgrains, pulses, oilseeds and cotton.
8. Movement of essential commodities from surplus areas to scarcity areas and helps in ease consumer supplies.

CONCLUSION

The Indian Co-operative Movement is more than 90 years old. The credit structure is fairly well organised and other functions such as marketing, grading, supply of agricutlural inputs and consumer co-operatives are yet to be firmly established in the co-operative sector. A planned approach towards integration of all activities and efficient functioning of co-operatives is required for evolving a strong co-operative system in our country.

QUESTIONS

1. How does co-operative marketing Act as a remedial measure to overcome the imperfections in rural marketing?
2. What are the reasons for the poor performance of co-operative societies in many states and what are the remedial measures?

CASE STUDY

The Case of a State Co-operative Federation

The vicious circle, the MARKFED is the apex Federation of Primary Marketing Co-operatives in the state. It came into being in October 1966 as a result of the reorganisation of the bilingual state. Earlier, it functioned for the entire unified state.

The objective of the State Federation is to arrange for marketing of agricultural produce brought to it by the member-marketing co-operatives and to the extent possible to arrange for the processing of it also. It is also expected to provide other allied and supplementary services such as storage, transport, interim financial accommodation, including supply of inputs. Under the accepted policies and programmes, it has been appointed as the agent of the State Government for procurement of foodgrains in the state.

The Board of Directors consists of 17 members. Representatives of member-marketing co-operatives (one for every 10 co-operatives in the district with a minimum of one representative for each district) find a place on the board. In addition, nominations of the Registrar of Co-operative Societies, Director of Agriculture, Director of Food and Civil Supplies Department have been placed on the Board. The Managing Director who is an IAS officer on deputation is the ex-office member of the Board of Directors.

For the past three years, the Board of Directors stands superseded and the State Government has nominated a board of administrators. The reasons given for supersession were the generally inefficient and unsatisfactory management of the State Co-operative Marketing Federation. The Government was concerned about its funds invested in the share capital as state partner (and it failed to safeguard the capital) and the public interest at large. It was constrained to supersede the top management.

The Managing Director is assisted by Financial Controller, 3 Managers (Marketing, Inputs and Processing) and Executive Engineer. At middle level, there are 13 field officers, one for each district, for coordination and supervision.

Initially, the Federation started distributing agricultural inputs. From 1970, it took up procurement work on behalf of the State Government. Today, it carries processing operations as well.

On the financial front, the Federation appears to have over-borrowed. The interest burden is disproportionately heavy in relation to returns on investment. It needs, therefore, a revamping to be able to function as a self-reliant, successful co-operative business federation. However, the Government nominees on the board of directors do not attend to the tasks assigned to them and irregularly participate in the periodical board meetings. The chief executive officer is hardly able to do anything about it. Unofficially, it has been experienced that nominees do not indicate any commitment to co-operative philosophy and need for development through co-operatives. However, the Board and the chief executive officer (who is an IAS officer), from the records available, it appears, have not been pulling together as they should in the interest of the organisation. In a period of past 5 years, 6 chief executive officers were changed. Duration of the CEO varied between 2 months and 16 months. There was a general impression amongst officers at the middle level that the Government officer who is sent on deputation exhibited his loyalty to the parent department and not to the organisation to which he was posted. He also lacked necessary managerial and professional orientation. Frequent transfers came in the way of required experience being gathered on the part of the CEO and affected adversely continuity and stability in policymaking. The whole environment was affecting the morale of the workers at the lower levels of management.

This is largely reflected in financial returns which have been progressively recording a decline.

Correspondingly, there were demands growing for funds from the State Government and in order to keep the organisation going, the Government was in a way compelled to sanction additional resources to the Federation. Thus, the State Government found itself in a vicious circle. In certain fields of operation the MARKFED had to compete with other State Undertakings like the FCI, the State Agro-Industries Corporation, the State Seeds Marketing Corporation, etc. Quantitatively, the size of operations in terms of money in certain spheres were recording some increase though not uniformly satisfactory. In a more pronounced manner, the State Federation was fast losing its co-operative character.

The co-operators in the State Co-operative Union were worried about the performance of the Federation and a spokesman of the State Co-operative Movement desires to represent to the State Government a case for the re-organisation of the MARKFED. Under the resolution of the Committee of the State Co-operative Union, the Chairman has been asked to represent the case of the MARKFED to the State Government.

QUESTIONS

1. Identify the main problems of MARKFED.
2. How can we revive MARKFED?

✿ ✿ ✿

18 RECENT TRENDS IN AGRICULTURAL PRODUCE MARKETING

INTRODUCTION

An efficient agricultural marketing system is an important requirement for the development of the economy of the country. In the present system of marketing of agricultural produce, the middlemen dominate the trade and farmers get low prices for the produce. Low prices dampen the enthusiasm of the farmers and they would be motivated to increase the yields only if they receive remunerative prices for their produce. The farmers are able to get fair prices for their produce by selling through regulated markets. The regulated markets are situated in district/taluka headquarters and are not easily accessible to the farmers. On an average, a regulated market covers about 450 sq. km. which is high. During the recent years, Corporate sector, State Governments and Co-operatives have taken a number of measures to improve the efficiency in the marketing of agricultural produce.

CONTRACT FARMING

Contract farming by private/co-operative units, can be a useful tool for overcoming inadequacies existing in agricultural production and marketing. Contract farming is a system of farming, wherein farmers grow selected crops under a buyback agreement with an agency engaged in trading or processing. It is a system for the production and supply of agricultural produce under forward contracts between producers and buyers. Contract farming ensures adequate on time supply of quality produce, maintenance of price stability and adoption of best agricultural practices. Industrial houses like Reliance, Bharti, United Breweries, ITC, HUL, Tata are entering the agriculture scene in an effort to corporatise agriculture and remove the uncertainties associated with agriculture.

Examples:

(a) Satnam Overseas Limited has established its supremacy in the Indian Basmati market under the brand name Kohinoor. They have covered about 4,000 acres under contract farming of rice.

(b) Punjab Agro Industries Corporation Limited has entered into collaboration with Rallis, ICICI Bank and LT Overseas Ltd. The project is implemented by Punjab Agro, Rallis provide solutions to farmers' field problems and supply agricultural inputs, ICICI extend finance to farmers and LT Overseas procure the agricultural produce, process and sell under Dawat.

(c) United Breweries is tying up with farmers to produce high quality barley for its distilleries.

(d) Bharti, the telecommunication company has a joint venture with Del Monte Pacific (Philippines). The company has contract farming arrangements with farmers in Maharashtra, J&K, Punjab and Gujarat for procurement of apple, sweet corn, baby corn and banana. It sells fresh produce under the brand "Fieldfresh" and processed foods under Del Monte branding. The company has established Field Fresh Centre of excellence in Ludhiana and collaborates with Punjab Agricultural University in the areas of agricultural research and development. It is putting up a plant in Hosur in Tamil Nadu for processing of agricultural produce.

(e) Golden Green Company (Thapar group) has undertaken cultivation of Gherkins in Andhra Pradesh and Karnataka. The company offers high quality seed materials and technical advice to farmers under buyback arrangement. The company has a turnover of over ₹ 100 crore and about 90 per cent of the produce is exported to foreign countries.

ORGANIC FARMING

The use of chemical fertilisers and pesticides has played a positive role in increasing agricultural productivity, making India a self-sufficient country in food production. However, there has been an increasing demand especially in developed countries like USA, Japan and Europe and among upper economic segment of the Indian population for organic food products, i.e., crops grown without the use of chemicals. Out of the total food production of over 260 million tonnes, the country produced 14,000 tonnes of organic food. At present, we have about 1,500 certified organic farms. Organic market analysts have forecasted annual growth rates of about 20 per cent a year. Knowing the value of organic food, many farmers have started cultivation of crops like chillies, vegetables, grapes without using chemicals. Similarly, organic tea cultivation is also followed in plantation areas of south and east. Most consumers are willing to pay a price premium of about 20 per cent for organic products and there are tremendous opportunities for export of fruits, vegetables, spices and beverages.

However, the consumer price for organic produce continues to be high compared to regular produce available in the market. ***Example:*** Moong Dhal (Green Gram) ₹ 160 compared to ₹ 80 per kg, Chana Dhal ₹ 130 compared to ₹ 70 per kg (2012).

The Government has set up National Institute of Organic Farming in 2003 in Ghaziabad. The purpose of the institute is to formulate rules, regulations and certification of organic products in line with International standards. The certification agencies include APEDA, Spices Board, Tea Board and Directorate of Cashew and Cocoa.

Examples:

(a) Alphanso mango grown without the use of chemicals like fertilisers and pesticides in fetching high price in Mumbai market. The organic mango has been certified by a German based agency.

(b) Andrew Yule and Company have introduced organic tea brands. (Himalayan delight, Specialty tea) all produced at company's tea estates in Darjeeling.

AGRICULTURE AND FOOD PROCESSING

Food processing industry covers fruits, vegetables, grains, cocoa, soyabean, plantation crops, milk, livestock and aquaculture products. Food processing involves all the activities from the harvesting of the produce till it reaches the final consumer in the desired form. The sector has large potential for growth and development especially in rural areas. While in foreign countries about 14 per cent of the workers are engaged in agriculture and food processing industry, in India it provides employment to only about 3 per cent of the labour force.

Socio-economic changes in the Indian society, i.e., increasing number of women workers, nuclear families, dual income, larger disposable income, fast life, etc., have contributed to the growth of the industry. Ready-to-eat food, beverages, processed fruits, frozen vegetables, marine, dairy and meat products are becoming popular in the country.

Food processing provides vital linkages between the industry and agriculture and therefore offers excellent opportunities for entrepreneurs, corporates and progressive farmers to set up agri-business and agro-industries. We are the largest producers of fruits and vegetables, yet only 2 per cent of the produce undergoes value addition.

As a part of the strategy to develop food processing industry, the Ministry of Food Processing has come out with a detailed plan for Mega Food Parks. There will be a three-tier structure consisting of collection centres at farm gate level, primary processing centres for sorting, grading, etc., and central processing centres with backward linkages with primary processing centres and forward linkages with the market. The Mega Food Parks would be located in Shirwal (Maharashtra), Ranchi (Jharkhand), Chikmagalore (Karnataka), Dharmapuri (Tamil Nadu), Jalandhar (Punjab), Haridwar (Uttarakhand), Jagdispur (UP), Jangipur (West Bengal), Chittor (Andhra Pradesh) and Nalbari ((Assam). The facilities include the following:

(a) **Infrastructure Development:** Food Park, packaging centre, cold chain facilities, irradiation facilities. Development of common facilities such as cold storage, warehouse, quality control labs, effluent treatment plant, etc., for food processing units in Food Parks.

(b) **Technology Upgradation:** Processing food industry in general.

(c) **R&D, Quality Assurance:** Food safety, bar-coding, quality control laboratories.

(d) **Human Resource Development:** Setting up of National Institute for Food Technology and Management, impart training to update skills, conducting diploma/degree courses.

(e) **Strengthening of Institutions:** Meeting expenditure, Information technology, strengthening of state nodal agencies.

NATIONAL HORTICULTURE MISSION (NHM)

The objectives of the mission are to increase production and productivity of horticulture crops (fruits, vegetables and flowers), reduce post-harvest losses, improve nutritional security, increase exports, increase farmers' income and generate employment opportunities for the unemployed. The floriculture export is expected to touch ₹ 1,000 crore by 2010. The domestic market is estimated at about ₹ 3,000 crore and is growing at 40 per cent per annum. The Government is setting up flower auction centres in Bengaluru, Kolkata, Noida and Mumbai and is to improve cargo handling facilities in Goa, Calicut and Coimbatore.

FARMERS MARKET

In many states, the Government has encouraged farmers to sell vegetables directly to urban consumers by setting up "Farmers' market". These markets are known as Rythu Bazaars (Andhra Pradesh) and Vivasayigal Santhai (Tamil Nadu). These markets are run by Government and only farmers are allowed to sell the agricultural produce to the consumers in the market. The market works both in the morning hours. The market committee in consultation with farmers fixes the rates for different commodities. The farmers come from about 25 villages surrounding the city and are allotted stalls by the market committee. The market committee also provides cold storage facilities for perishable commodities.

Example: **Uzhavar Sandai (Farmers Market) in Tamil Nadu:** The prices of vegetables and fruits are fixed on a daily basis at an average rate of 20 per cent higher than wholesale price and 15 per cent less than the retail price. The prices are exhibited in front of each shop. The first Uzhavar Sandai was started in Madurai in1999 and now there are over 100 such markets in Tamil Nadu managed by the Department of Agricultural Marketing, Agriculture and Horticulture.

ORGANISED RETAILING

Major retailers such as Spencers (RPG Group), More (Aditya Birla Group), Natures Basket (Godrej), Food Bazaar (Pantaloon Group), Reliance are setting up collection centres in vegetables growing areas of the country. The farmers sell the produce to the collection centres and earn a decent income as the middlemen (Arhatias, Hoondekeri, Commission agent) are not involved in the transaction. Further, they do not have to incur transportation costs. The vegetables are cleaned, graded and packed on the spot and sent to towns like Bengaluru, Hyderabad, Pune, Mumbai and Delhi.

Example: The company buys cauliflower at ₹ 8 per kg and the packing and transportation cost is about ₹ 2 per kg. The same vegetable cost about ₹ 16 in wholesale vegetable markets. Therefore, direct sourcing of vegetables from farmers benefits the company and the farmer.

(a) **Reliance** has rolled out "Reliancefresh" stores to sell fresh fruits, vegetables and staples (such as wheat, atta, rice, etc.), and is spread over 3,000-5,000 sq. ft. "Reliancefresh Plus" stores will, however be spread over 10,000-15,000 sq. ft., and stock fruits and vegetables, staples as well as apparel, consumer electronics, FMCG items and even medicines. Reliance sourcing model is based on rural business hubs (RBHs). These RBHs would procurefresh produce and also provide technical service to farmers to increase agricultural production.

"Reliancefresh Store"

(b) **Pantaloon**, the leader in apparel and retailing grocery is putting a big thrust on organic food business. The company has identified Pune for growing and sourcing vegetables and fruits without chemical contents. Other places to be covered would include Bengaluru, Hyderabad and Nashik. Pantaloon plans to set up 150 food bazaar stores in two years at an estimated investment of about ₹ 350 crore. The investment on the farm to plate initiative will be mainly on people, supply chain mechanism and development of business.

(c) **Aditya Birla Group** has launched "More" retail outlets in urban centres. These outlets deal in consumer goods, durables, fruits and vegetables.

"More Store"

(d) The Tata group has entered into a joint venture with "Total Produce" Europe's largest fresh farm produce company, to procure and sell fresh farm produce. The joint venture will have over 40 hubs over a period of 2-3 years.

(e) Godrej Aadhar sources premier quality vegetables for its retail venture **Natures basket** from villages surrounding Narayangaon near Pune. They have set up collection centre where farmers come in the evening to sell their produce. The retail outlet of Godrej Aadhar sells seeds, fertilisers and pesticides. It provides soil and water testing and technical advice to farmers on scientific cultivation of crops.

(f) NDDB: Mother Dairy has established Safal fruits and vegetables retail outlets in major cities and towns to meet the requirements of urban population.

"Mother Dairy – Vegetable Retail Outlet"

(g) The State of Jammu and Kashmir is one the biggest producers of Saffron (Kesar) in the world. The produce is sold through Government agencies and private traders.

"A Saffron Dealer (Srinagar)"

AGRI-TOURISM

Agri-tourism means travel organised around farming, small-scale food production or animal husbandry. Visiting a farm for education and enjoyment are the key features of farm tourism. In a mundane world, farm tourism offers the visitors to connect with the land providing hands on experience with the farm. It involves slower and leisurely activities that help a person to understand and appreciate the farm and the farmers who cultivate the land.

Farm tourism involves farm based activities such as ploughing the field, irrigating the land, weeding , applying nutrients, harvesting, riding bullock carts/tractors, milching animals, staying in farm house and enjoying local food, etc. Farm tourism provides employment and income to locals and brings in economic stability in rural areas. At the same time, it provides opportunities for urban people to go back to roots and live close to nature far away from the man-made urban environment.

Examples:

(a) Winers in Maharashtra have initiated Wine Tourism. The idea of having Wine Tourism is to have visitors stay in winery, see the vineyard and get a feel of wine-making process. This will also allow to relish the drink. There are about 50 wineries in and around Nashik and most of the Vineyards offer a guided tour along with a session on their tasting room. Wine tours are usually spread across the entire day. The wine festival held in Nahsik draws lakh of visitors. Efforts are being made for branding of Nashik Wine as it is made from good quality grapes.

(b) Konkan Bhumi Prathisthan, an organisation that promotes rural tourism in Konkan area in collaboration with Maharashtra Tourism Development Corporation conducts Konkan Alphonso Mango Tourism Festival and arranges a bus tour and stay in villages for the visitors.

(c) Gowardhan Dairy (Go Cheese) organises Milk and Cheese Tour of their dairy situated in Mancher, near Pune. It is one of the biggest dairies in Asia with a modern farm and 3,000 cows. It has an exclusive nursery for calves. The company is providing opportunities for students and Mahila Mandals to visit the dairy complex and understand the various operations in the dairy farm.

USE OF IT AND INTERNET

1. Farm Operations: Farming continues to be the main occupation of the rural population. While the Government has initiated several measures for improving production and productivity of crops, the farmers require support in the form of finance and remunerative prices for the produce. Further they require timely information on climatic conditions, sowing time, high yielding varieties of seeds, use of fertilisers and pesticides, technical advice on the cultivation of crops and information on marketing of agriculture produce. Over the last twenty years, our country has emerged as the leader in the IT services. The information and communication technology has played major roles in various sectors like finance, insurance, communication and transport and the potential of IT is yet to be fully tapped in agricultural sector. The various functionaries in agricultural sector, i.e., the farmers, traders in inputs and agricultural produce, agricultural research institutes, Central and State Governments, department of agriculture, NGOs working for the benefit of the farmers can contribute to the growth of the agricultural sector through IT. A few examples are given below:

(a) **Agricultural Technology Information Centre by Indian Council of Agricultural Research, New Delhi:** Call Centres, Researchers and farmers linkages on cultivation practices, technological developments and use of inputs.

(b) **Kisan Portal by Nagarjuna Group (Andhra Pradesh):** Portal in regional languages on agricultural practices, plant protection, weather and animal husbandry.

(c) **Village Knowledge Centre by MS Swaminathan Foundation, Chennai:** Knowledge Centre for agricultural practices, Govt schemes on agriculture, weather conditions, etc.

2. Agricultural Marketing: Information technology and internet play an important role in Agricultural Marketing by providing cost effective and commercially viable information to the farmers. Major areas of the use of IT in marketing are given below:

(a) **Agricultural Market Information System:** The system provides information on production practices, post harvest practices, agricultural meteorology, details of all the agricultural markets in the country.

(b) **Price Forecasting System:** "What Price Can I get" always remains a question mark in the minds of the producer. Low prices dampen the enthusiasm of the farmers and very high prices affect the consumers. The system can be used to workout future prices of agricultural commodities, on weekly basis in the interest of the farmers and also help the Government in market intervention.

(c) **Creation of National Market Atlas:** The common thrust areas include developing infrastructure facilities, identification of new markets, modernisation of existing markets, assessing movement of marketable surplus, developing sub-markets and matching the infrastructure with the availability of output.

(d) **Electronic Auctioning System:** The system provides facilities for auctioning agricultural produce through electronic and transparent auction process. This system has been implemented at Azadpur Mandi of the Agricultural Produce Marketing Committee, New Delhi and Safal Auction Market in Bengaluru.

(e) **Electronic Displayer System:** The primary objective is to increase the degree of knowledge of market participants about the market. The main focus areas are current prices of different crops and different varieties, prices in different markets, seasonal price trends and historical prices quantities supplied.

(f) **E-commerce** is a new phenomenon for marketing of agricultural products. The most important requirement for successful electronic commerce is access to market information system. Electronically linked, producers and retailers will be able to lower their costs by reducing intermediary transactions.

Example: The farmers society in Devgad Taluka in Maharashtra which grows managoes is selling its fruits online (devgadmango.com) with prices ranging from ₹ 400 to ₹ 1,800 per dozen (2013). Other sites are yummangoes.in, localbanya.com and bigbasket.com. DHL has e-commerce portal and offers to ship mangoes to several foreign countries (www.dhlestore.com/mango)

(g) **Information Kiosks** will help the farmers to know more about modern agricultural practices, source of agricultural inputs, availability of farm finance, past and present prices of agricultural commodities in different markets. These kiosks are connected to the national data bank through internet.

Mobile Information Service for Farmers
Reuters Market Light (RML) provides information on weather, crops commodity prices at different markets and future projections to 2,50,000 farmers at an annual subscription of ₹ 800. Similarly, IFFCO in partnership with Bharti Airtel provides crop related information to farmers. The farmers have to purchase special SIM card to receive voice mail containing requred information.

Source: *DNA* August 1, 2010.

ELECTRONIC AUCTIONING SYSTEM

The system provides facilities for auctioning agricultural produce through electronic auction process.

Examples:

(a) **The National Dairy Development Board (NDDB)** has established Safal Fruit and Vegetables Auction Market in Bengaluru. The market offers state-of-the-art infrastructure and world-class services to farmers and traders to transact business in the most convenient and modern way. Village level growers' societies have been formed in vegetable and fruits growing areas and the farmers deliver the produce to these societies. The societies send the produce directly to the auction centre in Bengaluru eliminating all middlemen in the process. Only registered traders are allowed to participate in the auction and once the trader confirms the price and the quantity of the agriculture produce, the total amount payable is directly credited to the account of the Safal. The farmers receive payment for the produce within a few days. The following are the facilities available at the Safal Auction Market.

- The market has computerised auction halls and traders, at the press of a button can do wholesale buying of over 200 graded items.
- The market has provisions for online bidding. The traders can place pre-bids for auction through internet or telephone from any place in the country.
- The market has temperature controlled cold rooms and ripening chambers.

- The centre has large areas for parking, loading and unloading of agricultural produce and high-tech food handling equipment for transportation of produce.
- The auction market has coffee shops, banks, post office, medical shop, telephone booth to make business an easy and enjoyable experience. The market will be open 24 hours, six days a week and has round-the-clock security to protect the property.

"Safal Auction Centre"

(b) National Spot Exchange for Agricultural Produce (NSEAP) is a joint venture of Financial Technologies (I) Ltd., (FTIL), Multi-commodity Exchange of India Ltd., (MCX), National Co-operative Marketing Federation (NAFED) and State Bank of India (SBI). The objective is to set up an electronic platform for commodity trading for the benefit of traders and farmers. The first commodity Soochana Kendra has been launched at agricultural produce market committee, Navi Mumbai.

(c) Fruit and Vegetable Market, Azadpur Mandi, Delhi has facilities for electronic auction, grading of potato and onion, vegetables, ripening rooms for banana and refrigerated vans and trucks.

(d) Flower Auction Centre at Noida, New Delhi: Set up at a cost of ₹ 15 crore at an area of over 10 acres, the flower auction centre is the most modern in the country with world-class facilities including electronic auction centre.

ITC LIMITED (e-Choupal)

ITC, one of India's largest corporations with a turnover of ₹ 26,000 crore (2008-2009) has presence in tobacco, hotels, paper boards, foods, fashion retailing and commodity export. International business started in 1990, is a division of ITC and is engaged in exports of a range of agricultural commodities. The range includes food ingredients — soyameal, rapeseed meal, grains — rice, wheat, pulses, coffee, black pepper, groundnuts and marine products like shrimps and prawns.

e-Choupal

ITC has been trying to find a solution to an old problem for years. The company used to buy soyabean for export and it had sourced supplies from the local mandies. This created two problems — one quality was not guaranteed and two since the supplies were sourced through middlemen, the company had no contact with growers — a crucial pre-condition for orders in many European countries. Direct contact with farmers was not possible as they lived in interior villages. The company looked for the solution in information technology through a project called e-Choupal, launched in 2000. e-Choupal in Hindi means village meeting place. The project e-Choupal is a unique initiative for carrying out agricultural commodity trading in a number of locations. ITC has set up e-Choupal which is an internet kiosk located in the house of an influential person in the village. The village official is appointed by the company and is known as Sanchalak. The Sanchalak acts as the interface between the farmer and the computer terminal. Full contents of the site is made available to registered Sanchalaks only.

The farmer brings a sample of his produce to e-Choupal. The Sanchalak inspects the produce and based on his assessment of the quality, gives the farmer a conditional quote. If the farmer chooses to sell his crops to ITC, the Sanchalak gives him a note containing his name, village, particulars about quality test (foreign matter and moisture content) approximate quantity and conditional price. The farmer takes the note from Sanchalak and proceeds with his crop to the nearest ITC procurement centre. At the ITC centre, the samples are tested by a chemist. After inspection and weighing are completed, the farmer collects his payment in full at payment counter. The farmer is also reimbursed transportation cost. ITC has also incorporated a local commission agent known as Samyojak (collaborator) as the provider of logistics support. Samyojak handles labour at the centre, bagging, storage of the produce and transportation from purchase centre to processing centre.

The previous days mandi closing price is used to determine the benchmark fair average quality price at e-Choupal. This information and the previous day mandi prices are communicated to the Sanchalak through e-Choupal portal. The commission agents at the mandi are responsible for entering daily mandi prices into the e-Choupal.

Power availability in rural India is unreliable and the quality of power is substandard. As power supply is usually available for only a few hours a day, the computer cannot be accessed when information is needed. ITC has overcome this problem by providing battery based UPS backup. ITC has set up e-Choupal in the villages which are within a radius of 15 kms. from town so that the technician can provide system support and maintenance of e-Choupal.

The total cost incurred on the initiative so far has been ₹ 50 million and the benefit accrued is ₹ 20 million, through procurement of 60,000 tonnes of soyabean.

Both ITC and the farmers make a neat saving by bypassing the middlemen in the mandi. For instance, the farmer saves as much as ₹ 250 per tonne on soyabean because he does not incur costs such as baggaging, transportation, loading and unloading, to haul his goods to the mandi. The company, on the other hand, saves over ₹ 200 a tonne by avoiding transporting the produce from the mandi to the company outlet even after reimbursing the farmer for transport and the Sanchalak, the local-level entrepreneur, also makes money by getting a 0.5 per cent commission on the total transaction made through this kiosk. The kiosk can be used for reverse trading also — for companies to sell products and services needed by farmers directly and ITC is already putting together a strategy to leverage the infrastructure to market and distribute goods and services that farmers require. The facility will be available for selling both ITC's products as well as those of other companies — of course, at a price.

The Status of Execution: Launched in June 2000, 'e-Choupal' has already become the largest initiative among all Internet-based inventions in rural India. 'e-Choupal' services today reach out to more than 3,50,000 farmers growing a range of crops — soyabeans, coffee, wheat, rice, pulses, and shrimp — in some 3,00,00 villages through 6,500 kiosks across seven states (Madhya Pradesh, Rajasthan, Maharashtra, Chhattisgarh, Karnataka, Andhra Pradesh and Uttar Pradesh). The problems encountered while setting up and managing these 'e-Choupals' are primarily of infrastructural inadequacies, including power supply, telecom connectivity and bandwidth, apart from the challenge of imparting skills to the first-time internet users in remote and inaccessible areas of rural India. This enthusiastic response from farmers has encouraged ITC to plan for the extension of the 'e-Choupal' initiative to 15 states across India by 2010. On the anvil are plans to channelise services related to micro credit, insurance, health and education through the same 'e-Choupal' covering one lakh villages through 20,000 'e-Choupals'.

CONCLUSION

Modern methods of marketing of agricultural produce establish linkages between agriculture and industry, increase employment opportunities, improve rural income and prevent migration of rural population to cities. This is an area that offers excellent opportunities for entrepreneurs, progressive farmers and corporates to set up agri-business and food processing industries leading to rapid transformation of the rural economy.

QUESTIONS

1. Describe with examples the recent trends in agricultural produce marketing.
2. Do you think that contract farming and organic farming will be beneficial to farmers in the long run.

CASE STUDY

Nisarg Nirman Agro Products, a Mumbai-based firm owned by Makrand Anjali Churi grows and sells exotic fruits and vegetables to five-star hotels in India.

The company has a business model similar to ITC's e-Choupal, but for the fact that the farmer only deals in exotic vegetables and fruits. So you have vegetables such as asparagus, artichoke, fennel, curled parsley and zucchini green (and yellow) being supplied to five-star hotels of the likes of Holiday Inn, The Leela, the Taj Group and also to luxury passenger liners like Libra and Star Cruises.

Nisarg Nirman, first approach the farmers and check their soil in a laboratory to explore which fruits and vegetables can be best grown. They then give a schedule and also the seeds that they want to source.

The company sources these from the farmers with a 100 per cent buyback guarantee and markets it to its five-star customers. Presently, around 300 farmers based in Maharashtra, Gujarat, Himachal Pradesh, Tamil Nadu, Punjab and other states supply to Nisarg Nirman, along side some sourcing from farmers in Thailand.

The company grows around 20 varieties of exotic vegetables in India. Churi says they will soon set up a factory in Mumbai for manufacturing root drip irrigation systems in collaboration with Easy Irrigation, an Israeli company.

The ₹ 2 crore project that is to be started in January 2009 would be a pilot project. The firm currently imports saplings and seeds from countries like UK and Thailand. There are plans to enter the Pune market and even supply exotic vegetables to retail buyers in Mumbai.

You have been appointed as consultant for Nisarg Nirman Agro Products.

QUESTIONS

(a) What hurdles Nisarg Nirman Agro Products will face in managing the procurement of their products from farmers.

(b) Suggest the sources of Finance for Nisarg Nirman Agro Products for expanding their business

(c) How would you develop the Sales Force for Nisarg Nirman Agro Products so that they are fully trained and are able to convince the farmers to become their partners?

✿ ✿ ✿

19 AGRICULTURAL FINANCE AND ROLE OF INSTITUTIONS

INTRODUCTION

Finance is an important requirement of agricultural sector. The farm activities are not managed systematically as in the case of industrial sector. The size of the farm varies even in the same village. Cultivation practices vary from farmer-to-farmer. The farmers do not keep separate accounts for farm operations and domestic expenses. The credit requirements vary from farmer-to-farmer.

In our country, success and failure of crops depend upon climatic factors. Favourable climatic conditions give bumper crops and unfavourable conditions result in very low yields. The markets for agricultural products are generally unorganised and unregulated and the farmers are very often forced to sell their produce at low prices. Further, majority of the cultivators are small farmers and they borrow money from different sources to meet household and cultivation expenses.

CREDIT NEEDS OF FARMERS

The farmers need credit and their credit needs can be looked at two angles, i.e., based on (1) Time, and (2) Purpose.

On the Basis of Time

(a) **Short-term** loans are required for agricultural operations, i.e., for less than 15 months.

(b) **Medium-term** loans for purchase of livestock, deepening of wells, etc., for a period from 15 months to 5 years.

(c) **Long-term** loans required for making permanent improvements on land, purchase of tractors, etc., and the period of loan extends beyond 5 years.

On the Basis of Purpose

(a) **Productive** loans are required for purchase of seeds, fertilisers, pesticides, payment of wages, digging of wells, making permanent improvements on land, etc. About 65 per cent of credit needs is production credit and balance is consumption credit.

(b) **Consumption Needs:** The farmers require money for running the family between marketing of agricultural produce and harvesting of next crop. In case of floods/drought situation, the crop is damaged and farmers are forced to avail loan facilities from village moneylenders.

(c) **Unproductive Purposes** include money required for litigation, performance of marriage, birth/death of family member, festivals, etc.

MARKETING FINANCE

Agricultural produce has to be moved from the place of production to the place of consumption. The produce passes through several intermediaries. The middlemen require finance for buying the produce and for undertaking other activities such as cleaning the produce, processing, warehousing, packaging, grading and transportation. During peak season, large quantities of produce come to the market and it is not possible for the traders to make cash purchases from the farmers. The requirements of finance depend upon the following factors.

(a) **Nature of Crops:** Crops like chillies, cotton and spices require high finance compared to crops like paddy and millets.

(b) **Nature of Business:** Wholesale business requires high finance than retail.

(c) **Seasonal Crops:** There are crops like groundnut, cumin, potato which are cultivated only during specific season and the traders have to carry the stocks to make them available throughout the year.

(d) **Terms of Buying and Selling:** Cash and credit sales will affect the requirements of finance.

The middlemen require two types of finance, i.e., **Fixed capital** for shops, warehouses and weighing equipment and **Working capital** for purchase and transportation of produce and salary to staff. Institutions such as commercial banks, co-operatives, etc., extend credit facilities to farmers and traders.

SOURCES OF FINANCE

Sources of finance can be divided in two categories, i.e., non-institutional sources and institutional sources.

NON-INSTITUTIONAL SOURCES

1. **Big Cultivators/Landlords:** They advance money to small cultivators on the understanding that the produce will be sold to them.
2. **Friends and Relatives:** Sometime farmers borrow money for a short period from friends/relatives to meet urgent financial requirements.
3. **Mobile Traders:** These traders move from village-to-village and generally advance money for short period and also procure agricultural produce from cultivators.
4. **Small Commission Agents:** They are generally known as Kachcha Arhatias in Northern India. They procure produce from villagers and arrange to sell it to the nearby mandis. As soon as the money is received from mandis, they make payment to the cultivators.
5. **Wholesale Commission Agents:** They are Pucca Arhatias. They deal in bulk quantities of commodities and finance traders as well as farmers.
6. **Professional Moneylenders:** In this case, money lending is the main business and they charge exorbitant interest rates.
7. **Non-professional Moneylenders:** They may be either village merchants or traders in agricultural produce and money lending activity is a side business for them.
8. **Indigenous Bankers or Shroffs:** They are basically moneylenders and their scale of operation is high. They finance traders, local industries and villagers and also receive deposits.

   Examples: Gujarati Shroffs, Multani Shroffs, Chettiars and Marvari Kayas.

It is seen that the most important non-institutional source of rural credit is the moneylenders. During pre-independent days, there was practically no other source for availing credit and the farmers were forced to borrow money from moneylenders. As per All India Debt and Investment Survey (1971-72), moneylenders were the main source of credit for rural households and they were meeting as much as 70 per cent of the credit needs of rural households. There are several methods by which the moneylenders were exploiting the rural people:

1. Obtaining pro-note for a large amount of money than what is actually paid.
2. Computation of interest at exorbitant rates as high as 48% per annum.
3. Deduction of interest in advance from the amount lent.
4. Forcing the farmers to sell the produce at low rate to the moneylenders.
5. They often exploited the villagers by not entering the money returned and the interest paid.
6. Moneylenders advanced long-term loan against security of land and over a period of time manipulated the records and seized the land.

It may be said that legislative measures alone cannot wipe out the evil of indebtedness completely, as the disease is widespread. A real solution to the growing indebtedness lies in the provision of productive and remunerative jobs to the rural poor and strengthening institutional lenders such as co-operatives and commercial banks. Considering the evils associated with money lending by private people, the Government has initiated the following measures for regulation of money lending.

1. Licensing of moneylenders.
2. The interest paid should not exceed double the principal amount.
3. In order to protect the debtors from manipulated accounts, states have prescribed form of accounts and insisted on the debtor being given statements regularly by moneylenders.
4. Act to protect the assets of the agriculturist from passing to the hands of non-agricultural moneylenders.
5. Exempting ancestral property from attachments and also standing crops.
6. Restoration of mortgaged land on payment of nominal compensation.
7. Empowering the court to direct payment of decremental amount by instalments.

INSTITUTIONAL SOURCES

The most important move was the expansion of institutional credit to the cultivators. The Government of India nationalised fourteen commercial banks in 1969 followed by nationalisation of six more banks in 1980. In 1975, Regional Rural Banks were established. Subsequently, National Bank for Agriculture and Rural Development (NABARD) was set up in 1982. As a result of these measures, the share of institutional credit has increased to 61 per cent in 2002.

The co-operatives are fully familiar with local conditions and problems and as such are ideal institutions to serve the rural poor. The rural co-operative structure mainly consists of credit co-operatives, land development banks and farmers' service societies.

CO-OPERATIVE BANKING

Definition of Co-operative Banking

A co-operative bank has been defined by Devine as "a mutual society formed, composed and governed by working people themselves for encouraging regular savings and granting small loans on easy terms of interest and repayment". A co-operative bank is a voluntary agency formed by needy persons themselves to get credit facilities on the basis of the securities they have, not from the rich or from the public, but by their own resources — resources of the credit society. In the twentieth century, co-operative banks have become popular and mainly finance agriculture and its allied activities.

Importance of Co-operative Banking

Co-operative banking is useful in the following ways:

1. It is a superior institutional arrangement for financing agricultural operations. Co-operative banks offer loans to farmers so that they might utilise the amount for increasing agricultural production and raising their standard of living. In a country where the farm population is composed of small farmers who have small means and small lands, co-operative banking is most advantageous. As the society consists of farmers themselves, it knows at firsthand, the credit problems of the rural poor and strives to find out suitable solutions for them.
2. Co-operative banks make persons dynamic by offering them the necessary financial assistance. This encourages farmers to engage in productive activities which benefit them as well as the banks. Co-operative banking changes the whole attitude of farmers and enables them to adjust to the changing environment.
3. Co-operative banking teaches the farming community to borrow at the right time, in the right amount for the right purpose and repay the loan on the due dates. Therefore, we may say that co-operative banks assist in developing a healthy attitude among farmers, which enables them to step up agricultural production.
4. A strong and stable co-operative bank in rural areas will free a large number of borrowers from the clutches of moneylenders and constrain the latter to reduce their rate of interest if they want to continue in business.
5. Co-operative banks provides easy credit facilities to farmers and stimulate economic activity. Secondly, farmers learn to develop the habit of saving so that they may not have to borrow in future. The savings of the people promote investment activity, which ultimately results in prosperity.
6. As co-operative banks grant loans for agriculture and allied activities, they supplement the income of the farming community by enabling them to engage in dairy farming, sheep rearing, vegetable growing, etc.
7. Co-operative banks not only stimulate several economic activities, but help in bringing about rural re-orientation by changing the thinking and behaviour of the people for their own advantage and the benefit of the nation.

Objectives of Co-operative Banks and Societies

Co-operative banks or co-operative credit societies operate with a view to attaining the objectives mentioned below.

1 Co-operative credit societies function with the prime objective of making available loans at concessional rates to needy members. They lend funds against any kind of security. To enable even the small farmers to avail of the credit facility, loans are often granted against personal security.

2. Co-operative banks try to bring about the most effective use of the loans they advance. For this purpose, the loans are advanced only for productive purposes. Secondly, the bank supervises the activities of those members who have borrowed from it to ensure that the amount is used for the purpose for which it was granted.
3. The financial resources of a co-operative bank alone may not be sufficient to cater to the requirements of a large number of its members. Therefore, the other objective of a co-operative credit institution is to draw on the sources of funds outside the society to finance the productive activities of its members. Even though a co-operative bank is an association of small farmers, who are often creditworthy, it does not encounter much difficulty in securing loans from other financial agencies.
4. The aim of the co-operative bank is also to reduce the risks in lending by a careful handling of its activities. Its insistence on the utilisation of the loan amount only for productive purposes ensures that the borrowers will repay back the amounts on the due dates. If no close watch is kept on the activities of the borrowers, it is very likely that the borrowed funds would be used for consumption purposes, in which case the borrower becomes a defaulter; and with it, the risk of lending increases.
5. When small farmers easily receive co-operative loans, they are motivated to invest the borrowed funds in productive ventures with a view to increasing their incomes. As a result of this, the savings of members go up, leading to larger amounts of funds at the disposal of the co-operative bank. In other words, co-operative credit institutions promote the thrift habit among its members.

Comparison of Commercial Bank and Co-operative Bank

1. Commercial banks are primarily profit-making institutions. All their activities are therefore directed towards the making of profit. Obviously, the rate of interest charged by these banks is high. Co-operative banks, are guided by service considerations, and therefore they make available loans at lower rates of interest.
2. Commercial banks, mostly finance trade, commerce, and industry, where the risks are low and the amount of profit is high. Co-operative banks are different from commercial banks in the sense that they provide credit to agriculture and its allied sub-sectors with the object of assisting in the promotion of the productive activities of the small farmers.
3. While sanctioning loans, commercial banks carefully examine the creditworthiness of the borrower. Only after their creditworthiness has been established, do they grant loans. Co-operative banks, on the other hand, bear in mind the purpose for which the loan is granted. Even if a person is poor, he gets the loan if the co-operative bank is convinced that the purpose for which the loan would be utilised would enable him to repay the borrowed money in time.
4. Under the commercial banking system, we find commercialisation of credit. In order to secure credit from the bank, one has to offer some tangible security. In co-

operative banks, we have the personalisation of credit, the funds are supplied even on the basis of personal security — for example, honesty, good reputation, etc.

5. The commercial banking structure is not federal in character. But the federal set-up is evident in the case of co-operative banking system. The co-operative banking structure is a two or three-tiered set-up where each tier is independent in the performance of its set functions but is federated with a view to earning higher gains.
6. Commercial banks do not receive any financial assistance from the Government. But state participates in the activities of co-operative banks. The state assists co-operative banks in meeting the requirements of small farmers.
7. The management of commercial banks works on remuneration, whereas a co-operative bank does not offer any financial rewards to its management committee. But there is a justification for the co-operative bank in doing this, for it has to operate at the lowest management cost and make available loans at lower rates of interest than the rates the commercial banks charge.
8. In order to minimise risk, commercial banks generally provide short-term loans. Co-operative banks grant both short- and long-term loans with a view to assisting the farmer in executing the plans which would increase agricultural production.
9. In the commercial banking structure, one man is in charge of sanctioning loans up to a specific limit. The loans in the co-operative banks are always sanctioned by the management committee, irrespective of the loan amount.
10. The accounts of commercial banks are audited by its head office. But in the case of co-operative banks, it is the responsibility of the Registrar of Co-operative Societies to have the accounts audited.
11. Commercial banks declare substantial dividends for their shareholders at the end of every year. Co-operative banks declare small dividends for their members. A substantial part of dividend is used for the provision of better services to members.

Co-operative Banking in India

Independent India has accepted co-operation as an indispensable agency for rural upliftment and national development. Among different types of co-operative societies, co-operative credit societies in India are very important.

A co-operative bank is a three-tiered structure offering short- and medium-term credit. Its base is the primary co-operative credit society while state co-operative banks are at the apex and the central co-operative banks in between the two. A study group of the National Credit Council, headed by D.R. Gadgil, observed: "The co-operative banking system is an integrated one and, because of its three-tier structure, has been able to extend credit to agriculturists, artisans, etc. The three-tier system also allows a rationalised flow of resources from the metropolitan centres to villages and combines this with a fairly low cost of operations."

As for long-term credit, the organisation of co-operative credit structure is a two-tiered one, with central land development banks at the apex and primary land development banks at the base. Co-operative credit institutions in India "constitute an integrated system for mobilising resources and are an efficient means of supplying credit".

PRIMARY CO-OPERATIVE CREDIT SOCIETIES

Primary co-operative credit societies operate at the village level to attain the following objectives:

1. To accept deposits and provide short-term loans on reasonable conditions;
2. To develop the habit of savings among the rural masses;
3. To assist in a better implementation of the five-year plans in so far as they relate to agriculture;
4. To take up educative, advisory and welfare functions for the benefit of farmer members.

Individual farmers are members of primary credit societies. Each society secures its funds by way of share capital, deposits, loans and the Reserve Fund. The share capital is directly contributed by members and indirectly by State Governments. Deposits are accepted both from members and non-members with a view to effective mobilisation of rural savings. To get larger deposits, primary co-operative encourages rural people to save a part of their income and deposit it with it. Loans constitute an important source of working capital for primary credit societies. Loans are procured from the State Government and central co-operative banks.

Primary credit societies advance loans to their members for short periods, varying between six months and one year, to enable them to conduct their ongoing agricultural operations. The loan amount sanctioned varies among members depending upon:

1. The purpose of the loan;
2. The character of the individual;
3. His repayment capacity; and
4. The type of security that he can pledge to the society.

A short-term loan is sanctioned for the purchase of seeds, fertilisers, pesticides and minor repairs. Medium-term loans are granted by the society for the purchase of cattle, pumpsets, agricultural implements, etc., for periods varying between one to five years. Short-term loans are lent against personal security or against the security of other members up to a certain limit. For medium-term loans, tangible securities have to be pledged. The success of a co-operative credit society lies in the extent to which the management committee members and office bearers are in a position to recover the loans from the borrowers on due dates.

Primary co-operative credit societies in India suffer from the following defects:

1. Many of our primary credit societies are non-viable, for the membership of each is small and capital is inadequate. In this connection, the All-India Rural Credit Review Committee says: "A large number of primary agricultural credit societies are neither viable nor even potentially viable, and must be regarded as inadequate and unsatisfactory agencies for disbursing production-oriented credit".
2. The credit facilities granted by credit societies are very inadequate when compared with the requirements of the farming population. This being so, the farmers continue to be exploited by moneylenders.
3. There is no uniformity about the growth of the credit movement in different states. We come across wide fluctuations in their area of coverage and their pattern of functioning.
4. There is much delay in sanctioning loans. Farmers, therefore, fail to get money in their hour of need.
5. The supervisory machinery of many primary credit societies is not efficient.
6. Due to selfish motives, the operational efficiency of the credit societies is very low.
7. A significant proportion of the weaker sections in rural areas has not been in a position to receive any worthwhile assistance from these societies.
8. Credit societies have failed to develop to any significant extent the savings habit among the rural masses.

The structure and working of primary co-operative credit societies need to be modified to make them more responsive to the needs of small farmers. The non-viable units must be amalgamated with the viable ones, and their resource base must be strengthened. Their operational efficiency should be enhanced by the appointment of a paid secretary. Suitable arrangements, both coercive and persuasive, will have to be made for the speedy recovery of loans on due dates. Loan policies will have to be modified to provide greater assistance to the weaker sections of the community. In this connection, the Banking Commission report says: "The progress of reorganisation of primary societies with a view to building strong and viable primary societies has been slow and halting due to various factors, such as reluctance on the part of some State Governments to enforce compulsory amalgamation, unwillingness on the part of primary societies to amalgamate, absence of legal provisions in many State Co-operative Acts for compulsory amalgamation; and various administrative and other delays due to administrative inefficiency and political and other pressures".

"A Service Co-operative Bank"

CENTRAL CO-OPERATIVE BANKS

G.M. Laud in his book 'Co-operative Banking in India' says: "The necessity for a central co-operative banks is that there should be an intermediary agency between the primary credit society with a rural bias run by agriculturists having no touch with the money market and the provincial co-operative bank run mainly by city men with urban bias and having no close association with the countryside". We agree with this viewpoint, for an intermediary structure is essential if the co-operative credit movement is to become effective.

Central co-operative banks function at the district level with the primary co-operative credit societies in that district as its members.

We also have central co-operative banks which admit both individuals and primary societies as their members. The Standing Advisory Committee on Agricultural Credit of the Reserve Bank of India (1952) was in favour of only one central bank for each district. This suggestion was supported by the All-India Rural Credit Survey Committee as well. But still, in certain districts, we have more than one central co-operative bank.

The share capital of central co-operative banks consists of the shares purchased by individual members, by primary credit societies and by State Government. The bank gets loans mainly from the state co-operative bank and the Reserve Bank of India. Deposits of various types — savings, current, recurring and fixed deposits — are received from primary co-operative societies and individuals. It is binding on the bank to create a Statutory Reserve Fund out of its profits. The functions of the central co-operative bank are guided by the following motives:

1. To act as the connecting link between primary credit societies and state co-operative banks;
2. To provide credit facilities to its member societies to enable them function more effectively.

3. To act as a balancing centre by diverting funds from surplus primary credit societies to deficient primary credit societies;
4. To guide and control the working of its member societies;
5. To maintain a supervisory staff to watch carefully the activities of its member societies; and
6. To strengthen the co-operative credit movement in the district.

Central co-operative banks lend money to member societies for short- and medium-terms on the basis of the security of land, houses, gold, fixed deposit receipts, life insurance policies, etc. Loans are granted up to a certain limit fixed for each society, depending upon its repayment capacity. The rate of interest charged by the bank is 3 per cent higher than the rate at which it has borrowed funds. This constitutes the incorne of the bank, which is used to meet its operational expenses. It is also used to pay dividend on share capital and to build up the reserve fund. Lending by central co-operative banks differs from that of commercial banks in that the former do not have any choice in the investment of its funds, for it has necessarily to finance its members. It invests a large proportion of its funds on financing agriculture.

Defects of Central Co-operative Banks

Central co-operative banks suffer from the following defects:

1. The average number of member societies affiliated to a central bank is small because the number of central co-operative banks is very large. This has made the central co-operative banks weak and non-viable.
2. Like primary credit societies, these banks are also short of adequate capital. The working capital of central co-operative banks in many states is less than ₹ 25 lakh.
3. The amount credited to the Reserve Fund is not sufficient to enable the bank to overcome its financial difficulties when they crop up.
4. The deposits position of these banks is not satisfactory.
5. Proper books of accounts are not maintained. As a result, there is scope for irregularities to a considerable extent.

Central co-operative banks, to attain their objectives, will have to improve their financial position. The Government should help them in this task. Co-operative banks and the co-operative department should work in co-ordination with each other and take right decisions. The defaulting societies must not be allowed to continue on the Board of Directors. To ensure quick sanctioning and disposal of loans, decentralisation of powers is necessary. The operations of the bank will have to be stepped up, both quantitatively and qualitatively.

STATE CO-OPERATIVE BANKS

State co-operative banks are the highest agencies for the supply of co-operative credit for short- and medium-terms. They are at the top in the three-tiered co-operative credit structure. The jurisdiction of these banks is the whole state. The central co-operative banks in the state are the members of the state co-operative bank, individuals and primary co-operative credit societies are also admitted as members by some state co-operative banks. The main functions of a state co-operative bank are:

1. It acts as a intermediary between the central co-operative bank and the money market. State co-operative banks borrow money from the money market and make available loans to central co-operative banks.
2. The state co-operative bank functions as the balancing centre by borrowing from those central co-operative banks which have excessive funds and disbursing this amount to the deficient central co-operative banks.
3. It inspects the working of central co-operative banks and gives them timely guidance and help as and when necessary.
4. It operates as an agency of the Reserve Bank of India to finance agriculture. The Reserve Bank of India grants loans to state co-operative banks which, in turn, are disbursed to farmers with the help of the three-tiered structure.
5. It aids State Governments in drawing up plans of rural development and in their implementation.

Central co-operative banks and the State Government subscribe to the share capital of state co-operative banks. Formerly, individuals were also permitted to purchase the shares of these banks. But now this practice has been dispensed with. They accept deposits from member societies, non-members, companies of various types and individuals. Special deposits are accepted from local boards, educational institutions and municipalities. Loans constitute the major source of funds for state co-operative banks. Money is borrowed from the Reserve Bank of India, the State Government, the State Bank of India and its subsidiaries. The state co-operative bank enjoys an overdraft facility with the State Bank of India. Sometimes, the state co-operative banks borrow from one another. But borrowings from the Reserve Bank of India are the chief source of loans for state co-operative banks.

State co-operative banks do not lend funds directly to farmers. Loans are sanctioned to central co-operative banks. These banks distribute them to primary credit societies. And these societies, in turn, lend the funds to the ultimate borrowers. The lending operations of state co-operative banks cover loans, cash credit and overdraft facility made available to member banks. A certain limit is fixed for each central co-operative bank, up to which it can borrow from state co-operative banks. Short-term loans are given for a period of less than 12 months and medium-term loans for less than three years.

Defects of State Co-operative Banks

State co-operative banks often suffer from the following defects:

1. While investing their funds, many state co-operative banks have not acted cautiously. Some of the banks have invested large amounts of money in the purchase of the shares of other co-operative institutions. A few others have made huge advances to primary credit societies. Such practices have come in the way of the successful working of state co-operative banks.
2. The loans advanced by some state co-operative banks have posed serious problems of recovery.
3. The overdues of state co-operative banks have been mounting year-after-year. This is due to the dishonest and inefficient management of the bank.
4. State co-operative banks have been unable to make full use of the medium-term loan facility extended to them by the Reserve Bank of India. If it is properly utilised, the medium-term needs of a larger number of farmers can be met.
5. Many state co-operative banks have not carefully fixed the credit limits for central co-operative banks. This has resulted in excessive borrowing by central co-operative banks and created the problems arising out of the non-recovery of loans.

The defects in the working of state co-operative banks can be eliminated if State Governments and the Reserve Bank of India come forward with larger assistance to help them tide over their difficulties. Adequate staff should be appointed to raise the efficiency of the banks. The state co-operative bank, as a measure for effectively controlling central co-operative banks, should open its own branches in those places where these banks (central co-operative banks) are not working properly. The Reserve Bank of India must, in turn, guide and inspect the working of state co-operative banks more effectively.

PRIMARY LAND DEVELOPMENT BANKS

It is not enough if farmers are provided with short- and medium-term credit. Equally important is the long-term credit, which is essential because it would facilitate structural changes in the agricultural sector. If short- and medium-term credit assists farmers in making immediate gains, long-term credit brings about lasting benefits. Long-term credit is provided by primary and central land development banks.

Primary land development banks either operate at the level of a district or a taluka, depending upon the circumstances in different states in the country. Their main function is to supply long-term credit to its members against the security of land and other immovable property. Its other function is to assist farmers to raise their standard of living. Members and non-members subscribe to the share capital of primary land development banks. Deposits are accepted from the public. There is a restriction on the number of shares to be held by each member and on the amount to be distributed as dividend on shares. Members subscribing to a large number of shares will not receive more privileges while electing the management committee.

Primary land development banks lend money only to members for a period varying between 15 to 30 years for carrying out permanent improvements to land. On a careful examination of the immovable assets of the borrower which are to be mortgaged with the bank and the purpose of the loan, amounts are sanctioned to the members. The rate of interest on these loans varies between 6 per cent to 9 per cent. The loan is to be repaid in equal annual instalments, consisting of both the principal amount and the interest. Loans sanctioned for the purchase of additional land, costly agricultural implements, for the construction of wells, the conversion of dry land into wet land, building of farm houses, cattle sheds, etc., have become more extensive in recent years than the loans given for the redemption of old debts. In the case of loans advanced for the repayment of old debt, the amount is paid to the creditors themselves to prevent the misuse of funds by members.

CENTRAL LAND DEVELOPMENT BANKS (CLDBs)

The membership of a central land development bank is composed of primary land development banks. In a few states, individual members are also permitted to acquire its membership with certain restrictions. A board, consisting of 16 to 18 members, of which two-thirds or three-fourths are representatives of member land development banks elected for a period of three years with Registrar of co-operative societies all its ex-officio member, is the management committee of the central land development bank. Paid officials are appointed to handle the routine office matters of the bank.

Central land development banks perform such functions as the financing of its member banks, arranging for proper supervision and guidance of primary land development banks, acting as intermediaries between Reserve Bank of India and long-term banking institutions, and preventing the farmers from mortgaging their lands with greedy moneylenders. The prime motive in doing all this is to protect the farmers from falling victims to the middlemen and give them the necessary encouragement to save so that the process of capital formation is stimulated.

The share capital of central land development banks is contributed by member banks and the State Government. Only long-term deposits are accepted by the bank because it has to lend funds for longer periods. The bank raises loans by issuing three kinds of debentures, namely, ordinary debentures, rural debentures and special development debentures. Ordinary debentures are guaranteed by the State Government and are issued to the general public. The rate of interest on these debentures depends upon market conditions. Rural debentures are issued against the guarantee of mortgaged land to be purchased by rural people and institutions. These debentures are floated to mobilise rural savings. The rate of interest on rural debentures is one per cent higher than that given on ordinary debentures. Special development debentures are issued in order to raise funds for financing special agricultural development schemes. The Agricultural Refinance Corporation contributes 90 per cent of the amount of special debentures; the balance is collected either from the concerned State Government or the general public. Central land development banks finance primary land development banks which, in turn lend funds to farmers. In those areas where primary banks do not exist, central land development banks themselves supply finance directly to the farmers. In certain circumstances, even if primary banks exist, central land development banks advance loans to agriculturists.

Defects of Land Development Banks (LDBs)

The defects of land development banks are many and varied. Some of the more important ones are:

1. There is no uniform development of land development banks in India. Different State Governments have different attitudes towards these banks. Their organisational structure, therefore, is not same in all the states.
2. Many land development banks are non-viable because of the scarcity of financial resources.
3. There is an absence of honest and efficient supervisory machinery for the inspection of the activities of primary units.
4. As the loaning policy of many banks is defective, they are faced with severe problem of overdues.
5. There is lack of co-ordination between the different credit agencies operating in rural areas, leading to competition among themselves.

In order to improve their working and raise their efficiency, a proper loaning policy will have to be pursued by land development banks. The policy has to be such as to extend the benefits of banking to a larger number of farmers and at the same time, to see to it that the problem of non-recovery of loans does not arise. The State Government should develop a positive attitude towards these banks by providing financial, technical and other forms of help. Land development banks and the State Bank of India, commercial banks, State co-operative banks and regional rural banks should not indulge in unnecessary competition, but work in a co-ordinated manner to intensify the process of economic growth. The management committee must take to innovational activities so as to promote the business of land development banks.

ASSESSMENT OF CO-OPERATIVE CREDIT MOVEMENT IN INDIA

The co-operative credit movement in India, having a history of about more than eight decades, has now developed to a substantial extent. With separate credit structures for short- and long-term financing, it has played a useful role in the rural areas of our country. The effectiveness of co-operative credit has been considered in the paragraphs that follow.

1. Coverage

The number of primary agricultural credit societies has been on the increase year-after-year. Co-operative credit institutions have made much progress by covering nearly 95 per cent of our villages. But when we compare this geographical expansion with their population coverage, we find that the figures are not encouraging. A significant proportion of our farming population lies outside the operations of these institutions.

2. Monetary Assistance

Co-operative credit organisations have made available short- medium- and long-term loans to farmers to enable them to undertake such activities as would raise the productivity of land and the efficiency of labour. Though the amount of the credit advanced by them is far lower than the actual requirements of farmers, their role as agencies providing monetary help to agriculturists is not so small as to be ignored. Because of their meagre resources, they are unable to serve larger sections of members.

3. Reduction in the Importance of Moneylenders

The reliance of the rural community on moneylenders has declined as a result of the operations of co-operative credit organisations, though their complete elimination has not been possible. They have also succeeded in diverting the borrowed funds from consumption purposes to production purposes. This has promoted economic activities in the country to a certain extent. Co-operative banking has assisted in a proper channelisation of rural savings in India.

4. Social Effect

The co-operative credit movement has had a welcome social impact on the country in the sense that it has educated and trained rural masses to avoid the clutches of exploiters and help themselves by practising the co-operative ideology. With the provisions made by the co-operative organisation for educating and training its members, it has facilitated the establishment of a suitable infrastructure for national development.

The co-operative credit movement in India should not be judged in merely quantitative terms, but should be analysed on an altogether different basis. That is why Dr. R.C. Dwivedi says: "Overemphasis on the commercial aspect of co-operatives, measuring their efficiency with the yardstick of the volume of profits, ignoring the social content of their business operations and obligations to execute the Government's policies — this is the visible trend which is a matter of anxiety and concern. Just because we are not in a position to achieve all that we expected from it, we cannot write off the co-operative credit movement as a failure. We should rather revitalise and reorient it so that it may play a more purposeful and meaningful role in stimulating the growth of the national economy."

FARMER'S SERVICE SOCIETIES (FSS)

The main objective of FSS has been to help farmers, particularly small/marginal farmers, agricultural labourers and rural artisans by providing them integrated credit, i.e., credit linked with input supply and marketing. Each FSS has to cover a block so that it can maintain an expert and trained managerial and technical staff for undertaking the diverse activities. Societies provide short- and medium-term credit for agriculture and allied activities mainly for productive purposes. They supply agricultural inputs to farmers and required raw materials, machinery, appliances, etc., to cottage and small-scale industrial activities and provide marketing and agricultural extension services to members. These societies are organised and financed by commercial banks, central co-operative banks and regional rural banks.

THE LEAD BANK SCHEME AND REGIONAL RURAL BANKS

In August 1969, the Reserve Bank of India (RBI) had appointed a committee of bankers, which made specific recommendations for setting up lead banks for each of the underdeveloped districts. Accordingly, the Lead Bank Scheme was introduced in December 1969.

Under this scheme, a particular commercial bank is entrusted with the responsibility of playing a major role in relation to rural development in a defined area. The leading bank co-ordinates the activities of co-operative banks, other commercial banks and financial institutions. It initiates an integrated approach for financing small-scale industries, cottage industries, farming activities by assessing the credit needs of the area and allocates the total requirements among all recognised credit agencies.

The RBI allotted various districts in the country other than metros and union territories to the public sector banks and private sector banks. The lead bank established contacts with other banks and Government agencies and prepared district-wise reports on banking potentiality, information about economy of the districts, population, administrative set-up, infrastructure, industries and trade. Also information was collected on unbanked and underbanked centres for expanding banking facilities. The task of identification of credit gaps and scope for institutional finance was also undertaken. The major objectives of lead bank scheme are:

1. To specify suitable areas for branch expansion.
2. To formulate a phased programme for expanding the branch offices with the object of providing banking facilities to the entire area covered.
3. To earmark the potential area for promoting agriculture and small-scale industrial schemes inducing local entrepreneurs.
4. To assess the major constraints on the development of the district and to induce appropriate agencies for taking up the follow-up remedial action.
5. To experiment with financial schemes which can help in mobilising deposits and promoting investment among the local people.

    Example: Syndicate Bank plays the role of lead bank in Karnataka and they have sponsored Regional Rural banks (Grameen Banks) in important rural markets in the state.

Regional Rural Banks

The Government of India promulgated the Regional Rural Banks Ordinance on 26th September, 1975, which was later replaced by the Regional Rural Bank Act 1976. The distinctive feature of a rural bank is that, though it is a separate corporate body with perpetual succession and common seal, it is closely linked with the commercial bank, which has sponsored the proposal to establish it. The total number of regional rural banks functioning in the country as at the end of June 1999 was 196, covering 451 districts spread over 23 states with the network of 14,467 branches.

Regional rural banks were established with the following objectives in mind:

1. Taking the banking services to the doorstep of rural masses, particularly in hitherto unbanked rural areas.
2. Making available institutional credit to the weaker sections of the society who had by far little or no access to cheaper loans and had by force been depending on the private moneylenders.
3. Mobilise rural savings and channelise them for supporting productive activities in rural areas.
4. To create a supplementary channel for the flow of the central money market to the rural areas through refinance.
5. Generating employment opportunities in rural areas and bringing down the cost of providing credit to rural areas.

The authorised capital of each regional rural Bank is ₹ 1 crore, divided into one lakh fully paid-up shares of ₹ 100 each. Fifty per cent of the capital issued by a Rural Bank is subscribed by the Central Government and thirty-five per cent by a sponsoring bank and the balance by State Government. A rural bank may in particular undertake the following types of business, namely:

1. The granting of loans and advances, particularly to small and marginal farmers and agricultural labourers, whether individual or in groups and to co-operative societies (including agricultural marketing societies, agricultural processing societies, co-operative farming societies, primary agricultural credit societies or farmers' service societies) for agricultural purposes or agricultural operations or for other connected purposes.

2. The granting of loans and advances particularly to artisans, small entrepreneurs and persons of small means engaged in trade, commerce or industry or other productive activities within the notified area of a rural bank.

Future of Rural Banking: The demand for finance will also go up on account of intensive use of modern technology, increase in consumption of fertilisers and pesticides, creation of irrigation facilities, growing use of high yielding variety crops and diversification of agriculture to various allied activities. The rural banks would continue to play a major role in financing agriculture.

COMMERCIAL BANKS

The Banks offer financial assistance to farmers in the form of: 1. Crop loan — to meet cultivation expenses, 2. Produce marketing loan — to avoid distress sales, 3. Farm merchandisation loan, 4. Land development loan, 5. Minor irrigation project loan, and 6. Land purchase loan. Many Commercial Banks provide the following facilities:

(1) **Crop Loan:** The bank offers financial assistance to meet cultivation expenses for various crops as short-term loan. With a repayment period not exceeding 18 months, the crop loan is extended in the form of direct finance to cultivators, tenant farmers and share croppers who actually cultivate the lands. All categories of farmers — small/marginal (SF/MF) and others are included. The bank verifies Service Area Approach land records to ascertain cultivation rights, acreage under different crops, scale of finance per acre and sources of other borrowings, before granting the loan.

(2) **Produce Marketing Loan:** The bank extends financial assistance to help farmers store produce on their own to avoid distress sale. The repayment period of the produce marketing loan (PML) does not exceed 6 months. Further, this facilitates immediate renewal of crop loans for the next crop.

(3) **Land Development Scheme:** The bank gives credit solutions for land development programmes in the form of direct finance to cultivators aimed at better productivity.

Loans under this head cover various activities like land clearance (removal of bushes, trees, etc.), land levelling and shaping, contour/graded bunding, bench terracing for hilly areas, contour stone walls, staggered contour trenches, disposal drains, reclamation of saline/alkaline soils and fencing.

(4) **Minor Irrigation Scheme:** The bank provides credit for creating new source of irrigation by exploiting underground water, energisation of wells, conveyance of water, judicious use of available water, etc. Loans cover various activities like digging of new wells (open/borewells), deepening of existing wells (traditional/in wellbore), energisation of wells (oil engine/electrical pump and laying of pipelines) installing drip/sprinkler irrigation system and lift irrigation system. The repayment schedule of this mode of credit may span 5 to 15 years, depending on the farm income.

Micro Irrigation – State Bank of India Enters into a Tie-up with Finolex Plasson Industries Ltd.

SBI, the premier bank in rural lending has entered into a national level tie-up with Finolex Plasson, a part of the ₹ 5,000 crore Finolex group. The company is engaged in manufacturing and selling micro-irrigation systems and crop management services. The tie-up will help; farmers increase their acreage under irrigation by minimum use of available water and will increase productivity and profitability. The company will assist the bank in identifying eligible farmers and providing loans for purchase of micro-irrigation systems.

(5) **Farm Mechanisation Schemes:** The bank provides credit for purchase of farm equipment and machinery for agricultural operations. This mode of finance covers

activities ranging from purchase of tractors, trailers, cultivators, cage wheels, power tillers, harvesters, power sprayers, dusters, etc. Eligibility is ascertained on the basis of minimum area requirements: Tractors – 8 acres of irrigated area, Power tiller – 5-6 acres, Combine harvester – 20 acres. The repayment schedule of this mode of credit may span 5 to 9 years, depending on the income generation patterns.

(6) **Land Purchase Scheme:** The scheme is applicable to small/marginal farmers, tenants, owning less than five acres of non-irrigated land or 2.5 acres of irrigated land and landless agricultural labourers. Own land (in their own name) before and after purchase should not exceed five acres of unirrigated or 2.5 acres of irrigated land. Maximum loan amount will be ₹ 2 lakh with a minimum 15 per cent contribution from the farmer. The loan could be used for land development and related activities also. Repayment will be in half-yearly instalments for over 10 years.

(7) **Kisan Plus Scheme:** This is a scheme for financing tractors to rural youth. The objective is to promote young entrepreneurs in rural areas to take up the activity of custom hiring. The scheme is applicable for the purchase of new tractors and implements only subject to a maximum amount of ₹ 4 lakh. 10 per cent of the cost of tractor has to be paid as margin money. Repayment period is 5-7 years and security by hypothecation of tractor financed.

(8) **Arhatias Plus:** The scheme provides finance to commission agents against receivables from farmers and the loan amount will be maximum of ₹ 25 lakh. Security by hypothecation of assets and receivables.

(9) **Kisan Credit Cards:** The Kisan Credit Card scheme was launched in 1998-99 so as to facilitate short-term credit requirements of the farmers. The scheme was aimed to provide timely and adequate support to the farmers for their cultivation needs.

"Kisan Gold Card Scheme"

All farmers having a good track record for the last two years are eligible for Kisan Credit Card. The minimum credit limit for this scheme is ₹ 3,000 and the credit limit is based on operational landholding, cropping pattern and scale of finance.

The withdrawal is made easy and convenient with withdrawal slips. The card has a validity period for three years subject to an annual review.

Under Gold Card Scheme, loans up to ₹ 5 lakh can be availed for land development, purchase of pumpsets, bullocks, tractors, machinery, etc. Eligibility is based on credible repayment record for minimum of five years. The loan amount will be maximum of 5 times the annual farm income or 50 per cent of the value of mortgaged land whichever is less, subject to a maximum of ₹ 5 lakh.

Farmers are issued a credit card and a passbook or credit cards-cum-passbook incorporating the name, address, particulars of land holding, borrowing limit and validity period. This card also includes a passport-size photograph of the holder, etc., which may serve both as an identity card and facilitate recording of transactions on an ongoing basis.

(10) Loan Amount

(a) Crop loan up to 18 months and loan amount normally up to ₹ 50,000.

(b) Produce marketing loan (up to 6 months) and loan amount up to 60 per cent of the value of the produce.

(c) Land development scheme and amount normally up to ₹ one lakh.

(11) Crop Loan – Security to be Furnished

(a) Up to ₹ 50,000 hypothecation of the crops.

(b) Above ₹ 50,000 hypothecation of the crops and mortgage of the land or third party guarantee.

(c) Above ₹ 1 lakh hypothecation of the crops and mortgage of the land.

(12) Movable Assets – Security to be Furnished

(a) Up to ₹ 10,000 based on track record and personal guarantee.

(b) Above ₹ 10,000 and up to ₹ 50,000 hypothecation of the asset.

(c) Above ₹ 50,000 hypothecation of the asset and mortgage of the land.

"State Bank of India is Bringing About a Major Revolution in Rural Business"

PROBLEMS FACED BY BANKERS IN RURAL AREAS

1. The density of population is low in rural areas and therefore the cost of providing service is high compared to urban market.
2. Many of the rural consumers are not able to provide security in the form of physical assets while applying for loans.
3. Rural households need low value loans and bankers find it difficult to recover the transaction costs.
4. Due to low literacy and low awareness, the villagers find the procedures laid down by banks for availing loan to be very cumbersome and they prefer to approach moneylenders.
5. The loan waiver scheme initiated by Government has encouraged even well-to-do farmers to become defaulters.
6. Crop production is influenced by Agro-climatic conditions and there are wide variations in the quantity and quality of the yields obtained by farmers. The yields are low under adverse climatic conditions and they are unable to repay the loan amount.
7. Due to lack of infrastructure facilities, bank officials are reluctant to work in rural areas. Some of them even consider working in rural areas as 'Punishment Posting'.

SUGGESTIONS FOR DEVELOPING BANKING SERVICES

1. Considering vagaries of monsoon, seasonal income, the banks have to come out with rural-specific products and services to meet the requirements of rural people.
2. The banks may consider lending at different interest rates based on the creditworthiness and risk profile of borrowers.
3. Kisan Credit Cards have become very popular and can be integrated with ATM network. This will enable the rural consumers to draw money easily and at the same time, the bank can save expenses in running the conventional bank branches in these markets.
4. Banks can consider franchisee model of bank operations to increase their reach in rural areas.
5. The banks are already extending loans to SHG members for starting income-generating activities such as candle making, pottery, tea stall, vegetable garden, etc. This activity could be extended to important rural markets by all the banks.
6. Many consumer goods and agri-input companies are developing channels of distribution to service the rural markets. The banks can provide finance to channel members.

7. The banks can integrate the products and services with stakeholders like agri-input suppliers, food processing units, NGOs, traders in agricultural produce, cottage industries, etc. This will reduce the risk involved in granting loan in rural areas.
8. The rural bank manager should have genuine concern for the welfare of people and commitment for serving them. He should attract new customers while retaining existing members. He should create awareness among villagers about products and services and mobilise deposits apart from giving loans. The management should provide incentives to bank officials who volunteer to work in rural areas.

NATIONAL BANK FOR AGRICULTURE AND RURAL DEVELOPMENT (NABARD)

The Government set up the National Bank for Agriculture and Rural Development in 1982. The core product of NABARD is credit loan, but NABARD does not finance directly, instead it deals with refinancing. It acts as a link between the bank and the farmers who require finance.

NABARD provides refinance for various types of production and procurement activities:

1. Seasonal agricultural operations which include preparation of land, sowing, weeding, application of fertilisers, pesticides and labour charges for raising the crop.
2. Provides refinance facility to weavers society, rural artisans, village industries and to persons engaged in trade and business.
3. Extends short-term refinance to enable farmers to hold on to the produce and obtain remunerative prices for their produce.
4. Provides refinance for procurement, stocking, distribution of fertilisers to co-operatives.
5. Provide medium- and long-term credit to farmers for purchase and development of land and purchase of high-value agricultural machinery.

NABARD stipulates contribution by the beneficiary in order to ensure his stake in the investment. Such margin money varies from 5 per cent to 25 per cent depending upon the type of investment and the category of borrowers. NABARD operates throughout the country with Head office in Mumbai, and 28 regional offices and 320 district development offices.

1. Self-help Group (SHG)

Villagers do not need money in lakh, they need a small amount and for this Self-help Group (SHG) came into existence. People from the same background and involved in similar economic activities are encouraged to make a natural cohesive group of 15-20 people. This group formation helps them to save some money and if somebody is not, he is disciplined. When the group is formed and saving habit is developed, then the banks step in to support the group. The bank normally extends 1-4 times of SHG savings as loans. The loan is issued in the name of the group. The group is responsible for repayment of the loan amount. The SHG grants loan to members for various purposes, i.e., illness in the family, marriage, candle making, starting a pan shop/tea stall, etc., and charges interest as decided by the group. This is usually between 2 to 3 rupees per month per hundred rupees of loan.

The SHG has to pass resolution in the group meeting signed by all members indicating their decision to open saving bank account with the bank. The Reserve Bank of India has issued instructions to all commercial banks and regional rural banks permitting them to open saving bank account of registered or unregistered SHGs. The SHG authorises at least three members and any two of them to jointly operate the account. The resolution along with the application is to be submitted to the bank for opening an account. The bank issues a passbook in the name of the SHG and not the name of members. NABARD has taken a big stride with SHG. All commercial banks and as well as a large number of NGOs are also involved in this effort. The total credit disbursed through this programme is ₹ 3,000 crore with NABARD contributing about ₹ 1,500 crore. The 98 per cent recovery rate speaks for its success. The group comprises of nearly 85-90 per cent of women. SHG programme is the largest micro credit programme in the world, conceived and implemented by NABARD.

"A Self-help Group Engaged in Making Scented Sticks"

2. Kisan Credit Card (KCC)

Introduction of Kisan Credit Cards (KCC) scheme through banks was another innovation conceived by NABARD in the recent past. Under this scheme, farmers are issued credit cards by banks for meeting the expenditure of the farming operations in the most flexible way. Farmers have been given the freedom to operate the credit limits at will, including payments of bills for farm inputs like seeds, fertilisers, etc. About 30 million KCCs have been issued by all banks put together with a total credit limit of over ₹ 80,000 crore.

3. Agri-export Zones

NABARD has identified financing of farmers in 45 Agri-export Zones for cultivation/ production of identified crops/commodities as a priority item.

4. NABARD Consultancy Services

With a view to meet the growing demand for technical and financial consultancy services for agriculture and rural development projects, a separate unit — NABARD Consultancy Services (NABCONS) has been constituted. It provides consultancy services in agriculture and agro-processing projects, infrastructure, microfinance, watershed development, non-farming enterprises, evaluation, training, identification of potential and policy and related areas through a pool of qualified, well-trained manpower in various disciplines. Although its services will be provided on payment of consultancy charges, it has more than just commercial interest in extending its competence to all those who have similar vision and objectives. To place Indian agriculture on the global map, it intends to support the R&D efforts.

5. Agriculture Insurance

Agriculture Insurance Company (AIC) of India Limited was established in 2002 with authorised and paid-up capital of ₹ 1,500 crore and ₹ 200 crore respectively. NABARD and General Insurance Company and four other Insurance Companies have contributed to equity. The company has obtained Certificate of Registration from Insurance Regulatory and Development Authority (IRDA). One of the objectives of the AIC, is to act as an implementing agency for the Governments National Agricultural Insurance Scheme (NAIS). NAIS is in operation since 2000 and is being implemented in 23 states and about 6 million farmers have been covered under the scheme.

Crops Covered: The scheme covers all cereals, pulses, millets, oilseeds, annual horticultural crops subject to past 10 years' yield data available with State Government.

Unit of Insurance: The size of unit area varies from state-to-state and from crop-to-crop. Presently, the defined area is Block/Taluka/Gram Panchayat or Village.

Limits of Sum Insured

(a) **Loanee Farmers:** The amount of crop loan availed for the notified crop is the minimum amount of sum insured which has to insured on compulsory basis. Further, the farmer may opt for additional coverage up to 150 per cent value of average yield by paying premium at actuarial rate as communicated by AIC and notified by the State Governments.

(b) **Non-loanee Farmers:** Coverage at normal flat rates of premium is available up to the value of threshold yield, i.e., normal coverage. Additional coverage up to 150 per cent of the value of average yield can be availed by paying actuarial rate. The value of sum insured is arrived at by multiplying the threshold yield/average yield with the last available Minimum Support Price (MSP) announced by Government or the market price provided by the State Government, in case MSP is not announced.

Premium: For Kharif crops, the premium rate is 3.5 per cent of sum insured for bajra and oilseeds and 2.5 per cent for all other food crops including pulses. For rabi crops, premium rate is 1.5 per cent for wheat and 2 per cent for all other food crops and oilseeds. The premium for small and marginal farmers is subsidised to the extent of 10 per cent which is shared by the State Government and Government of India in equal proportion.

Procedure for Insurance Coverage: All crop loans disbursed including those through Kisan credit cards or otherwise, for insured crops are automatically covered by banks. Non-loanee farmers willing to avail insurance can contact the nearest bank before the stipulated cut-off dates and submit the proposal forms along with proof of land/crop cultivated.

Settlement of Claims: Claims in Notified Area becomes automatically payable if there is shortfall in yield, i.e., the current seasons yield is less than the guaranteed yield. The shortfall is converted into claims by multiplying the percentage shortfall with sum insured. The yield data considered for the assessment of claims is the production series date which is obtained through the General Crop Estimation Survey used for the purpose of production estimate of the state. Separate yield data for crop insurance is not allowed. The threshold yield or guaranteed yield from a crop in an insurance unit is the moving average of the preceding 3/5 years multiplied by the indemnity level (90/80 per cent or 60 per cent depending upon the variability in the yield of the crop. The claims are automated and credited to the farmers account in the banks and farmers or banks need not lodge a claim with AIC.

COMMODITY MARKET

Agricultural commodity prices are highly volatile due to several reasons:

(a) Agricultural commodities are perishable and they cannot be stored indefinitely.

(b) The farmers do not have proper storage facilities to protect the produce from insects and dampness and are forced to sell the produce immediately after harvest.

(c) They do not have access to latest information on current prices of commodities.

(d) The farmers are compelled to sell the produce even at low prices to meet their commitment, i.e., to meet day-to-day household expenses and creditors. The lower price is beneficial to consumers and at the same time, it has adverse impact on the large number of farmers living in the rural areas of the country.

In order to help the farmers to get a remunerative price for the produce, the Government has come out with Minimum Support Price for commodities such as paddy, wheat, and sugarcane, etc. The Government procures foodgrains and distributes through Public Distribution System. Also the Government maintains buffer stocks and regulates import and export of commodities to protect the local producers as well as consumers.

Many farmers sell their produce in the village market or in the nearby mandi to traders against cash payment. This is known as the Spot Market. In practice, the traders make payment over a period of time. The spot prices are subject to wide price fluctuations. In the case of crops like mango, forward sales takes place between the contractor and the farmer based on private negotiations. Under this system, the producer sells his anticipated future produce in advance to the trader directly at a price fixed at the time of striking the deal either in the village or at the business place of the trader. This is only an oral contract and is not enforceable in any court of law. The trader usually enters into a contract with a speculative motive and when the price declines subsequently he may force the seller to reduce the price by refusing to lift the produce. The price is usually coated in lump sum for the entire crop and the seller may receive 50 per cent of the value of the sale transaction in advance. Usually, the sale goes against the agriculturalist as the price is fixed and determined by the buyer on the basis of the urgency to sell and not on the basis of the prevailing market rates. There is a need to find ways to reduce the losses arising out of uncertainty in price fluctuations and to protect the normal profit from farming operations.

Commodity Derivatives

Commodities are commercial articles which are deemed as assets similar to stocks. For example gold, steel, rice, wheat, cotton, coffee, pepper, etc. They are physical products as compared to bonds or stocks which are pieces of documents. Commodity derivatives are derived products and the asset involved is a commodity. The most commonly traded derivative instruments are Forwards and Futures.

(a) Forward Contract is an agreement to buy or sell an asset at a certain future time for a designated price. The contract may be between two financial institutions or a financial institution and a client. It is traded not on an 'Exchange' but as an 'Over the Counter Product'. The variable is the market price of the asset. The agreed upon price is known as Delivery Price. As time passes, the Forward Price is liable to change, but the Delivery Price remains the same.

(b) Futures are trade contracts to buy or sell financial instruments or physical commodities for future delivery at an agreed price. Trading takes place in Commodity Exchange. At present, trading is permitted only in Futures. The contract has certain specifications such description of the commodity, price per quintal, contract quantity of the asset, delivery month, delivery location, etc. The Commodity Futures traded are basically agricultural commodities, basic metals and petroleum products.

Commodity Exchanges perform two important functions in respect of commodities, i.e., Price Discovery and Price Risk Management. Price discovery through future trading provides useful information to producers about the likely future prices of commodities. Consumers get an idea about future costs. Exporters are able to quote a realistic price to overseas buyers. The trading is conducted under a three-tier regulatory framework, i.e., at the Apex level is the Department of Consumer Affairs in the Ministry of Consumer Affairs, Food and Public Distribution. Forward Market Commission is the market regulator, the second tier in the regulatory set-up. The exchanges are responsible for carrying out the trade as stipulated under their own rules, regulations and by-laws which are framed as per Forward Market Commission.

COMMODITY EXCHANGES IN INDIA

Future trading was introduced in India on the Bombay Cotton Exchange in 1921. The Government has given recognition to about 25 associations to run Commodity Exchanges. A few examples are given below:

(a) The Indian Pepper and Spice Trade Association established in 1957 with headquarters in Cochin is probably the only exchange engaged in trading Pepper futures. Malabar Garbled Black Pepper and Black Pepper are the commodities traded in the exchange.

(b) Cotton Futures Exchange: Indian Cotton Contract in Mumbai is the exchange for trading in Cotton. Trading is conducted in the trading hall of Cotton Green, Sewri, Mumbai by 'open outcry' system.

(c) Coffee Futures Exchange India Limited has been functioning since 1997 in Bengaluru.

Apart from Regional Exchanges, there are three nationwide exchanges in India as per details given below:

(a) National Commodities and Derivatives Exchange of India (NCDEX) is promoted by the ICICI Bank, Life Insurance Corporation of India, National Bank for Agriculture and Rural Development and National Stock Exchange of India Limited (NSE), Punjab National Bank, CRISIL, Indian Farmers' Fertiliser Co-operative Limited and Canara Bank and it commenced its operations in 2003. NCDEX trades in about 45 commodities through its members spread over 110 locations in the country.

(b) National Multi-commodity Exchange (NMCE) is promoted by Central Warehousing Corporation, National Agricultural Co-operative Marketing Federation, Gujarat State Agricultural Marketing Board, Gujarat Agro-Industries Corporation, National Institute of Marketing and Neptune Overseas Limited in 2002 and trades in 24 commodities.

(c) Multi-commodity Exchange is promoted by State Bank of India and Associates, Financial Technologies, Fidelity International, National Stock Exchange, National Bank for Agriculture and Rural Development, HDFC Bank, SBI Life Insurance, Union Bank of India, Canara Bank, Bank of India, Bank of Baroda and Corporation Bank in the year 2003.

CONCLUSION

Majority of the farmers have small holdings and they require credit to meet cultivation and consumption expenses. Similarly, the traders and service class in rural areas also require credit to meet business and household requirements. The institutional agencies have to continue to play a major role towards development of agriculture and rural areas.

QUESTIONS

1. Discuss various kinds of credit requirements in agriculture. What are the major agencies currently involved in granting credit to agricultural community?
2. Discuss the main objectives and functions of financial institutions in rural areas.
3. Describe the role of NABARD in agriculture and rural development.

✿ ✿ ✿

20 AGRICULTURAL PRICING

INTRODUCTION

In our country, over 70 per cent of the population lives in villages and agriculture and agricultural related activities continue to be the major source of income in rural areas. Industries also depend upon agriculture for raw materials. For example cotton, sugarcane, etc. Vagaries of monsoon, unorganised markets and superfluous middlemen are the major reasons for wide fluctuations in the prices of the agriculture commodities. The farmers would be motivated to increase the yields only if they receive remunerative prices for their produce. An efficient agricultural marketing system should benefit all the sections of the society. However, the expectations vary from group-to-group as can be seen below:

Producers: The farmers (producers) want the maximum possible price for their produce. They also want the inputs such as fertilisers, seeds and pesticides at the lowest possible price.

Consumers: The consumers want the produce to be made available at the lowest possible price. This objective is in conflict with the objective of the producers.

Middlemen: The middlemen are interested in buying the produce at low prices and selling them to the consumers at high prices.

Government: The Government wants to protect the interest of all the groups by giving remunerative prices to the farmers, supplying commodities at reasonable prices to the consumers and providing enough margins to middlemen so that they remain in the trade. The Government, thus, wants to have a marketing system that will benefit all sections of the society. Therefore, agricultural pricing is very important for growth and development of agriculture.

FACTORS INFLUENCING AGRICULTURAL PRICES

1. **Uncertainty of Supply:** The supply of agricultural produce depends upon agro-climatic conditions and therefore they are inelastic to price fluctuations.
2. **Financial Problems:** The farmers are compelled to sell their produce even at a lower price to meet their commitments (household expenses and creditors).

3. **Perishable Commodities:** The produce has to be sold immediately.

4. **Superfluous Middlemen:** There is huge difference between what the consumer pays and what the farmer receives for his produce as middlemen take away the profits. ***Example:*** In the case of foodgrains, growers receive only 55 per cent, vegetables 40 per cent and fruits only 35 per cent of the price actually paid by the consumers.

5. **Variation in Quantity and Quality:** The production depends upon vagaries of nature, i.e., monsoon and incidence of pests and diseases and therefore there are wide variations in quantity and quality of agricultural produce.

6. **Inadequate Storage Facilities:** In the absence of proper storage facilities to protect the produce from insects and dampness, the farmers are forced to sell their produce even at low prices.

7. **Improper Weights and Measures:** Even today, primitive weighing measures are used in the markets to the disadvantage of the farmer.

8. **Lack of Adequate Market Information:** The villagers do not have access to the latest information on current prices and therefore they sell the produce at low prices.

IMPORTANT FEATURES OF THE POLICY

1. To reduce the margin between producers and consumers.
2. To ensure reasonable relationship between prices of foodgrains and non-foodgrains and between agricultural commodities and manufactured articles.
3. To maintain relationship between prices of competing crops so as to fulfil the production targets in respect of different commodities commensurate with the rise in demand.
4. Integration of prices between various regions.
5. To ensure proper relations between input costs and output prices.
6. To protect the interest of consumers by supplying commodities at reasonable prices.

Considering the above objectives, the Government established Agricultural Price Commission in 1964. The National Commission on Agriculture was asked to study the problem of prices and to consider:

(a) The ingredients of agricultural price policy,

(b) What should be the policy for supply of key inputs and credit? and

(c) What are the factors to be considered in fixing the prices of individual commodities?

The commission set up a study group and the group submitted its report in 1975 and made the following recommendations.

APPROACH TO AGRICULTURAL POLICY

1. Regarding assurance of remunerative price to the farmers, the policy should be formulated keeping in view of its impact on the general situation and economy as a whole.
2. Reliance should not be placed on price as the principal mechanism for augmenting production. Such a policy will only add to price rise without yielding higher production. The increase in output and farmers income will have to be brought about mainly through technological improvement and availability of crucial inputs rather than manipulation of prices.
3. The interests of the producers should be protected through price support operation, when there is sharp fall in prices. The interests of the consumers, particularly the vulnerable sections of the population should be protected, through procurement and distribution of a part of marketable surplus at below the market price where there is a sharp rise in the prices of basic necessities such as paddy and wheat.
4. Public distribution of essential commodities will have to be permanent or semi-permanent feature of economic management in the country in the context of shortages.
5. Dual pricing and dual availability system is in vogue in our country in respect of cereals and sugar should be continued until an overall balance between supply and demand is achieved on a durable basis in respect of these commodities.
6. The price fixation should take into account the fluctuations in the prices of inputs.
7. As the prices of agricultural commodities are expected to take into account changes in input prices, widespread use of input subsidy as incentive to increase production should by and large be avoided except in the case of small and marginal farmers.

MINIMUM SUPPORT PRICES

The Commission also recommended minimum support prices and important features are:

1. The minimum support price should be fair to the farmers and should cover his cost of production and leave him a reasonable margin of profit. In the calculation of costs, the family labour should continue to be evaluated.
2. No specific allowance need to be made in the cost of managerial account, when it is not actually incurred by keeping hired managers.
3. Existing practice of fixing uniform all-India minimum support price should continue.

Agricultural price can be regulated through various measures and suggest the following regulatory measures:

1. Fixation of minimum and maximum prices or both. From producers' point of view, the minimum price should cover the cost of production and provide a fair margin of profits. From the consumers' point of view, the maximum price should not be too severe and should give rise to a demand for the whole quantity produced.
2. Guarantee to buy the farm produce at declared prices if the prices fall below the minimum fixed by the state.
3. Regulation of exports and imports to maintain the prices.

CONCLUSION

Agricultural price regulates market conditions such as supply and demand and quality of the products. It also improves standardisation and grading of agricultural products, transportation of these products from the fields to the markets, storage of these products and finally selling these products through various outlets to the consumers. Agricultural price policy exhibits a co-ordinated effort of all factors such as grading, standardisation, purchasing and distribution measures.

QUESTIONS

1. Discuss briefly the features of pricing policy.
2. "An efficient agricultural pricing system should benefit the producers, intermediaries and consumers." Discuss.

CASE STUDY

Agricultural Subsidies

Agriculture and related activities continue to be the major source of income in rural areas. The farmers would be motivated to increase the yields only if they receive remunerative prices for their produce. An efficient agriculture marketing system should benefit all the sections of the society, i.e., producers (farmers) and consumers. The Government wants to protect the interest of the farmers by giving remunerative prices to the farmers and supply commodity at reasonable prices to the consumers.

Considering the importance of pricing, the Government established agricultural prices commission and the National Commission on Agriculture recommended minimum support price (MSP) for important agricultural commodities. The minimum support price/procurement prices for wheat and paddy have gone up during the last 10 years as shown below:

Year	MSP – Price/Quintal	
	Wheat	Paddy
1992-93	₹ 330	₹ 270
2003-04	₹ 630	₹ 550-580
2012-2013	₹ 1,285	₹ 1,250-1,280

The increase in subsidies on foodgrains has added to the fiscal deficit of the Government. The food subsidy bill has been rising at an alarming pace. It increased from about ₹ 3,000 crore in 1991-1992 to about ₹ 25,800 crore in 2004-2005 and the amount for 2011-2012 was ₹ 72,000 crore and the fertiliser subsidy has gone up from ₹ 505 crore in 1980-1981 to about ₹ 16,000 crore in 2004-2005 and ₹ 74,000 crore in 2011-2012. Further, in many states, irrigation water and electricity are made available at subsidised rates. Many agricultural scientists and economists feel that the subsidies and exploitation of groundwater will have a long-term effect on sustainable agriculture.

QUESTIONS

1. Do you think that agricultural subsidies have contributed to the growth and development of agriculture in our country.
2. Should agricultural subsidies continue?

CASE STUDY

Marketing of Agricultural Produce

Arvind Patil, a vegetable farmer in Nashik district in Maharashtra was very upset. He had cultivated tomato during the Kharif season of 2008 along with a large number of other farmers in the village. He sold the first consignment of tomato to the local trader. The price he received was just sufficient to meet his cost of cultivation. The arrivals in local mandi were also very high during the season. His friend Jayram Patil informed him that he had visited Mumbai market and found the prices of tomato to be very high. Both of them felt that there is something wrong in the marketing of the produce.

A few days later, Arvind Patil and Jayram Patil met a few other tomato growers in the market. One of the farmers felt that "The middlemen are responsible for the problem. They buy at low prices and sell at high prices and earn a good profit. We have to eliminate the middlemen in the market and sell directly to consumers. By this method, we can get a high price for tomato."

Arvind Patil remarked, "It is a good suggestion, but can we enter into distribution of tomato". Jayram Patil said, "I have no expertise or experience in marketing of tomato".

QUESTIONS

1. What are your recommendations to Arvind Patil and Jayram Patil and other farmers regarding direct marketing of tomato to consumers?
2. Do you think that we can eliminate middlemen? Discuss.

✿ ✿ ✿

21 GLOBALISATION AND AGRICULTURE

INTRODUCTION

Globalisation involves integrating the economy of a country with the global/world economy. It means that our economy is open to foreign direct investment by providing facilities to foreign companies to invest in different fields of the industry. Multinationals can enter a number of crucial sectors and have freedom to import foreign capital. Indian companies can enter into foreign collaboration in India and also set up joint ventures abroad. Import duties are considerably reduced. New Economic Policy since 1991 has introduced globalisation in India.

GLOBALISATION

International Monetary Fund (IMF) defines Globalisation as "the growing economic inter-dependence of countries worldwide through increasing volume and variety of cross-border transactions in goods and services and international capital flows and also through the more rapid and widespread diffusion of technology". The IMF definition has highlighted the important aspects of globalisation in terms of international economic inter-dependence and borderless movement of products and factors.

Four Important Components of Globalisation

(a) An environment that facilitates free flow of capital.

(b) Free flow of knowledge (technology).

(c) Free movement of labour across national boundaries.

(d) Free flow of goods and services without trade barriers.

Examples:

Automobile majors like General Motors, Hyundai, Honda are active in Indian market and we have a choice of several models of cars. Mobile phones have become common in villages. McDonalds and Pizza Hut fastfood restaurants are seen in small towns also. We are exporting spices, pulses, fruits, vegetables, processed foods, etc., to foreign countries. Internet has created a revolution in communication across countries. IT companies like Infosys, Wipro, Tata, Mahindra have established offices and research centres in foreign countries and have provided employment opportunities for Indians in foreign countries as well as in domestic market. Software and allied services export rose to US dollars 40.4 billion in 2007-08 from US dollars 9.56 billion in 2002-03.

Features of Globalisation

1. Expansion of business globally.
2. Setting up production and distribution facilities in various parts of world.
3. Development of products and services to meet global market demand.
4. Globalisation of factors of production.
5. Organisational structure, culture, strategy, management practices based on global outlook.

Benefits of Globalisation

1. **Economic Efficiency:** Countries will focus on production of those goods and services in which it has competitive advantage over others. Countries have to innovate and ensure superiority on cost and quality of products and services.
2. **Flow of Capital:** Globalisation and liberalisation lead to non-restricted flow of capital across countries. Foreign Direct Investment (FDI) increases the financial capacity of the countries without the problem of debts or interest payments. FDI reduces borrowings and dependence on foreign aid.
3. **Human Resources:** The developed countries enjoy the benefit of having enriched human resources at a lowest cost. The human capital normally flows from developing countries to developed countries. The developing countries are benefited from the remittance of expatriates. Employment gets a boost when free trade is encouraged. The software boom in India has certainly increased the income level of employees and trade associated with the industry.

Problems of Globalisation

1. Income Inequality: The gap between the rich and the poor continues to increase. The number of people earning less than two dollars per day has gone to about, ₹ 28 crore in our country.

2. Influence of Multinationals: These corporations with Patents and Intellectual Property Rights (IPR) may dominate the Seeds, Pharmaceutical and Biotechnology areas in the country.

3. Employment Opportunities: There will be job opportunities for skilled and technically qualified people but at the same time manual and non-skilled labour would face employment problems. In order to achieve production efficiency, companies may shift their manufacturing centres to areas where wages are low.

4. Cultural Issues: Younger generation is influenced by music channels and print media and national culture is slowly being replaced by new alien culture.

GLOBALISATION AND INDIAN AGRICULTURE

India's participation in global trade is negligible and is less than one per cent. Agriculture provides about 16 per cent of India's GDP and agricultural export constitutes about 25 per cent of total export revenues.

World Trade Organisation (WTO)

With a view to liberalise trade flows, WTO has asked for removing trade barriers by all members. India had expected that with dismantling of domestic support in developed countries and reduction of export subsidies by these countries, market for Indian agricultural products would increase. However, the developed countries continue to offer high subsidies and follow other trade practices to the disadvantage of countries like India. Therefore, the share of agricultural exports dropped from 19 per cent (1995-96) to about 10 per cent in 2005-06. However, we have provided increased market access to other countries by removing quantitative restrictions.

Foreign Competition

We need to protect Indian agriculture and Indian farmers from foreign competition.

1. Subsidies by Developed Countries: Developed countries provide high level of subsidy and support to their agriculture. India along with other countries should put pressure for reduction in subsidy during various WTO negotiations.

2. Volatility in Market Prices: Meeting WTO obligations may lead to fluctuations in domestic prices and farm income. For example, Chinese garlic, apple, etc., are already competing with domestic produce. There are chances of dumping of agricultural commodities in Indian market. Government has to take measures to protect the interest of farmers.

3. Self-sufficiency in Food Production: A country which globalises in agricultural sector cannot achieve self-sufficiency in production because globalisation will require specialisation on those agricultural commodities in which it has a comparative advantage. With a large population and low purchasing power, availability of foodgrains at lower prices is a basic requirement of Indian economy and should not be sacrificed by the Government.

4. Trade Related Intellectual Property Rights (TRIPs): Agreement under WTO stipulates that all member countries must grant Intellectual Protection Rights (IPRS) for plant varieties. This stipulation favours the developed countries and multinationals (MNCs). This will enable MNCs to control the market for seeds and plant varieties in the developing countries and capture the 'seed market' of these countries.

5. Protection and Enforcement of Intellectual Property Rights: The value of technology intensive products like computer software, medicines and plant varieties lies in the amount of invention, innovation, research, design and testing involved. The creators of such innovative products can be given the right to prevent others from using their inventions, designs or other creations and to use the right to negotiate payment in turn from others using them. These are Intellectual Property Rights (IPRs). They take a number of forms like Patents Copy Right, Logos, Brands, etc.

Farmers and consumers in developing countries are highly apprehensive of the misuse of patent laws by the developed countries. Patents in developed countries relate to Turmeric, Neem, Darjeeling Tea, Basmati Rice have generated lot of controversies in our country.

Example: In 1995, two expatriate Indians were granted US Patent for turmeric used to heal wounds. The Indian Council for Scientific and Industrial Research filed a case with US Patent office challenging the Patent on the ground of prior art, i.e., existing knowledge. Turmeric is being used for healing wounds for thousands of years and therefore, its use as a medicine is not a new invention. The US Patent cancelled the Patent. Basmati rice was patented as Texmatic. The Government of India is aware of these problems and has already passed the "Protection of Plant Varieties and Farmers Rights" legislation in 2001.

Agricultural Exports

The striking features of India's export has been distinct changes in its composition. Exports used to be classified into two categories — traditional and non-traditional products.

Traditional products include tea, jute, cotton, cashew, spices, coffee, etc. Non-traditional products consist of engineering goods, leather goods, marine products, software, and allied service, etc.

Exports of some of the important agricultural products are given in Table 21.1.

Table 21.1: Export

(Value in crore)

Product	2006-07	2011-2012
1. Rice – Basmati	7,036	16,860
2. Pulses	764	1,042
3. Groundnut	800	3,775
4. Tea	1,956	2,842
5. Coffee	1,969	1,200
6. Spices	3,122	9,783
7. Tobacco	871	4,373
8. Floriculture	381	365
9. Fruits and vegetables	2,890	4,801

Agriculture and primary products constitute about 25 per cent of our exports (2006-07). In the case of agricultural products, demand of the domestic market is very high and has to be met and only surplus can be exported.

While we have made progress in the export of agricultural products, it should be remembered that some of these products are produced by other developing countries and offer stiff competition.

Example: Competition from Sri Lanka, East Africa, and even Vietnam for Tea.

First Generation Agro Entrepreneurs

A new crop of first generation entrepreneurs has combined their hands on approach with their expertise in technology and marketing to emerge as dollar earning global leaders in agri-business in Punjab and a few examples are given below:

Agro-dutch Industries Limited Promoted by Malvinder Singh Bhinder is the world's largest mushroom producing firm. The fully integrated plant spread over 150 acres produces about 60,000 tonne of processed mushrooms in a year. The company located in Chandigarh supplies to international food chains like Unilever, Heinz and US Food Service and accounts for 85 per cent of India's exports clocking a ₹ 200 crore turnover.

Jagjit Singh Kapoor of Kashmir Apiaries (Annual sales: ₹ 100 crore) based at Doraha near Ludhiana is the country's biggest honey producer-exporter. It collects 9,000 tonnes of honey from about 2,000 farmers and processes it as the state-of-the-art plant spread over 20 acres. The company markets its honey under brand name "Little Bee" in foreign countries.

Jitendra Singh of Kodos Chemie is the largest producer and exporter of caffeine alkaloid to global Cola and energy drink majors.

R.T. Aromatics Limited, Promoted by Maninder Pal Singh and Manjit Singh Toor, has set up the first aromatic agri-business by cultivating and processing roses for export to perfume manufacturers. The company has about 120 acres of rose plantation and has inhouse rose oil extraction and processing plant. R.T. Aromatics is now the country's largest rose extract manufacturer.

Jang Bhadur Singh Sangha and Family (Ludhiyana) are the largest producers of potato and maize in the country with more than 5,000 acres land spread over Punjab. The Sanghas grow 45,000 tonnes seed potato and 75,000 tonnes maize in an year. They have three types of association with farmers, i.e., cultivation in leased land, technical advice to farmers and procuring the produce and contract farming.

Source: *Business World*, May 28, 2008.

RECOMMENDATIONS

1. It is estimated that about 65 per cent of the rural population is involved in agriculture. Even though modern technology keeps reducing the employment potential in agriculture as well, this workforce cannot be redeployed quickly into other sectors since they lack the knowledge and skills to work in service and manufacturing sector. One obvious solution is to increase our production and export agriculture products. This will be very difficult since agriculture in the developed countries is subsidised to a great extent and the international prices of agriculture products have been falling over the last two decades. Farmers are a powerful vote bank all the world over and they force the Governments to keep the subsidies as well as high import tariffs.

2. There is tremendous potential in the area of Agro Industries and Food Processing industries. The value addition to agriculture will open up the international and domestic markets in a very big way, and as these are labour-ntensive, they will lead to better employment potential.

3. Almost all major horticultural crops such as fruits, vegetables, medicinal specialities, spices, plantation crops, mushrooms, etc., are produced in our country. India produces 40 million tonnes of fruits and nearly 70 million tonnes of vegetable, but the post-harvest losses are as high as 30 per cent of fresh fruits and vegetables due to lack of adequate post-harvest handling and storage facilities. Loss of the produce due to bad handling and storage, pest infestation, damages, loss-in-transit and transport are very high. Lack of attention to all these factors hinders the growth of this industry. The Government should get fully involved with the help of a highly knowledgeable technical group and get these facilities established in a professional manner. The employment potential and export prospects are so high that it has to be taken up on priority bases.

- Provide cold storage facilities wherever needed.
- Give all possible facilities to convert as much of the cultivable wasteland (it is estimated that we have 250 million hectares of cultivable wasteland) to hi-tech horticultural farms with all the latest facilities.
- Encourage export oriented units, and foreign collaborations wherever needed with the necessary infrastructural support.
- This country has excellent agricultural universities and research set-ups, and they should be utilised to give the necessary inputs for supply chain management and packaging and transport, as also product development.
- Encourage organic farming as it has a growing and profitable niche in the world market.
- The markets for fruits and vegetables are huge, both nationally and internationally and the employment potential, especially for the rural unemployed is very great indeed.

4. In 'Service Sector', there is a good scope for improvement. BPO centres can be established in small towns as real estate and labour costs are low compared to urban centres. This will provide employment to educated rural youth.

5. There is big potential in the tourism sector where both the State and Central Government should take initiatives with the help of the private sector. Rural tourism offers tremendous opportunities in our country. We can provide opportunities for tourists to visit villages and stay in well developed farm houses. The tourists can participate in farming operations like land preparation, sowing, weeding, irrigation, etc., and live close to the nature, away from the polluted atmosphere in cities.

6. The need of the hour is to take steps — Government and private sector working together — on a national basis to get India moving forward and show the world that it can meet these challenges that will make India a developed country by the year 2020.

CONCLUSION

Globalisation presents challenges and opportunities for the country. Our country is blessed with agro-climatic conditions favourable for cultivation of a variety of crops. The value addition to agriculture through agro-industries and food processing will open up the domestic and international markets in a big way and also provide employment opportunities. Government and private sector should work together on a national basis to move forward and to establish our position in the global market.

QUESTIONS

1. Define globalisation. What are its features?
2. Discuss the benefits and problems of globalisation.
3. How can our country face the challenges of globalisation?
4. Discuss the role of WTO and its impact on Indian agriculture.

✿ ✿ ✿

22 MARKETING OF AGRICULTURAL INPUTS

INTRODUCTION

In olden days, agriculture was viewed as a traditional occupation and the production from the farm mainly catered to the requirements of the family. During British period, not much attention was paid for the growth of the agricultural sector and there was poor growth in agricultural production. The Bengal Famine (1942-1943) claimed the life of about 20 lakh of people, due to hunger. The gap between food production and requirement widened and the Government had to import foodgrains. With the increase in population, there was an urgent need to increase food production and the Government adopted a pragmatic policy towards agriculture. Use of modern agricultural inputs such as high yielding varieties of seeds, chemical fertilisers and plant protection chemicals helped our country to attain self-sufficiency in food production in 1971. Our country is the second largest producer of agricultural produce in the world and we are exporting agricultural commodities to several countries. Of late our agricultural productivity is stagnating and what we require is a Second Green Revolution. The key requirements for successful agriculture are high yielding seeds, balanced use of fertilisers and pesticides, modern cultivation practices, institutional sources of finance and marketing facilities.

FEATURES OF AGRICULTURAL INPUTS

1. Derived Demand: The agricultural inputs are purchased mainly for production of crops. The cultivators do not buy these inputs like consumer goods but they use the same as per the demand. One input decides the need for the other input.

Example: Use of hybrid vegetable seeds in farming requires intensive use of pesticides since they are highly susceptible to a number of pests and diseases compared to traditional varieties of vegetables.

2. Similarities with Consumer and Industrial Goods: We find that agricultural inputs fall between consumer goods and industrial goods due to the following reasons:

(a) Promotion and distribution of agricultural inputs are similar to that of consumer goods.

(b) They are bulky and high cost items. They have technical features and personal selling is an important aspect of marketing. The demand for these inputs is derived demand and therefore they are similar to industrial goods.

3. Heterogeneous Customers: The target customers are the farmers. They form a heterogeneous population as they live in heterogeneous agro-climatic zone. The use of agricultural inputs depends upon the size of the farm, type of crops grown, irrigation facilities, output prices, etc. Further, they also differ in terms of income, age, education, tradition, value, beliefs, lifestyles and these factors influence the use of agricultural inputs.

"Farm House of a Landlord"

Example: It is seen that about 75 per cent of landholdings consist of small and marginal farmers and therefore the marketers have to identify large and progressive farmers for selling high value agricultural machinery like tractors.

4. Demand Forecasting: The demand for agricultural inputs is dependent on a number of uncontrollable factors such as rainfall, output prices, Government schemes, incidence of pests and diseases etc., and are subject to wide variations.

Example: The survival and growth of the pesticides industry to a large extend depends upon the incidence of bollworms and other pests on cotton crop. The incidence depends upon agro-climatic conditions and may vary even on a weekly basis during season. Demand forecasting is indeed a challenging job under such dynamic environmental conditions.

5. Technical Selling: The farmers want solutions to their field problems such as insect pests, diseases, weeds, nutritional deficiency, low yields, etc. Therefore, the salesperson has to make farm-to-farm visits, identify the problems, conduct demonstration and offer solutions to their problems. He should have good knowledge of crop husbandry and has to play the role of a Plant Doctor among farmers.

"A Company's Technical Officer Educating the Farmers on Modern Agricultural Inputs"

6. Distribution: As we have seen, the demand for inputs is highly seasonal and the products have to be made available with village/mandi level dealers even at short notice failing which the company will lose the sales in the market.

Example: Delay or advancement in sowing of crops due to changes in weather conditions will affect the movement of fertilisers in the market. The retailers play a major role in agri-input business as they have direct contact with farmers and extend credit facilities. They also focus on products with high margins. For the marketer, they are the most important source of information about performance of different products and competition.

7. Management of Stocks and Receivables: Normally, companies build up stocks based on past sales and future projections. In case of a poor season, the movement of stocks will come down leading to piling up of stocks at dealer, distributor and company level and delayed payments. In the past, many companies had financial problems due to high inventories and receivables in seeds, fertilisers, pesticides and agricultural machinery business.

8. Promotion Media and Methods: The marketers have to make use of rural-specific media and methods such as group meeting of farmers, village-level film shows, field demonstrations, field days, jeep campaign, etc., to reach the target customers.

"A Group Meeting of Farmers"

CLASSIFICATION OF AGRICULTURAL INPUTS

Agricultural inputs can be broadly classified into two categories as shown below:

1. Consumable Inputs: Seeds, fertilisers, manure, pesticides, animal feeds, veterinary products, energy (petrol, diesel, oil), materials such as ropes, baskets, gunnies, etc.

2. Durable Inputs: Farm machinery, irrigation equipment, construction materials (cement, bricks), transportation equipment (tractors, trailers, tempos, carts), etc.

MARKET SEGMENTATION

The market for agricultural inputs is scattered over a wide range of crops covering a large geographical area. Therefore, the marketer has to identify the most potential markets for promoting products and services. Important characteristics which will help us in segmenting the market are given below:

1. Irrigation Facilities: Irrigation plays a major role in agricultural development. Crops grown under irrigated conditions give higher yields and this enables the farmer to increase farm income. Also efficiency of fertilisers, hybrid seeds and pesticides depend on quantity and timing of water supply. In rainfed areas, the yields are low and depends upon the timely arrival and distribution of monsoon rains.

2. Electricity: Electric power is required for pumping water for irrigating the land and use of electrically operated farm equipments.

3. Size of Land Holding: A farmer with a large holding and variety of crops require more agricultural inputs.

4. Types of Crops and Varieties: Long duration crops like sugarcane and irrigated crops consumes more quantities of fertilisers. Use of hybrid seeds is high in the case of crops like cotton, sunflower, jowar, maize, vegetables and flowers and these segments offer lot of opportunities for marketing of seeds.

5. Incidence of Pests and Diseases: Cotton crop is more susceptible to attack of insect pests and therefore insecticides market is high on cotton crop. Fungicide market is high on grapes as the crop is damaged by a number of diseases.

6. Use of Farm Implements Like Tractors, Tillers and Harvesters are indicators of the progressive nature of the cultivators.

7. Based on socio-economic conditions, the farmers could be segmented into the following six groups, i.e.,

(a) Landlords

(b) Affluent farmers

(c) Medium farmers

(d) Small farmers

(e) Marginal farmers

(f) Tenant farmers

"A Grape Farmer Spends About ₹ 30,000 per Acre on Pesticides"

Identifying the right farmer and meeting him at the right time is a challenging job considering widely disbursed farming community living in about six lakh villages. Normally, marketers focus on first two categories of farmers for promoting the use of existing and new agricultural inputs.

"An Affluent Farmer"

8. Adopter Categories: The market for agricultural inputs is heterogeneous and all the farmers do not adopt an innovation at the same time. They adopt it over a period of time. The farmers can be classified into five adopter categories based on when they adopt a new product or idea in farming.

- **Innovators:** They are venturesome and are eager to try new ideas. They have financial resources to absorb losses due to failure of an innovation in the field conditions. Some of the characteristic of innovative farmers are: Willingness to take risks, large farms, well informed about farming practices, read farm magazines and publications, keep in touch with agricultural research stations, universities and input companies and have formal and informal contacts with people outside the village.

- **Early Adopters:** While they may not be interested in testing untried products/ideas, they are quick to use tried products/ideas in the field. They read farm journals and are considered as opinion leaders in the village. Government agencies make use of their services to hasten diffusion process. They have fairly large farms and earn high income from farming.
- **Early Majority:** They have medium to high socio-economic status. They may not be formal leaders in the village, but they actively participate in meetings and field demonstrations. They deliberate about new ideas and take longer time for taking innovation decision. Many farmers approach them for seeking information about new farming practices.
- **Late Majority:** They are relatively skeptical and cautious about innovations and adopt them due to economic necessity or when many people have adopted the idea in the village. Normally, they have less education and read fewer magazines and papers.
- **Laggards** follow traditional practices and they are suspicious about innovations and change agents. They rarely participate in village meetings and Government activities. They are the last one to adopt an innovation.

Normally, companies focus on the first two groups for promoting the use of new agricultural inputs.

Example: The landlords, affluent farmers, rural youth engaged in farming are the innovators and early adopters in the village.

PERSONAL SELLING

Personal selling plays a major role in marketing of agricultural inputs. It involves face-to-face communication and presentation with the farmers, dealers, wholesalers and opinion leaders for the purpose of making sales. Personal selling involves two-way communication. During personal interview, the salesperson understands the needs and wants, highlight product benefits and convinces the customer to buy the product. The salesperson is responsible for achievement of sales target, managing credit, effective use of resources, development of the market and enhancing company's image. In addition, he has to develop himself to take up higher responsibilities in the organisation.

PROMOTION MEDIA AND METHODS

(a) Formal Media: It includes Print, TV, Cinema, Radio, Wall Paintings, Signboards and Hoardings, POP Materials, etc.

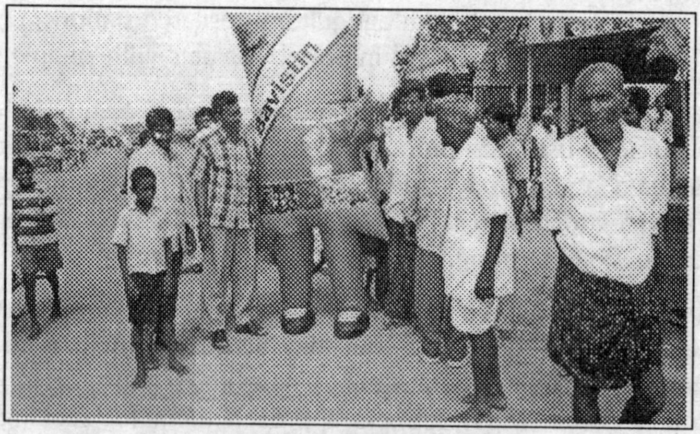

"Brand Promotion"

(b) Rural-specific Media:

- Farm-to-farm visit
- Group meeting
- Audio-visual publicity van
- Field demonstration
- Field day
- Jeep campaign

"An AVP Van"

"A Company Executive Highlights Product Benefits during a Farmers Meeting"

While we have already covered formal media and rural specific methods such as farm-to-farm visit, group meeting and use of audiovisual publicity van in Chapter 10, details about field demonstration, field day and jeep campaign are given below:

1. Field Demonstration is based on the extension principle "Seeing is believing" and is one of the most effective methods to show the superiority of the company's products to the customers. A progressive farmer who is an opinion leader is selected and the demonstration is conducted in his field in the presence of a group of farmers in the village. The farmers observe the results in the field and the local dealer and company representative call on them in their farms and persuades them to buy the particular brand of pesticide, seed or fertiliser. A few points to be observed while conducting field demonstrations are:

1. Potential village and the group of farmers to be identified.
2. The date, time and place of meeting to be informed to the farmers.
3. The salesperson should have good knowledge of the products, needs and wants of the customers and also be fluent in the local language. He should explain in simple language using local idioms and proverbs.

Examples:

(a) Demonstrating the use of tractor/implements for different agricultural operations.

(b) Application of urea fertiliser in paddy fields to show the luxurious growth of the crop.

(c) Spraying a particular brand of insecticide against insect pests and showing the farmer how effectively the insects are controlled.

"A Demonstration Plot in Grapes Garden"

2. Field Days are extension of field demonstrations. One of the main objectives of following modern agricultural practices is to the increase the yield. The company organises demonstrations in a piece of land belonging to a progressive farmer. All the fertilisers, pesticides, nutrients, etc., are applied after making field observations. Just before harvest, all the important farmers are invited to see demonstration plot and see for themselves how the yields are better in the plot compared to other fields. Field demonstrations/field days consume lot of time and efforts and therefore have to be planned well.

"Field Demonstration/Field Day"

3. Jeep Campaign is normally organised for promoting the use of fertilisers, pesticides and seeds. The programme starts in the morning and about 4-6 trained agricultural field assistants travel in a jeep. As soon as the jeep reaches the village, all the field assistants get down and move in different directions in the village. They meet the farmers, talk to them about the products, hand over the leaflets and move to another village. Depending upon the size of the village, crops grown, number of villagers to be contacted and the distance between villages, the group covers about 4 villages per day. By organising jeep campaign, the company is able to pass on the messages about products/services to a large number of farmers during a short period.

"A Jeep Set Ready for the Campaign"

4. Cycle Rickshaw Campaign: During agricultural season, farmers visit mandi towns to purchase agricultural inputs. A mike set is mounted on the Cycle Rickshaw and trained sales assistant talks about the benefit of the company's products and distribute handbills to the farmers in the mandi. By this method, the company is able to pass the message about its products like seeds, fertilisers and pesticides to a large number of people during a short period during the agricultural season.

"Cycle Rickshaw Campaign"

A brief account of the important agricultural consumable inputs, i.e., seeds, fertilisers, pesticides and capital input, i.e., tractors is given below:

SEEDS

The thrust on agriculture during the Five Year Plans and Green Revolution in late 1960s and early 1970s which mainly focused on high yielding varieties of paddy and wheat led to significant increase in yields. Further, the Government has taken the following initiatives for development of seed sector.

1. Seed Act of 1966 for regulating the quality of seeds sold, by providing for compulsory labelling and voluntary certification.

2. Amendment of the industrial licensing policy in 1987 which removed restrictions on investment by FERA/MRTP companies such as foreign companies, large Indian companies in Indian seed business.
3. The new seed policy of 1988 which allowed import of vegetable and flower seeds under open general licence.
4. Considering the need for increasing food production, Indian Council of Agricultural Research launched a project on hybrid rice in 1989 and 16 hybrids have been released for commercial cultivation.
5. Trade Related Intellectual Property Rights (TRIPs) under which it is expected that the developer of new seed varieties will have right on the product and process developed and this could lead to more investment in research and development activities in the seed sector.
6. After extensive trials, hybrid cotton containing Bacillus thuriengenesis (Bt) was released for commercial cultivation by the Government in the year 2000.
7. The Genetic Engineering Approval Committee in the Ministry of Environment has given approval for Bt brinjal which will considerably reduce the application of pesticides for controlling the pest and help the farmers in increasing the yield and quality of brinjal crop. However, Government approval is pending.

Brinjal Economy

Almost 40 per cent of the brinjal product in India is destroyed by the fruit and shoot borer. Attacks by *leucinodes orbonalis* (the biological name for the FSB borer) is so widespread that production has barely increased by 9 per cent in the last 10 years despite a 15 per cent larger cultivation area. Yet, India remains the world's second-largest producer of brinjal, accounting for nearly 26 per cent of the global production. China tops with 30 per cent global share.

India's Vegetable Economy

Vegetable	Total acreage (Lahh hectares)	Annual production (Million tons)	Share in total veg prodn (%)	Annual sales (₹ crore)	No. of farmers (lakh nos)	Loss in prodn (%)
Brinjal	5.5	8.5	10.4	9,600	14	40
Potato	12.8	22.5	27.8	20,800	22.3	18
Tomato	4.6	8.3	10.2	6,200	15	22
Cabbage	4.3	6.3	7.8	3,150	14.5	15
Cauliflower	2.6	4.8	5.9	6,240	8	18
Onion	5.3	7.5	9.2	7,500	18	30
Others	45.0	23.4	28.7	18,720	20	22
Total	80.0	81.2	100	72,210	112	

Source: BioSpectrum.

Potentially, the approval to Bt brinjal, India's – and world's first – genetically modified variety, is expected the change all that, and can very well catapult India into the numero uno producer. India's brinjal economy is estimated to be close to $2 billion (₹ 9,600 crore) with 1.4 million farmers cultivating it annually in nearly 5,50,000 hectares (1.4 million acres). The technology, developed by multinational Monsanto, was taken up by Mahyco and two public institutions – Tamil Nadu Agricultural University, Coimbatore and University of Agricultural Sciences, Dharwad, Karnataka.

In addition, scientists at Cornell University, US, at the University of Philippines and at the Bangladesh Agricultural Research Institute (BARI) were also involved in the development of the technology. So far, India has approved only one genetically modified crop – Bt cotton – which was allowed to be cultivated commercially in 2002. The runaway success of this – more than 85 per cent of cotton farmers have shifted to it – must have influenced the Government decision. Bt brinjal seed companies, experts said, could expect annual seed sales in excess of ₹ 500 crore over the next few years.

The net gains for farmers are expected at ₹ 4,000 crore, including annual savings of about 40 per cent of input costs involved in the use of pesticides. The regulatory approval marks a new beginning for India's $ 300 million biotech seed industry.

CROP SEGMENTS

Some of the important crop segments that offer tremendous opportunities for Seed Industry are given below:

1. Wheat: The total area under wheat cultivation is about 27 million hectares and the average yield is 2.7 tonnes per hectare. The most productive state is Punjab with average yield well above global standard, i.e., 4.5 tonnes per hectare. About 90 per cent of seed planted is farm saved and the balance 10 per cent represents the purchase seed. Out of purchase seed market, hybrid wheat seed market is only about 1 per cent and therefore there is tremendous potential for growth in this crop segment.

2. Paddy: The area under paddy is 45 million hectares, the largest in the world. Average yield per hectare is only 1.9 tonnes per hectare, half of the global average. The highest productivity is in Punjab. Around 75 per cent of the seed planted is farm saved. Currently, only about 5% of the total purchase seed market is under hybrid rice. From the seed industry point of view, there are tremendous opportunities to expand seed market on rice. Some of the leading private sector companies engaged in hybrid rice research are Advanta, Hybrid Rice International, Indo-American Hybrid Seeds, Nath Seeds and Syngenta.

3. Maize, Millets and Sorghum: The majority of the seeds used in the country are from farmer saved sources. Out of the purchase seed market, hybrid seeds represent about 45 per cent for maize, 20 per cent for sorghum and 22 per cent for millets by value and there is a great scope for increase in the use of hybrid seeds in these crops.

"Papaya Farm"

4. Vegetables: India is the second largest producer of vegetables with an annual production of 84 million tonnes. There is a need to increase the production in coming years. In vegetables, both open pollinated varieties and hybrid seeds are cultivated by farmers. The use of hybrid seeds has been increasing in tomato, okra, cabbage, chillies, papaya, cauliflower and watermelon. Almost entire quantity of cabbage seed is imported followed by cauliflower seeds. Among open pollinated varieties, seeds of cucumber, carrot, coriander, onion, peas are popular among farmers. About 80 per cent of the hybrid vegetable seeds are produced in Karnataka. Produce with good keeping quality will be preferred by consumers and traders. Many mega stores in towns and cities have started selling high quality vegetables and fruits. In addition, novel produce like baby corn, coloured capsicum and cabbage, cherry tomato, etc., will be attractive to the rising middle-class population in the country.

5. Cotton: India has the largest area under cotton cultivation, but we are ranked only third in annual cotton production. There is a gap between production and demand, necessitating import of cotton annually. Cotton is a risky crop as the yield depends upon agro-climatic conditions and pests' damage. Hybrid cotton occupies over 80 per cent of the total area under cultivation. Many private and Government institutions are engaged in research and development activities of hybrid cotton. The major production centres are in Andhra Pradesh, Maharashtra, Gujarat and Tamil Nadu. Many interior villages have become seed production centres leading to increase in employment opportunities and higher income. Mahyco-Monsanto Biotech, a joint venture between Maharashtra Hybrid Seeds Company and Monsanto was the first company to commercialise Bt cotton in our country. Nuziveedu seeds, an unlisted company has a share of about 30 per cent in hybrid cotton seed market and it is the largest BT cotton seed company in India (2009-2010).

6. Oilseeds: We are the fourth largest producers of vegetable oil, behind USA, China and Brazil. We produce about 6 million tonnes of vegetable oil and the balance requirement of about 3.5 million tonnes is met through import of mainly palm oil. Advanta, Mahyco and Syngenta are some of the companies who have high share in oilseeds seed market.

MARKET

The organised seed industry is just forty years old. Indian seed industry has evolved to become the sixth largest in the world. During the last five years the industry has been growing at 12 per cent compared to global growth of 6 per cent. The major growth has come from Bt cotton hybrids, corn hybrids and hybrid vegetables. Hybrid seeds account for about 60 per cent of the industry's turnover. Hybrids seeds are increasingly used in the case of crops like Cotton, Jowar, Maize, Sunflower and vegetables. Cotton seeds contribute to about 30 per cent of the total sales. The Indian seeds market has been estimated at about ₹ 10,000 crore for the year 2012-2013. The consumption of seeds was low due to low monsoon rains in 2012-2013. The market for different crops seed are given below:

Table 22.1: Indian Seeds Market

Crop Seed	Value (in ₹ crore)
Wheat	1,000
Paddy	900
Maize	800
Pearl millet	300
Sorghum (Jowar)	400
Hybrid Vegetable	1,200
Open Pollinated Vegetable	1,000
Cotton	3,200
Sunflower	600
Others	600
Total Market	**10,000**

Source: Industry Estimate for 2012-203.

SEED COMPANIES

There are about 400 private companies and 14 Government/Public Sector organisations operating in the Seed Industry as given below: National Seed Association of India is the apex organisation representing the Indian Seed Industry with more than 250 companies as members.

1. Public Sector Firms: They are engaged in production and marketing of seeds of paddy, wheat,oilseeds and millets and account for 30 per cent of the turnover of the industry.

Example: National Seeds Corporation, State and Central Seeds Farms.

2. Private Seeds Companies with R&D Facilities: These companies have developed R&D facilities to evolve high quality hybrid crops such as cotton, sunflower and vegetables. Depending upon the demand, they also undertake sometime multiplication of seeds by obtaining basic breeding materials from Government research stations.

Example: Maharashtra Hybrid Seeds Company Ltd., (MAHYCO) Jalna, Indo-American Hybrid Seeds Limited, Bengaluru, Nath Seeds, Aurangabad, Nuziveedu Seeds, Rasi Seeds, Salem.

3. Private Seeds Companies with Foreign Collaboration

Example: Bejo Sheetal Seeds (Private) Limited, Jalna have joint venture with Dutch Seeds Company Bezo Zadem for development of vegetable crop seeds.

4. Contract Seeds Producing Companies: They enter into contract with domestic/ international companies and undertake production of seeds as per requirements.

Example: Exim Seeds, Bengaluru and Unicorn Agrotech, Hyderabad.

5. Subsidiaries of Multinational Companies: They normally obtain basic seed material from parent companies, conduct adaptability trials, select high quality varieties/hybrids suitable for Indian conditions.

Example: Syngenta, Bayer, Monsanto.

Public sector companies handle high volume seeds of cereals, pulses and oilseeds. The market shares of different categories of companies are: Large Private Sector (40 per cent), Public Sector (30 per cent), Medium Private Players (17 per cent) and unorganised sector (13 per cent).

PRODUCT

Seed is a living organism and is a perishable product. It has limited shelf-life and has to be used in the season. Unsold stocks cannot be stored since the quality deteriorates during long storage.

Example: Depending upon the crop and variety, vegetable seeds have to used within nine months of production.

The seeds used by the farmers may be traditional, improved, high yielding or hybrid varieties. Normally, farmers save some quantity of seeds after harvest and use the same as seeds for the next season. In the case of hybrids, he cannot use the farm saved seeds due to loss of hybrid vigour leading to low yields and poor quality of the produce. They have to buy fresh seeds from the market.

The demand for a particular variety depends upon agro-climatic conditions, price of the crop/competing crop (for example, Cotton versus Chillies, Cotton versus Jowar/Maize). These factors may lead to high or low demand for a particular crop seed. Even if the demand is high, the supplies cannot be geared up at short notice like consumer goods. The seeds production has to be taken up at least one year in advance to meet the seasonal requirements. Similarly, low demand will lead to carry over of stocks and deterioration of the quality of seed material.

Normally, production of seeds is carried out in cultivator's field and the companies enter into written agreement with the farmers for production and supply of seeds as per specifications. The foundation seed required for production of certified seeds is generally supplied by the company to the growers. The farmers meet all the cultivation, harvesting, processing, grading and packing expenses. They are paid as per agreed price subject to quality checks.

Many companies organise seed production, through agents, popularly known as Seed Production Organisers. These organisers get in touch with farmers; organise the production of crop seeds. They guide the farmers regarding effective use of agricultural inputs. Sometimes, they advance money and also supply inputs to the farmers and the amount is adjusted while making final payment to the farmers.

The harvested seeds are tested to see whether they conform to specifications at Government. Seed testing centres. Once the seeds are certified by the Government agencies, they are released for sale. In the case of proprietary seeds like vegetables, the companies after testing the same in their own labs release the stocks into the market. Important specifications are also printed on the product packing for the benefits of the farmers.

Example: Germination, Physical purity, Inert materials, Moisture, Genetic purity, Shelf-life and MRP.

"Capsicum Crop"

PRICING

Pricing of seeds is based on the expenses of parent seeds, cultivation, harvesting, processing, grading, packing, storing and distribution and marketing. Another factor is demand and supply position of the particular seed variety. Similarly, there are fluctuations in the price of the seed material depending upon the rainfall. The prices are lower for public varieties/ hybrids, compared to proprietary crop seeds. Branding of crop seeds has enabled the companies to differentiate the product from that of competition with regard to quality and yield and earn higher price for the product.

Example: Sunflower (SUNBRED 275) and Tomato (Avinash) are very popular among farmers.

DISTRIBUTION

Seeds business is highly seasonal and the demand is unpredictable. The seeds have short shelf-life and have to be made available as and when required by the farmer. The demand for a particular crop seed lasts for about a month and therefore distribution has to ensure that the right crop seed is available with village/mandi level dealers during the sowing season. During the season, seed movement in a particular area depends upon rainfall and therefore the companies have to take quick decisions for moving the seeds from a dry area to wet area.

The different channels of distribution of seeds are given below.

(a) **Production centre → Distributor → Retailer → Farmers**

(b) **Production centre → Co-operative Marketing Federation → Primary co-operative Societies → Farmers**

Apart from selling seeds, the retailers also deal in allied lines like pesticides, fertilisers, cement, sprayers, etc., for continuation of the business. The discounts payable to channel members are:

Distributors: 5-7.5 per cent

Retailers: 10-15 per cent depending upon the crop and the varieties.

Example: In the case of hybrid tomato/chilli seeds, the retailer margin is about 20 per cent. Normally, the companies come out with attractive promotion schemes and try to secure the business for the year by collecting advance orders and payments from the distribution chain.

"A Pesticides and Seeds Shop"

PROMOTION

A. Formal Media

- Printed materials (Leaflets, posters in regional languages)
- Regional Newspapers, Radio
- Wall painting.

B. Rural-specific Media and Methods

- Farm-to-farm visit
- Opinion Leader
- Group meeting of farmers
- Participation in Melas and Haats
- Field demonstrations
- Field days
- Jeep campaign.

OPPORTUNITIES AND CHALLENGES

The seed industry has grown significantly with involvement of both public and private sector and has provided high yielding and quality seeds to the farmers for increasing agricultural productivity. Due to favourable agro-climatic conditions and availability of technical manpower companies are able to take 2-3 breeding generations of crops in an year and thereby reducing the time for release of new seed varieties. Our country has emerged as one of the leading seed producing centres in the world.

With a total cropped area of 190 million hectares that is one of the highest in the world and 60 million hectares of irrigated land, the seed industry has tremendous opportunities in growing in the coming years. On the other hand, the arable land is plateauing, the scope for increase in irrigation facilities is limited due to depleting water sources. The farmers are concerned with increasing incidence of pests and diseases and the need for weekly sparying of pesticides. There are reports that the companies are charging very high prices for seed materials. Considering these factors, the seed industry could initiate research and come out with improved varieties that are adaptable to local conditions and resistance to pests and diseases for the benefit of Indian farmers.

FERTILISERS

Fertilisers are the most important inputs used by the farmers for increasing the yield of crops. The consumption of fertilisers has increased dramatically during the last decades- from 2.66 million tonnes of NPK in 1971-72 to 28 million tonnes in 2010-2011. This has been made possible due to Government initiatives such as favourable pricing schemes, encouraging distribution of phosphatic and potassic fertilisers and establishing quality control laboratories. Increased fertiliser consumption is also one of the important factors which have lead to increased foodgrain production in our country, i.e., from 105 million tonnes in 1971 to 260 million tonnes in 2011-2012. Global fertiliser demand is estimated at 160 million tonnes (2010) and China and India account for 40 per cent of global consumption. Nutrient consumption is low in India (133 Kg/HA) compared to China (333 Kg/HA).

MARKET

Fertilisers are mainly used by large and medium farmers. Further, about 25 per cent of the farmers do not use fertilisers regularly and such non-users are high in Bihar, Odisha and Rajasthan. The consumption is high during the Rabi season (53.40 per cent) compared to Kharif season (46.60 per cent). Uttar Pradesh continues to be the highest consumer of fertilisers (Sugarcane, Paddy), followed by Andhra Pradesh, Maharashtra, Punjab, and West Bengal. The average consumption across different states varies considerably as shown in Table 22.2.

States like Punjab, Andhra Pradesh, and Haryana have average consumption in the range of 237 kg, 253 kg and 197 kg per hectare respectively, whereas Madhya Pradesh, Odisha and Rajasthan have consumption of 90 kg, 60 kg and 57 kg per hectare respectively. In states like Arunachal Pradesh, Nagaland and Sikkim the consumption is less than 10 kg per hectare.

Table 22.2: Fertiliser Consumption Across Selected States in India ('000 Tonnes)

States	Total consumption of fertiliser nutrients in 2007-2008	Total consumption of fertiliser nutrients in 2010-2011	Per hectare consumption of fertiliser nutrients (Kg) in 2010-2011
East Zone			
Arunachal Pradesh	.73	.83	3.00
Assam	213.94	276.70	69.40
Bihar	1,205.64	1,352.35	173.50
Jharkhand	145.00	126.00	74.60
Manipur	19.01	6.61	28.00
Meghalaya	4.08	5.03	14.90
Mizoram	3.87	5.60	59.00
Nagaland	.84	1.29	3.20
Odisha	451.89	541.64	59.70
Tripura	12.33	20.63	69.80
West Bengal	1,374.74	1,685.60	172.00
North Zone			
Haryana	1,220.36	1,274.83	196.60
Himachal Pradesh	49.96	55.53	59.30
Jammu & Kashmir	78.24	121.33	106.70
Punjab	1,697.76	1,887.30	237.30
UP	3,755.92	4,571.11	179.00
Uttaranchal	150.48	159.08	133.90
South Zone			
Andhra Pradesh	2,667.80	3,496.79	252.80
Karnataka	1,507.38	2,110.43	170.60
Kerala	208.30	283.54	105.20
Tamil Nadu	1,075.65	1,229.19	211.00

West Zone			
Gujarat	1,623.26	1,939.10	167.60
Madhya Pradesh	1,301.70	1,867.50	90.40
Chhattisgarh	441.87	610.58	107.40
Maharashtra	2,325.85	3,315.51	150.00
Rajasthan	986.70	1,307.80	57.40
Goa	7.13	7.88	47.50
All India Total	**22,570.13**	**28,282.93**	**145.00**

Note: Consumption of fertiliser nutrients per HA is based on the available data on Gross Cropped Area.

We are the third largest producers and consumers of NPK fertilisers in the world, the largest is China, followed by USA. However, we are not yet self-sufficient in production of fertilisers and are dependent on import of finished fertilisers and raw materials. There are 64 large and about 80 medium and small-scale plants in the country manufacturing a wide range of NPK fertilisers and mixtures. Some of the leading companies are IFFCO (Indian Farmers' Fertiliser Co-operative), KRIBHCO (Krishak Bharti Co-operative Limited), GSFC (Gujarat State Fertiliser Company), Chambal Fertiliser and Chemicals Ltd., Zuari Fertilisers, Rastriya Chemicals and Fertilisers Limited, Coramandel Fertilisers' Limited, Nagarjuna Fertilisers, SPIC (Southern Petrochemical Industries Corporation), FACT (Fertilisers and Chemicals Travancore Limited).

"A Fertiliser Plant"

IFFCO

Indian Farmers Fertiliser Co-operative Limited is the largest fertiliser co-operative federation and it is registered as a multi-state co-operative society. The society was registered in 1967 and has over 40,000 co-operatives as members. IFFCO has five manufacturing units producing fertilisers such as urea, diammonium phosphate, complex fertilisers, ammonium phosphate and biofertilisers. The society has achieved an all time high turnover of ₹ 26,000 crore for the year 2011-2012 and has paid dividend @ 20 per cent to its shareholders for eighth consecutive year. The products are marketed through co-operative societies. The marketing set-up consists of five zonal offices, 500 sales executives stationed in district/taluka headquarters. Through ITGI (IFFCO-TOKIO General Insurance), the society offers insurance services to farmers. Bharti Airtel and IFFCO joint venture offers voice messages, mandi prices and weather forecast along with handsets bundled with Airtel connections.

PRODUCT

It is known that at least 16 plant food elements are necessary for the growth of the plants. In the absence of any of these elements a plant fails to complete its life cycle. These 16 elements are Carbon, Hydrogen, Oxygen, Nitrogen, Phosphorus, Potassium, Sulphur, Calcium, Magnesium, Iron, Manganese, Zinc, Copper, Molybdenum, Boron and Chlorine. Carbon is obtained from carbon dioxide of the air, oxygen from air and water, hydrogen from water and all other nutrients from the soil. Soil is the most important source of plant food. The nutrients have been classified as follows:

(a) **Primary Plant Nutrients:** Nitrogen, phosphorus and potassium.

(b) **Secondary Plant Nutrients:** Calcium, magnesium and sulphur.

(c) **Micro Plant Nutrients:** Iron, manganese, copper, zinc, boron, molybdenum and chlorine.

Of the elements listed above, carbon, hydrogen and oxygen are supplied by air and water and therefore not treated as nutrients by the fertiliser industry. The main objective of the industry is to provide the primary and secondary nutrients which are required in macro quantities. Materials which are commonly used to maintain and improve soil fertility may be classified as follows:

1. Manures: These are relatively bulky materials such as animal or green manures, which are added mainly to improve the physical condition of the soil. They also supply small quantities of plant nutrients.

Examples: Farm yard manure, oil cakes, bone meal, etc.

2. Fertilisers: These are concentrated materials and are applied mainly to increase the supply of one or more of the essential nutrients.

Examples:

(a) **Nitrogenous Fertilisers:** Ammonium sulphate, Urea

(b) **Phosphatic Fertilisers:** Super phosphate, Rock phosphate

(c) **Potassic Fertilisers:** Muriate of potash

(d) **Compound Fertilisers:** These fertilisers are multiple plant nutrients supplying two or three plant nutrients simultaneously.

Example: Diammonium phosphate

(e) **Mixed Fertilisers:** They contain two or more fertilisers in suitable proportions and are prepared to meet specific crop requirements.

"Urea Fertiliser"

The concentration of nutrients in fertilisers is expressed as a percentage of total nitrogen (N), available phosphate (P_2O_5) and soluble potassium (K_2O). Thus, urea contains 46 per cent nitrogen, ammonium sulphate 20.6 per cent nitrogen, single superphosphate 16 per cent phosphorus, muriate of potash 60 per cent potassium and so on.

The fertilisers are applied as basal dressing, i.e., before sowing or as top dressing after the crop has established. They are applied into the soil or broadcast over the field as in the case of paddy crop. The quantity of fertiliser used per acre depends upon the fertility of the soil, type of crops, and irrigation facilities.

The fertiliser consumption has been growing, though slowly, during the last few years as shown below.

Table 22.3: All India Consumption of Fertiliser Nutrients-NPK (in Million Tonnes)

Year	Consumption of Fertiliser Nutrients	Consumption: Kg per HA
2007-08	22.57 Million tonnes	116.50
2008-09	24.90	127.70
2009-10	26.48	135.80
2010-2011	28.28	145.00

Marketing of fertilisers is regulated under The Fertiliser (Movement Control) Order (1973), Fertiliser Control Order (1950) and Essential Commodities Act (1955) and they have to be sold under generic name only. However, many companies add their name to the generic name for identifying the product from that of competitors. For example, Jai Kisaan Urea (Zuari Fertilisers), Vijai Urea (Madras Fertilisers), Nagarjuna Urea (Nagarjuna Fertilisers).They also use symbol/logo for easy identification by farmers. Elephant brand for FACT fertilisers. The fertilisers are packed in HDPE bags of 50 kg.

Biofertilisers

Several beneficial microorganisms occur in soils naturally. They are isolated, artificially cultured in adequate count and mixed with suitable carriers or as it is with some changes in artificial culturing. These are known as biofertilisers or microbial inoculants. Biofertilisers include Rhizobium, Azotobacter, Azospirillum, Phosphate solubilising microorganisms, Nitrogen fixing microorganisms, Pseudomonas, Thiobaccillus, etc. Biofertilisers are inexpensive and eco-friendly. Many agricultural universities, agricultural departments and a number of commercial units in private and public sectors are producing and distributing biofertilisers.

PRICING

With a view to protect the interest of the farmers, fertiliser pricing is basically regulated by the Government of India. The prices are fixed at a low level to encourage farmers to use fertilisers for increasing agricultural productivity. Fertilisers have to be sold at uniform price and selling prices are notified by Government for different fertilisers. The policy prescribes the quantity of fertiliser allocated for different geographical zones in the country, freight charges, distribution margins and manufacture have to comply with these requirements. Any amount incurred over and above the limits will have to borne by the manufacturers and it will affect the profits. The Government determines the retention price payable for different fertilisers' units and they are eligible for a subsidy as per the scheme. An apex body known as Fertiliser Industry Coordination Committee (FICC) does the process of fixing retention price and its administration. The retention cost consists of variable costs, fixed cost and return on investment. The difference between retention price and actual selling price is paid as subsidy by Government. Increased consumption of fertilisers has also increased the financial burden on Government as the subsidy amount has increased from ₹ 505 crore in 1980-1981 to ₹ 74,000 crore in 2011-2012.

Considering the huge subsidy burden, the the Government has a taken policy decision to decontrol the prices of all fertilisers except urea. The price of urea may be increased by 10 per cent effective 2010. The Government has introduced a Nutrient Based Subsidy (NBS) in the place of product-wise subsidy effective 1.4.2010. Subsidy amount payable to the company will be fixed annually for each nutrient of the products sold based on the nutrient content. Practically, all fertilisers except urea will come under NBS.

The Government is buying fertilisers at a high price from manufacturers and they are made available to farmers at a low price. Price at which the Government is buying fertiliser and the price at which it is made available to farmers are given below (2011-2012).

Table 22.4: Prices of Fertilisers

Fertiliser	Indigenous Price	Price per tonne (in rupees) to Farmers
Urea	13,017	5,400
Diammonium Sulphate	58,584	20,100
Muriate of Potash	-	12,040
Complex Fertilisers (17:17:17)	43,274	18,000

Source: Ministry of Chemical Fertilisers (2011-2012).

DISTRIBUTION

The fertilisers are produced at selected locations and imported fertilisers arrive at seaport near to the area of operation of the company. Fertilisers are very bulky materials and their consumption is highly seasonal. Therefore, distribution is the most important aspect of fertiliser marketing, as they have to be made available with village/mandi level retailers. Transportation account for about 60 per cent of the marketing cost. Fertilisers are distributed through co-operatives and private dealers. Important channels of distribution are given below.

1. **Factory → Warehouses → Retailer → Farmers**
2. **Factory → Wholesaler → Retailer → Farmers**
3. **Factory → District wholesale society → Taluka level society → Village-level society → Farmers**

The number of retailers has increased from 82,000 in 1970-1971 to 2,80,000 in 2002-2003. Each retailer deals with many fertiliser companies based on product popularity, range of products offered, speed of supplies and the demand at farmer level. The commission earned by wholesaler/retailer is only 1-3 per cent of the farmer's price and therefore the retailers place orders only against demand. The company has to build up stocks and keep it ready to meet the demand at short notice. When the supply is less than the demand during a specific season, the retailer charges a higher price than normal price. Credit plays a major role for increasing the sales through trade and consumption at farmer level.

"A Fertiliser Shop"

PROMOTION

The farmer is the target customer in fertiliser promotion and his response depends upon a number of factors such as education, income, size of the farm, types of crops grown, output prices, yield and past experience. Important media and methods used in fertiliser promotion are given below.

1. Formal Media

- Printed materials (Leaflets, posters in regional languages)
- Regional TV
- Radio
- Regional newspapers
- Wall paintings
- Bus boards

2. Rural-specific Media

- Farm-to-farm visit
- Opinion Leaders
- Group meeting of farmers
- Field demonstration
- Agricultural fairs
- Field day
- Village level film shows
- Screening of films in rural cinema halls
- Farmers' training programme
- Village adoption
- Soil testing.

One Stop Solution to Farmers' Problems

Coramandel Ltd., (Sales: ₹ 4,589 crore in 2011-2012), has established over 500 Mana Gromor centres in Andhra Pradesh. The centres are located at Taluka/Mandal headquarters. Each centre covers 30-40 villages and provides quality agricultural inputs and one stop solution to the farmers' problems.

OPPORTUNITIES AND CHALLENGES

1. Our population is expected to grow by about 15 million per year in the coming years. At present, we are producing about 260 million tonnes of foodgrains annually and this has been made possible by application of about 28 million tonnes of NPK and other inputs. By 2025, the scenario would be as given below:

Population: 1,400 million

Foodgrain requirements: 380 million tonnes

Fertiliser requirements: 40-45 million tonnes.

2. Revival of defunct plants of Fertiliser Corporation of India and Hindustan Fertiliser Corporation of India located in Gorakhpur, Sindhri, Durgapur, Baruni, Haldia, Ramagundam, etc., has to be taken on priority basis. The estimated cost for revival of these plants is about ₹ 36,000 crore.

3. In the coming years, we must look into both quantitative and qualitative use of fertilisers. The imbalance in the use of NPK needs to be corrected. Repeat use of fertilisers without addition of organic manures can impair fertility of the soil. Promoting integrated nutrient management should form an integral part of fertiliser marketing.

4. Considering the burden on subsidy, surviving outside the protected environment of price scheme is a major challenge awaiting the industry. Cheaper imports could threaten the domestic industry. Indian industry should also increase its efficiency to meet the challenges from these imports.

PESTICIDES

All our cultivated crops are subject to the attack of organisms like insects, fungi, bacteria, and viruses affecting the growth and yields of crops. It has been estimated that our country is losing over ₹ 1,40,000 crore (2007) of produce due to damages caused by these harmful organisms. A few of the economically important insect pests, diseases, weeds and viruses are given below.

(a) **Insects:** Paddy stem borers and leaf rollers, cotton bollworms, vegetable shoot and fruit borers, groundnut leaf miners.

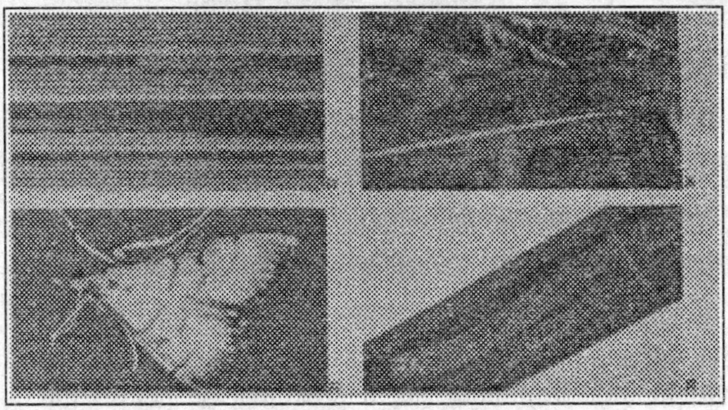

"Leaf Roller — A Serious Insect Pest of Paddy Crop"

(b) **Fungal Diseases:** Paddy blast, Grape mildews, Chilli dieback, Apple scab, coffee rust.

(c) **Weeds:** Phalaris in wheat, Echinocloa in Paddy.

(d) **Viruses:** Bunchy top of banana, Mosaic on chillies, Tomato leaf curl.

It has been observed that these pests cause enormous crop losses as shown below:

Type of pest	Losses (per cent)
Insects	26
Weeds	33
Fungi, Bacteria and Viruses	26
Rodents and others	15

Fig. 22.1: Crop losses due to pests

While there are several methods of controlling the pests such as use of physical, biological and cultural methods, the use of chemicals have been found to give immediate control and our farmers are increasingly using the same. These chemical compounds are popularly referred to as pesticides. The different types of pesticides are insecticides, fungicides, weedicides and rodenticides.

"A Farmer Spraying Fungicides in Potato Farm"

Biopesticides

Chemical pesticides are poisonous products and misuse results in damage to human life, crops and environment. Indiscriminate use of chemical pesticides has lead to development of resistance among, cotton bollworms, diamond back moth on vegetables and brown plant hopper in paddy. Nowadays farmers have started using biological products like parasites, predators, pathogenic bacteria, fungi, viruses to control pests and diseases. Similarly, botanical pesticides like neem based products containing azadirachtin are used as insect repellant, antifeedant and insect growth regulator by farmers. Nimbecidine, Neemguard, Margocide, Neem Gold, Margosom are some of the popular brands available in the market.

Botanical Pesticide – "Nimbecidine"

MARKET

The consumption of pesticides is closely linked to factors such as type of crops, agro-climatic conditions, incidence of pests and disease and output prices. Two kharif crops, i.e., cotton and paddy account for about 50 per cent of pesticides consumption in our country. Though the area under cultivation is low, the usage of pesticides is very high in cotton due to high susceptibility to pests and diseases. In recent years, with the introduction of Bt cotton varieties that are resistant to bollworms, there has been reduction in the use of pesticides on cotton crop. The peak season for consumption of pesticides in our country is during July-October.

Pesticides use in India at present is at a very low level. The annual average consumption of pesticides in our country is only 480 gm/ha compared 10.7 kg/ha in Japan, 4 kg/ha in USA and 3 kg/ha in Europe. Our country consumes only 3 per cent of the world consumtpion of pesticides. Currently, only about one-fourth of our cropped areas is treated with pesticides.

Out of total pesticides consumed in agriculture, the share of insecticides in value terms is 65 per cent, fungicides 15 per cent, weedicides 17 per cent and others 3 per cent. Weedicides are used in wheat, paddy and plantation crops mainly due to shortage of labour and high wages in these segments. About 60 per cent of the sales of pesticides are in Andhra Pradesh, Punjab and Haryana. The size of the domestic pesticides market was about ₹ 12,000 crore for the year 2013-14.

PESTICIDE COMPANIES

There are six large manufacturers who control 75 per cent of the Global Pesticides Market, i.e., Bayer, Syngenta, DuPont, Monsanto, BASF and Dow. Among them Bayer, Syngenta, Monsanto and DuPont are also Seed Industry leaders. The Indian pesticides industry comprises of basic manufacturers, formulators, importers, distributors and dealers.

1. **Multinationals Organisations** such as BASF, Bayer, Cheminova, Dow, DuPont, Isagro, Monsanto and Syngenta.

2. **Indian Companies** like Excel industries, Hyderabad Chemicals, Indofil, Nagarjuna, Northern Minerals, Parry & Company, Pesticides India, Rallis and United Phosphorus.
3. **Public Sector Firms** like Hindustan Insecticides Limited and State-level Agro-Industries Corporations.

We are the largest manufacturers of basic pesticide chemicals in South Asian and African countries next only to Japan. Our export of pesticides materials was about ₹ 10,000 crore in 2009-2010. Currently, 145 pesticides have been registered and 85 technical grade pesticides are manufactured in our country. The pesticides industry is regulated by the Insecticides Act (1968). The registration procedure requires submission of authentic data on chemistry, bioefficacy, residues, toxicity, packing, labelling, and pesticides presence in water, soil, crop, environment and carcinogenicity. The manufacturers and dealers have to obtain licence for selling pesticides from the Government. The local market is characterised by large capacities with low capacity utilisation and has resulted in a steady decline in the selling prices of many generic products. The uncertain weather conditions coupled with long credit period for farmers have resulted in low margins for the players in the industry.

PRODUCT

The products are formulated in different forms such as liquids, dusts, granules and wettable powders and in different concentrations. The products are available from 50 gm to 20 kg pack in tin, aluminium, multilayer and laminated cartons. There are products which are insect, disease, weed specific and can be used on many crops. Liquids and wettable powders have to be mixed with water and applied on the crops using sprayers. Dusters are used for application of dust and granules are broadcasted over the field. MRP, date of manufacturing and expiry date are printed on the packing. Some of the popular brands available in the market are:

(a) **Insecticides:** Actara, Curacron, Ekalux, Karate, Regent, Proclaim, Confidor.

(b) **Fungicides:** Bavistin, Contaf, Dithane M 45, Ridomil, Amistar Section.

(c) **Weedicides:** Gramoxone, Topik, Leader, Rifit, Roundup.

PRICE

The prices of pesticides are not regulated by Government and the manufacturers are free to fix the prices. The business is highly seasonal and is very competitive and therefore companies offer attractive schemes towards annual targets, off-season/bulk purchases, and early/timely payment to distributors and dealers.

DISTRIBUTION

The most important objective of distribution is to ensure that the right product and packing are made available with the village/mandi level retailers during the season to meet the requirements of the farmers. Normal distribution channels in the industry are given below.

1. **Manufacturer → Depot/C&F Agent → Distributor → Retailer → Farmers**
2. **Manufacturer → Depot/C&F Agent → Preferred dealer → Retailer → Farmers**

The company establishes own depot or appoints C&F Agents in major towns and make supplies to distributors/preferred dealers who are operating in major agricultural centres. The distributors/preferred dealers service the retailers in the villages/mandis. The commission payable to different channel members are C&F Agent: 3-4 per cent, distributors: 5-7.5 per cent, preferred dealers 3-5 per cent and retailers 10 per cent. In addition, the companies extends credit period of 60-90 days to distributors who in turn pass on the credit facility to retailers. The retailers play a major role in pesticides business as they have direct contact with farmers and extend credit facilities. They advise the farmers regarding the type of products to be used for conrolling pests and diseases. In order to achieve the annual targets and to liquidate the stocks in a competitive market, it is a common practice for the dealers to sell the product below MRP. The farmers also bargain with the dealers and try to get the lowest possible price for the product.

PROMOTION

A variety of promotion media and methods are used as per details given below:

1. **Formal Media**
   - Printed materials (Leaflets, posters in regional languages)
   - Regional TV
   - Radio
   - Regional newspapers
   - Wall paintings
   - Bus boards
   - Tree Boards

"A Farm Wall Painting"

2. Rural-specific Media:

- Farm-to-farm visit
- Group meeting of farmers
- Field demonstration
- Field day
- Village-level film shows
- Screening of films in rural cinema halls
- Farmers' training programme
- Jeep campaign
- Participation in melas

"A Large Gathering of Farmers in Connection with a New Product Launch"

"A Company Stall in Agricultural Fair"

MANAGING CHANNEL CONFLICT

Types of Conflict

Even when a company has an effective distribution set up in the market, some conflict between channel members and between the company and channel members may take place. This is normally due to conflicting business interests.

Example: The company wants the distributor to extend the activities to new and uncovered markets and appoint new dealers for increasing sales volumes. But the distributor focuses on existing, developed markets and loyal dealers and is comfortable to work in the established market. He is reluctant to explore new and unknown markets. There are three types of channel conflict.

1. **Vertical Channel Conflict** relates to conflict between different levels within the same channel.

   Example: Conflict between distributor and the retailer.

2. **Horizontal Channel Conflict** means conflict between members at the same level of the distribution channel.

   Example: Price cutting between retailers in the same market.

3. **Multichannel Conflict:** Here, the company selects two or more channels to sell its products in the same market.

   Example: Company makes direct supplies to wholesalers as well as key retailers in the same market. The wholesaler is hurt since this arrangement affects his sales in the market.

Causes of Channel Conflict

1. **Conflicting Objectives:** The objectives of the company and the channel members differ. *Example:* The company wants the distributor to offer sales incentives for bulk purchases. The distributor wish to work with high margins and is concerned with his profitability.

2. **Demand for Extra Discount:** The channel members may ask for additional discount for pushing the products and the company may not be in favour of such proposal, leading to conflict.

3. **Unethical Practices:** Channel members, i.e., distributors and dealers may resort to unethical practices like charging more than MRP (particularly during shortages), selling unwanted products like plant tonics, spurious products, etc., leading to conflict between company and channel members.

4. **Direct Supply to Consumers:** Some companies may supply directly to key customers bypassing the area distributor. The distributor looses the business and the commission, and this leads to conflict between the company and the distributor.

5. **Competitive Products:** The distributor may sell competitors' products and this will affect company's business.

6. **Reduction in the Area of Operation:** In order to improve dealer coverage and sales, the company may reduce the area of operation of the current distributor and add one or more distributors in the same area. The distributor is upset with the decisions of the company as his area of operation has been reduced and his sales may be affected.

Managing Channel Conflict

Channel members play a major role in growth and development of business. They perform specialised marketing functions such as buying, selling, warehousing, financing, risk taking and provide valuable marketing intelligence to the company. Chosen channels cannot be terminated overnight. Channel decisions require special attention as they are key external resource equally important like internal resource (employees).

1. **Communication:** Regular communication between the company, distributors and dealers will certainly go a long way in minimising channel conflicts. Circulars, e-mails, newsletters, personal one-to-one discussions can be used to communicate with channel members. Taking feedback from key distributors/dealers and involving them in discussions will help the company in improving relations with distribution channel.
2. **Aligning Goals of the Company with that of Channel Members:** The sales and field activities plan of the company should be discussed and communicated to the distributors/dealers so that both the company and channel members can work together for achievement of common objectives.
3. **Dealer Councils** can resolve conflicts between company/distributors/dealers. It provides an opportunity for dealers to represent the problem in the market.
4. **Arbitration and Mediation** facilitate settlement of channel conflicts. If these methods prove ineffective, the member may go to the court. However, it is a time-consuming and very often an expensive option.

OPPORTUNITIES AND CHALLENGES

Agricultural sector contributes to about 16 per cent of GDP and is expected to maintain a similar contribution in future as well. The high growth of population along with limited availability of land will be a challenge for increasing food production. The country is witnessing a boom in consumer goods sector and increasing affluent middle-class is demanding quality and processed foods. The increased share of cash crops and greater awareness levels will lead to higher pesticides' usage. The agricultural sector will grow by 7 per cent to 10 per cent per annum in value terms in the next few years. This will result in pesticides' sector growth of at least 10 per cent per annum on value terms.

Pesticides are poisonous chemicals and misuse results in damage to human life, crops and environment. Continuous use of pesticides has resulted in residues on crops, produce, soil, water and air. Indiscriminate use of chemical pesticides have led to development of resistance among cotton bollworms, diamond black moth on vegetables and brown plant hopper in paddy. Misuse of pesticides is mainly because of lack of awareness. Hence, there is a need to educate the farmers and dealers about integrated pest management and promote safe and efficient use of pesticides for sustainable agricultural development in our country.

The general public is easily frightened when the newspapers talk about pesticides residues because they have been told that all pesticides are killers. It should be noted that pesticides are designed to kill insects, weeds, rodents, etc., and not humans. Pesticides are the products of modern chemistry offering immense benefits to the society. Right use of pesticides will help to increase per hectare yields of crops, thereby ensuring the prosperity of our farmers. In the coming years, the industry must look into both quantitative and qualitative use of pesticides.

In the present business environment characterised by overcapacity, intense competition, less product differentiation, uncertainties with regard to pesticides market in cotton, carryover stocks, huge outstandings with distribution chain, the marketers have moved away from a purely sales approach and become more market-oriented to meet the challenges facing the pesticide industry.

TRACTORS

The tractors are mainly used for three basic purposes, i.e., farming operations, transportation and as a power source. In farming operations, the tractors are used for seedbed preparation. Tractors are used in transportation of people, fodder, foodgrains, etc., from rural area to nearest marketplace. They are used as a power source in farms for harvesting, pumping of water, etc.

"Land Preparation"

INDUSTRY

The industry is segmented on the basis of the power of the tractor engine expressed in terms of Horsepower. The market share of each segment being, less than 30 HP (13 per cent), 31-40 HP (42 per cent), 41-50 HP (28 per cent) and more than 50 HP (17 per cent) (2012).

North India constituting UP, Punjab and Haryana leads among the regions in tractor sales. The soil in these states (UP, Haryana, Punjab) is alluvial in nature and requires a low-powered tractor for tilling it. In Western and Southern parts of the country, where the soil is harder, it needs high-powered tractors. The largest segment continues to be for 31-40 HP tractors.

The tractor sales grew from 2,48,000 in 2005 to 5,45,000 in 2011 as shown below:

Tractor Sales (in Lakh)

Year	Sales in Lakh
2005	2.45
2006	2.96
2007	3.53
2008	3.47
2009	3.43
2010	3.94
2011	5.45

Note: During the year 2012, the sale was low (4.19 lakh) due to adverse monsoon conditions.

Out of the total sales of tractors, the replacement market is about 40 per cent and this segment will grow in the coming years. Export of tractors stood at 50,000 units in 2012-2013. The industry is controlled by six major players, i.e., M&M, TAFE, Escorts and International Tractors. John Deer and New Holland tractors. With plants in Mumbai, Nashik and Nagpur, Mahindra and Mahindra are the market leaders in the highly competitive Indian market. M&M launched "MAHINDRA VISHWAS" in 2001 to bring prosperity to small farmers by providing pre-owned tractors of good quality.

Table 22.3: Company-wise Market Shares

Company	Market share (percentage) (2012-2013)
Mahindra and Mahindra	40.10
TAFE	23.20
Escorts	10.20
International Tractors (Sonalika Group)	8.40
John Deer	9.40
New Holland	5.80
HMT and Others	2.90

Note: Escorts plans to sell Ferrari Tractors, priced at about ₹ 8 lakh for 30 HP machines. Similarly, Lamborghini is planning to enter the market. These companies are targeting affluent farmers in Punjab, UP, Maharashtra and Andhra Pradesh.

The major factors which influence the demand of tractors in India are given below:

1. Land Holding Pattern: The optimal land holding required for different HP tractors is approximately 8 to 10 hectares for 25 HP tractors, 25 to 30 hectares for 35 HP and beyond that, it is higher HP tractors. But the actual relationship between different land holdings and the power of tractors is dependent on earning stability, type of soil, type of operation and affordability by farmers.

2. Irrigation Potential: Purchase of tractors require high financial investment and therefore they are preferred for use in irrigated areas.

3. Monsoon: A poor monsoon leads to hardening of soil and greater need for tractors and at the same time, a poor monsoon also leaves the farmers with low purchasing power.

4. Availability of Credit: Over 90 per cent of the purchases of tractors are through loans taken from banks and agricultural institutions. Any variation in availability and cost of credit affects the demand.

5. Income from Agriculture: The improvement in procurement prices of agricultural produce leads to increase in disposable income of farmers and in their purchasing power.

6. Scientific Farming Practices: Considering the capital cost, the tractors are to be used optimally in the farm and scientific farming practices are a prerequisite for use of tractors. Multiple Cropping requires repeated tilling of the land and the need for tractors.

7. Increase in Literacy will help in understanding and implementing farm mechanisation in India.

8. Priority of the Farmer: When the farmers starts earning, he invests the money on jewellery, two-wheelers, land and purchase of tractor is the last priority for him.

Greaves Cotton Enters Mini Tractor Segment

Greaves Cotton has developed Mini Tractor "USTAD" aimed at small farmers having 3-5 acres of land. With scarcity of labour and increasing wages, the farmers are in need of affordable tractors. Priced at around ₹ 2.5 lakh, the farmer can attach plough, cultivator, harvester, seed drill to the Mini Tractor. The Farm Equipment Division contributes to about 15 per cent of the company's turnover of ₹ 1,800 crore. The market size of small tractors is about 500 crore and about 25,000 units are sold annually. Ustad will directly compete with Yuvaraj of Mahindra and Mahindra.

MARKETING-MIX

Product

Indian tractor market is characterised with low price, no frills, rugged, versatile and low to medium power tractors. The price varies between ₹ 2.80 lakh to ₹ 5.0 lakh depending on the HP of the tractors. The following are the various kinds of tractors:

- Tractors below 30 HP
- Tractors between 30 – 40 HP [e.g., Bhoomiputra – 42 WP]
- Tractors above 40 HP [e.g., Sarpanch – 45 WP]
- Tractors of 60 HP [e.g., Arjun – 60 WP]

Implements are tools or machinery used with the tractor for carrying out activities like tilling, ploughing, sowing seeds, etc., and some of the implements are:

- Mounted Offset Disk Harrow
- Mounted Disk Plough
- Leveller
- Mounted Mould Board Plough
- Heavy Duty Tiller.

DISTRIBUTION

The company appoints dealers in important agricultural centres. A dealer either covers one district or two-three tehsils. The dealer looks after the sale and service of tractors. A dealer earns between ₹ 30,000 and ₹ 60,000 depending upon the model of the tractor and accessories sold.

"Display of Tractors by a Dealer"

Tractor Mandis: Large number of tractors are sold in Punjab and UP mainly due to large farms, fertility of the soil and affluent farmers. There is a big replacement market for tractors in these states. There are several tractor mandis where buying and selling of used tractors takes place. The commission payable to the agent varies from .5 per cent to 1 per cent depending upon the model and the value of the tractor.

PROMOTION

- **Advertisements** in Regional TV, newspapers, agricultural magazines.
- **Farm-to-farm visit.**
- **Melas:** Many companies promote its products in melas. It could be a religious mela like "Kumbh Mela" or a non-religious mela like "Pushkar Mela" or "Agri fairs".

- **Demonstrations:** Field staff conduct product's demonstrations in the presence of farmers.
- **Outdoor** advetisement like wall paintings, hoardings, signboards and paintings on buses and bus stops.
- **Opinion Leaders:** Over 90 per cent purchases of tractors are through bank loans and therefore the companies/dealers regularly call on the bank managers and brief them about tractor models and promotion schemes.

OPPORTUNITIES AND CHALLENGES

India is a vast country with varied agro-climatic zones. Farm holdings are small due to higher population density and fragmentation of land holdings. The farmers have limited financial resources to modernise farming. Draught animals will continue to be used in farming operations. Cost of maintenance of animals is increasing. Use of animal power is economical when labour wages are low and land holdings limited. In the present circumstances, when labour wages are increasing and their availability at peak times of sowing and harvesting is decreasing the farmers are now moving towards use of agricultural machinery. Custom hiring of tractors for tillage and transport is being practised in many states.

"Draught Animals are Still used in Farming Operations"

A few points to be considered for making available adequate farm power to farmers are:

1. Encourage tractorisation of farm operations through: (a) group loans for tractors, (b) self-employment scheme for rural youth, and (c) subsidising tractor costs. It has been observed that 60 per cent of the life of tractors is used in transporting men and materials and only 40 per cent of the time is spent in the field. The average farmer utilises his tractor only for about 500 hours in a year as against 1,000 hours required by bankers to recover the fixed cost.
2. Liberalise norms for tractor financing especially in areas like dry land, drought-prone and hilly areas.

3. Availability of spare parts, after-sales service and repair facilities for the benefit of tractor owners.
4. Insurance cover for tractors.

CONCLUSION

While we have achieved self-sufficiency in food production, the value addition from agriculture is coming down due to higher income from industry and services. One-third of the population from non-agricultural sector contributes to about 85 per cent of national income. Under this situation, agricultural inputs play a major role in increasing the yield of crops and we have to continue to focus on increasing agricultural production to meet the food requirements of growing population. There is a need to evolve integrated agricultural input management along with modern farming practices in our move towards sustainable agriculture.

QUESTIONS

1. What are the features of Agricultural Inputs? How are they different from consumer goods?
2. Discuss the importance of pull and push strategies in marketing of agricultural inputs.
3. The salesperson has to play the role of a plant doctor among farmers – Discuss.
4. Discuss the important promotion media and methods used in promotion of agricultural inputs.

✿ ✿ ✿

23 AGRICULTURAL INPUTS AND CUSTOMER RELATIONSHIP MANAGEMENT

INTRODUCTION

The opening up of our economy through liberalisation and globalisation has led to increase in production and availability of agricultural inputs such as seeds, fertilisers and pesticides agricultural machinery. The market is flooded with different brands of these inputs and product differentiation is becoming more and more challenging. The users have wider choice and are demanding more and more benefits and the competition is increasing in the marketplace. The companies are wooing the customers with flexible credit and additional discounts. Channel choking well in advance of the season and sales reversal at the end of the season have become common features of business. There are cases where the business performance of the company has been affected due to sticky outstanding and huge take back of stocks sold during the previous years.

In this dynamic market situation, delivering superior service, enhancing customer value and enriching the brand play a major role in the profitable growth of the organisation.

CUSTOMER RELATIONSHIP MANAGEMENT (CRM)

Parvathiar and Sheth (2001) have defined CRM as "a comprehensive strategy and process of acquiring, retaining and partnering with selective customers to create superior value for the company and the customer. Gronroos (1990) stated "CRM is to establish, maintain and enhance relationship with customers and other partners, at a profit, so that the objectives of the parties involved are met".

Practitioners and consultants use Customer Relationship Management (CRM) to refer to technology enabled processes for customer interactions and relationship building, while marketing academicians prefer the term "Relationship Marketing" [Ref.: G. Shainesh and Jagadish N. Sheth, Customer Relationship Management, MacMillan India Ltd., New Delhi (2006)].

The customer relationship management (CRM) initiatives focus on building and maintaining profitable and long lasting relations with the customers and creating superior customer value and customer satisfaction. CRM focuses on co-operative and collaborative relationship between the firm and its customer. The focus is creating, growing and retaining customers. Some of the aspects of customer relationship marketing are mutual benefits, trust, and transparency, inter-dependency and shared values. Normally, a customer buys a product that offers the highest perceived value, i.e., the difference between all the benefits and the cost of the product compared to that of competition. Customer satisfaction denotes the extend to which a product's performance matches with the expectation of the buyer. If the product matches his expectations, the customer is satisfied. If the performance exceeds expectations, then the customer is delighted. Sometimes, companies focus too much on mechanics such as IT and database rather than the ultimate user, i.e., increasing the value of customer relations. If the customer is taken care, sales volume, market share and profits will grow.

Focusing on the Customer

In CRM, a sale is considered as the beginning rather than an end of a company's interaction with the customer. The firm can make a start with CRM by understanding individual customers and their specific needs and requirements.

Example: Large pack requirements of pesticides, advance purchase of seeds, technical service to farmers, etc. The firm should initiative suitable and well-defined strategies to meet the requirement.

The sales staff should be able to establish good rapport with the customers. They should have the ability to suggest solutions according the customer needs. So, in CRM, studying clients and their background are of utmost importance.

Examples: Crop-wise acreages, method of cultivation (modern/traditional), level of mechanisation in the farm, pest problems, cash/credit sales, role of opinion leaders, etc.

CRM is based on the premise that important customers (distributors, dealers, key farmers, opinion leaders) need focused and continuous attention. The sales staff normally visit the customers when they are ready-to-place orders. In fact, they should meet them during off-season also.

Examples: Off-season calls to understand the customers' experience of the previous season, provide information on new products, new technologies in crop production, off-season schemes, performance of competitive products and their sales. Off-season calls will be very useful in the case of agricultural machinery like tractors, harvesters, etc., which requires high investment.

The sales staff should act as representative of the organisation they are working for. They are the main contact point for the clients for the product or services provided by the company. They have to ensure that customers' expectations are taken care of in the best possible manner.

Development of Customers

The firm identifies the prospects who have interest in the product and the ability to pay for it. The prospects are rejected if they are not creditworthy or would not be profitable in the long run. The firm tries to convert most of the prospects to first-time users and then to repeat customers. First-time users and repeat customers may continue to buy from competitors also.

The next challenge is to make them members by starting membership programme. (Farmers club, Privileged dealers) that offers a whole set of benefits to customers who join. Most probably, may of the members would turn into advocates who recommend the company and its products/services to others.

Examples of advocates: Important contact farmers, opinion leaders, preferred dealers and influencers such as scientists attached to universities. The ultimate challenge is turn advocates into partners (Distributors, big dealers, large plantations, key farmers) where the customers and the company work together. It is likely some of the customers will become inactive and it is the responsibility of the sales staff to reactivate the customers through new products, handling complaints, etc. It is relatively easy to bring back ex-customers because the company knows their background and action to be taken to bring them back.

While loyal customers may bring in more revenue, the company has to spend time and money to build customer loyalty. The company has to ensure that the costs do not exceed the gains. Our objective should be to increase our share from the total purchases of individual customers and therefore the focus should be on big customers such as large progressive farmers, plantations, distributors and big dealers.

RELATIONSHIP SELLING

Rural people prefer face-to-face communication and therefore personal selling plays a major role in inputs marketing. The sales executive has to take a lead in developing a CRM plan for the territory. Based on the marketing strategy, he has to evaluate the relative importance of the different categories of customers and discuss the same with his reporting manager. Some executives feel that all customers are important and all should be treated equally. This approach is good for building relations with public but does not take into account customer value and contribution to company sales and profits. It is a well-established fact that all customers do not contribute the same value to the company. Further, only a small percentage of the customers contribute to a large percentage of the total sales volume and profit. Another critical aspect is that of product strategy. Many sales executives insist that the company should offer full range of products to meet the needs of all customers. The focus should be on tailoring products to meet the needs of those customers who drive profitability. The sales executive should focus on users (farmers), channel members (wholesalers and retailers), influencers and the brands.

CRM Process

CRM is an interactive process and consist of four steps, i.e.,

1. Collecting customer data and constructing data base
2. Analysis of the customer data and identify target customers
3. Develop appropriate CRM programmes
4. Effective implementation of CRM programme

1. Selection of the Villages: Keeping district/taluka/block as a unit, the sales executive has to select the villages based on important crops and varieties grown, area under different crops, area under irrigation and nature of cultivation, i.e., traditional/modern methods cultivation, consumption of agricultural inputs and accessibility. Arrange all the villages in the order of potentiality and select the most potential villages for undertaking farmer-oriented activities.

2. Selection of the Farmers: The sales executive has to select most potential farmers based on size of the farm, type of crops/varieties grown, irrigation facilities, readiness to try new products (i.e., innovators and early adopters) volume of different agricultural inputs used and past consumption of company's range of products. The sales executive should also consider farmer-buyer behaviour as given below:

- **Benefits:** Concerned about quality, price, service
- **User Status:** Non-user, ex-user, potential user, occasional user and regular user
- **Usage Rate:** Light user, medium user and heavy user
- **Shop/Brand Loyalty:** None, medium and strong
- **Attitude to Product:** Enthusiastic, positive, negative and hostile

3. Frequency of Visit to Selected Villages: This depends on allocation of time between pull (farmer calls) and push (retailer calls) activities. Many sales executives feel that they have to maximise the number of farmer calls and they go on meeting farmers at random without follow-up visit. This is similar to the large number of people met by politicians during election and we are all familiar with the outcome of such calls. The farmer wants solutions to his problems, i.e., nutritional defeciencies, low yields and pest problems and the sales executive has to play the role of a Plant Doctor among farmers.

It is essential that identified farmers are met regularly as per plan to build up long-term relations and obtain higher share from his purchases of agricultural inputs. Some executives feel that they have to meet customers only during agricultural season when they think customers might to ready to place orders. In fact, they should visit them during off-season, when they are relatively free, to understand the customer's experience of the previous season, feedback on product performance and find out his plans for the next season. The sales executive could even recommend a competitive product and experience shows that such recommendations are appreciated by the farmers. Some of the activities which could be conducted to develop relations with farmers are:

- Field visit along with the farmer
- Identification of field problems
- Recommendations to solve the problems
- Demonstration
- Training programme for contact farmers
- Off-season meeting with the farmers
- Incentives for bulk purchase of products for own consumption
- Visit of farmers to agricultural universities

"Field Demostration in Cotton Crop"

4. Distribution Channel initiatives are designed to improve sales and profitability of the territory by developing a network of committed retailers and offering value-added services and solutions. In order to be successful in the marketplace, the channel partners should align their activities with the marketing objectives of the company. Companies are using internet and other IT tools to avoid manual processing of data and promote positive channel partner experience.

(a) Distributor: The channel members consist of wholesalers (distributors) and retailers and the sales executive has to develop relationship with these channel partners. The company should initiate at least on an annual basis, business development plan meeting with all the distributors. The meeting should focus on business performance during previous year, areas for improvement (applicable to the company as well as the distributor) and plans for the next year. Incentives for achievement of agreed targets should also be discussed and finalised during the meeting. This meeting provides an opportunity for the senior managers of the company to interact with distributors and sort out pending issues, if any. The plan should not remain in paper and therefore the sales executive and the reporting manager should do necessary follow-up and assess the progress made during the course of the year. All genuine problems have to be addressed in the interest of the distributor and the company. The sales executive and the distributor could undertake joint tours and sort out the problems of retailers. The sales executive should also organise training programmes for distributors' promotion and sales staff to improve their performance.

(b) Retailer: The retailers play a major role in input sales, since they have close association with farmers and very often advise them on the type of products to be used in crop cultivation. Further, they extend credit facilities to farmers and push products where the margins are high. While there may be a large number of retailers engaged in selling agricultural inputs, only a small percentage of retailers contribute to large percentage of the sales and profits of the company. The sales executive should collect retailer-wise information such as total sales value, volumes of different products sold, cash and credit transactions, influence with farmers and company's share in his total business. It has been observed that 20-30 per cent of the retailers contribute to about 70-80 per cent of the business done by a company in a sales territory and therefore the sales executive should identify potential retailers and develop relations with them. Some of the activities which will increase the involvement of the retailers are:

- Detailing the products and highlighting product benefits.
- Imparting knowledge of pests and disease and product recommendations.
- Meeting the farmers in the field along with the retailer.
- Involving him in product demonstrations and farmers meetings.
- Assisting him in liquidating the stocks of company's products.
- Undertaking field activities in the villages suggested by the retailer.
- Credit facilities.
- Sales incentives for achievement of agreed targets.
- Training programme for retailers.

"A Company Executive Highlights Product Benefits to a Dealer"

5. Influencers: This group includes gramsevaks, agricultural officers, research scientists, etc., and the sales executive should find out the relative importance of this group in product recommendations in his sales territory. Of late, the role of influencers in product recommendation has come down and they are also pre-occupied with administrative work. Therefore, the sales executive has to identify influencers who have good contact with farmers and meet them regularly. He could involve them in group meeting of farmers, dealers' training programmes and product demonstrations.

Over 90 per cent purchases of tractors take place through bank loans and therefore the sales executive/dealer should call on bank manager and brief them about tractor models and promotion schemes.

It is not possible for a sales executive to meet all the customers and develop relationship with them. To start with he has to select a few potential villages, farmers, retailers and influencers in each market so that he can offer more personalised service which makes them feel happy and important.

6. Brand: Many people feel that brand relates to product name, company name or logo. In fact, brand is much more than that. Brand includes company products, services, behaviour of company staff, distribution channel and use of technology and marketing processes. It is the sum total of the experience of customers with the company.

Example: A company may have high quality products, but if a distributor has to make repeat calls/send reminders for settlement of genuine claims, then the inordinate delay is damaging the brand. The company has to integrate the activities of sales, marketing, accounts and logistic department to develop positive brand image

REACHING THE CUSTOMERS

1. Direct Mailing

It is a way of sending information relating to goods and services directly to prospects and customers. It can be used for sending an offer, reminder or announcement to a particular customer, i.e., farmer, retailer, influencer or distributor at a particular address. It is employed by company to bring in a personal touch. If cities a lot of junk mail is received by all of us and very often such mails are thrown into the dustbin, whereas a villager get very few letters and he is receptive to such mailers. Some of the points to be considered in preparing mailers are: design of the envelope, personalised sales letter, reply form and postage free reply envelope. The mailer has to be sent as per agricultural season in the sales territory. Greeting cards could also be sent during festivals such as Diwali, X-mas, Baisakhi, Durga Pooja, etc. E-mail service is useful in the case of customers like planters and distributors. The message arrives immediately and many companies have started using the same for sending product information and schemes.

2. Telemarketing

Telemarketing involves use of telephone to contact new and existing customers, to take order and to know the market situation.

Examples: Sowing of crop seed and application of fertilisers depend upon rains and there are wide variations in the receipt of rainfall even among adjoining villages. During peak agricultural season, the pests and diseases incidence changes even on a weekly basis, leading to wide fluctuations in the demand for pesticides.

Under such a dynamic market situation, telemarketing would be an additional support to the sales executive. Creating a central database of customers, timely communication and answering queries are essential for success of telemarketing programme.

EXPLORING THE NICHE MARKET

Niche market is a market segment having distinctive features and requirements and with focused working provides higher returns to the marketers. There are three important elements in niche marketing, i.e., the market segment, the product (brand), and the unique product benefits.

The niche market segment consists of all potential buyers, i.e., growers, sellers and influencers such as technical personnel, extension and research agencies. The growers have distinctive requirements and they want solutions to the field problems, i.e., control of pests and diseases and correcting nutritional deficiencies. They are willing to use even expensive branded products once they are convinced. Most of them are cash customers or prompt pay masters and are prepared to pay premium price for the products. They expect the marketers to have sound technical knowledge to solve their field problems. They are also concerned about pesticides, residues and phytotoxicity.

The product should have unique qualities and offer superior benefits to the growers compared to other products. The product should have been tested and approved against specific pest problems by authorised agencies and should not cause residue problems and phytotoxicity. It should be made available even at short notice. The marketer has to identify such niche markets in all sales territories based on the following factors:

- What is the current size of the market and growth prospects?
- Will it be attractive in the long run?
- Who are the key customers and what are their requirements?
- What will be the resources required to enter the niche segment?
- Who are the competitors and what are their strengths?
- What is the relative advantage of our products *vis-a-vis* competition?
- Do we have sufficient knowledge and experience to enter the market?
- Whether the customers will pay premium price for the products and services offered by us?

Examples:

(a) The floriculture segment consists of flower plants such as roses, jasmine, marigold, chrysanthemum, etc., and the niche market segment includes cut flowers such as roses, gladiolus, tuberose, lily and carnation. Our country is blessed with fertile soil, cheap labour and technical manpower and several export-oriented units have come up near Delhi, Bengaluru, Hyderabad and Pune. The cut flowers are being exported to countries such as UAE, UK and Netherlands. The crops are subject to attack by a number of pests and diseases and about 4-6 rounds of spraying are given in a month during the peak season. The growers have to meet the stringent requirements of importers. The cut flowers have to be free from pests and diseases and should not show phytotoxic symptoms.

(b) Number of units has taken up cultivation of edible mushrooms and they are located near Pune, Bengaluru and Delhi. They make bulk purchases of fungicides and other products to get a healthy crop.

(c) Capsicum (popularly known as Shimla Mirchi), cabbage and watermelon, brinjal are cultivated in villages near big cities and towns and consumption of hybrid seeds, fertilisers and pesticides is high compared to traditional varieties.

(d) Gherkin is cultivated in Karnataka and Andhra Pradesh and fungicide consumption is high in this crop.

The company has to identify all such special segments in each sales territory and initiate focused working in all identified territories to build up high sales volumes and profits. It should be noted that niche marketing requires putting the customer first and genuine customer involvement through communication and sharing of knowledge. The customer is not to be treated as one-time purchaser, but as a person who patronise the brand for lifetime. This means one-to-one communication will play a major role in niche marketing.

CONCLUSION

Customer relationship management focuses on cooperative and collaborative relationship between the firm and its customer. A few important customers have to be selected so that the firm can offer more personalised service which makes them feel happy and important and this leads repeat orders from highly satisfied customers. The focus is on creating, growing and retaining customers to maximise customer value, corporate profitability and in turn shareholder value. Further, companies can focus on niche segments to increase sales volume.

QUESTIONS

1. Discuss the scope of Customer Relationship Management in the marketing of agricultural inputs.
2. Assume you are the Sales and Service Executive for a tractor manufacturing and marketing company. Prepare a plan for development of CRM in your area of operation.
3. Do you feel that niche marketing of pesticides will be profitable to the company in the long run?

CASE STUDY

SEEDS

M/s. William George and Company Limited are in the business of manufacturing and marketing of pesticides and seeds with a turnover of over ₹ 1,500 crore. The company markets a wide range of pesticides used for controlling insect pests, fungal and bacterial diseases and weeds of a variety of crops, i.e., paddy, cotton, vegetables, fruit crops, plantation crops like tea, coffee, cardamom, oilseeds like groundnut, pulse crops such as green gram, red gram, flowers such as roses. They are the subsidiary of a multinational company operating in the country for the last twenty years.

The seeds' division contribute to about 40 per cent of the total sales of the company and markets hybrid seeds of cotton, chillies, cabbage, tomatoes, sunflower, maize and jowar. Performance of a new seed variety, depends upon agro-climatic conditions, i.e., soil type, moisture, temperature susceptibility to pests and disease and therefore, the company regularly conducts field trials and demonstrations in different locations in the country before launching the same.

In the year 2009, the company introduced a new hybrid tomato, which did extremely well in terms of yields and customer acceptance in South India. The marketing plan was prepared well in advance and there was excellent coordination between the technical and sales team. During the campaign, the technical team and sales team conducted a large number of field trials and demonstrations respectively.

The sales and marketing department were very enthusiastic about the new hybrid tomato and they have already announced plans to position the product in other markets in 2010. However, in order to ensure full success in all parts of the country, it had agreed with technical department to conduct planned trials and demonstrations and then position the product. The technical department accordingly laid out plans for trials and demonstrations.

In a particular state where conditions were similar to those prevailing in South, the sales manager was overenthusiastic and decided to introduce the product in this state in 2010 without detailed trials and demonstrations being carried out in advance by the technical department. The technical department was upset about this approach since such short-cut approach could affect the long-term future of the product. The technical department also could not fulfil their agreed targets with regard to field trials and demonstrations.

The hybrid tomato met with initial success. However, by the end of the season, many product performance-related complaints had come up and the company was faced with product returns and dissatisfied customers.

QUESTIONS

1. What is that we can learn from this case study?
2. What managerial qualities could have helped avert this situation?

CASE STUDY

FERTILISERS

Rastriya Chemicals and Fertiliser Limited (A Government of India undertaking with mini-ratna status) is engaged in manufacturing and marketing fertiliser and industrial chemicals. The company has two manufacturing units, i.e., Trombay and Thal and achieved turnover of ₹ 7,000 crore in the year 2012-2013.

Product

Important products are Ujjwala urea (46 per cent nitrogen), sulpha (N15:P15:K15 and 20:30) and industrial chemicals such as methanol, nitric acid, formic acid and sulphuric acid. While urea is under price control, phosphatic and potassic fertiliser continue to be under the indirect control of the Central and State Governments. The company's market share is about 9 per cent of the total fertiliser sold in the country. Company's market depends upon monsoon and its primary market is in Maharashtra, Karnataka and Andhra Pradesh. The company's manufacturing units, some of which were commissioned in 1965, have been maintained with utmost care to operate at optimum capacities and therefore able to produce low-cost urea. The company also markets Micro, a 100 per cent water soluble fertiliser in liquid form and contains vital micro-nutrients and biola — a bio-fertiliser. The "Ujjwala" urea and complex fertiliser "Suphala" brands of fertiliser manufactured by RCF carry a high brand equity and are recognised brands all over the country.

Pricing Strategy

Fertiliser being a farm/field input for agriculture is targeted towards the rural village people. The company being a public enterprise would like to provide its products and services at Government rates so that the farmers are not exploited for money. The price of the major product, i.e., urea is fixed by the Government. The complexes which are produced at RCF's establishments, their basic component is purchased at a controlled rate from Government and companies add their margin after adding value to basic products. The complexes are made of one or more raw materials called basic, e.g., Suphala (15.15.15) is made up of nitrogen, phosphorus and potassium; all in fixed equal quantity.

The traded and imported products are purchased by the company and are sold on commission basis in the market.

Subsidies form an integral part of the pricing strategy and the Government fixes the subsidy plan and the appropriate pricing strategy. Consumers are price-conscious and the company has no flexibility in fixing prices as it is a complete Government initiative.

Prices of Fertiliser

Type of Fertiliser	Selling Price/Tonnes (₹)
Urea	4,830
Di-Ammonium Phosphate	9,350
Complex Fertilisers	6,980-9,080
Single Superphosphate	Varies from state-to-state.

Source: Ministry of Chemicals and Fertilisers.

Packing

The fertilisers are packaged in high density plastic carry bags. The ideal weight of each unit of bag is 50 kgs.; 25 kgs. may be given on a custom-made order but is optional. The colour of the bag is tracer orange with shining done for consumer recognition. Recently, the colour of the bags was changed as rural customers are very conscious about physical attributes like packaging.

Promotion Mix

The company provides a full range of marketing services including sales, fertiliser promotion, agricultural research and free agronomical services. Some of them are- Soil Testing and farm services, Experimental Farms, Farmers' Trainings and association with Agricultural Universities, RCF own two farmers Training Institutes, one at Nagpur in collaboration with the Punjabrao Krishi Vidya Peeth, Nagpur and the other at Thal.

1. Cable TV
2. Regional TV channels
3. Radio
4. Posters and Leaflets.
5. Soil testing helps diagnose soil health and evolve soil specific and crop specific solutions. It helps to identify problematic soils, their nutritional status, texture and structure. Based on the analysis, farmers are advised on soil fertility management through rational use of manure, fertilisers and amendments to make agriculture more productive and sustainable. Recognising this paramount need, RCF has established six static soil testing laboratories since 1967 at Mumbai, Kolhapur, Nagpur, Ahmednagar, Hassan and Vijaywada.
6. Sample plots: The company takes sample plots and cultivates the land after enriching it with fertilisers and showing the farmers the change in productivity of crop and also the quality. When they see the quality of the produce and learn how to use it, they would like to replicate the same in their farms also.
7. Farmer Training Centres: The adoption of agricultural technology for increasing crop yield and land productivity is greatly facilitated by training and adequate

dissemination of knowledge. RCF sought to bridge the gap between Research Scientist and the farmer by setting up its State-of-the-Art Farmers' Training Centre (FTC) in 1988 at Nagpur and in 1998 at Thal. These early steps have paid rich dividend since then. More than 30,000 farmers have attended and benefited from these training programmes conducted at the two Farmers Training Centres These institutes are equipped with the latest audio-visual aids, classrooms and also hostels providing residential accommodation to the farmers. The company's dedicated training facilities are manned by in-house professionally qualified faculty, eminent research scientists from agricultural institutions, Agro experts, progressive farmers and senior Agriculture departmental officials are invited on regular interval as visiting faculty members. The curriculum covers aspects of farm management and specifics of farm technology, with special reference to regional needs.

8. Schemes: The company also has certain schemes so as to attract farmers to buy their product. The schemes are free coupons, free torch with bag of fertilisers, gifting motor cycle to a lucky winner, umbrella free with purchase of bulk fertilisers, etc.

Distribution Strategies

RCF being a public sector company has reservations policy and has to abide by the same. It has to reserve its dealership for scheduled tribes and castes as specified by the Government from time-to-time.

The company has 6,500 dealers all over India with majority of them being in Maharashtra as it comes under key area of operations. The transportation is done through rail and road, out of which 85 per cent is by railways and 15 per cent by roadways.

The channels of distribution are:

A. RCF → Customers (direct to Farmers)

B. RCF → Dealer → Customers (Farmers)

C. RCF → Warehouse Retailers → Customers (Farmers)

The company has also some satellite distribution chains running in villages of Maharashtra where the sugarcane belt is more prominent.

Challenges Faced by the Company

(1) Seasonal Sales: Fertilisers are used to enhance the quality of soil and thereby increase the productivity and gain surplus in agriculture. Once the soil is given all requisite nutrients, then it is ready for cultivation. So, once cultivation starts, fertilisers do not have much role to play until next season. The whole process generally happens once or maximum twice in traditional farming. So the demand for fertilisers is seasonal. The dealers who deal in fertilisers work only for 4-5 months as rest of the time there is no demand. In spite of seasonal nature of demand, the production of fertilisers is continuous throughout the year. The companies have to manage the whole production cycle with lowest inventory.

(2) No Control over Pricing: The fertilisers manufactured are ultimately for the benefit of the farmers, and they should be able to afford the prices of the same. Hence, the Government keeps a strict vigil on the price fixation of basic components like urea, ammonia, etc., the subsidy schemes are also decided by the Government and RCF being one public sector enterprise has to comply with Government norms and policies. Since the company cannot fix the price, it cannot increase the prices in spite of increasing costs of fertiliser production. Thus, the business is to be sustained at the discretion of Government and no autonomy in such case can be offered.

(3) Awareness: If the company needs to sustain and maintain its pedestal in business, it has to increase its sales and the margin it is earning thereby. The company needs to make the customers, i.e., the farmers aware of what is the use of fertilisers and how can they increase their productivity and quality of produce. Such awareness will be beneficial for both the farmers and the company. For creating awareness, the company has adopted many villages and is developing them to bring them in line with other prosperous villages. It has taken up demonstration plots to create awareness amongst the locals of the area.

(4) Spurious Products: This has been a grave problem for FMCGs as spurious products eat into their market share and hence their profitability decreases. In case of fertilisers, a small percentage of such cases have been reported till now and appropriate action was taken promptly.

Major Competition

The company faces competition from companies like Deepak Fertilisers and Petrochemicals Ltd., (DEPCL), ZUARI, KRIBHCO, IFFCO, etc.

Sector-wise Market Share

(a)	For Urea		
	RCF	45%	[PSU]
	KRIBHCO	19%	[Co-op.]
	IFFCO	13%	[Co-op.]
	ZUARI	12%	[private]
	OTHERS	11%	
(b)	For Complexes		
	RCF	40%	[PSU]
	ZUARI	35%	[Private]
	OTHERS	25%	

Ref.: Annual Report 2007-2008.

QUESTIONS

1. Discuss the promotion strategies followed by the company. Can we follow similar strategies in the case of consumer goods?
2. What are the challenges in fertiliser marketing?

CASE STUDY

Pesticides

Summary

Pesticides companies in India have growth strategy planned around new generation solution for pests and diseases. Registration and clearance are time-consuming processes and hence are focused on a few crops prior to the launch. After launch, they are extended to other crops. Aggressive sales personnel explore opportunities in different avenues to meet the ambitious sales plan.

The Case

Lonka was shattered. Keshav, the banana farmer, had filed a complaint with the Consumer Dispute Redressal Forum, demanding ₹ 5 lakh from Research Incorporated. He claimed he had followed the advice of the company executive and sprayed the new product "Prove" and burnt four acres of the crop. Keshav is from Dahanu, Lonka's territory. Lonka, however, had not met him before.

Early Days

Vinod and Lonka have been friends for long since their days in college together. Both completed their bachelors and masters in horticulture and joined Research Inc. Both were studious and chosen through competitive examinations and interviews into Research Inc., and were posted in two similar markets but in two different geographical regions under two different Zonal Sales Managers. That was six years back. In the last six years, both have grown their territories substantially. Vinod's market potential was twice that of Lonka's but both markets were predominantly unexploited and remained at less than ₹ 50 lakh, when they joined. Vinod had taken his territory to ₹ 6 crore and Lonka to ₹ 3 crore. Vinod, however, had far more recognition because of the size of operations. Both were growing at a healthy 10 per cent every year. Both kept their friendship alive and kept in touch.

The Current Issue

Research Inc., had launched 'Prove' in paddy. Despite excellent demand generation activities, the product was proving to be a slow starter. Vinod's boss Shyam was an aggressive go-getter with a series of memorable successes in crop diversification for new products being launched by Research Inc. He tried 'Prove' in banana and had hit success. The technical officer reporting to him had a series of findings to establish its effectiveness. Shyam usually believes in launching the idea with a bang. He conducts large-scale farmer meeting with scientists and agricultural officers. Product managers participate from HO. When Lonka came to know about this, with the help of Vinod, he could get an opportunity to participate in the "Prove" in banana meeting. In this meeting, scientists and agricultural officers talked about all the agronomical aspects of banana cultivation. Shyam and his technical officer focused on 'Prove' in banana. Five farmers gave their opinions on 'Prove'. Four of them were in favour. One of them hinted at crop burning but said it recovered soon after. Mementos were distributed, lunch was served and the meeting was declared a huge success. Farmer testimonials were printed and circulated. A small booklet was issued.

Supply chain shipped 1,000 litres to Shyam, which was billed immediately. The HO was also relieved to find another crop segment to add volumes. Returning back, he persuaded his boss, Ram to have a large-scale meeting to launch this idea with a bang. Ram did not encourage this, as it could cost him another ₹ 25,000. Not to be dissuaded, he trained his Field Assistants (FAs), translated and printed "Prove" in banana literature from Vinod and launched a serious fieldwork initiative. Initial results with his contact farmers were encouraging. He could invoice 20 litres. Slowly the crop burn symptoms were appearing in some fields. Lonka and his FAs could explain to the farmers that while the control was excellent, the crop damage was transient. Many contact farmers accepted this. The demand grew and was now going beyond Lonka's close set of contact farmers, as dealers started promoting the product. The sale grew to 100 litres. Keshav was one such farmer who was recommended "Prove" by the dealer Venkat. He quickly came back with a crop burn complaint over four acres and demanded compensation of ₹ 5 lakh. The dealer visited the field and was shocked. When the FA came to visit him, he took the recommendation in writing from him in the presence of Keshav, claiming that the literature was exhausted. Not knowing the problem, the FA promptly obliged. The dealer and Keshav now approached Lonka for the compensation but learnt that he was on leave. The dealer Venkat escalated this matter through his distributor to the zonal sales manager Ram. The distributor and the dealer convinced Ram that the best course of action would be to settle the issue through a small compensation of ₹ 25,000. Ram felt the best thing to do is not to put anything in writing. The distributor did not take anything in writing from the dealer or the farmer in good faith.

The Situation Today

Two weeks later, Lonka came back and learnt about the entire issue. Ram scolded him for selling a product without fully understanding it and advised him not to repeat it. Lonka was stung but thankful to his boss for relieving him of this tension.Two weeks later, the message about the compensation was out in the market. All dealers and farmers were talking about it. "Prove" sales stopped abruptly. Lonka learnt from his friends in other companies that Keshav and his dealer Venkat had earlier taken compensation from two other agro-chemical companies. Unfortunately, his distributor did not know that and had advised Research Incorporated also to pay. Lonka rang up his friend Vinod to see how "Prove" was doing in banana, Vinod told him that crop burning had got serious and so he stopped promotion after informing his boss Shyam. Lonka called up the product manager in Mumbai who did not seem to know much about the problems in both areas. Neither Ram nor Shyam had told him anything. He still felt that "Prove" in banana was a successful crop diversification. Supply chain Mumbai received a phone call from Shyam. After telling them of the excellent sale the previous month, Shyam told them about the 900 litres of "Prove" lying in his state and requested them to move elsewhere. Lonka came to know about this, as supply chain had called him wanting to know if he can sell it.

There was notice from the Consumer Redressal Forum. Keshav has filed a complaint with evidence to prove his case of crop burn in banana. He has the translated literature, the FA letter, and the money from the distributor, which he claims was paid to buy his silence by Research Inc. He would like to bring such bad practices out into the open and demanded a compensation for ₹ 5 lakh from the company for his crop loss and loss of peace of mind. The complaint was being addressed to the Managing Director of Research Incorporated.

QUESTIONS

1 Assume you are Vinod and Lonka, how would you avoid such risks but continue to grow?
2. Assume you are the head of sales and marketing, what would be your actions in this situation and similar situations if they emerge in future.
3. Comment on the rural consumer behaviour with reference to this case.

Source: The case prepared by M/s. B.Viswanathan and R. Krishnamoorthy, Syngenta Limited, Crop Protection Division, Mumbai.

CASE STUDY

Pesticides

Standard Industries Ltd., which has emerged as a multitechnology group, has meaningfully diversified into the manufacturing and marketing of pesticides, fertilisers, essential drugs, portable tools and exports and has achieved a turnover of ₹ 1,500 crore. It has a strong and independent R&D cell within each division, with an objective of adapting to newer technologies to the realities of the Indian market. Agro-chemicals account for 35 per cent of Standard Industries' turnover and fertilisers/seeds account for 30 per cent of the turnover.

Pesticides' Market

Pesticides are chemicals or mixtures of chemicals which are used for destroying pests, that is any organisms, insects, rodents, weeds, bacteria, which are injurious to the health of the crop. Pesticides protect the plant from pest attacks, reduce infestation, and make plants grow better, increase yields and make farmers prosperous. Pesticides may be phosphorus based, chlorine based, mercury based or synthetic pyrethroides based. They may be sold in technical grade, formulations or in dust form, tablet form or granule form.

Insecticides are substances that prevent, inhibit, destroy, kill or mitigate insects. Herbicides are substances used for preventing the growth of plants or for killing or destroying unnecessary plant growth. Fungicides are substances that prevent or destroy or inhibit the growth of fungi in plants or crops. Rodenticides are substances that prevent, inhibit, destroy, kill or mitigate rodents.

India is the largest producer of pesticides in Asia, next to Japan. More than 60 technical grade pesticides are manufactured by about 125 units, and another 500 units are making pesticide formulations. The market for pesticides was ₹ 3,500 crore in 2005 and is expected to grow by 10 per cent per annum.

Peculiarities of the Pesticide industry are: It is heavily dependent on monsoon, there are numerous manufacturers including multinationals and large Indian companies, R&D cost are high and they are hazardous to health. There is a need to develop safer formulations of pesticides.

Pesticides' Marketing

Personal Selling: Salesman has to educate the farmers to use the right pesticides, at the right time, in right doses; otherwise the farmers may not get the desired results, and he will blame the company for the product failure, in protecting his crop. Also, the salesman has to demonstrate on the farmer's field, the product effectiveness.

Group Meetings: Salesman arranges group meetings with the farmers so that not only it saves time, but also farmers learn from each other's experience.

Demonstration Seminars: For farmers, seeing is believing; they follow the village opinion leaders. Large farmers' experience and endorsement is very necessary for farmers' conviction.

Pre- and Post-sales Services play an important role in relation building exercise with the farmers.

Government Policy

In the early sixties, when there was a pressing need to augment the food supplies in India, pesticides were given at 25 per cent subsidy by the Government and the procedures for the registration of the molecules were simplified. As a result, many formulators entered the market thereby increasing the competition in the industry. In the process, the farmer was the major beneficiary. A large variety of pesticides were available to the Indian farmer at cheap prices.

In 1994-95, the subsidies were withdrawn for insecticides and weedicides used for wheat, rice and oilseeds. In the 1996-97 budget, import duties on all the raw materials were rationalised and lowered from a high of 85 per cent to 50 per cent. Yet, the industry suffered a setback due to imposition of 10 per cent excise duty on all the raw materials. The Government in furtherance of its liberalisation policy, has extended MODVAT facility for the industry in the budget, owing to which, the impact of duty has been minimal, around 6-7 per cent. Also, the industry faces opposition from the environment lobbyists, as excessive exposure to the chemicals used in pesticides is dangerous to human, animal, bird and plant life.

Pesticide Distribution

Standard Industries has a strong national distribution network of about 50 company depots and 2,500 preferred dealers (PDs), through whom it serves million of farmers throughout the country. The PDs perform the pivotal role in the relationship chain, which the company has built with its end-consumers, namely the farmers. The PDs sell either directly to the farmers through their own retail outlets or sell to the retailers, who then sell it to the farmers.

Depots

The finished products from the factory are transported to the company depots, where they are stored. Such storage is needed, firstly because the demand for pesticides is seasonal, while production process is throughout the year, and secondly because the demand is to be met as soon as the need is felt due to the sudden occurrence of pests and diseases. So the depot has to be not only located near the point of final consumption but also has to be stocked adequately to meet sudden demand.

Madan Transporters are appointed as Transport Contractors, who have the responsibility of transporting goods from the factory to various depots. Madan Transporters are also responsible for despatch of goods from the company depots to the preferred dealer's warehouse. Madan has the responsibility to appoint various sub-transport contractors locally to undertake this function. Madan Transporters are paid the transport charges from factory to PD's doorstep and they settle directly the local transporters' charges, without involving the company.

Preferred Dealers: Many of the preferred dealers work both as wholesalers as well as retailers. Hence, some business is transacted by them as retailers, with the ultimate consumers, that is village farmer. Small retailers, however, buy pesticides from the PDs and then sell to the farmers, who are unable to reach the PDs directly, due to longer distance or poor transport facilities.

The PD margin is around 12.5 per cent out of which he passes on 7.5 per cent to the retailers as their margin. If he sells through his retail outlet, he keeps this 7.5 per cent as his retail margin.

Credit: Standard Industries gives its PDs credit for 30 days from the date of despatch of the goods. Unsold goods are not taken back by the company and as such, the PD incurs a loss.

Preferred Dealer Survey

A survey was conducted among the pesticides' dealers, during which the following facts emerged:

- PDs feel that the credit period of 30 days is not adequate; they claim that other competing companies offer 45 days of credit;
- At times, the supplies are inadequate to meet full demand; the company should increase its production capacity;
- The PD is expected to pay 30 per cent of the overall amount of the bill as a booking price; the preferred dealers are unhappy about this and they want the abolition of this system;
- The PDs want the company to take back unsold stock as pesticide is a product which does not have a long shelf-life.

Change in Distribution System

A consultant has suggested to the company, to abolish preferred dealer as a channel member. Sales promotion task is done by the company salesmen and the PD's role is only to distribute and sell the product through his retail outlet. Salesmen can book the order and depot can arrange for delivery of the goods to the retailers. Part of the saving of 12.5 per cent margin can be given to salesmen as incentive.

QUESTIONS

1. What are the special problems of pesticides distribution and how the company tries to solve them?
2. Are the preferred dealers justified in demanding certain additional benefits as the survey has revealed? What will be the company's response to these demands?
3. Should the company abolish the preferred dealers system and make direct supplies to retailers as recommended by the consultant?

CASE STUDIES ON AGRICULTURAL INPUTS

(Annexure for Reference)

Indian Agriculture: General Information	
Total area	329 million ha
Total cropped area	190 million ha
Net area sown	142 million ha
Net irrigated area	60.20 million ha
Population	1,210 million
Rural	833 million
Number of villages	6,41,000
Number of rural markets	36,000
Official languages	18

Cropped Area (142 million ha) (in per cent)	
Rice	30
Wheat	17
Pulses	16
Oilseeds	11
Millets	10
Cotton	6
Others	10

Production of Major Crops

Crop	Million MT	World Ranking
Rice	97	2 (China)
Wheat	79	2
Groundnut	7	2 (China)
Cotton	14	3 (China, USA)
Potato	10	3 (Russia, China)
Pulses	15	1
Tea	80	1
Sugarcane	340	2 ((Brazil)
Vegetables	125	2 (China)

Crop	India (in kg/ha)	World Best (in kg/ha)
Cotton	300	1,500 (Aus)
Rice	2,600	6,300 (Japan)
Wheat	2,400	6,900 (UK)
Groundnut	1,000	2,800 (USA)

Major Agricultural Season

India is a land of many climates and varieties of soils affording scope for much diversity in agriculture. With the exception of Jammu and Kashmir in the extreme North and Tamil Nadu in South, 80-90 per cent of the rainfall over the country occurs mostly during the south-west monsoon season. Normally, the south-west monsoon reaches the Kerala coast by the end of May, advances along the Konkan coast in early June and extends over the entire country by the end of July. The rains continue up to the end of September when the south-west monsoon recedes.

In November and December, the North East Monsoon is the main contributor to the amount of rainfall over the south eastern portion of the country.

Kharif season (South-west monsoon season), i.e., May-September: Rice, Cotton, Millets, Groundnut and **Rabi season** (North-east monsoon season), i.e., October-April: Rice, Wheat, Potato, Pulses, Vegetables.

Major Crops – State-wise Details

Practically, all the crops are grown and the acreage varies from state-to-state depending upon agro-climatic conditions.

Punjab, Haryana	Rice, Cotton, Wheat, Potato, Vegetables
Rajasthan	Cotton, Wheat
UP/Bihar	Rice, Wheat, Sugarcane, Mango, Potato
East	Rice, Tea
Madhya Pradesh	Cotton, Pulses, Soyabean, Rice
Maharashtra	Cotton, Vegetables, Sugarcane, Fruits
Gujarat	Cotton, Groundnut
Karnataka	Cotton, Vegetables, Pulses, Coffee, Flowers
Andhra Pradesh	Cotton, Rice, Chillies
Tamil Nadu	Rice, Cotton, Sugarcane, Tea
Kerala	Rice, Tea, Cardamom, Pepper.

Indian Agriculture – World Recognition

Examples: Basmati rice, Darjeeling tea, Mysore coffee, Kerala cardamom and pepper, Saurashtra groundnut, Bengaluru and Poona flowers, Uttar Pradesh sugarcane, Andhra chillies and rice.

Progress in Agricultural Front

Items	1970-71	2011-2012
Pesticides	24,000 Tonnes	(90,000 Tonnes)
Fertilisers	2.3 Million Tonnes	28 Million Tonnes (2010-2011)
Tractors	20,000 Nos.	5,45,000 Nos. (2011-2012)
Food Production	108 Million Tonnes	260 Million Tonnes

(2011-2012)

Note: From a food deficit nation in mid-60s, our country became self-sufficient in food production in 1971 and we are now exporting agricultural produce to other countries.

✿ ✿ ✿

24 ETHICS IN SALES AND MARKETING

INTRODUCTION

Ethics in Latin language is called Ethicus and in Greek it is called Ethicos. The word has originated from the Greek Ethos meaning character or manners. Another term that is considered synonym of ethics is morality. However, they are different. The word morality means behaviour and therefore ethico-moral actions pertains to actions initiated by the character and expressed through behaviours. Ethics focuses on standards, rules and codes of conduct that govern the behaviour of individuals or groups. It is the science of morals, which is concerned with human character and conduct. It also refers to the code of conduct that guides an individual while dealing with a situation. Of late, many companies are entering rural markets and they have to follow ethical marketing practices and create positive image in the mind of rural consumers.

FEATURES OF BUSINESS ETHICS

1. Business ethics are moral principles that define right or wrong behaviour in the world of business. What is right or wrong behaviour in business is determined by public interest groups, business organisations and individual's personal values and morals.

2. The coverage of business ethics is wider, as it deals with norms in relation to customers, shareholders, employees, dealers, Government and competition. Dealings with all the above groups should be honest and fair.

3. Every professional activity has rules of conduct and professionals like lawyers, doctors, accountants are expected to follow ethical standards.

4. Business ethics deals with moral standards and extend beyond legal limit. The statement "if it is legal, it is ethical too" is inadequate.

Example: Giving inadequate information in an advertisement may be legally permitted, but is unethical.

The popular statement "if it is business, then it cannot be ethical and if it is ethical, it does not represent business at all", amounts to saying that business can make profits only by being unethical. There are many ethical companies who have discharged their social responsibilities and made profits too.

Examples: Tata Group, Wipro, Infosys.

5. Ethics is subjective and it is a relative concept.

Example: An advertisement for a slimming centre may highlight the benefits of joining the centre, but may be silent on the side-effects of the treatment. The advertiser may feel that this is ethical, but the consumer, the Government and the Advertising Standard Council of India may not feel so.

6. The concept of ethics is universally applicable and all organisations are expected to follow ethical business practices.

IMPORTANCE OF MARKETING ETHICS

1. When a company charges fair prices, offer quality products, provides after-sales service and pay regular taxes to Government, it creates good image in the mind of people.
2. It helps the company to increase sales.
3. The morale of the employee is high as the company enjoys a good reputation in the market.
4. Business ethics is required to check malpractices and offer protection to consumers.
5. To develop the confidence of consumers regarding price, weight, quality.
6. To protect the interests of all the stakeholders, i.e., employees, dealers, suppliers an shareholders.

UNFAIR SALES AND MARKETING PRACTICES

Marketing is recognised as one of the important functions of the business enterprise. Sales alone generates revenue to the company. In these days of intense competition, the emphasis is on increasing sales volume, market share and profit even at the cost of consumer satisfaction and service. Marketers adopt an aggressive sales approach in selling unsought or unwanted goods.

Examples: Sales of insurance policies, toys, cosmetics, credit cards, chocolates, etc. Many types of criticism have been levelled against marketing and in general they are related to unfair marketing practices.

1. Product

(a) Product Safety: Consumers buy products believing that they would not harm or injure them. Consumers lack technical knowledge to judge many of the sophisticated products and it becomes the responsibility of the marketer to ensure consumer safety.

Examples: Safety of toys, medicines, pesticides, etc., to man and environment. Business should give safety the priority warranted by the product. They should abandon the misconception that accidents occur due to product misuse and it is absolved of responsibility.

(b) Product Quality: The manufacturer and marketer should take responsibility to ensure that the quality of the product measures up to the claim made about it and meets reasonable consumer expectations.

Example: Many people believe that bottled water is purer and safer than tap water. When the seller claims that the saree is shrink proof/fast colours, the moral concern is whether the product lives up to its claims.

(c) Spurious Products: Several spurious drugs meant for cold, cough, bodyache, fever are available in rural market. The main ingredients of such products are sugar, wheat and chalkpowder which do not have any negative effects on human beings. Illegal traders sell such products as they get attractive discounts. Similarly, counterfeit suitings are available in major wholesale markets in India. While original manufacturers build brands, through heavy advertising and sales promotion, counterfeit fabrics are offered at a low price to such wholesalers. There are dealers who sell adulterated fertilisers and pesticides to the farmers.

2. Pricing

(a) Many consumers feel that higher prices mean better products and manufacturers increase the price of the product to show it as a superior product. The price may be higher compared to products' extra quality.

(b) Price Fixing is another unethical marketing practice followed by some companies. It is an agreement between two or more firms on the price they will charge for a product or service or bidding the lowest price on a contract.

(c) Predatory Pricing covers the practice of selling at a very low price or below the cost of production so as to eliminate competition.

3. Packaging and Labelling

The marketer has the responsibility to provide accurate and adequate information through packaging and labelling. Many companies have come out with catchy words such as organic, biodegradale, recyclable, environmentally safe, ayurvedic, etc., without providing scientific evidence to back them up. Tall and narrow cereal boxes look larger in the shelves. Terms such as large, extra large and economy size are misleading and consumers would require a packet calculator to calculate the relative prices of such packs.

4. Distribution Channel

(a) **Exclusive Dealing** refers to manufacturers insisting on its distributors to sell only its products and not to deal in competitors' products.

(b) **Tying Contracts** require distributor/dealers to purchase unwanted/slow-moving products as a condition for obtaining fast-moving brands.

(c) **Full Line Forcing:** Here, the buyer is forced to purchase all the products when only part of the line is required by the buyer.

UNFAIR ADVERTISING PRACTICES

Advertising has become an integral part of not only of our marketing process but also of our entire economic and social life. It is a double-edged instrument or tool in the marketing-mix. If it is properly used, it can be a boon or a blessing in distribution. But if it is abused or misused, it can also act as a curse in distribution. By itself, it is no doubt a very fine device of demand creation and demand stimulation, and can contribute a lot to investment, economic growth, rising income, rising standards of living and economic prosperity in any country. Most impartial studies of the economic value of advertising point out, beyond the shadow of doubt, that favourable economic effects do counterbalance the unfavourable effects which are primarily due to unsocial and unethical advertisers. Fortunately, such unscrupulous advertisers are in a very small minority in our country.

1. Deceptive Advertising: Advertising should win the confidence of consumer to achieve its objectives. Many feel that advertising is deceptive and claims made in the advertisement are exaggerated and untrue. Misrepresentations, ambiguous statements and misleading interpretations are considered as deception. Deception will not work in the long-term as consumers can verify the claims from their own experience. They will discard the product despite the great claims made for the product in advertisements.

Example: Deceptive advertisements for curing baldness, weight reduction and fair skin. The advertisement on fairness cream — is this not an exploitation of the weakness, Indians have for fair skin? Is this advertisement ethical?

2. Harmful Effects: The appeal to sex, nudity, violence, fear, adventure, has become the most adverse aspect of advertising. Some advertisements have created emotional disturbances and long run anxiety conditions among younger generation. Advertising repeats several messages and becomes uninteresting and boring. It exposes several messages which are undesirable. The growing desire to possess the products advertised becomes a source of conflict in the family.

Example: Fairness creams, soft drinks, fast foods, namkeens, durables like refrigerators, air-conditioners, two-wheelers, etc.

3. Confuses People: Advertising creates confusion in the minds of people. Consumers do not take rational decision. They are biased by unethical and emotional advertising.

(a) Power of advertising is so high that it has the potential to manipulate consumers. Consumer welfare and interest may not be given much importance. It is used to exploit the emotions and sentiments of people.

(b) Due to proliferation of brands, companies are forced to advertise to show the superiority of the products. This has encouraged unnecessary differences in the brands of products and consumers are confused by such advertisements.

Example: Soap, toothpaste, shampoo, etc.

(c) Uniformity and conformity refer to people's desire to buy products similar to the one purchased by relatives, neighbours and friends. It exploits the sentiment of status symbol and advertising creates unnecessary desire for satisfaction of status ego. It created demand for luxuries.

(d) Degrading of women: Women are irritated when, they are shown as a sex symbols, servants or housewives in advertisements. Women's organisation have objected to such advertisements.

(e) Advertisements creates unnecessary comparison between two products. Such advertisements conveniently hide the weaknesses and highlight only favourable attributes of the products.

4. Forceful Selling: (a) Emotional appeals are used to induce prospective buyers to buy their products. Producers are interested in the sale of their products without caring for the impact of emotional advertisements on ethics and moral value of consumers. The consumers live in an imaginary and exciting atmosphere generated by these advertisements.

(b) Manufacturers use persuasive advertising to influence people. Real and factual information is often concealed from the people.

(c) Advertisers try to sell those products which are not required by consumers. The advertisers create wants not really felt by consumers.

Example: A middle-class man is lured into purchasing a car, though he is unable to maintain it.

(d) Many worthless products/insignificant products have been sold under heavy advertising.

5. Media Misuses: Newspapers, magazines, television, etc., are crowded with advertisements.

(a) Many advertisers buy advertising time or space to present their messages. They try to sell stores favouring the products and small newspapers accept such advertisements to improve their financial position.

(b) Many magazines contain advertisements offering cure for cancer and baldness! In the case of TV serials, the advertisements continue sometime for half of the time of the serial.

(c) In a democratic country, the press is given full autonomy and is used for the welfare of the people. Advertisers purchase the freedom for money. Many irrelevant advertisements, ignoring the interest of people are released in press advertisement.

6. Message Problems: The messages are often emotional and sexy. If people start liking such advertisements, there would be violence and immoral activities in the society. Advertisements should carry acceptable messages.

7. Moral Influence: Advertising motivates people in such a way that people have come to believe that success is evaluated primarily based on material possessions. Spiritual, mental and intellectual satisfaction also determine the level of success.

Advertisements drives people to a fairy land. The consumers try to realise their dreams. If they cannot achieve their dreams objectives, it leads to dissatisfaction and frustration.

8. Advertising Impact on Children: Advertising has adverse impact on children as given below:

(a) Children are more susceptible to deception because they lack the conceptual defence of adults.

(b) They are unable to assess the advantages and disadvantages of advertising and many advertisers have used this innocence of children to create a particular impression about a product.

Example: Chocolates, fruit juice. Children put pressure on parents to purchase advertised products.

(c) Children enjoy seeing commercial advertisements. They are easily attracted towards using food products which are playfully advertised. Children and teenagers are vulnerable to this kind of advertising.

(d) Children recall the commercial messages and slogans and asks for the products when they go for shopping with parents.

(e) Advertisements showing violence, anxiety, sex fever, etc., creates emotional disturbances in children. They are a few cases where children have been seriously injured trying to repeat 'a scene' they have seen in TV programme. After seeing advertisement for toys, many children start fighting with toy guns. Advertisements on feminine/family planning products may arouse the curiosity of children.

AGRICULTURAL INPUTS

Marketers make use of promotion-mix consisting of Personal Selling, Sales Promotion, Advertising and Publicity to create awareness and increase the use of agricultural inputs among farmers. Some of the unfair marketing practices observed are given below:

(a) Tall claims are made about the yield potential of high yielding and hybrid seeds. This approach will not work in the long run, as the farmers can verify the claims from their experience and they will discard such varieties.

(b) Sometimes old stocks of seed materials are sold to farmers and this leads to poor germination and lower yields.

(c) Marketers adopt an aggressive approach in selling unsought products such as micronutrients, enzymes, etc., through channel members. Many dealers push such highly profitable products to farmers along with pesticides.

(d) Only benefits of the pesticides are highlighted conveniently avoiding side-effects of the products to man and environment.

(e) Leaflets are printed in local language highlighting the benefit of the particular product against a major pest/disease problem even though the product has not been tested and approved by universities or central authorities.

(f) Due to proliferation brands, companies are forced to highlight the superiority of the products against competition. This has encouraged unnecessary differences among brands and confusion in the minds of the farmers and dealers.

(g) Slow-moving products are pushed along with fast-moving goods.

(h) During period of shortages, unscrupulous dealers increase the prices of fertilisers and sell adulterated products to the poor and innocent farmers.

ADVERTISING STANDARDS COUNCIL OF INDIA (ASCI)

Registered in Oct. 1985, u/s 25, as a Not-For-Profit Co., under the Companies Act, 1956.

Main Objectives

1. To monitor administer and promote standards of advertising practices in India with a view to:
   - ensuring the truthfulness and honesty of representations and claims made through advertising and safeguarding against misleading advertising.
   - ensuring that advertising is not offensive to generally accepted norms and standards of public decency.
   - safeguarding against the indiscriminate use of advertising for the promotion of products or services which are generally regarded as hazardous to society or to individuals or which are unacceptable to society as a whole.
   - ensuring that advertisements observe fairness in competition and the canons of generally accepted competitive behaviour.
2. To codify, adopt and from time-to-time modify the code of advertising practices in India and implement, administer and promote and publicise such a code.
3. To provide facilities and machinery in the form of one or more Consumer Complaints Councils having such composition and with such powers as may be

prescribed from time-to-time to examine complaints against advertisements in terms of the Code of Advertising practices and report thereon.

4. To give wide publicity to the Code and seek adherence to it of as many as possible of those engaged in advertising.
5. To print and publish pamphlets, leaflets, circulars or other literature or material, that may be considered desirable for the promotion of or carrying out of the objects of the company and disseminate it through any medium of communication.

Consumer Complaints Council

The Board of Governors shall appoint Consumer Complaints Council (CCC), the number of members of which shall not be more than twenty-one. The Consumer Complaints Council shall examine and investigate the complaints received from the consumers and the general public, including the members of the company, regarding any breach of the Code of Conduct and/or advertising ethics and recommend the action to be taken in that regards.

Power of the Consumer Complaints Council

1. Each Council shall be entitled to receive complaints from the Board of Governors, the consumers, the general public and members of the company.

2. Each Council shall enquire, investigate and decide upon the complaints received by it within the framework of the Code of Conduct adopted by the company.

3. All the decisions of each Council shall be by simple majority, in writing and may specify the action to be taken in respect of the offending advertisement.

4. The role and functioning of the ASCI and its Consumer Complaints Council (CCC) in dealing with complaints received from consumers and industry, against Ads which are considered as false, misleading, indecent, illegal, leading to unsafe practices, or unfair to competition, and consequently in contravention of the ASCI Code for Self-regulation in Advertising.

5. ASCI is a voluntary self-regulatory council, registered as a not-for-profit company under Section 25 of the Indian Companies Act. The sponsors of the ASCI, who are its principal members, are firms of considerable repute within industry in India, and comprise Advertisers, Media, Ad. Agencies and other professional/ancillary services connected with advertising practice.

6. The ASCI is not a Government body, nor does it formulate rules for the public or for the relevant industries. The purpose and the mission of the ASCI is spelt out clearly in the literature provided.

7. If an AD is to be reviewed for its likely impact on the sensibilities of individual viewers of TV, or readers of press publications, they require to convey to the Advertiser concerned, the substantial issues raised in the complaint, in the exact context of the specific Ad, as conveyed by the perception of the complainant, and to elicit the appropriate response by way of comments from the Advertiser.

Only then will the CCC, of the ASCI, be in a position to deliberate meaningfully on the issues involved, and to arrive at a fair and objective conclusion, which would stand the scrutiny of all concerned with the right to freedom of expression, and the freedom of consumers to choose the products/services made available to them in the marketplace.

For this, they require in each case a clearly readable copy or clipping of the Ad under complaint, with full particulars of name and date of publication, or a printout of an Ad or promotion on a website or in case of a TV Commercial, the channel, date and time or programme of airing, and a description of the contents of the TVC, along with a hard copy of the complete complaint preferably signed by the complainant.

8. As a policy, they do not disclose the identity of the complainant to the Advertiser.

9. The ASCI receives and processes complaints against Ads, from a cross-section of consumers, the general public and industry, in the interests of all those who rely on advertising as a commercial communication, and this covers individuals, practitioners in advertising, advertiser firms, media, Ad agencies, and ancillary services connected with advertising.

10. In the case of complaints which were upheld by the CCC, during the past year, it may interest to know that over 80 per cent of such Ads have been withdrawn or modified appropriately by the Advertisers/Agencies involved, and the concerned Media have also confirmed that they would not carry such offending Ads/TVC.

Corporate Codes

Companies have to operate within the ethics and moral principles of the society to which it belongs. There are three types of code of ethics, i.e.,

(a) Code of ethics are statements of the value and principles that define the purpose of the organisation,

(b) Code of practices are those which guide decision making, and

(c) Code of conduct states how one must behave.

COUNCIL FOR FAIR BUSINESS PRACTICES (CFBP)

The Council for Fair Business Practices is an association of businessmen which is playing an important role in making businessmen conscious of business ethics. It is a voluntary non-profit and non-political association promoted by enlightened businessmen. One of the objectives of CFBP is to create awareness among trade, business and industry as to their social obligations and duties towards the consumers. One important feature of CFBP is Code of Fair Business Practices. The following fundamental obligations are included in this code:

1. To charge only fair and reasonable prices and take every possible step to ensure that the prices to be charged to the consumer are brought to his notice.
2. To take every possible step to ensure that the agents or dealers appointed by him do not charge prices higher than fixed.

3. In times of scarcity, not to withhold or suppress stocks of goods with a view to hoarding and/or profiteering.
4. Not to produce or trade in spurious goods or goods of standards lower than specified.
5. Not to adulterate goods supplied.
6. Not to publish misleading advertisements.
7. To invoice goods exported or imported at their correct prices.
8. To maintain accuracy in weights and measures of goods offered for sale.
9. Not to deal knowingly in smuggled goods.
10. Not bribing public servants and corrupting the democratic structure of the country.

Member of the CFBP are expected to adhere to the Code of Ethics with discipline and dedication in the interest of consumers' welfare. This code of ethics of the CFBP is now recognised nationally as well as by the International Chamber of Commerce as a basis for winning confidence of consumers. Following the example of the CFBP, many trade associations and their apex bodies like FICCI, ASSOCHAM, IMC, AIMO and Advertising Standard Council of India have decided to adopt code of ethics for their members.

CONCLUSION

Ethics are moral principles that define right or wrong behaviour in the world of business. The coverage of sales and marketing ethics is wider as it deals with norms in relation to customers, employees, shareholders, Government and competition. When a company charges fair prices, offer quality products, provides after-sales service and pay regular taxes, it creates good image in the minds of people. There are many ethical companies who discharge their social responsibilities and make consistent profits too.

QUESTIONS

1. Explain marketing ethics and its importance.
2. Explain how marketing ethics will be useful to consumers?
3. An organisation can follow ethical practices and still earn profit. Discuss.
4. Discuss fair business practices. Do you think it is being practical by business enterprise.
5. Discuss unfair marketing practices with examples.
6. Discuss the role of Advertising Standard Council of India in promoting ethical advertising practices.

✿ ✿ ✿

25 UNDERSTANDING THE RURAL MARKET – A PRACTICAL APPROACH

INTRODUCTION

As described in earlier chapters, the rural market presents huge opportunities for the companies. Increase in rural income, expansion of TV network, mobile phone services, internet facilities, rising aspirations of rural people and packaging revolution have contributed to the growth of rural market. There has been a shift from an agricultural economy to manufacturing and service economy and this development has resulted in increase in job opportunities, income and demand for goods services in rural markets. Many companies have taken the initiative to establish their products through innovative marketing programmes.

Marketers face several challenges. Rural markets are heterogeneous in nature. There are wide variations with regard to availability of infrastructure facilities among villages. Villages close to towns and cities and villages connected by transport facilities have high level of urban orientation and interior villages continue to have traditional outlook. Availability of retail outlets and reach of mass media is low in small villages. The market consists of individuals and groups of people and their needs, resources, preferences and buying habits differ. There are different groups based on caste, occupation, income, age, education and politics and each group exert influence on the behaviour of people in the village. Traditional life, traditional occupation and traditional belief are some of the features of rural life. The traditional population has strong reservations about Westernisation of their culture. Rural markets are highly scattered and spread over a wide geographical areas. The marketers has to be address two major problems, i.e., (a) How we reach the scattered rural market through different media and methods, and (b) How do we ensure that goods and services are made available to the rural consumers at the right time and at the right place?

VISITING RURAL MARKET

The younger generation of management students and executives who are brought up and educated in cities should have an understanding of the rural realities. Visiting villages and interacting with various categories of consumers will enable them to understand the challenges and opportunities in the growing rural market.

Lessons from the Road

Some of the country's marketing professionals have met their biggest challenges not in the boardroom but on the road. Mayan Pareek, Managing Executive Director – Marketing and Sales for the leading car maker in the country – Maruti has visited over 500 districts in India. It's a simple philosophy he works by: "You can't do marketing from the corner office". Our country, he says, changes every 50 kilometres and therefore it is essential to witness the change for yourself and more importantly share your consumer's experiences. It's surely a better classroom, the open road. Maruti has been running a very successful rural marketing programme for over five years now and it has most certainly paid-off. Today, one in every three cars sold in the rural market is a Maruti. For instance, now Maruti has over 7,500 rural dealership sales executives, locally recruited salespeople who double up as agents of influence.

Each time Hemant Bakshi, executive director, home and personal care, HUL, travels within the country he returns with "incredibly eye-opening", extraordinary experiences and insights. The consumer's aspirations are growing and evolving at a remarkable pace, say Bakshi and that's why it is critical to clock-in some serious face time with consumers across geographies and economic strata. HUL has as intense programme that requires every employee working on one of their brands which include Surf, Wheel, Lux, Dove, etc., to accumulate at least 100 hours with consumers when they first join the company.

N. Krishna Mohan, CEO – sales, supply chain and human capital, Emami got a lesson in this one night in Bihar. "We were travelling through the state at about 8 0' clock at night, having covered 350 kilometres. We stopped for a cup of tea in a village. But the entire place was shut. We were seared (legacy of old Bihar in our minds). We were about to return to our car and rush out when we heard a loud applause. We turned back just in time to see the entire population at the village panchayat. They were cheering at the sight of Sachin's half century."

Atul Singh, president & CEO, Coca-Cola India and South West Asia was visiting a rural market in UP. During this visit he noticed some of the outlets were operating out of ice boxes, with very little ice, because electricity supply is temperamental in most of India, rural or urban it doesn't quite matter when it comes to power. As a result people weren't buying too many Cokes because they weren't cold enough. Soon after Coca-Cola deployed solar coolers in the affected areas. "Most businesses, and more so the food and beverage business, are a people's business," says Singh. Modern day companies must start from the consumer's requirement and then workback wards if they have to run a sustainable business. For a beverage company like Coca-Cola it helps when they can decode the consumer's voice, not just for launching new products, but also newer packages, price points' etc. "Market visits are therefore a part of the plan when I am travelling. Even otherwise my leadership team and I spend time with consumers and in the marketplace to keep our finger on the pulse."

Source: Brand Equity, *The Economic Times*: February 6, 2013.

The following factors have to be considered while undertaking village visits and meeting various categories of consumers.

1. Selection of Villages

(a) Population: The villages can be categorised based on population, i.e., large villages (> 5,000 population), medium villages (2,000-5,000), small villages (1,000-2,000) and very small villages (<1,000 population).

(b) Nearness to Cities and Towns: Villages close to towns and cities have high level of urban orientation compared to interior villages.

(c) Availability of Services such as schools, banks, hospitals, libraries, sewerage, street lighting, and public transport and telecommunication facilities will influence the lifestyle of people in rural areas.

(d) Occupation Pattern: There are three sectors that provide employment to rural population, i.e., Primary, Secondary, and Tertiary sectors. About 65 per cent of the rural population is engaged in agriculture and allied occupations. However, there is a shift towards secondary and tertiary occupations especially in large villages and villages situated close to towns and cities.

(e) Land-use Pattern: Cash crops like cotton, chillies, vegetables and fruits give higher returns compared to crops like jowar and maize.

(f) Irrigation Facilities: Crops grown under irrigated conditions give higher yields, leading to higher farm income.

2. Selection of Markets Where Buying and Selling Take Place

(a) Village Market: In small villages, there are pan shops selling tobacco products, candies, local soft drink, etc. Large villages have grocery shops selling foodgrains, edible oil, FMCGs, minor electrical items, over the counter medicines, etc.

(b) Weekly Market: Also known as Haats, Shandies, Hatwari, Chindies, Angadi, Peta, etc., are held once in a week in villages. The sellers in the haat are mobile. They arrive in the morning and remain till late evening. Next day, they go to another haat.

(c) Feeder Market: The rural consumer visits nearby towns for selling agricultural produce and buying consumer goods. These are the Feeder Markets/Mandis which are situated at Taluka/District headquarters or in important agricultural centres. The companies appoint dealers for consumer durables and wholesalers for FMCGs. Sales representatives of the companies are also normally stationed in Taluka/District headquarters.

(d) The Melas are different types, i.e., commodity fairs, cattle fairs, religious fairs and exhibitions. The melas can be successfully used to give information about products and services among villagers and also make spot sales.

3. Selection of Sellers

There are two categories of sellers, i.e., wholesalers, and retailers/dealers. While retailers for FMCGs operative at village level, dealers for consumers' durables have shops in Feeder Markets/Mandi towns.

(a) **Village Retailer** deals in a variety of consumer goods. He keeps in touch with wholesalers in the Feeder Market and collects information about new products and services. They have direct contact with consumers and extend credit facilities. The village retailers can provide valuable information about the markets and consumers.

(b) **Wholesalers/Distributors:** They are located at Taluka/District Headquarters or important agricultural centres. They buy in bulk and sell to retailers after breaking down the bulk into smaller quantities. They offer special services such as collection of orders, despatch of stocks, credit, collections of dues, after-sales service and market information.

4. Selection of Users/Consumers

There are broadly three categories of consumers in rural market, i.e., farming community, traders and service class. Income from agriculture is seasonal and therefore the demand for goods and services depends upon agricultural situation.

(a) **Farmers:** Based on size of land holdings, there are five categories of farmers, i.e., Marginal, Small, Semi-medium, Medium and Large farmers. 75 per cent of land holdings consist of small and marginal farmers.

(b) **Traders** include merchants dealing in grocery items, fertilisers, cement, agricultural produce, electrical and hardware items, dress materials and general stores.

(c) **The Service Class** has regular income and they include teachers, clerks, mechanics, and electricians in the villages and office and factory workers, who work outside the village.

The traders, service class, landlords and affluent farmers are the target audience for branded consumer durables.

5. Selection of Opinion Leaders

Opinion leader is a person who is considered to be knowledgeable and is consulted by others and his advice is normally followed by villagers. They give valuable information and advice and are credible source of product-related information. Teachers, progressive farmers, local agricultural offers, vaidyas, bankers, village president are some of the opinion leaders in villages.

6. Selection of Officials

Government Officials working in departments such as Agriculture, Health, Public Works, Education, Revenue, Rural Development and Managers of Co-operative Marketing and Credit Societies, Banks and Insurance can provide valuable information on agriculture and rural development activities. They can be contacted at large villages, taluka/mandal/district headquarters.

PERSONAL INTERVIEW OR FIELD SURVEY

In the questionnaire method, we can collect information through mail, telephone or personal interview. Experience shows that the personal interview with respondents gives the required information. It offers a sense of participation and it is more flexible for data collection. Rate of refusal is low. Depth interview is possible. Complex questions can be asked. Visual aids such as pictures, exhibits, etc., can used to get views, opinions of respondents.

The important areas that could be covered during field surveys are given below. The list is not complete and more areas could be added depending upon the objective of the survey. A suitable questionnaire has to be prepared for collection information. It would be preferable to pre-test the questionnaire on sample of respondents before it is used for wider use.

Chapter 1: Nature and Scope of Rural Marketing

(a) Availability of infrastructure facilities.

(b) Occupation pattern of rural people.

(c) Are there differences between villages with regard to (a) and (b).

(d) Problems faced by agricultural labourers and rural artisans.

(e) Feedback from villagers on various developmental programmes initiated by Government in rural areas.

Chapter 2: Exploring the Growing Rural Market

(a) The factors that have contributed to the growth of rural market.

(b) The role of private agencies in agricultural and rural development.

Chapter 3: Rural Consumer Behaviour

(a) Beliefs, perceptions and customs prevalent among villagers and their influence on the buyer behaviour.

(b) Shopping habits of rural consumers.

(c) The consumer buying process for TV, insurance policy, computers, mobile phone, and tractors.

(d) Who are the opinion leaders for different categories of products and services?

Chapter 4: Rural Marketing Research

(a) Buying motives with reference to durables like TV, mobile phones, computer and two-wheelers.

(b) From where (like village shop, weekly market, mandi towns/taluka/district headquarters) do they buy grocery items, packed consumer goods, agricultural inputs and durables like TV and mobile phones and why?

(c) Do rural people patronage a particular shop in the village? If so, why?

(d) How many brands of biscuit, toothpaste, soap, hair oil, washing cake/powder are kept by the retailers? What are the reasons for keeping these brands?

Chapter 5: Rural Market Segmentation

(a) Segment the population based on socio-economic factors.

(b) Find out who are the target customers for television, mobile phone, computer, two-wheeler and refrigerator and why?

Chapter 6: Rural Marketing-mix

Do you think that rural consumers are concerned with utility of the products rather than mere looks in the case of consumer durables?

Chapter 7: Product and Pricing

(a) Find out important brands of soap (bathing/washing), detergent powder, shampoo, biscuit, toothpaste/toothpowder sold by the retailers. What are the factors considered by retailers for stocking these products?

(b) Do you think that rural people are brand-conscious/price-sensitive while buying consumer packed goods and durables like watches, television and transistors?

Chapter 8: Distribution in Rural Market

(a) The channels of distribution followed by the companies (FMCGs and Consumer durables) in the rural market.

(b) What are the services provided by the distributor/stockist to the retailers (grocery merchants) and dealer to consumers in the case of durables?

(c) Study the functioning of 'Haats'/'Weekly markets'.

Chapter 9: Organised Rural Retailing

Study the functioning of an organised retail store situated in a taluka/district headquarters and compare with organised urban stores in major towns and cities. You may meet store officials and visitors for collecting the information.

Chapter 10: Rural Promotion

1. Take any company (FMCG, consumer durable and insurance, etc.), and find out the promotion media and methods followed by the company in rural market. You can meet company representatives, distributors, retailers for collecting the required information.
2. Meet officials of a commercial bank in rural area and find out how they go about mobilising fixed deposits from villagers.
3. Visit a Commodity/Cattle/Religious fair (MELA) and study rural promotion.

Chapter 11: Developing the Sales Force for Rural Market

1. Meet the sales representative/sales executive of a company/distributors promotion staff dealing in FMCGs, durables or pharmaceutical products and find out the nature of job and activities performed by them to increase the sales in rural market.
2. What are the challenges faced by the salesperson in rural market?

Chapter 12: Marketing of Consumer Goods and Services

Meet the wholesalers/dealers selling products of Asian Paints, Nokia and Colgate in taluka, mandal or district headquarters and find out as to how the companies are marketing their products (with reference to 4 Ps) in rural areas.

Chapter 13: Corporate Initiatives in Rural Market

Meet the sales executives of FMCGs, durables, insurance companies and find out the marketing strategies followed by the companies in rural market.

Chapter 14: Agricultural Marketing

Visit village, primary and secondary market and find out the following:

(a) Type of products sold.

(b) Methods of sales followed in these markets.

(c) Channels of distribution of agricultural produce

(d) The role of middlemen.

Chapter 15: Defects in the Agricultural Marketing System and Lines of Improvement – Part I

(a) What are the problems faced by farmers in selling the agricultural produce?

(b) Collection information on forced sale, market charges, commission payable to middlemen, number of middlemen in agricultural produce marketing, delays in payment, if any, the difference between consumer price and farm gate price in the case of vegetables, fruits, grains and cotton.

Chapter 16: Defects in the Agricultural Marketing System and Lines of Improvement – Part II

(a) Study the working of regulated market, Government warehouses and AGMARK laboratories.

(b) What is the perception of farmers about regulated market, standardisation, grading and AGMARK.

Chapter 17: Co-operative Marketing

(a) Study the working of credit and marketing societies.

(b) What are the problems faced by village-level societies?

(c) Obtain feedback from farmers regarding working of societies.

Chapter 18: Recent Trends in Agricultural Produce Marketing

(a) Find out the working of e-Choupal and compare with mandi operations.

(b) How organised urban retail centres are procuring vegetables, fruits and grains from farmers?

(c) Is there a scope for development of "contract farming" in the villages visited?

Chapter 19: Agricultural Finance and Role of Institutions

(a) Find out the credit needs of farmers.

(b) Study the working of commercial banks and credit societies.

(c) What are the problems faced by these institutions in extending credit to farmers.

Chapter 20: Agricultural Pricing

(a) Find the out the differences between consumer price and farm gate price in the case of fruits, vegetables and grains.

(b) Do you think farmers are aware of the subsidies given by Government on fertilisers, electricity and irrigation water and waiving of farm loans?

(c) What are your recommendations for increasing the income of small and marginal farmers who are depending upon only agriculture as a source of income?

Chapter 21: Globalisation and Agriculture

Meet farmers/companies growing flowers, vegetables and fruits for export and find out to what extent they are able to meet requirements of the importers with regard to price, quality and delivery schedule.

Chapter 22: Marketing of Agricultural Inputs

(a) Use of high yielding/hybrid seeds, chemical fertilisers and pesticides in the cultivation of crops. Are there differences between small and large farmers in the use of these inputs?

(b) The role of Government and private agencies in advising the farmers on modern cultivation practices.

(c) Who are the opinion leaders in the case of new hybrid crops and pesticides in the village?

(d) What are the services provided by agricultural input dealers to farmers?

(e) What are the problems faced by dealers and distributors in the marketing of agricultural inputs?

(f) The job of sales executive in agri-input business.

Chapter 23: Agricultural Inputs and Customer Relationship Management

(a) Meet distributors, dealers and company representatives and find out customer relationship management activities followed by agricultural input companies in rural market?

(b) Are there any niche market segments in the villages visited? If so, explain.

Chapter 24: Ethics in Sales and Marketing

Meet distributors, dealers and company representatives and find out details of ethical/ unethical marketing practices followed by companies, distributors and dealers of consumer goods, durables, agricultural inputs and insurance companies/agents and banks in rural market.

Chapter 25: Understanding the Rural Market — A Practical Approach

Define the objective of the field visit and prepare questionnaire accordingly. Form small groups, collect required information, exchange with other group members and make presentations in the class for the benefit of all the students.

✿ ✿ ✿

BIBLIOGRAPHY

Acharya S.S. and Agrawal N.L. (1999), *Agricultural Marketing in India*, Oxford and IBH Publishing Company Private Limited, New Delhi.

Anjila Saxena, Samiuddin, Harsh Dwivedi and Rahman M. (1997), *Rural Marketing, Thrust and Challenges*, National Publishing House, Jaipur.

Badi R.V. and Badi N.V. (2010), *Rural Marketing*, Himalaya Publishing House, Mumbai.

Gopalswamy, T.P. (2009), *Rural Marketing, Environment, Problems and Strategies*, Vikas Publishing House Private Limited, New Delhi.

Habeeb-Ur-Rahman K.S. (2008), *Rural Marketing in India*, Himalaya Publishing House, Mumbai.

Handbook of Agriculture, ICAR Publication, New Delhi (2005).

Kamat G.S., Krishanamoorthy R., Chakravarty Pulak, Kamat Minouti (2012), *Co-operatives and Rural Markets*, Himalaya Publishing House, Mumbai.

Kotler Philip (2007), *Marketing Management*, Prentice-Hall of India Private Limited, New Delhi.

Krishnamacharyalu, C.S.G. and Lalitha Ramakrishnan (2006), *Rural Marketing, Text and Cases*, Pearson Education (Singapore) Private Limited, Delhi.

Krishnamoorthy R. (July, 2000), *Managing the Sales Force*, Team Power.

Krishnamoorty R. (October, 2000), *Indian Rural Market, Problems and Prospects*, Indian Management.

Krishnamoorty R. (November, 2000), *Closing the Sales Deal*, Human Capital.

Krishnamoorty R. (December, 2000), *Winning the Heartland*, A&M.

Krishnamoorthy R. (2001), *Reaching the Rural Customers through Haats and Melas*, Bombay Management Association Review.

Krishnamoorthy R. (2001), *Effective Communication Media and Methods for Rural Audience*, Saket Digest.

Krishnamoorthy R. (January, 2005), *Carving out a Career in Rural Marketing*, Agriculture Today.

Krishnamoorthy R. (2006), *Challenges in Marketing of Farm Inputs*, Agriculture Today.

Krishnamoorthy R. (2012), *Exploring the growing rural market*, Sydenham Management Review, Mumbai.

Marketing White Book (2012-13), *Business World*, ABP Private Limited, Kolkata.

Minouti Kamat and Krishnamoorthy R. (2006), *Textbook on Rural Marketing*, Himalaya Publishing House, Mumbai.

Parthasarathy R. (2005), *Rural Marketing, Concepts and Cases*, ICFAI University Press, Hyderabad.

Pradip Kashyap (2012), *Rural Marketing Book*, Pearson Education, New Delhi.

Prahalad C.K. (2006), *The Fortune at the Bottom of the Pyramid,* Pearson Education (Singapore) Limited, New Delhi.

Praxis, Kasturi and Sons, Chennai (July, 2003).

Ramaswamy V.S. and Namakumari N. (2008), *Marketing Management, Planning, Implementation and Control*, Macmillan India Limited, New Delhi.

Ramkishen Y. (2002), *New Perspectives on Rural Marketing,* Jaico Publishing House, Mumbai.

Rao K.L.K. and Ramesh G. Tagat (July-September, 1985), *Rural Marketing, A Developmental Approach,* Vikalpa.

Sanal Kumal Velayudhan, Rural Marketing (2005), *Targeting the Non-urban Consumers*, Response Books, Sage Publications, New Delhi.

Sanjay K. Patro (2000), *Rural Marketing, the Relevance, Challenges and Strategies*, Management and Labour Studies.

Sathyasundaram L. (2002), *Rural Development*, Himalaya Publishing House, Mumbai.

Sherlekar S.A. and Krishnamoorthy R. (2012), *Marketing Management Concepts and Cases*, Himalaya Publishing House, Mumbai.

Singh Rakesh (February, 2004), *New Corporate Initiatives in Indian Agriculture,* Indian Management.

Singh Rakesh (January, 2006), *Rural Hyper Market,* The Rural Marketing Journal.

Singh Sukphal (2011), *Rural Marketing*, Vikas Publishing House Private Limited, New Delhi.

Survey of Indian Agriculture (2010), *The Hindu*, Chennai.

Swaminathan M.S. (2010), From *Green Revolution to Evergreen Revolution*, Academic Foundation, New Delhi.

Vedamani Gibson (2012), *Retail Management*, Jaico Publishing House, Mumbai.

✿ ✿ ✿